Evelyn Wood VC

Pillar of Empire

Evelyn Wood VC
Pillar of Empire

Stephen Manning

With a Foreword by Saul David

Pen & Sword
MILITARY

Published in Great Britain in 2007 by
PEN & SWORD MILITARY
an imprint of
Pen & Sword Books Ltd
47 Church Street
Barnsley
South Yorkshire
S70 2AS

ISBN 978-1-84415-654-2

A CIP catalogue record for this book is
available from the British Library.

Typeset by Concept, Huddersfield, West Yorkshire
Printed and bound in Great Britain by CPI UK

Pen & Sword Books Ltd incorporates the Imprints of
Pen & Sword Aviation, Pen & Sword Maritime, Pen & Sword Military,
Wharncliffe Local History, Pen & Sword Select,
Pen & Sword Military Classics and Leo Cooper.

For a complete list of Pen & Sword titles please contact
PEN & SWORD BOOKS LIMITED
47 Church Street, Barnsley, South Yorkshire, S70 2AS, England.
E-mail: enquiries@pen-and-sword.co.uk
Website: www.pen-and-sword.co.uk

To Michaela, Alexander & Dominic –
with Much Love

Contents

Acknowledgements

I must first thank Evelyn Wood himself, for his two-volume auto-biography, *From Midshipman to Field-Marshal*, which provided an essential basis to begin my interest and research. I am indebted to the following institutions and individuals for allowing me to access research material: to Bobby Eldridge, Senior Archivist at Killie Campbell Africana Library whose helpfulness, combined with her natural cheerfulness, made this work a viable research project; Janie Morris at the Special Collections department of Duke University, Zoe Lubowiecka at Hove Reference Library, Sally Day at the Army Museum, Aldershot, Lucy McCann, the librarian of the Rhodes House Library, Oxford, Colin Harris at the Bodlein New Library, Oxford, Alastair Massie and his staff at the National Army Museum, and the archivists at the Public Records Office, the House of Lords and the Imperial War Museum. I am most grateful to the descendants of Dr Norman Moore for allowing me to access Moore's private papers. I would also like to thank Her Majesty Queen Elizabeth II for permission to quote from the Royal Archives.

For their help, support and encouragement I would wish to thank Ian Beckett, Saul David, Jeremy Black, John Laband, Huw Davies, Ian Knight, and Tony Morris. I am particularly grateful to Saul David for kindly agreeing to write a foreword to this book. Finally I would like to thank and praise my wife Michaela, and our two boys, who have lived this book with me for nearly two years. It is to them that this work is dedicated.

Abbreviations

BNL	Bodleian New Library, Oxford
C-in-C	Commander-in-Chief
DRO	Devon Records Office, Exeter
DUK	Duke University, Raleigh, North Carolina – the Evelyn Wood Papers
FLH	Frontier Light Horse
H/L	House of Lords Archive, London
HOV	Hove Library Archive
IWM	Imperial War Museum, London
KCM	Killie Campbell Africana Library, University of Kwazulu-Natal, Durban, South Africa
NAM	National Army Museum, London
PIET	Pietermaritzburg Archive, South Africa
PRO	Public Records Office, Kew
QVJ	Queen Victoria's Journal, to be found in the Royal Archives, Windsor Castle
RA	Royal Archives, Windsor Castle
RH	Rhodes House Library, Oxford
WO	War Office – Papers held at the Public Records Office, Kew

List of Maps

Foreword

The career of Field Marshal Sir Evelyn Wood VC was nothing short of extraordinary. Born in 1838, the son of an Essex vicar, he joined the Royal Navy and fought with distinction in the Crimea where he was badly wounded. He then switched to the army and saw further action in India, the Gold Coast, the Cape, Zululand, the Transvaal, Egypt and the Sudan, winning a Victoria Cross and a knighthood in the process. A qualified barrister and a graduate of the Staff College, Wood was a protégé of Sir Garnet Wolseley, the most talented and ambitious officer of his generation. He served under Wolseley during three African campaigns and in 1897, by which time his old mentor was Commander-in-Chief, Wood became Adjutant-General at the War Office. It was during this period that Wood acquired a deserved reputation as a reformer and an innovative trainer of troops.

Wood is, along with Wolseley and Sir Frederick Roberts, one of the three great British generals of the late Victorian period, and yet comparatively little has been written about him. There was, until now, only one biography and that was penned during his lifetime. Wood himself is partly to blame: he wrote an excellent two-volume memoir, *From Midshipman to Field Marshal*, and a separate book of military recollections, *Winnowed Memories*. But that still left a gaping hole in the historiography of Victorian generalship. Stephen Manning has filled it with his impeccably researched, fluently written and judiciously honest account of Wood's life. Never afraid to criticise his hero – Manning attributes the humiliating defeat at Hlobane in Zululand to 'Wood's lack of intelligence gathering' – he is also alive to his many qualities, concluding: 'Evelyn's legacy was more than his evident bravery and an ability to inspire and organise ... He introduced a way of thinking, among all the officers that served under him, that encouraged a respect for the abilities of the rank and file, as well as initiative from officers.' In this respect, at least, he was well ahead of his time.

Saul David

Prologue

Evelyn Wood slept very little on the night of 28/29 March 1879, for he knew that the new day would bring a massive onslaught of 20,000 Zulu warriors upon his small force of 2,000 British soldiers, entrenched on the slopes of Kambula Hill. Evelyn had seen these same warriors decimate a smaller mounted force the day before, at the battle of Hlobane, and Wood had been forced to bury many of his comrades where they had fallen, including his beloved friend Captain Campbell. Evelyn would not have been the only British soldier who awoke on the morning of 29 March with a sense of dread and loss. The thick mist which shrouded the dawn would have produced a chill to match the shivers of fear which must have pervaded the British camp. Nearly 100 men, who had laughed and joked with their comrades only the day before, were now lying butchered on the slopes of Hlobane and all the ranks, from Wood to the most junior private soldier, would have heard recounted the stories of how, after the crushing Zulu victory at Isandlwana two months before, the British had been slaughtered and mutilated by the enemy.

Yet, amid the atmosphere of fear and apprehension, the commanding officer of Number 4 Column, Colonel Evelyn Wood, had a clear understanding of the enemy he now faced and what his force had to do. Ever since Lord Chelmsford, the Commander-in-Chief of British forces in South Africa, had instructed Wood to harass the enemy, Wood's men had been most active in numerous skirmishes with the Zulu forces under the command of Prince Mbilini. Such actions had culminated in the costly attack by mounted infantry on the Prince's mountain headquarters at Hlobane. This British reversal now placed the men of Wood's command in a precarious position, but Wood was quietly confident that the entrenched position, which he himself had been instrumental in designing, and the ground that he had chosen for the forthcoming battle, would produce a decisive victory.

Wood was fortunate in that he was ably supported by Colonel Redvers Buller, who commanded the mounted infantry and whose bravery the day before at Hlobane would win him the Victoria Cross. The Zulu army had received strict, and direct, instructions from the Zulu king, Cetchwayo, not to attack the British if they were behind entrenched positions, but, as the warriors approached the Kambula camp, Wood ordered Buller to provoke the enemy into an attack. This plan was successful and so began a four-hour struggle to the death as the Zulu army repeatedly threw itself at Wood's forces. Despite their outstanding bravery, the Zulus were unable to penetrate the British defences and so attempt to gain the upper hand in close combat. Yet, throughout the battle, a British victory hung in the balance, as the Zulu warriors nearly succeeded in entering Wood's prepared position. Indeed, at one point the danger was so severe that Evelyn himself took a rifle from his orderly and was able to shoot and kill two Zulus who were urging their comrades forward. When the exhausted Zulus finally began to retreat, Wood unleashed his mounted infantry, who pursued and slaughtered the defeated enemy for several miles.

Wood's success at Kambula made him a Victorian celebrity. He was propelled into the hearts and minds of the British newspaper-reading public and into the higher circles of society. He became a firm favourite of the Queen and frequently stayed with Her Majesty at both Balmoral and Windsor. There he would recount his exploits from the many campaigns in which he had already participated, and, as the years passed, the friendship between the monarch and her General would remain constant.

Wood certainly viewed himself as a campaigning soldier, and indeed his active participation in, and important contribution to, many of the great Victorian conflicts would place him alongside the most the famous officers of this period. Yet, above all, Wood had a unique understanding of the needs of his men. His concern for their welfare on campaign was well known in the army, and this not only gained his men's respect and appreciation, but also allowed him to see beyond the simple requirements needed to achieve a battlefield victory. His attention to detail would see him fill perhaps his most important role as an army reformer and trainer of men, a legacy of which he could be proud, and one which was recognised, certainly within the army, during the opening years of World War One. By 1901 Evelyn held the rank of Adjutant-General, second only in rank to the Commander-in-Chief, and in the following year Commander Robinson published *Celebrities of the Army*, in which he described Wood as 'a strong pillar as well as a fine ornament of the British Empire.'[1]

So how did a young naval Midshipman, who first saw active service during the Crimean War, end his military career as a holder of the three greatest honours a British soldier could achieve; a Field Marshal's baton, the Victoria Cross and the Colonelcy of the most illustrious cavalry regiment, The Blues? How could this deaf, accident-prone hypochondriac rise to the highest rank in the British army? The answer centres on Wood's determined and single-minded approach to the advancement of his career, combined with a vanity he found impossible to contain, which would place him firmly in the position of a 'General of Empire' and a 'Soldier of the Queen'. The determination and coolness that he displayed on the slopes of Kambula would appear again and again, throughout his career and private life, and would ensure that he would become one of the most successful and respected soldiers of his time.

Chapter One

A Family Tradition

The future Field-Marshal, Evelyn Wood, did not come from a long line of distinguished military men. In fact his father was vicar of the parish of Cressing, near Braintree, Essex. Henry Evelyn, the youngest son and one of thirteen children of Emma and Sir John Page Wood, was born on 9 February 1838. Altogether seven of Evelyn's brothers and sisters died before their seventeenth birthday, including, at the age of four, the second born son, John, who had been considered a prodigy and could speak both Latin and Greek before his premature death.[1] Evelyn would have learnt from an early age of the service that his grandfather, Alderman Matthew Wood, had given to members of the Royal family, a tradition that the young Evelyn would continue.

Wood's family were originally from the small Devon village of Brixton, near Plymouth. A cadet branch settled in Tiverton, where they established themselves as manufacturers of lace and serge.[2] It was here that Matthew was born, although he would eventually migrate to London, via a brief stay in Exeter. In the capital, Matthew established successful businesses, both as a chemist and a hop merchant, and developed a taste for radical politics which saw him elected twice as Lord Mayor of London, in 1815 and again in 1816, and as Member of Parliament for the City of London in nine successive parliaments.[3]

As a consistent supporter of the more radical Whigs, who campaigned for popular rights and opposed the King, Matthew undoubtedly saw a political opportunity in the chaos and furore surrounding the decision of Princess Caroline to return from her self-imposed exile in Italy to attend the proceedings of the Milan Commission. This was a parliamentary investigation into allegations of her adulterous behaviour. In addition, with the death of George III, Caroline was determined to claim her position as Queen at the coronation of her estranged husband George IV. The marriage of George and Caroline had been a disaster from their wedding night onwards, and Caroline's apparently numerous love affairs had scandalised society, humiliated

1

her husband, despite his own many liaisons, and produced a lively 'soap opera' for the masses.

Matthew Wood not only offered political support to Caroline, for he apparently believed her return to England would precipitate the fall of the Tory Government, but also material assistance in that he arranged for, and escorted the Princess on, the boat back from France. Arriving at Dover on 5 June 1820, he escorted Caroline through cheering crowds to London. Here the people loudly and excitedly welcomed Caroline's return, and Wood was so delighted that he occasionally stood up from the carriage, where he was seated next to the Princess, to return the cheers of the masses that thronged the streets. For the next three nights Caroline stayed with Alderman Wood at his home in St James Street, and both were greeted by cheering whenever they appeared.[4]

A Secret Committee, which was composed, amongst others, of the Archbishop of Canterbury, the Lord Chancellor and various Cabinet members, examined the evidence of Caroline's adultery, as compiled by the Milan Commission. The Committee viewed the charges as so potentially damaging to 'the honour of the Queen ... the dignity of the Crown, and the moral feeling and honour of the country', that its members had no hesitation in recommending a 'solemn inquiry in the form of legislative proceeding'.[5] In practice, this meant a parliamentary Bill of Pains and Penalties, which was introduced in the House of Lords in July 1820 and sought to deprive Caroline of her title, prerogatives, rights and privileges and to dissolve the marriage between her and George. Caroline attended the five-month proceedings throughout, much of the time accompanied by Matthew Wood. Both displayed their disdain for the hearing by playing backgammon to while away the time. Despite the apparently strong case against her, the government supporters failed to produce conclusive evidence and the bill was abandoned, without producing the required result for the King. Caroline and the masses who had followed the passage of the bill were euphoric, and the popular support the Queen now received encouraged her to seek even greater humiliation for her estranged husband.

Although the King had failed to obtain his required divorce, he could still gain some satisfaction by ensuring that Caroline would not be crowned queen, nor even be allowed to attend his coronation. Despite actually arriving at the doors of Westminster Abbey, Caroline was firmly refused entry, and had to suffer an embarrassing and ignominious retreat. Matthew Wood was at her side throughout this painful experience. Soon after, in her distress, Caroline fell ill and rapidly became extremely unwell. On 8 August 1821, just three weeks after the coronation, she died. At her bedside sat Alderman Wood, as well as his new daughter-in-law, Emma, who in 1820 had been appointed Bedchamber Woman to the Queen and had helped nurse Caroline through her painful final illness.[6] Alderman Wood later accompanied the coffin through London to Harwich, from where the body was to be transported to Caroline's family in Brunswick for burial. On route, at Chelmsford, Wood attempted one last gesture of support for the uncrowned Queen when, in accordance with Caroline's instructions, he attempted to screw a silver plate to the coffin, on which were inscribed the words, 'CAROLINE OF BRUNSWICK: THE INJURED QUEEN OF ENGLAND.'[7] However, the King's representative ensured that the plate was removed before the coffin continued its journey. Thus ended Matthew Wood's association with Caroline, but it had not been his only involvement with royalty.

Earlier, in 1819, Matthew Wood had been instrumental in aiding the Duke and Duchess of Kent in their return to England from the continent, so as to ensure that their expected child would be born in Britain. The issue of succession to the throne had become a burning question ever since the earlier death of the Prince Regent's and Princess Caroline's only child, Charlotte, in 1817. For clear reasons of the succession, Wood wrote to the Duke to urge him, at all costs, to guarantee that the birth took place on English soil. The Duke could only agree, but replied that he had difficulty returning because he was 'totally deprived of all pecuniary means'.[8] The Prince Regent attempted to prevent the return by refusing to pay the Duke's outstanding debts or pay his travelling expenses.[9] Wood saw a political opportunity to frustrate the King and he persuaded Lord Darnley to sign a bond for £10,000 'to make the removal and settlement in England possible.'[10]

Although George had no choice but to agree to the Duke of Kent's return, he did take the opportunity to chastise his brother for forcing the Duchess to make the arduous journey in such an advanced stage of pregnancy. However, the trip was safely and successfully completed and, on 24 May 1819, the Duchess gave birth to a healthy child, 'a pretty little Princess, as plump as a partridge', who was named Victoria.[11] Wood later assisted the Duke in his unsuccessful attempts to sell his country home, Castle Hill, so as to relieve his debts, and even procured a seaside residence in Sidmouth, Devon, so that both the Duchess and the little Princess might benefit from the sea air. Just as Matthew Wood provided a great service to the little Princess in arranging for her royal birth in London, so his grandson Evelyn Wood continued the family tradition of service to royalty by becoming one of Victoria's most successful generals, as well as her great friend.

Evelyn Wood's family on his mother's side were also originally from the west country. The Michell family represented Truro in Parliament from as early as the reign of Queen Elizabeth I and had leases on Cornish tin mines that went back over 300 years. Wood's mother, Emma Caroline, was the youngest of the three daughters of Admiral Michell and had been born in Lisbon when her father was an Admiral in the Portuguese Navy. One of Emma's brothers, Sir Frederick Michell, became an Admiral in the British navy and he was very influential in Evelyn's early career. Likewise, Evelyn's uncle on his father's side, William Wood, was able to exert influence and support in his nephew's later life, when he became Lord Chancellor of England and took the title of Lord Hatherley.

Although the Wood family may have had an illustrious background, this had not shown itself in terms of family wealth. Evelyn's father was always in financial difficulties as he tried to maintain the social position of his family. The family's financial situation became particularly fraught by the end of the 1840s, since the vicar's stipend did not grow with the increase in the number of children. In 1846 Evelyn's father was forced, due to monetary concerns, to dismiss the governess, which had a major impact on Evelyn's education. As a result, when he went to Grammar School in Marlborough, at the age of nine, he could only read words of one syllable.[12] Fortunately the family did receive some financial help from Lady Emma's wealthy and widowed sister, who was known affectionately as Aunt Ben. This assistance was to increase after the death of Evelyn's father.

Evelyn admitted in later life that he owed any redeeming feature he may have possessed to his mother. It is clear that he was very close to her, and she to him, and their relationship caused some jealousy in the large Wood family. Evelyn's sister Katharine, seven years his junior, who as Mrs Kitty O'Shea would cause great family turmoil as a result of her affair with the Irish Nationalist Member of Parliament Charles Stewart Parnell, considered that Evelyn was their mother's idol and admitted to being jealous of the relationship between them. Evelyn fully reciprocated the devotion of his mother. Kitty wrote of him in 1914 that it was 'in his nature to work hard at the thing in hand,' and for his mother's sake the thought of failure became impossible.[13]

Whilst Evelyn had a very close relationship with his mother, this was not the case with his father, and indeed it was Kitty who received more attention from her father than any of her brothers or sisters. What little is known of Evelyn's early personality has been gleaned from the writings of Kitty. She was evidently the much teased younger sister and resented the manner in which Evelyn treated and patronised her.

She clearly did not relish Evelyn's advice to her that in the company of men she should 'look lovely and keep your mouth shut!'[14] Kitty also recalled that Evelyn had a malicious streak by recounting an incident that occurred when out riding together: he deliberately whipped her already excited mare, causing it to bolt.[15] It appears that whatever trials and tribulations the brother and sister put themselves through, there was finally mutual respect when Kitty's patience with her teasing brother exploded in an outburst, during which she shouted, 'I shan't be sorry at all when you're killed in a war ... and I wish you'd go away and be a dead hero now, so there!' The horrified silence of their mother was broken by howls of laughter from Evelyn, and Kitty stated that her brother 'was very good to me after this'.[16] However, their relationship was to be shattered when Kitty's affair with Parnell became public knowledge.

Another of Evelyn's sisters, Anna, gained national fame as a popular novelist, writing under her married name of Anna Steele. Evelyn's relationship with Anna was less turbulent than that with Kitty and it seems that they were very close. Anna's marriage to Lieutenant-Colonel Thomas Steele proved a disaster from the wedding night onwards, when Anna, to her horror, discovered what was expected of her. She fled home a week after the ceremony, still a virgin, and never returned to her husband, despite his repeated attempts to win her back. These attempts were to result in a court appearance for Evelyn when on one occasion Colonel Steele saw Anna with Evelyn in a cab travelling through London and tried to join them. Evelyn's protectiveness towards Anna, and his temper, resulted in him knocking the Colonel to the ground. Wood was subsequently sued for assault and forced to pay substantial damages of £500.[17]

After the death of his mother, Evelyn seems to have transferred much of his affection to Anna, who herself became absorbed in her brother's career and was his adviser in all matters. After Evelyn had left the family home at Rivenhall in Essex they corresponded every day, sometimes twice a day, and over 16,000 letters from Evelyn to Anna were found by their niece, Edith Bradhurst. Edith described how all the letters breathed the greatest tenderness and affection, and anxiety for his sister's opinion. Knowing Anna's financial position and increasingly eccentric behaviour, Evelyn supplied her with stamps, envelopes and the note paper for her to reply.[18] In later life, as Anna's mental health and behaviour became more worrying, Evelyn would be forced to offer material support to his sister, and he clearly stood by her in every way.

Evelyn followed in his father's footsteps and attended Marlborough Grammar School from the age of nine, when he was described as small but strongly built with reddish hair. Two years later he graduated to the College at the end of town. Here Wood seems to have enjoyed the greater liberty he was allowed, but was critical of the food, which he described as 'poor and scanty'.[19] This may have been a rather generous description as one of his contemporaries described the fare as a 'near-starvation diet.'[20] Evelyn was remembered by his classmates for his amiability and a degree of combativeness. The Rev. John S. Thomas, two years older than Evelyn, recalled him at Marlborough as 'an exceedingly high-spirited active little fellow, who entered with delight into every enterprise which suggested a lark, and a vent for the superabundance of his own spirits, but always with absolute good nature.'[21]

Wood was unfortunate in that his time at Marlborough coincided with a near mutiny amongst some of the pupils, which appears to have been provoked by the weakness of the Headmaster and a rather haphazard, random and indiscriminate approach towards discipline. Although Evelyn was rather generous to his former Headmaster in his autobiography, describing him as 'a learned scholar and kind-hearted man', he did admit that he considered him not strong enough to master 500 boys.[22] Wood witnessed a series of acts of what can only be considered as vandalism by the older boys. These included the setting alight of the Headmaster's desk and the attempted firing of some of the school's outbuildings.[23] In later years, this period of insubordination became known in the school's history as the 'Dark Ages', but it seems clear that the young Evelyn played no part in the malicious damage done to school property.[24] However, the sense of paranoia amongst the staff, caused by the disturbances, did directly lead to Evelyn's departure from the school.

Writing in his 1906 autobiography, the sense of injustice that Evelyn felt at his departure from Marlborough could still be seen, although the grievance did not stop him from speaking at the school's speech and prize-giving day in July 1888. He told the boys that despite Marlborough teaching him a little Greek and Latin the greatest life lesson the school had taught him was always to be truthful, for his arithmetic master, the Rev. J. Biden, had once told him that 'only cowards tell lies'.[25] In his autobiography Wood clearly blames the decision to leave Marlborough on the 'travesty of justice' which saw him fined, forced to recite 300 lines from the Aeneid, as well as caned in front of his classmates in December 1851. Wood's punishment was as a result of being out of bounds from school on a Saturday, although he argued, he thought correctly, that he had not been confined to school like other boys and was thus not breaking any rules. Wood assumed that after defending himself in front of the Headmaster the matter was then closed. However, at a school assembly later in the month Wood's punishment was announced and duly carried out. In the five years of his school life Wood had never been flogged before and the fact that it was now done for an offence that he felt he had not committed made his sense of hurt and grievance even stronger.

This incident seems to have taught Evelyn another 'life lesson', and throughout his career he clearly possessed a sense of fairness and justice in dealing with both the men under his command and his senior colleagues. It has also been recently argued that Wood's later ability to endure pain and discomfort whilst campaigning can be understood by the 'conditioning' he received from the harsh environment at school. It is clear that throughout his career Evelyn was a very driven individual, and it has been likewise argued that this too can be explained by the very competitive nature of his schooling.[26]

After receiving such an indiscriminate punishment, Evelyn was determined to leave the school he had come to hate. Throughout the Christmas break of 1851–2, Evelyn begged and pleaded with his parents that he might leave Marlborough and he even offered to go and work in a merchant's office in London rather than remain. Wood's persistence paid off as he gradually wore down his parents', particularly his father's, resistance. However, his parents had no intention of seeing Evelyn working in a merchant's office and it is probable that his mother used the influence of her brother, Admiral Frederick Michell, then a post captain, to obtain a nomination for Evelyn for the Royal Navy. The fourteen year old Evelyn was ordered to report for examination at the Royal Naval College, Portsmouth Dockyard, in April 1852. Wood left Marlborough in February of that year and received six weeks' arithmetic cramming in order to satisfy the Naval Examiner, as so much of his school time had been spent learning Latin and Greek at the expense of other subjects.

It appears that Wood need not have worried about arithmetic, as the entrance examination he undertook when he arrived at Portsmouth on 15 April 1852 was, at best, perfunctory. The test consisted of an English comprehension, based on a half page of the *Spectator* magazine read by the examiner, and a paper on English history, which Evelyn found easy enough as he had been taught this subject by his mother at home even before he could read.[27] Having successfully navigated his way through the examination, Wood joined HMS *Queen*, a 116-gun, 3,000-ton three-decker, under Captain Wise, on 3 July 1852. This was to be the beginning of a successful, if brief, naval career.

Evelyn described his first Captain as a 'strongly-built, active man, much feared, and still more disliked, by all hands on account of his severity'.[28] Captain Wise's face was scarred by powder marks, caused

7

when a Marine fired too close to him whilst he was at the head of a landing party in Malta. However, much as his men disliked him, Wise was respected for his courage and practical seamanship. Wood quickly learnt the basic skills of seamanship and he joined a more than competent ship's company who were famous at the time for being the fastest crew in the Navy to reef the topsails of a three-decker. Undoubtedly the watchful eye of the feared Captain spurred his men on to achieve this record. Evelyn seems to have had only two encounters with his Captain. On the first, Wise caught the small boy on deck with both hands in his trouser pockets. The Captain duly summoned a sail-maker's mate to sew up the pockets with Evelyn's hands still in them. As the first stitch went in, the Captain instructed the mate to stop sewing, but informed Wood that if he saw his hands in his pockets again they would remain there for a week. Ten days later, Evelyn was summoned to the Captain's cabin where Wise, without looking up from his desk, informed the young boy that he had received a letter from Wood's uncle, Captain Frederick Michell, asking him to look after Evelyn. A long silence followed, Evelyn not knowing whether the Captain had more to say or if he had been dismissed. Eventually Wise looked up and shouted at the young seaman, 'Well, get out of the cabin.'[29]

Wood's relationship with Wise was brief, as the Captain was soon transferred from HMS *Queen*. The new Captain duly arrived on 2 July 1853 and it must have been with excitement, but also a little foreboding, that Evelyn welcomed on board Captain Frederick Michell, his uncle! Wood shared his fears about how his uncle would treat him with his messmates, who to a man advised Evelyn to ask for a transfer to another ship. This he indeed tried, but on two separate occasions was unsuccessful. When his uncle discovered that his nephew had tried to leave the ship he summoned Evelyn to ask why he had volunteered for a transfer. The young man bravely and frankly informed his uncle that his actions were taken in an attempt to get away from him.[30] There is no record of how the Captain behaved towards his nephew up to this point, but there is some evidence that after this moment the Captain attempted to be strictly impartial and show no favour toward Evelyn.[31]

Evelyn, writing in his autobiography, described two occasions when he encountered his uncle's wrath. The first of these occurred in January 1854, when after nearly two years on board Evelyn considered himself a more than competent sailor. HMS *Queen* had been despatched to the Black Sea to monitor the Russian Fleet and, if required, to provide material assistance to the Turkish Navy, at a time of growing tension in the region. Wood was given responsibility, although not overall command, of a launch to sail to the assistance of a Greek brig which was flying signals of distress. After a hard day's work, Wood and his men succeeded in stopping the brig from running ashore and returned to HMS *Queen*. His superior officer, being as Wood described rather stout, insisted that he ascend to the ship via a rope ladder, rather than pulling himself up by rope. Evelyn pointed out that to get alongside the rope ladder would risk the launch damaging itself against the side of the warship. However, the superior officer insisted and damage did indeed result to the launch. Wood was severely reprimanded by his uncle, who refused to accept his nephew's defence that he had been obliged to obey his superior officer's order after he had pointed out the risk to the launch. His uncle's reply of, 'I don't care, sir; you were in charge of the boat, so you are responsible', was considered rather unfair by Evelyn.[32]

Similarly, three months later, Wood was censured by the Captain, this time for trying to assert his command. Once again he was responsible for a launch, under the command of a Lieutenant, collecting some of the ship's crew from Kavarna Bay, where they had enjoyed a brief shore leave. Returning to the ship, the men, who had enjoyed a drink or two on shore, became noisy, and the Lieutenant ordered Wood to keep the men quiet. Evelyn replied that it was useless to try to talk to the men in their drunken state. On return to the ship, Wood was reported to his uncle for hesitating to obey an order. Evelyn received a severe lecture from his uncle and a prediction that if he continued with such behaviour he would end his days on the gallows. The Captain's attitude towards his young nephew can be viewed as little more than one of high expectation and it does seem that the Captain, himself a very driven and ambitious man, was trying to establish the same drive in his nephew. Certainly this last incident did not harm Evelyn's naval career, for a few days later the Captain gave his nephew his first independent command, when he ordered him to take sections of the ship's anchor chain to the Constantinople dockyards for repair. This involved Wood being absent from the ship for two days and required some tact in dealing with the Turkish workers, a job which also presented language difficulties. Wood rose to the responsibility, and this far from straightforward task was successfully carried out by the young boy of just sixteen.[33]

More command and responsibility was to follow soon for Evelyn as the long expected conflict between Britain and Russia finally broke out in April 1854. By the conclusion of the war Wood was to earn fame for his courage, be recommended for the Victoria Cross and be severely wounded; moreover, by the end of the fighting he would hold a commission in the Army rather than the Navy. He would gain the respect and favour of the Army Commander, Lord Raglan, and would experience the purgatory of one of Florence Nightingale's hospital wards, returning to England physically broken. All this was to occur within less than two years, yet the sixteen year old Evelyn, who in April 1854 had not yet heard a shot fired in anger, could not have imagined such adventures and tribulations.

Chapter Two

Under Fire – The Crimean War

The Crimean War of 1854–6 arose from Russia's attempts to expand its empire southwards at the expense of the Turkish Ottoman empire. Both Britain and France were determined to stop such expansion, which had first seen the Russians occupy Turkey's Danubian provinces in July 1853. Turkey finally declared war in October of that year and, despite the show of force by both the British and French navies in the Black Sea over the winter of 1853–4, of which HMS *Queen* had been a part, the Russians could not be deterred from their expansionist policy, and France and Britain declared war on Russia in March 1854. The allies focused their attention on the Crimean peninsula and aimed at the destruction of the Russian naval base at Sebastopol, which exercised control of the Black Sea and thus threatened Constantinople. The Captain and men of HMS *Queen* first learnt that war had broken out between Russia and the alliance of France, Britain and Turkey on 9 April 1854.[1] The sixteen year old Evelyn Wood was soon to experience his first action but, before he heard the sound of guns fired in anger, he received two pieces of good and encouraging news from Captain Michell.

On 14 April 1854 Evelyn proudly received from his uncle a certificate which clearly demonstrated that any belief that the Captain had been vindictive towards his nephew because of his family connection had been wrong. The certificate, which was addressed to the Lords Commissioners of the Admiralty, stated that Evelyn had served on HMS *Queen* for two years 'during which time he conducted himself with diligence, sobriety, and attention, and was always obedient to command.'[2] Furthermore, at the end of 1853 Wood had taken his examination for the rank of midshipman and the following day he received written confirmation that he had passed. According to the citation, Evelyn had 'a due knowledge of arithmetic, geometry, and trigonometry, and a practical acquaintance with the use of the quadrant and the manner of making observations for ascertaining the latitude and longitude ... also a due knowledge of steering and managing a boat under oars and sails.'[3] His uncle approved the promotion the same day and Evelyn was then entitled to wear the white patch of a midshipman on his collar.

HMS *Queen* was assigned to the fleet that bombarded Sebastopol, as the allies began their year-long siege of the Russian city. The war began for Michell and his crew on 22 April, when the British warships began a bombardment of the port of Odessa. HMS *Queen*, and several other British and French vessels, circled around in succession, firing broadsides at the Russian batteries. Allied casualties were low, despite the fact that HMS *Terrible* was hulled eleven times and the *Vauban* set on fire by a well aimed red-hot shot. Wood believed that the Russian gun crews were not as well trained as the Allies and that the exchange of fire was not an even contest. When the Allied fleet had destroyed four of the Russian magazines, their guns were silenced.[4] However, the young midshipman would have cause to change his view of the Russian gunners in his subsequent encounters with them.

Having survived his first action, Evelyn then narrowly escaped death at the hands of his own shipmates. Writing in 1894, Wood described how, in the summer of 1854, every evening aboard HMS *Queen*, the twenty-five midshipmen would skylark around, with the favourite game being 'follow my leader'. This involved the midshipmen pursuing each other around the more dangerous parts of the ship, normally ending in the leader on the main trunk of the mainsail. Evelyn did not enjoy this game, as at such heights he had been unable to cure himself of giddiness. One evening in early July, the normal skylarking was taking place and the young Wood had crawled from the main yard to the brace, where he was resting, when a messmate opened the quarter-gallery window, and shouted out 'Boo!'. Wood was so startled that he let go of the rope and fell over forty feet to the water, turning over twice in the air. His head narrowly missed an open gun port on the way down, which, if he had hit, would have surely killed him, but he did strike his shins, making them bleed freely, on the 'round' where the sides of the ship swell out on nearing the water line. Shocked and in pain he had some difficulty swimming back to the ship and ascending the stern ladder. It seems that Evelyn managed to keep his latest exploit from his uncle.[5]

After so narrow an escape, Evelyn, together with the rest of the Allied forces, was now to face even greater danger as cholera broke out among the men and soon began to take a heavy toll. The disease was first seen in the British camps near Varna, in modern day Bulgaria, in early August 1854. Nearly 2,000 men became victims of cholera, and insufficient medical equipment meant that nearly 600 of these did not recover. An unfortunate decision was made to move a battalion to the Bosphorus, in the hope that a change of air would improve their condition. This resulted in the spread of the illness amongst the fleet and it was first seen on the French flagship, where 140 of the crew passed away. The British flagship lost ten per cent of her men and casualties were proportionally greater amongst the naval forces than the army, probably because of the cramped conditions experienced on board a man-of-war which facilitated the spread of the disease. Wood was fortunate in that only two British ships, *London* and *Queen*, escaped the outbreak. Nevertheless, the sixteen year old midshipman would lie awake in his hammock tormented by the screams of the sufferers aboard the other ships, who were gripped with the cramps of this terrible disease.

Within a few days of the first outbreak, so many of the crews had been weakened by intestinal complaints that some of the ships, carrying between 700 and 1,000 men, had not sufficient men fit enough to work the sails. Wood was sent to the British flagship to assist in the furling of the sails but soon became involved in the burying of the ship's dead, which, as he described, took place for days on end.[6] This first direct encounter with death must have been a harrowing experience for young Evelyn, but he was soon to be surrounded by carnage as he ventured ashore.

By the end of August, Lord Raglan, commanding the British land forces, had decided on a site for the landing of the invasion force, that being Kalamita Bay, roughly twenty-five miles north of Sebastopol. The forces, weakened by disease, began landing on 14 September 1854. HMS *Queen* and the other men-of-war covered the movement of the landing transports, which advanced towards the shore in columns. Over 20,000 Allied soldiers were landed on this first day and no resistance from the Russians was experienced. Casualties were remarkably low and the only tragedy was when twenty French troops, weighed down with their packets, sank to the bottom of the bay when their pontoon capsized.[7] The majority of the Allied infantry were on shore by the evening of 15 September, and for the following four days cavalry, artillery and ammunition were landed. By 19 September, over 1,500 men weakened by cholera were taken back to the ships as they were too ill even to march. The Allied advance towards Sebastopol began on that day, and on the following the British and French forces clashed with the Russian army at the battle of Alma. The young Wood was able to watch the spectacle from the top mast of HMS *Queen*, anchored off the mouth of the river Alma, and he was to recall in later life to his personal physician, Sir Norman Moore, how he had witnessed Lord Raglan advance with his forces. Evelyn stated to Moore that he believed that Raglan had advanced further forward than was safe for a General; a criticism that was to be later directed at Wood during the Zulu conflict.[8]

On the evening of 20 September, the midshipman was instructed by Captain Michell to transport him and some of the officers of HMS *Queen* to shore in a cutter, so that they might view the battlefield. Wood took the opportunity to inspect what must have been the sobering sights of the aftermath of battle. Over the next three days he assisted in the burial of some 700 bodies, found in and around the Russian breastwork where the fiercest fighting had taken place. By the end of the month Wood was back on board ship and on 1 October he was on duty as Signal Midshipman of the watch and took a message which read 'Line-of-battle ships will send 140 men and proportion of officers for service with land forces'.[9] This message was to change for ever the direction of Evelyn's life.

Michell was summoned to see the commander of the British naval forces, Commodore Lushington, to discuss who to send as part of this land force. It seems clear that it was Michell's idea to send his nephew, and not Evelyn's determination to go, that sent the young midshipman ashore. Writing later to his sister, Evelyn's mother, Lady Emma Wood, Michell stated that, 'As I could not go myself, I was determined that our family should be represented.'[10] It was Michell who recommended Evelyn to Lushington, and the midshipman joined his new friends aboard HMS *Firebrand* for passage to Balaklava, arriving on 2 October.

For the next six days Wood and the men of this new so-called Naval Brigade, which would reach a strength of 1,400 men, hauled guns and ammunition to the top of a rise overlooking the Balaklava Plain. The following week was spent erecting wooden batteries, and later Wood described how hard the men worked during this period. Turning out daily at 4.30 am and allowing only half an hour for breakfast and an hour's rest for lunch, Wood and his comrades laboured continuously until 7.30 pm, when they were replaced by a night shift.[11] All this endeavour meant that by 17 October the guns were ready to begin the bombardment of the Russian defences. On the eve of the action, Wood joined with the other officers of the Naval Brigade in betting on how long the Russian batteries would hold out. Short odds were given that the Russians would be silenced in a matter of hours, whilst some of the older and perhaps more prudent men thought the exchange might last forty-eight hours, but Wood recalls that this was considered the extreme option. Months later, Wood and his surviving comrades must have looked back at these conversations and considered them foolish beyond measure.[12]

Evelyn was not amongst the first gun crews to begin the bombardment at 6.30 am on 17 October 1854. He had to wait anxiously in camp, listening to the artillery duel. The first news of the exchanges arrived at around 9.30 am and it was not encouraging. A gunner from the initial gun crew arrived in camp with the information that the British had suffered many casualties and brought an order from Captain William Peel, the third son of the former Prime Minister, for every available man in camp to go forward to the batteries, bringing additional powder. Wood seized the opportunity, and before his senior officer could react he had ordered men from HMS *Queen* to load four carts with powder and headed for the batteries. When he and his men got within 500 yards of the British guns, the Russian gunners began shelling them from the Redan, about 2,000 yards away. A shell burst over the cart alongside which the midshipman was walking and carried away one of the wheel spokes. The men of this cart, and the other three, ran for cover. Wood later admitted that it did not occur to him to follow suit, despite his nerves, and he ordered the men to return to their carts. He was 'thus enabled to make a good start [with the men] by peremptorily recalling them to a sense of duty.'[13]

The smoke was so thick from the continuous firing that visibility was restricted to a few yards, but fortunately Evelyn had been to the batteries at night so frequently that he knew their position well. Leaving his men and the carts nearby, he advanced to inform the gun crews of the arrival of the fresh men and powder. He was forced to stoop when a Russian shell passed close over his head and he stood on something soft. Looking down, the sixteen year old sailor saw to his horror the first of many gruesome sights that he was to see in the coming months, as he realised he was standing in the disembowelled stomachs of two gunners, killed earlier in the day. Trying to conceal his shock, Evelyn reported his arrival and handed over the men and powder. He was then employed for the rest of the day in bringing fresh powder to these British guns. On one of the journeys, Wood passed close to a sergeant just as he was cut into two pieces by a Russian round-shot, which struck the man between the shoulders; this was to be the first of many occasions when Evelyn came so close to death.[14]

The British batteries had some successes on the first day of the bombardment: at about 2.00 pm, magazines in the Russian batteries, christened the Malakoff and the Redan, exploded in rapid succession, resulting in these batteries being able to bring only five guns in total to bear. However, Evelyn's initial disdain for the Russian gunners at the bombardment of Odessa was changed to respect, if not admiration, by the end of the first day. The Russians had not only inflicted casualties on the British gunners, but had silenced the French guns by 1.00 pm and had forced the Allied fleet to withdraw. By the evening, before he snatched some sleep, Evelyn realised that he had nearly been killed on several occasions during the day. He turned to pray, to thank God for his survival, and from then on he was ever mindful of his religious duties and prayed every day.[15] It was with some relief that Evelyn received news that the next day he was to command three guns in the battery, as he later admitted that the delivery of powder had been trying on his nerves.

It must have been with some trepidation that Wood awoke on 18 October, not only to his new responsibility as a gun commander, but also to the realisation that he was again to be in the thick of the artillery exchanges. If he had any fear as to whether he would survive the day, he did not show it, and by the end of the day the midshipman, and now artillery commander, was to receive the first of two recommendations for the Victoria Cross, the highest award for bravery in the British armed services. The day began with Evelyn witness to an extraordinary act of bravery by his commanding officer, Captain Peel, for which Peel would receive the coveted medal. A 42 lb Russian shell penetrated the British parapet and rolled into the centre of one of the gun crews, without exploding. The crew threw themselves to the ground, paralysed with fear. Peel lifted the shell up to his chest and carried it back to the parapet. With great difficulty, he managed to roll it over the side and down the slope, where it exploded. He then instructed the crew to recommence firing.[16] At noon, Evelyn was relieved, in order that he could have some lunch. While he was eating, a Russian shell burst over one of the magazines and set fire to the roof. Wood later admitted that he was, at first, more concerned for the safety of his lunch than at the prospect of the fire setting off the magazine. However, this view soon changed when it became clear to Wood that the danger of an explosion was very real. With his comrades lying flat on the ground, Evelyn reluctantly put down the remains of his lunch and got up on top of the magazine, stamping out the burning bags and kicking earth into the crater made by the explosion. All the time, Wood was exposed to Russian fire, both shell and bullet, yet, with the aid of Peel, he successfully extinguished the flames. Peel was full of praise for the midshipman, and this action, combined with Wood's evident bravery in bringing up ammunition and powder under constant fire, was reported at the time to the Commander-in-Chief, Lord Raglan, who, when the Victoria Cross was instituted a year later, put Evelyn's name forward for the decoration.[17]

As each day passed and Evelyn continued to survive, his confidence grew. He would later admit that he was always nervous under fire, but that his sense of duty carried him through many actions and helped

16

him overcome his fears. However, aged sixteen years, his youthful enthusiasm led him to acts of bravery and defiance that he would not consider as he grew older. For example, Captain Peel was very keen that his battery flew the Union Jack but the flag was too tempting a target for the Russian gunners and it was constantly shot off the improvised pole that Peel had rigged up. On one occasion, the Russians succeeded in cutting the staff, and sent the flag crashing to the ground. Wood jumped up, collected the flag and mounted the parapet. He was able to plant it on the parapet with what remained of the pole. He had hardly climbed down when a second shell hit the staff. Wood mounted the pole a second and then a third time on the parapet, exposing himself to enemy fire each time, until finally, with no pole remaining, he spread the flag over the top of the parapet to the cheers of the gun crews.[18] Such acts of foolish bravery began to get Evelyn a reputation for courage and determination.

Unlike the battle of the Alma, Wood was not to witness the next major clash of arms between the Allies and the Russians, at the battle of Balaklava on 25 October 1854. Although, whilst in camp, he was to hear the sounds of the fighting, Captain Peel was the only officer of the Naval Brigade to see the famous 'Charge of the Light Brigade', from the heights above Balaklava Plain. Peel returned to camp that evening and told Wood and his other officers of what he had seen, but Wood later admitted that the 'Charge' made little impact on the men at the front, and that he and his brother officers had little idea that the cavalry action was going to become such a worldwide story.

Wood and his Naval Brigade colleagues were to have an active part to play in the next major battle of the war, Inkerman, on 5 November 1854. Unbeknown to the Allied commanders, Lord Raglan and the French general Canrobert, the Russians had been gradually bringing up reserves from the Danubian theatre, with the aim of launching a surprise attack on the thinly held Inkerman ridge, overcoming, by superior numbers, the Allied forces and driving them off the Crimean peninsula. The early morning Russian advance caught the Allies by surprise, and it was only poor Russian coordination of their attack and the bravery of local commanders, such as Brigadier General Pennefather, who, rather than retreat in the face of superior forces, advanced to meet the enemy, that slowed the advance. Even so, Wood recalls that as the sound of battle grew closer, spikes were issued to all gun commanders, to ensure that if their position was overrun, the enemy would not be able to capture the guns intact. The head of the leading Russian column was spotted only 1,100 yards from Wood's battery, which opened a destructive bombardment that gradually dissolved the column's advance. Wood himself saw one of the British shells land on a

17

Russian powder wagon, and the resulting explosion threw men and horses far into the air.[19] Inkerman was, however, not primarily an artillery duel, but a confused infantry battle, in which stubborn resistance from the Allies and the heavy use of the bayonet in hand-to-hand fighting ensured that the superior Russian forces withdrew, with heavy casualties. The impact of the battle was far-reaching. The Allies had been badly shaken and the planned assault on Sebastopol was abandoned, with both sides preparing for a siege of the port. The siege continued throughout the winter of 1854–5, which would result in great privations and losses, as ill-equipped and ill-fed men succumbed to the elements. Evelyn himself would experience great hardship, as he and his comrades battled to survive the appalling conditions.

Three days after the battle of Inkerman, Wood visited the battlefield, this time not just as an interested observer, but more out of necessity. The supply problems which were to plague the Allies over the winter period had already begun to have an effect. When Evelyn had landed at Balaklava in early October, he was instructed only to bring with him two blankets and to wear light shoes. His footwear had long since worn out, and Evelyn was in effect barefooted. His visit to the battlefield was to acquire some much needed replacement boots. Despite the fact that over the preceding month Wood had been witness to much death and destruction, he became squeamish and could not bring himself to take the boots off the Russian dead, so he instructed one of his men, to whom he promised half a sovereign, to obtain for him a satisfactory fit. With so many dead, this task was soon accomplished, and Wood would later praise the good workmanship of the Russian boot makers.[20] As with so many of his comrades, Wood's resistance to illness was weakened by the severe conditions in which they found themselves. After Inkerman the weather became much colder, and from 10 November incessant rain fell for several days. It was on this day that Wood himself succumbed to sickness. He had been suffering from constant diarrhoea, the result of eating salt pork, the only available ration, often uncooked. The cold and rainy weather experienced in the trenches was to push him towards serious illness, and he now had to battle for his life.

The doctor who examined the young midshipman was only able to recommend that Evelyn be excused as much activity as possible, but what rest Wood was able to get was rudely disturbed by a great storm that hit the peninsula on 14 November. The strength of the winds was such that the tent in which he was gaining some shelter was blown away, as were many of the others, including those housing the most seriously sick and wounded, exposing all to the worst of the elements. The winds were so fierce that Wood was forced to crawl on his hands and knees to try to reach a stone wall, which was providing some cover and respite from the worst of the storm. His comrades observed that Evelyn did not even have the strength left to crawl to the shelter, and three of them carried Wood the remaining distance and placed him in the most shielded spot. Despite this limited cover, it seems clear that the weakened Evelyn would have perished from exposure had it not been for the efforts of his friends who, spotting two tents still standing in the refuge of the wall, carried him to them. The senior officer in the first tent refused the seriously ill midshipman entry, but the occupants of the second tent were more accommodating and allowed Evelyn to stay, even providing him with their own blankets. He immediately fell into a long deep sleep. The worst of the winds eased after eight hours, only to be followed by snow, which added further to the tribulations of the weakened men.[21]

When Wood awoke the next day, he witnessed a scene of utter devastation. The camp had been flattened, and although weak, Wood helped his comrades find and repair their battered tents. Several of the men who had been out on sentry duty were found frozen to death and over sixty horses had died of exposure.[22] Losses at sea were even more damaging. Twenty-one vessels were wrecked off the mouth of Balaklava harbour, including a Turkish battleship, which sank with all hands; the British transport ship *Prince* was also lost, together with its cargo of warm clothing for the troops. This loss was to claim even more British lives as the harsh winter continued.[23] With both the Russians and the Allies now resigned to a long siege, Wood and his companions focused on the need to survive the winter months. Writing over fifty years after the events of the Crimean war, Wood was to state that 'the storm on the 14 November was the commencement of misery so great as to defy adequate description',[24] and the evident bitterness in his tone reflected the fact that he clearly felt he and his comrades had been let down by the Army High Command and the Government of the day.

Although Wood and his comrades in the Naval Brigade did indeed suffer from want of adequate shelter, clothing and food during the long winter, he saw their suffering as nothing to that of the troops in the Army. It seems clear that the Army had not foreseen the probability of a long struggle and had made no provision for a winter campaign. Wood states that the ten and a half per cent losses of the Naval Brigade during the winter months, from disease and exposure, were slight compared to the seventy-three per cent losses suffered by the eight Battalions which served immediately to the front of the Naval Brigade. Wood attributes this huge difference to the ability of the sailors to establish a better supply chain from Balaklava harbour to the front for the meagre food and supplies that were available, and to the more active approach adopted by the Naval command. For example, Commodore Lushington visited the Naval Brigade several times over the winter months, and he himself initiated adequate sanitary measures in the camp, organised parties to carry supplies of food and warm clothing from the harbour, and even ensured that the men had an area where they could dry their wet clothing. Wood's experience of the hardship he and his comrades suffered undoubtedly had a huge influence on him, for in later years he always expressed a great concern for the men under his command, whether it was to ensure that they had sufficient rations during the fighting in Zululand or adequate accommodation whilst in barracks.

The weather continued to be deplorable and the food ration meagre. Without fuel for fires, the men not only suffered from the extreme cold, but until January had no means by which to cook the small meat ration. They lived on salt meat, usually pork, as this was easier to eat raw, biscuits and a rum ration. Even when fuel was issued to cook the meat, many of the men could not eat it, as their teeth were loosened by scurvy. To add to their woes, cholera reappeared on 2 December. Wood almost lost his beloved Russian boots in December, when they were sucked off his feet by the tenacious mud which covered the camp. In the second week of December, whilst still awaiting a proper supply of tents, Wood fell asleep in the gun battery. Anxious to get out of the freezing wind, he sheltered by crouching in the trench. When the wind dropped in the early hours, it began to rain, and Wood felt himself getting wet but was too tired to move. When he awoke at daybreak, he discovered that he was unable to move as the water on his clothing had frozen solid. Fortunately, his comrades reacted quickly and carried the midshipman back to camp, where he was surrounded by hot bottles to his feet and body and with much care and attention he was saved from frostbite.[25]

Life in the battery now centred on the need to somehow survive the winter. When not at the front, Wood was given the responsibility of daily visits to Balaklava or Kamiesh Bay to beg, borrow or buy food for the Mess and the men of the battery. During one of these trips, Wood was ordered to take a message to the Army Headquarters. Here he met Lord Raglan for the first time and, to Wood's satisfaction, the Commander-in-Chief recalled Evelyn's bravery of October. More welcome than the praise was the gift of food which Raglan gave to Wood to share with his men. Wood's 'raiding-parties' seem to have been very ingenious in always ensuring that his comrades had some food each day. How Evelyn managed to obtain such supplies is not dwelt on in his autobiography, but he does mention that some of the French officers who were billeted next to the Naval Brigade did complain to

Commodore Lushington that the disappearance of their horses would have to stop or there would be retaliation![26]

The daily hardship, and what must have been intense periods of boredom, were relieved by only two pieces of excitement for the young midshipman during the long winter. Military activity from both the Russians and the Allies was limited to the occasional firing of artillery. However, on 11 December 1854, Wood, whilst in command of the battery, received a request from an infantry officer in one of the forward trenches to train his guns on a party of Russians, who were working to extend the trenches around the Malakoff battery. Wood himself aimed the gun at the work party, which was over 1,700 yards away. One well directed shell not only halted the work of the Russians, but, as Wood observed, actually hit one of the enemy, cutting the unfortunate man into two pieces. This was the first man that Wood could claim for certain had died at his hands, but it was not to be the last.[27] On Christmas Day the Russians decided to send over some accurate artillery fire as unwelcome gifts. Again, Evelyn narrowly escaped death. One of the shells lodged in the parapet, close to where Wood was talking to a sergeant in charge of a work party, and failed to explode. Now hardened to such experiences, Wood recalled that the arrival of the shell did not even break the conversation he was having with the sergeant. Suddenly the shell exploded and a fragment lifted his cap clean off his head, but Evelyn survived without even a scratch.[28]

By February the weather had improved somewhat and, much to the relief of all the men involved in the siege, the ground began to dry out. Fresh reinforcements began to arrive from both France and England, and Wood's battery was rearmed with further 32 and 68-pounder guns. Perhaps of greater importance was the arrival in Balaklava harbour of Admiral Boxer, who was given the brief by the High Command to improve the unloading and transfer of supplies to the front. Wood states that the Admiral effected 'vast improvements'.[29]

The build-up of Allied supplies and men seemed to indicate a fresh willingness to attack Sebastopol, but before any action could be taken the Russians renewed their attempts to break the siege. On 22 March 1855, Russian troops centred their attack upon the French forces around the Mamelon battery. Like the British troops during the battle of Inkerman, the French army were not reluctant to use the bayonet, and, after severe hand-to-hand fighting, the Russians withdrew to their lines. The next day a truce was agreed, so as to allow for the collection and burial of the dead. Wood, again using his initiative, siezed the opportunity offered by joining the burial parties to ascend the ridge joining the two Russian batteries of Mamelon and Malakoff, in order to assess the fall of the ground on the other side of the ridge. Wood had calculated that in any future Russian attack this would be the ground on which the Russian troops would assemble, before launching themselves forward. From his reconnaissance Wood hoped to be able to judge the best angle for his guns to lob their shells on to the Russian concentration. Wood's espionage was successful and he duly obtained the desired information, before being spotted by a Russian officer and sent packing back to the British lines.[30]

It is clear that the experiences that Wood and Peel had shared during the early artillery exchanges of October 1854 had created a bond between them and, although Peel was senior to Evelyn in both rank and years, it is evident from Peel's later letters to Wood that a strong friendship existed between them. Evelyn was delighted when Peel took him for his aide-de-camp on 2 April. However, two incidents over the following week almost made this a very short appointment as, once again, Evelyn narrowly escaped death. First, on 6 April, a Russian mortar shell fell within six feet of Evelyn in the battery. Fortunately the shell was fitted with a long fuse, and Wood reacted quickly and managed to run for cover before it exploded.[31] Three days later Evelyn had an even narrower escape from death whilst in command of the battery. He was looking through a telescope in an attempt to assess the accuracy of his battery's firing, and he rested the telescope on the shoulder of a Charles Green, First Class Boy of HMS *Queen*, and Wood's friend and messmate aboard ship. The daily grog ration had just been issued and Green asked Wood to move the telescope so that he might raise the grog to his lips. As Evelyn lifted the telescope, a Russian shell cut across his face, its wind within an inch of his nose, and hit Green with such force that it took off his head. The headless body slumped at Evelyn's feet. The contents of Green's skull hit gunner Michael Hardy standing behind Wood, who did not flinch but, wiping the brains and blood from his face, continued to load his gun and ordered the rest of the crew to continue their work. Wood was as much stunned by the closeness of his own death as that of Green's, but the impressive action of Hardy in continuing his duty snapped him out of his shock. Wood later recalled that he found Hardy's actions inspirational, and he clearly had much respect for the gunner whom he described as 'a remarkable man ... who never felt danger'.[32]

Over the next two months, Evelyn fulfilled his role as aide-de-camp to Captain Peel, and Peel and the midshipman, who had now turned seventeen years of age, spent a great deal of time together. If anything, Wood's admiration for Peel grew even greater during this period, and it is clear that Peel valued the opinion of his aide-de-camp. For example, on the eve of a French attack on the Russian Mamelon battery, which was to be supported by fire from the Naval Brigade, Peel and Wood inspected the Naval batteries together, to ensure their readiness and establish that the officers in charge of the guns knew their targets. On 7 June 1855 the British batteries commenced an accurate fire on Mamelon and Malakoff, which silenced them by the early afternoon. Wood and his comrades then fired in support of the French infantry attack on the Mamelon battery. Although the initial attack was successful and drove the Russians from the battery, a large Russian counter-attack from the Malakoff overwhelmed the French, who had to return to their lines. However, Wood's reconnaissance of the ground between the two Russian batteries during the earlier truce of March brought dividends, when his battery was able to direct fire upon the advancing Russians, who were using the ridge as cover for their counter-attack. Although Wood's fire did not stop their advance, it did inflict substantial Russian casualties.

This French attack was part of a concerted attempt by the Allies to overwhelm the Russian batteries. A coordinated attack by both British and French forces was planned for later in June. Before this attack, however, Wood was to fall ill once more. Throughout the week of 10–17 June, Evelyn, along with many men of the Naval Brigade, suffered from fever and intestinal complaints. Knowing that an attack was being planned, he managed to evade the doctor and remain at the front, although much weakened by the effects of the illness.[33] By 17 June the fever had forced Wood to his bed, and as a result he missed the visit of Captain Peel to his battery. On awakening and learning of Peel's visit, Wood somehow mounted his pony and cantered off to find the Captain. However, he had only travelled a few yards when his pony refused to go on and stood still trembling. Despite Wood's encouragement and urging, the animal refused to move. Suddenly, a mortar-shell smashed into the ground in front of rider and horse, just where they would have been travelling. Evelyn had had another close encounter with death.[34]

On finding Peel, Wood was informed by his Chief that he considered him too ill to take part in the attack planned for the following day. Peel was moved by Evelyn's show of extreme frustration and disappointment and relented, stating that Wood could accompany Peel to the Russian Redan, but could not take part in the storming of the position. That evening, Wood and his messmates enjoyed a meal together, their bravado boosted by making bets as to who would be killed during the attack. One officer bet five sovereigns that Wood would not survive the day.[35]

Wood retired to bed at 10.00 pm, giving orders to a nearby sentry to rouse him for the attack. Peel, aware of Evelyn's poor physical condition, gave the same sentry a counter-order not to wake the midshipman, but Wood was stirred from his slumbers by the sound of the men getting ready for the advance. Wood had been taking high doses of laudanum over the previous days and this, combined with his general condition, meant that he now found it difficult to keep awake. He was roused once more by gunner Michael Hardy who, despite Evelyn's drug-induced protests that he was too ill to take part, dressed the midshipman, saying that Wood would not forgive himself in the morning if he missed the attack. Wood was so weak that he could not keep a grip on his pony and Hardy had to hold him in the saddle. Even when he did join Peel and the attack party at the front line, Wood was forced to sit down to recover some of his strength. In an attempt to remove him from the coming dangers of the assault, Peel sent Evelyn on three separate errands, delivering messages to other parts of the line. Evelyn believed this was done by Peel in the hope that, whilst the midshipman was away, the attack would be launched and he would miss it.[36]

The advance itself was badly coordinated. Unfortunately, the French launched themselves into the assault too early, before the two British columns had concentrated for their attacks. Nor was there any bombardment in advance of the attack. The Russians were apparently forewarned of the impending assaults and poured down a vicious fire on the French, who withdrew after forty minutes. The British then launched their attacks and were met by the same storm of Russian shell and bullet. Wood was one of the first over the British parapet, following his Chief, Captain Peel. Their appearance drew fire from the Russian guns and several men preceding them were swept off the parapet by grapeshot. Wood was later to describe the intensity of Russian fire as similar to the tropical rain when a monsoon breaks, sweeping down the hill and 'felling our men as a reaping-machine levels standing crops.'[37] The scene must have been an early preview of the battles of the Western Front during World War One, which Wood would live long enough to read of. Captain Wolseley, later Commander-in-Chief of the British Army and close associate of Wood, witnessed the British advance and exclaimed to Lord Raglan, 'Ah! there is no chance for them'; and Raglan himself, a survivor of the storming parties of Ciudad Rodrigo and Badajoz (1812) during the Peninsular War (1808–1813), stated that he had 'never before witnessed such a continued and heavy fire of grape and musketry.'[38]

In the mêlée, Wood soon lost contact with Peel and did not realise that his Chief had been wounded in the left arm and forced to retire. Evelyn, with his adrenaline pumping, continued to advance, all thoughts of his illness gone. Men from the Naval Brigade were falling all around him and he too was struck whilst waving on his men with his sword. The bullet struck first his thumb and then his sword. His arm was paralysed by the jar and he fell to the ground. On realising that he was not badly hurt, he stood up and picked up his sword, which he found had been twisted like a corkscrew. Discarding his weapon, he continued to advance unarmed. What Wood did not now realise was that all his fellow Naval officers had either be killed or wounded and he was the only officer still advancing. The ladder parties of both naval and army forces were being decimated by the Russian fire, and Wood noticed that he had outstripped the surviving men by about 100 yards. He reluctantly retraced his steps to help a man struggling alone with a ladder. Wood grabbed one end of the ladder and helped carry it towards the Redan, but after only a few minutes his comrade was shot dead. Wood later admitted that the first sensation he experienced at the death of his ladder companion was the relief that he felt he had done his duty and that no one could expect him to carry an eighteen-foot ladder by himself. He thus discarded the ladder and ran to join the few men who had reached the limited safety of the base of the Russian parapet.

From this position, Wood could look up and see the Russians fifteen feet above him, four or six deep, trying to fire down on the remaining British troops. Here he witnessed many disturbing sights which would never leave him. One Army officer tried to rally his men to advance, only to be cut down by Russian bullets. A young Sergeant, likewise, tried to encourage his men forward by threats and coercion. He even threatened to shoot one of his men, but before he could carry this out he too was killed. However, the most upsetting scene, Evelyn later recounted, was when he was discussing with an Army officer the futility of their position and this officer was struck by a bullet in the stomach. By now the seventeen year old midshipman had seen more death than most would ever see, and the sight of a dying Army officer in great pain, calling on the Almighty, did not perturb him. Yet when the officer, with his last breath, called for his mother, Wood was seriously affected and had to leave the man. He climbed in an attempt to find any weaker spots in the Russian defences and, as he did so, he was aware of four Russians above him training their rifles on him. He instinctively threw up his left arm to protect his face, just as one of the Russian guns fired case shot into the remaining British attackers. One of the shots, weighing five and a half ounces, struck Wood in the elbow and sent him rolling down the slopes of the hill, where he lay insensible.[39]

Wood lay unconscious for a few minutes until roused by an Irish corporal, who grabbed the lifeless body by its arm. Unfortunately, the soldier held Wood by his wounded arm and the sudden pain not only brought Wood back to his senses, but also earnt the corporal a stream of abuse. The Retire had been sounded, and despite being less than 100 yards from the Russian position, which was still firing down on the now retreating British, the corporal calmly helped Evelyn to his feet, being careful not to hurt his arm once again. Wood was now overcome with a feeling of faintness and it was with the greatest difficulty that he managed to stagger back to the British lines. On reaching the parapet, he was struggling up when he was pushed out of the way by a fleeing rifleman. Wood caught hold of his rifle to pull himself up the slope. The soldier turn around to see what Wood was doing just as a round shot passed over Wood's shoulder and hit the rifleman in the chest. Wood stepped over the remains of the body, too exhausted and indifferent to death to care about yet another close shave.

The bloody scenes in the casualty station soon shocked Evelyn out of his indifference. The sight of piles of already amputated and discarded limbs as well as the screams from the operating tables provoked a sense of panic within Wood and a desire to be away from this living hell. However, he was unable to escape an examination by one of the doctors, who insisted that Evelyn would have to have his arm amputated as the risk of infection was high and he would never regain the use of the arm. He managed, by doubling his fist, to raise his arm despite the severe pain, and he convinced the doctor to try to save it. Dr Liddell extracted the shot that day. When Evelyn recovered consciousness, he was visited by Captain Peel. The two men shared their own stories of the assault and, although Wood was overjoyed that his Captain had survived, he was bitterly upset to learn that the body of Michael Hardy had been recovered below the Russian parapet.

The news of Evelyn's exploits soon spread amongst the troops, both French and British. After Peel's visit Wood fell asleep, only to be woken by a messenger from Lord Raglan, who offered his carriage and his personal physician for Wood's transfer from the hospital to HMS *Queen*. News also reached Commadore Lushington, who wrote to Evelyn's uncle, Captain Michell, informing him that his nephew had been wounded, but that he had borne the wound well and had acted like a hero. Lushington rather candidly informed Michell of the reasons for the failure of the attack. He claimed that 'the assault was a total failure from the first ... bad in detail and worse in execution ... at all events we were well thrashed ... they [French and British Command] stormed the forts first and bombarded it afterwards. Our Allies are odd fellows, I suppose there will be a row.'[40] Wood took advantage of Lord Raglan's offer of his carriage and on 20 June travelled the eight miles from the hospital to the beach for transfer to HMS *Queen*, where his uncle gave Evelyn one of his cabins in which to recuperate. Michell wrote to Raglan thanking him for the kind use of his carriage, and the following day, 21 June, Lord Raglan replied to Michell, saying: 'I am very glad to have had the opportunity of being in any the smallest degree useful to your Nephew whose distinguished career cannot fail to enlist everybody in his favour.'[41]

Evelyn now became something of a celebrity amongst the Allied fleet and he received a succession of distinguished visitors, including the French Naval Commander, who called on him on 30 June. Michell was at first surprised by all the attention that his young nephew was receiving, but by the first week of July it suddenly dawned on him that Evelyn was a popular and deserving hero. On 4 July he wrote to his friend Captain Burnett, describing Evelyn's exploits. His own liking and respect for his nephew is clear from the letter. Michell wrote, 'if his Parents [Evelyn's] are not satisfied with his reputation he has won for himself, by his quiet steady courage they do not deserve such a son ... I suspect his actions leading the ladder party must have attracted attention, for even all my French friends have heard of the "young midshipman who was wounded in the arm". I have asked no questions of anyone about him, it is enough for me that my Brother officers and particularly Peel and Lushington speak so highly of him ... Were I to show the pride I feel and take in this Boy it would be the signal to start an "if" or a "But" against him.'[42]

Frustratingly, although Wood's arm was never in any danger once he had persuaded the doctors not to amputate, it refused to heal completely, and by the end of July Evelyn reluctantly accepted his doctor's advice that he should return to England to continue his recovery. Much to his uncle's disappointment, this is what Evelyn did, reaching his parents' home in early August 1855. He immediately began to work for his return to the Crimea, although it is clear that despite the recognition he had received whilst serving in the Navy, he did not see his future in this service. His biographer Charles Williams believed that Evelyn considered there was not much fame left for him to earn in the Navy and he yearned for something more active than keeping harbour watch or any of the daily duties on board a warship.[43] Having obtained his parents' consent to join the Army, at the end of August, Wood wrote to the Commander-in-Chief, Viscount Hardinge, asking for a Commission in any Light Cavalry regiment, and enclosed a copy of Lord Raglan's letter which had been written to his uncle in June.

It only took one week for Wood to receive the news that he had been accepted as a cornet in the 13th Light Dragoons, and the haste of the decision, together with the fact that Evelyn was not obliged, as others were at that time, to purchase his Commission, suggests that his fame and the support given by Raglan's letter had allowed him an easy transfer. This move, however, does seem to have cost Evelyn his Victoria Cross, for despite the support given to him by Raglan and Lushington, and the fact that his name was third on the list of recommendations, he was turned down for the award. Lushington wrote to Wood in February 1857 and offered some explanation as to why Wood did not get the medal. He stated that the Navy had pressed for a number of candidates from the Naval Brigade and that there was a general feeling that the number of awards needed to be curtailed.[44] It seems that the Navy was not going to insist on the award going to an officer who was no longer in their service. Evelyn did receive some recognition for the bravery he displayed in the Crimea, but it was not immediately from his own nation. His French Imperial Majesty conferred upon Evelyn the Knight Legion of Honour for his exploits in attacking the Redan, and he also received grateful thanks from the Turkish authorities when he was honoured with the Medjidie medal.[45] Finally, Wood did receive an award from his own country when he was presented with the British Crimean War Medal, with the two clasps of Inkerman and Sebastopol.[46]

In later life Evelyn became well known for his hypochondria, but at the age of seventeen, with his arm still refusing to heal properly and a summons to attend the cavalry barracks of the 13th Light Dragoons in Dorchester, he felt compelled to take action, and he displayed enormous bravery by operating on his arm by himself. It is clear that Evelyn was not squeamish. He placed his arm on a firm cushion, opposite a mirror, and with great patience he extracted eight pieces of splintered bone from his elbow, one of which was an inch and a quarter in length. Such drastic action meant that by the end of September he was fit enough to begin his cavalry training in Dorset. Fortunately, Wood had considerable experience of riding and progressed well, yet after less than a month's training his determination to return to the Crimea led him to write again to the Commander-in-Chief, now the recently appointed Duke of Cambridge, requesting active service. Wood received a stinging reply in which he was told to place all such requests via his Commanding Officer, and informed him that the Commander-in-Chief understood it took more than twenty-four days' depot training to make a perfect Cavalry officer.[47]

This evident determination to return to active service carried Evelyn through the training course, despite the handicap of his arm, whose injury he aggravated in the barracks when the accident-prone dragoon fell down the stairs. However, he managed to conceal his physical weakness from his riding instructors and passed out in the top half of the class. The order Wood was waiting for came through from the

28

War Office at the end of 1855 and he left the barracks on 1 January 1856 to return to the seat of war. The voyage to the Crimea took three weeks, and the new dragoon, still not yet eighteen years of age, stepped ashore at the port of Scutari with renewed optimism and energy for the fight before him. Soon Evelyn was to fight the toughest battle of his young life, but this time not against the Russians.

Within a month of his arrival Evelyn found himself in the hospital at Scutari, under the care and supervision of Florence Nightingale and her band of nurses. Wood considered that his survival was not due to their care, but to the persistence of his Commanding Officer, Captain Percy Smith, who managed to persuade his namesake, Doctor Smith, President of a Pathological Committee who had been sent out by the Government to report on conditions, to examine Evelyn. Although the staff at Scutari hospital had been treating Wood for the effects of typhoid, Doctor Smith diagnosed that Wood would first die of pneumonia if it was not treated immediately. With the applications of mustard poultices, Evelyn survived the initial threat. However, he was not out of danger, and a telegram was sent to his parents stating that he probably did not have long to live. On receipt of this news, they boarded a ship, in the hope they would reach Evelyn in time.

The treatment that Evelyn was now receiving at the hands of Nightingale's nurses can only be described as barbaric. Although one nurse, Susan Cator, was devoted to Wood and did everything in her power to aid his recovery, the other nurses were less caring. One in particular, whom Wood did not name in his autobiography, would deliberately inflict pain on the ailing dragoon. Evelyn had lost so much weight that the bones of both hips had pierced his skin. When changing his bandages, this nurse, rather than wetting them first, would tear off the lint roughly, ripping off skin and drawing blood. She would also slap and hit Wood when left alone with him. Evelyn feared this woman greatly, such torment soon affected his mental state and Wood shuddered and wept every time Nurse Cator had to leave him. Under such care his condition worsened, and Wood recalled that one day, whilst in a semi-conscious state, he heard the senior doctor instruct the ward doctor not to give him any more medicine and let him die in peace.[48]

Evelyn's parents finally arrived in Scutari on 20 March 1856, after experiencing dreadful weather and acute seasickness. Both Lady Wood and Sir John Page Wood feared that they might arrive only to discover the worst, that their beloved son was already dead. Indeed Evelyn's father, so sure his son had died, could not bring himself to visit the hospital. Lady Wood was clearly shocked by what she found there. At first she did not recognise her son, nor could she understand what he tried to tell her.[49] Lady Wood later described to one of her daughters, Maria Wood, how she found Evelyn a living skeleton, with ulcers covering his spine and hips.[50] After her initial five minute visit, Lady Wood returned to the hospital the following day and insisted that she would remain to care for her son. Suffering from delirium, Evelyn was still too ill to communicate to his mother the abuse he was suffering, but Lady Wood felt something was amiss, and contrived to catch Evelyn alone with the brutal nurse. Her worst fears were confirmed when she witnessed the nurse striking Evelyn across the face repeatedly. This was to be the first time, but not the last, that Evelyn's mother crossed swords with Florence Nightingale, for it appears that Nightingale initially refused to believe Lady Wood's tales of abuse, preferring to believe her nurse's protestations of her innocence. Ultimately Lady Wood's determination prevailed and she insisted that the offending nurse was dismissed from the hospital.

Writing in 1929, Lady Wood's niece, Edith Bradhurst, generously admitted that as Head of the Nursing Staff in the Crimea, Florence Nightingale was 'obliged to cater for the multitude rather than the individual.'[51] It is doubtful whether Lady Wood viewed her son's care in these terms. All she saw was a further deterioration in Evelyn's condition and she felt that he had but a slender chance of survival if left at Scutari. By the middle of April, despite protests from the doctors and Nightingale, Lady Wood was determined to return to England with her son. Evelyn's mother was told by the senior doctor that he felt Wood would not survive being carried from his bed to the beach to board a ship, let alone the voyage home. Evelyn had heard these comments, and when his mother asked him what he wanted to do he replied, 'Start tomorrow'.[52] Under the circumstances, the move from the unhealthy conditions of Scutari undoubtedly saved Evelyn's life, although he was to experience much pain and discomfort on the return journey. Whilst resting in Malta, Evelyn suffered from haemorrhaging in his lungs, and this and many other ailments meant that Wood and his parents were forced to break their journey back to England into several short stages. On 1 May, Evelyn's return to English soil at Folkestone was not a dignified entry. Dropsy had caused his feet to swell to an enormous size and, unable to find any footwear to fit him, he was forced to walk ashore in his stockings.[53]

Evelyn spent the next weeks continuing to recuperate, receiving friends and answering correspondence. At this time, he was frequently in touch with Captain Peel, who had also been invalided back to England. Peel, writing on 11 May, expressed his concern for Evelyn's health, and over the weeks Evelyn would write to Peel asking his advice as to his future career prospects.[54] Peel did his best to reassure the young dragoon that, despite all his health problems, he still had a future in the cavalry. Through the loving care of his mother, Evelyn made good progress and recovered his strength. By August he was fit enough to travel to France, to improve his French, and by the end of the year he was considered well enough to journey to Ireland to rejoin his regiment at Cahir, with the new rank of lieutenant, the commission having been purchased by his uncle, Sir William Page Wood.[55] For the next few months Evelyn joined his comrades on small patrols around the surrounding countryside, employed in keeping the peace during elections. It is clear that Evelyn found the work dull and this, combined with the expense of serving in a cavalry regiment, made him consider yet another transfer, this time to the infantry. Wood did not waste his spare time whilst in barracks, and he was fortunate that he made friends with Major Arthur Tremayne, a university graduate and classical scholar, who lent Evelyn many of his books and instructed him as to others he should read. Evelyn claimed that in five months he was able to make up for the five years schooling he had lost whilst serving on HMS *Queen*.[56]

On 26 June 1857 news reached England of events in India, where troops of the Indian Army (sepoys) had mutinied against the British. The mutiny began on 10 May and was first centred on the cities of Meerut and Delhi, but soon spread to much of Northern India. The long established view that the revolt began because of deep seated grievances against British rule, and was triggered by the issue of the supposed pig fat used to bind the Army's rifle cartridges, which was offensive to both Muslims and Hindus, has recently been questioned.[57] However, what is clear is that the uprising in India presented fresh opportunities to ambitious Army officers hoping for advancement. When the news of the Mutiny was debated in Parliament on 29 June, Lord Palmerston's Government was quick to announce the despatch of 14,000 troops to reinforce the British army now engaged in India against the rebels.

Desperate to be a part of the troop reinforcements, Evelyn at first considered a transfer to the 7th Hussars. When this proved impossible, his impatience grew and he obtained three months' leave on private affairs, but it is clear that he used this time to try to negotiate his transfer to a regiment destined for India. By September his endeavours paid off, when he was asked by the Commanding Officer of the 17th Lancers whether he wished to transfer into this regiment. Although such a move meant that he would be under officers who were junior to him, Evelyn jumped at the chance, and in early October, after a sad farewell to both his parents and the officers and men of the 13th Light Dragoons, he joined his new regiment and set sail for India. Lady

Wood was convinced that she would not see her son again. She felt that Evelyn, still not yet twenty, had not fully recovered from both his physical wound and his time at Scutari, and she told Maria Wood that she would 'despise Evelyn if he were not so anxious to go'.[58] Another chapter in Evelyn's career was about to begin, one in which he would yet again face extreme dangers, but would also gain more fame and recognition.

Chapter Three

The Search for Glory

Evelyn, still only nineteen years of age, once again left his home shores in search of active-service. On reaching Cape Town, Wood and all the other passengers aboard the *Great Britain* learned that Delhi had been recaptured by British forces, and some of his travelling companions confidently predicted the revolt would be over before they reached Bombay. Wood must have experienced mixed emotions at the latest news. Like many of his countrymen at home, reading of events in India in their morning newspapers, he must have experienced horror at the details of the British deaths at the hands of the Mutineers, particularly the massacre of women and children at Cawnpore, which led many in Britain to call for swift revenge and retribution. As an active soldier, Evelyn must also have known that India was now the best place to be if he were to gain rapid advancement and glory. Wood's ship docked in Bombay on 21 December 1857, and he must have disembarked from the vessel with the hope that there would still be some campaigning for him to do.

Evelyn was not to be disappointed, although his active service was to get off to a slow start. Wood was not to take part in the remaining set-piece battles which brought an effective end to the Mutiny. He was destined to join the Central India Forces, led by Major-General Sir Hugh Rose, and would take part in the pursuit of one of the rebel leaders, Tatya Tope. However, this would be in the future, as Wood's first priority was to oversee the unloading of the Regiment's baggage and to ensure its safe transfer to the new base at Kirki in northern India. The establishment of Wood's cavalry regiment in its new surroundings was somewhat delayed by the complete lack of horses. The import of suitable horses by the Government had been delayed, and it was not until February 1858 that Evelyn was able to journey back to Bombay to purchase his mount, which he christened 'Pig', as it would eat any food within its reach, from milk in a saucer to raspberry jam.

The 'Pig' was to serve Wood well as it carried him over 5,000 miles across India between May 1858 and April 1859.[1]

Wood had not wasted his time on the voyage, and he arrived in India with some ability to read and write Hindustani; he could even speak a few words. He now took advantage of the limited activity of his first few months to spend twelve hours a day learning the language under the tuition of two local teachers. Wood appears to have had something of a natural talent for languages, but he did admit that, due to the excessive temperatures, he sometimes found it difficult to keep awake during these lessons. He therefore worked at a stand-up desk, resting on an office stool. When he found that even in this position sleep still came too readily, he cut three legs off the stool so that he was forced to balance only on the remaining leg. If he drifted off to sleep, the delicate balance of the stool would be disturbed and he would wake up with a jolt.[2] His inventiveness and determination soon paid off when he was allowed to sit an examination for the position of Interpreter.

Evelyn was also able to use this time to correspond with his old commanding officer and friend from the Crimea, Captain Sir William Peel, who was also serving in India. In the last letter Evelyn was to receive from his old comrade, Peel expressed his delight that Evelyn had succeeded in becoming the Regiment's Hindustani interpreter, as well as frustration in that he felt it was unlikely that they would get to meet whilst they were both in India. Peel warned Evelyn not to be 'over anxious for employment in the field' as that day would surely come, and he predicted 'success, fame and promotion are pretty sure to attend you.'[3] It seems Peel felt certain that Evelyn's abilities and character would ensure his success. Sadly, the deep friendship that the two men had towards each other was to end with the death of Peel from disease only a few weeks later. The news of the death of his close friend was kept from Wood for several days, as at the time Evelyn was confined to bed with fever and the doctors considered that such terrible news would seriously affect his recovery.

By the middle of March, the Regiment had obtained sufficient horses to be able to form two effective Squadrons, and by May, the Colonel of the 17th Lancers acceded to Wood's request to join Captain Sir William Gordon's troop, which was assigned to General Rose's force. Evelyn was, once again, on active service. His first role was as part of a 100-strong squadron, which set off in pursuit of Tatya Tope. There followed a period of eleven months, during which Evelyn was on constant service, patrolling across a most unforgiving landscape and experiencing the most extreme climate. Such conditions took a toll of British officers and men alike, and Wood was no exception. The dangers of sunstroke were very real, sometimes fatal, and on numerous occasions Evelyn was forced to rest for a day or more to recover from the effects of the oppressive heat. Despite all this, as the pursuit of the rebels continued, Wood soon became indispensable; as the sole British officer with a knowledge of Hindustani, he soon found himself in the role of Quartermaster for the Troop, and the skills he had acquired in the Crimea as a supplier of food and forage came to be vital for the continued welfare of men and horses.

After months of continued pursuit of the rebel Tatya Tope, the British forces finally managed to get into a position to engage their elusive prey. On 14 September 1858, the advance guard, of which Evelyn was a part, finally closed on the rebels at a place called Rajghur. Tatya Tope believed his forces, which included over thirty artillery pieces, held a strong position and, rather than flee, decided to hold his ground. Evelyn was, as ever, impatient for action, but General Michel, commanding the British forces, considered that his weary infantry, many suffering from sunstroke, were too exhausted to advance. That night, as the British positioned their forces ready for battle on the following day, Tatya Tope changed his plans and decided to move off under cover of darkness. Gordon's Troop, including Evelyn, was ordered to maintain contact with the enemy and, in the early hours of 15 September, they trotted off in pursuit. The rebels had moved eastwards and it was not long before the Troop became engaged with the rebel rearguard. The rebel skirmishers commenced a heavy fire, which stalled the British advance.

Frustrated by the lack of progress, Michel summoned Evelyn and personally instructed him to advance through the line of rebels. At the head of a dozen native cavalry, Wood charged through the rebel skirmish line and advanced, in order to establish the position of the main body of the rebel army. Evelyn and his twelve men soon came across a number of cannons abandoned by the fleeing rebels. Suddenly, rounding a bend in the track, Wood came face-to-face with three rebel artillerymen, standing by their gun. One of the mutineers held a burning slow-match. Evelyn realised that he was going to light the fuse to the loaded cannon and that there was no time for his band of men to spread out and move off the track. Wood reacted quickly, ordering a charge at the gun, and the shot of the sighted cannon passed harmlessly over the cavalrymen's heads.[4] The native troops quickly cut down the three rebels and continued on their charge, with Evelyn unable to restrain them. He calculated that they would soon return when they encountered a larger body of the enemy, and this indeed happened.

With his restored Troop, Evelyn continued carefully to pursue the retreating rebels. He was accompanied by the orderly named Dhokul

35

Singh, who was to become Wood's devoted servant and friend. On this occasion, Singh was able to demonstrate his devotion by attacking a rebel who he saw taking careful aim at the young lieutenant. Singh immediately charged at the mutineer and, using his cavalry sword, cut the man's face in two. This blow, although horrific, did not kill him, and the determination and fanaticism of the rebels was clearly shown as the deformed man continued to fight. It was left to a squadron of the 17th Lancers, who were following, to finally dispatch this rebel. Both Wood's Troop and the remainder of the cavalry, under the command of William Gordon, lost contact with the main rebel army in the thick jungle into which the rebels fled; without infantry support, which was following behind, it would have been unwise to continue the pursuit in such terrain. Although Tatya Tope was able to make his escape, he was forced to abandon much of his artillery.[5]

As the mutineers continued eastwards, Wood and the pursuing British forces headed in a south-easterly direction, in the hope of eventually cutting off the rebel army. Once again, although the cavalry managed to regain contact with the rebels, the slow passage of the British infantry in the extremely hot conditions meant that it proved impossible to engage the enemy with sufficient numbers. At one point, eight cavalry officers and 350 Native troops confronted the rebel army of 10,000 men. Without the British infantry, any thought of attack had to be abandoned. After weeks of 'cat and mouse', in which Tatya Tope led his force first eastwards and then north, the British were finally in a position to force a battle. On 18 October, a patrol commanded by Wood came across an enemy cavalry picket just south of the town of Sindwaha, and beyond them Tatya Tope's main force. It seems clear that the rebel leader thought his army were only facing British and Native cavalry, and decided to make a stand against them, positioning his troops, along with four remaining cannons, on a low range of hills. What Tatya Tope did not realise was that the British infantry were only three miles away and that Wood had sent an urgent message to General Michel to rapidly bring up his troops.

The rebels advanced a small body of infantry on their left and centre, whilst the rebel cavalry took a position on the right. By this time, the British artillery had reached the battlefield and placed themselves centrally. Wood led his Squadron to the right, to act as an escort for the British cannons. Suddenly, he found himself in charge of the British forces then engaged, as his superior officer was forced to withdraw, giving the excuse that his poor eyesight prevented him from taking part in the battle! Wood sought and received instructions from General Michel to divert as much as possible of the enemy fire away from the British artillery and on to his own men. To this end, Wood's Squadron advanced to a ravine in the centre of the battlefield, where both the enemy's infantry and cannons rained fire down on them.

It did not take long for the rebels to find their range, and horses quickly started to fall. The squadron trumpeter, standing behind Evelyn, was struck by a bullet in the mouth and fell dead. This, combined with some very accurate cannon fire, produced a great deal of nervousness amongst Wood's men, which, by his own steadfastness and encouragement, he was able to curtail. Before General Michel could reach the field of battle, Wood and his men were placed in a dangerous position when the officer commanding the Native cavalry to their right withdrew his men to the rear, stating that he had received an earlier order from his commanding officer to avoid an engagement until he had received further instruction. With both Wood and Gordon now dangerously exposed, the rebel cavalry charged into the gap created by this cowardly withdrawal and almost succeeded in galloping into the rear of Gordon's troops. Gordon, however, managed to reverse his front and led his own men into a counter-charge at the rebels. The resulting clash witnessed the death of four Native cavalrymen, but the almost total annihilation of the rebel cavalry. This charge by Gordon and his men coincided with the arrival of the British infantry and the sudden attempted withdrawal of the rebels.

Wood, for one, was not going to let the mutineers get away that easily and, on seeing them once again in flight, ordered his own Squadron to pursue the retreating rebel army. He led his men off to the right, where they were confronted by about a dozen sepoys, who seemed determined to sell their lives dearly to delay the British advance. The warlike determination displayed by this small band of rebels certainly struck fear into Wood's men for, despite his orders, protestations and threats, the young lieutenant could not get his men to advance and attack them. Calling on his orderly, Dhokul Singh, to join him, the two men charged at the rebels. Wood headed for five sepoys, who had detached themselves from the rest of the group and took aim as he charged. As he lunged at the nearest man, the five fired simultaneously, and Wood ducked his head below his horse's crest as the shots passed over him and wounded two horses belonging to his reluctant troopers, 100 yards behind him. Wood now found himself engaged in trying to fend off bayonet thrusts from two of the sepoys, while at the same time attempting to fight off another, who was trying to kill him with a sword. Dhokul Singh saw the plight of his beloved officer and rode directly at the two bayonet men, knocking them over with his horse, then turned to engage the swordsman. Riding straight at his opponent, Dhokul Singh managed to miss him completely with his first thrust. Wood was by now something of a bystander and he could not resist uttering a sarcastic 'Bravo!' as his orderly missed his target. This infuriated Dhokul Singh, who again turned on the swordsman, and with renewed determination dispatched him with a thrust of his sword, his assailant falling dead, his head split in two.

Wood was now joined by Lieutenant Harding of the 8th Hussars who, seeing Evelyn's plight, galloped to his assistance. The two had been travelling companions on the *Great Britain* and Harding had given Evelyn the nickname of 'sailor' because he had insisted on boring Harding with his seafaring knowledge, acquired whilst on HMS *Queen*. Wood rode into the remaining body of sepoys, which now numbered about eight men, who pleaded for mercy. Evelyn, disgusted by their behaviour, used his fist to strike two of the rebels in the face before his advancing troopers captured them. With a shout of 'sailor!', Harding pointed to two of the mutineers who were trying to make their escape. Both Wood and Harding set off in pursuit. Harding reached his man first, who coolly turned, stood his ground and waited for the approach of the young Hussar. The rebel held his fire until Harding was about to cut at him and then pulled the trigger. Harding was so close that the cartridge set his jacket on fire and Wood's friend fell from his horse mortally wounded. The death of Harding enraged Evelyn, who now spurred the 'Pig' on towards the remaining rebel, who had stood his ground and awaited Wood's charge with his bayonet fixed. Evelyn rode straight towards the sepoy who, seeing Wood's intentions, decided to use his rifle as a club and lifted it above his head. Unfortunately for the rebel, as he raised his weapon, the point of the bayonet caught in his clothing and Evelyn was able to use the opportunity this presented to thrust his sword into the mutineer. The sword entered under his left armpit and went through him up to the hilt. The sepoy dropped off the point of the sword as Evelyn struggled to extract it. Evelyn then saw four more rebels and charged at them, but rather than make a stand, all tried to make their escape amongst some cedar trees; they were sighted by a Native Lancer, who dispatched all four before Wood could join him. It had only been a few minutes from the moment of his first charge at the dozen rebels to the death of the sepoy, but Evelyn was exhausted and he was forced to dismount and rest, both to recover his composure and to take a moment to mourn the death of his friend, Harding.[6]

The few rebels who had decided to stand and fight did succeed in delaying the British pursuit, but at the expense of their lives. Evelyn was again frustrated as the infantry failed to advance quickly enough and, in consequence, the main body of the rebel army was able to cross the Sujnaur river and make their escape. Wood was, however, pleased to learn that for their brave charge, Dhokul Singh had been promoted to Corporal and he had received a mention in dispatches. The next days were spent in the continued pursuit of the rebels, and on 22 October General Michel received intelligence that the mutineers were only eight miles to the south-west. The General, despite having promised his nearly exhausted infantry a rest, asked for another supreme effort from them. To avoid the unbearable heat, the British began their marches in the early hours of the morning and, after covering nearly eighty miles in just three days, again encountered the enemy at a place called Kurai. Such a pace took its toll not only on the British but on the rebels too, who were now exhausted. It is clear that they had no stomach for a pitched battle and again tried to flee. The mutineers split into three separate bodies in an attempt to divide the British forces, but each was pursued by the cavalry. Wood was, as usual, part of this pursuit and, once again, he led his troop over six miles, running the rebels to ground. Evelyn became engaged again in a fierce hand-to-hand struggle with a determined sepoy, who used his sword to cut the hocks of Wood's charging horse. Fortunately, the horse was not the 'Pig', due to the latter having a bad back, for this horse had to be destroyed after the engagement. The enraged Wood, in his best Hindustani, shouted at the rebel that he was not a warrior but a horse-slaughterer, but before he could turn his fatally wounded horse for another charge his troopers encircled the sepoy. The trapped man managed to keep the troopers at bay for several minutes by using his sword against the heads of the cavalry horses, until he was shot dead.

The engagement had cost the rebels dearly. The cavalry alone had killed around 150 of the mutineers, and their total losses were estimated to be around 350. At last the British cavalry and infantry had combined well and had inflicted significant losses on the rebels. A much weakened rebel force headed for Bhopal. This last rapid advance had taken its toll of the British, and Evelyn was not the only one to fall ill with exhaustion and fever. In early November, the rested British force reached the town of Hosingabad, where it was joined by Colonel Benson's 17th Lancers. The Colonel was given command of the Cavalry column of seven squadrons and a troop of Royal Horse Artillery. Evelyn was appointed Benson's Staff Officer, as well as fulfilling the duties of Interpreter and Quartermaster. Wood found the workload heavy and would surely have again succumbed to illness if Benson had not recognised his plight and supplied him with the assistance of a Corporal to ease his burdens. The pursuit of the rebels now turned into purely a cavalry action, as Tatya Tope recognised that his infantry were slowing him down and dispersed them into the Pachmarhi Hills. Colonel Benson and his force were now given sole responsibility for the capture of the remaining rebel horsemen. For the rest of November and early December the British, including Wood, were sent in circles by the rebel cavalry. Huge distances were covered, for example in one day, as Benson received intelligence that he was near to the mutineers, the force covered fifty miles in twenty hours in the most scorching heat. This effort was to no avail and the rebels managed to keep one step ahead of Benson's men.[7]

On 9 December, Colonel Somerset took over Benson's command and ordered a halt to the pursuit. Both men and horses needed rest and Somerset decided to await fresh intelligence on Tatya Tope's movements before setting off again. It was soon discovered that the rebels intended to raid and plunder the city of Jaora, so the British marched into the city on 14 December with the intention of surprising, or at least deterring, the rebels. The Nawab, or Prince, of Jaora was both relieved and delighted to receive the British and opened his palace to the British officers. After months in the saddle, this was a welcome break for Wood and his comrades and, while they were waiting for dinner, the Nawab insisted on showing them his small but varied collection of animals in the palace grounds. These included a giraffe, which was led around by a string through its nose. One of the officers laid a bet that Evelyn could not ride the giraffe. It was clearly not wise of the accident-prone Wood to accept the bet, but he was never one to turn down a challenge and, removing his spurs, he dropped down from the palace's balcony onto the beast. At first, as the animal walked around the grounds, Evelyn managed well, but when he tried a trot, the animal jumped up, throwing his rider to the ground. What now followed can only be described as pure farce as the animal bolted, dragging its attendant along for fifty yards before he lost hold of the reins. Evelyn now managed to hold on to the giraffe's neck and experienced a sensation of acute seasickness as the animal cantered through the formal grounds of the palace. When Wood realised that the beast was heading straight for its stables, he decided to lower himself off. Unfortunately, as he did so, the giraffe's knee hit Evelyn in his chest, knocking him backwards under the hind legs of the beast. Terrified, the giraffe stamped down on Wood's face, cutting both his cheeks and lips and 'mashing' his nose into a bloody mess. He was knocked insensible and had to be carried around in a doolie, or litter, for the next three days. His determination had won the bet, but it can only be imagined what Somerset thought of losing his staff officer for nearly a week as a result of such a prank.[8]

The last two weeks of December were frantic ones for the British. Various and contradictary intelligence reports placed the rebels in a number of locations at the same time, and Wood and his comrades, now rejoined by Colonel Benson, were obliged to investigate each

40

report, in the hope of discovering the position of Tatya Tope. The men found the alternation between severe cold and heat particularly draining. The thermometer could fall below zero at night and reach over thirty-five degrees centigrade during the afternoon. On 27 December, Wood climbed into the saddle at 3.00 am and rode continuously until 7.00 pm. Such long hours, combined with the harshness of the conditions, affected all the men. Both Benson and Gordon lost much weight and became ill, the former succumbing to a combination of illnesses the following year. Evelyn found that, whenever his troop halted, he could not keep awake and on one occasion fell asleep for over half an hour in the saddle. His troopers, themselves surrounded in a fog of fatigue, did not even notice and Evelyn, on awakening, was able to gallop after them, his absence being unnoticed. During this period, Wood was awoken one morning by the rising sun, only to discover that everyone in the British force, including the sentries, were fast asleep. Clearly, the men could not be expected to continue like this for much longer, yet into early January 1859 the British force doggedly marched on. General Michel rejoined the force on 12 January and appointed Evelyn to the position of Brigade-Major. Michel recognised that Wood and the rest of his force were close to total collapse and ordered all to rest for a few days. In the third week of January the force moved on to Kota and it was here that all the men were able to recover from the hardships of the pursuit.

Evelyn's idea of rest was different from many of the men now stationed at Kota, for the immediate area was celebrated for the amount of game that could be hunted. Wood could not resist the new challenge presented by the dangerous pastime of 'pig-sticking', in which a large number of native beaters walked through the undergrowth, driving wild boar towards mounted officers armed only with a lance. Once the boar was sighted the chase was something of a free-for-all, the winner being the first to spear the unfortunate beast. This demanding sport involved a very early morning start, so Evelyn certainly did not use his time at Kota to regain his strength. Indeed, he squeezed in his new leisure pursuit alongside his ever expanding role as Brigade-Major. On one occasion his day began at 2.00 am when he had to supervise the crossing of the nearby Chambal River by the Artillery and heavy baggage. He then returned to his tent to grab an hour's rest before he was up again to go 'pig-sticking', after which he returned to his duties until nearly midnight.[9] After two weeks of such activity, Evelyn and the rest of the British force set off again to try to locate the rebels.

Despite what Evelyn had already been through, he described the next period of the pursuit as one of continuous fatigue. During one intensive period he was without sleep for over eighty hours. It was not just physical exertion, since when the force did stop to rest Wood was responsible for issuing orders and payment to any spies the British used, as well as sorting and distributing letters from home and en-suring that the horses were fed and watered. Finally, after this par-ticular period, rest was forced upon Wood when he lost all strength in his legs and was unable to grip the flanks of his horse. Even during this time, Evelyn, much to the annoyance of his equally exhausted fellow officers, was renowned for his cheerfulness. Reflecting on this time, Wood was later to write that the force had now reached the limit of human endurance. Many officers could now only continue by sewing straps into their saddles with which they could tie their wrists so as to be able to sleep on the march. Nevertheless, such an approach did not stop three Lancers hurting themselves when they fell from their mounts. The horses themselves became so leg-weary that many just simply lay down and many refused even to eat.

It was not just the British who were suffering in such conditions. At the end of February, Wood's troopers captured some rebels whose horses' feet were worn to the quick, and others who were so exhausted that they were unable to remain in their saddles. As was the norm at this vengeful time, General Michel ordered the mutineers to be shot. However, the young Wood intervened and persuaded the General to spare the men. Evelyn did not base his argument on any humanitarian grounds, but he felt that if the British were close to the end of endur-ance, the rebels must be too, and by sparing these men, more might be encouraged to lay down their arms. Somehow word of this clemency reached many of the rebels and further mutineers offered to sur-render.[10]

This success was the only bright moment in the otherwise relentless and frustrating hunt for the rebels. After over 3,000 miles, several minor engagements, and much hardship, Tatya Tope was still at liberty; after two more fruitless marches an order was finally received to abandon the pursuit and break up the force. The 17th Lancers, along with Evelyn Wood, were ordered to Gwaliar, which was reached in May 1859. Whilst on route, Wood and his fellow officers learnt of the final capture of Tatya Tope as a result of betrayal by one of his own supporters, Raja Man Singh, who informed Major Meade and his Native Cavalry unit of Tatya Tope's whereabouts and received an amnesty in return for his treachery. Once captured, the British did not hesitate to hang the former rebel leader on 18 April.[11] After months in the saddle, Evelyn must have found the news that Tatya Tope had been captured in this manner somewhat bittersweet.

It is clear that Evelyn's conduct throughout the pursuit of the rebels had been exemplary and had attracted the attention of both Generals Michel and Somerset, who it seems endeavoured to obtain a Brevet Captaincy for Wood. This meant, in effect, a promotion in the field, which would have meant advancement without the purchase of a commission. It also entitled an officer to take a rank above that for which he received pay. It would be for the War Office later to confirm that brevet promotion and a pay increase. Although Evelyn had already received the title of Brigade-Major, this was little more than an administrative and honorary rank, which would not be recognised on Wood's return to England, where he would still be considered a Lieutenant. Michel wrote to the Chief of Staff on 14 April stating that, '[Wood] has so highly distinguished himself and his services have been of such extreme value to the state that I deem it my duty to bring these services to the notice of his Lordship the Commander-in-Chief in the hope that he may think fit to obtain for him from the Horse Guards [the War Office in London] such recognition of his services as will obtain for him Brevet promotion ...'[12] On the same day, Brigade General Somerset wrote to the Assistant Adjutant-General of Wood's 'unwearied zeal' as well as his 'highest intelligence and a facility in management of native Indians quite unusual in one so lately arrived in the country.'[13]

This concerted effort by the two Generals to obtain for Evelyn the promotion they clearly felt he deserved was to be met with disappointment, for Michel received a reply from Horse Guards dated 17 May, in which he was informed that the C-in-C, the Duke of Cambridge 'always declines to entertain such appointments'.[14] This brief and to the point response from Cambridge was to be typical of Wood's later relationship with the C-in-C, and it was not to be the last time that Evelyn was to receive disappointing news from His Royal Highness. Whether Wood knew of Michel's and Somerset's attempts on his behalf is not clear, but Lady Wood, Evelyn's mother, wrote to Michel in June 1859 to thank him for the kindness the General had shown towards her son and this, perhaps, indicates that Wood was party to the scheming.[15]

After a short period of rest at Gwaliar, Evelyn received news from General Michel that he had been appointed Brigade-Major of Beatson's Horse, an irregular cavalry unit of native troops, which was based at Arangabad. In his letter to Lady Wood, Michel clearly viewed this appointment as some sort of recompense for his failure to obtain a Brevet promotion for Evelyn, as Michel stated in the correspondence that 'I have ... been enabled to place him [Wood] in the irregular Cavalry: where his energy and talent will be sure to be appreciated.'[16] Once again, Wood set off on a long and arduous ride to his new post

43

and he reported to his new chief, Colonel Beatson, in July 1859. Although it is clear that Wood and Beatson enjoyed each other's company, Evelyn did not delight in some of his new commander's more eccentric ways. Beatson insisted that Evelyn move into his own quarters and, although used to hardships, the young Brigade-Major was shocked by his new chief's spartan living and neglect of hygiene. However, the two men were not to spend too much time together as Beatson was forced to return to England to pursue a lawsuit, and Evelyn found himself in charge of the Regiment, now named the 2nd Regiment Central India Horse or Maynes' Horse, after the commander of the 1st Regiment.[17]

Wood was later to complain that his new command showed all the imperfections of a unit raised in haste to meet the threat of the Mutiny. Most of the Native officers were illiterate, the majority of the men were poor riders, and little time had been given over to drill to improve this situation. Furthermore, the accounts of the Regiment were in a sorry state. Wood also found that the men had scant knowledge of basic care for their horses. With his usual vigour he set about rectifying these pressing problems.[18] The need for an effective fighting force had become urgent with the news that two rebels, Firoz Shah and Rao Sahib, had returned to the immediate vicinity and, although they offered no threat to British rule, were acting, Wood's words, as Indian 'Robin Hoods', flouting the rule of law and terrorising those individuals who had welcomed the end of organised resistance.[19]

Yet Evelyn discovered that his new command was unable even to advance a meagre twenty yards in a line, or wheel right or left without jostling into each other and becoming a tangled mess of horses and shouting men. Writing in March 1860 to the Adjutant-General, Evelyn described the situation he found on taking command and the improvements he had made, and stated that not a single Native officer could put his troop through the most simple drill.[20] Wood even found that two of his officers could not ride and he encouraged their resignation by ordering a weekly Officer's Ride without stirrups. A succession of falls resulted and the two men soon departed.[21] Relentless hours of drill allowed Evelyn to state, in his March letter, that 'All the Native Officers ... have gained a fair knowledge of simple Field movements.'[22]

More shocking to Evelyn than the sorry state of horsemanship he had found was the lack of basic care for the horses of the Regiment. Armed with a copy of *Youat on the Horse* and *Miles on Horse's Feet*, Evelyn was able to teach himself rudimentary veterinary skills and was able to reduce the sick list of horses, which was 80 out of 542 on his arrival, to 40 within three weeks and within three months to just 20.[23]

Wood was also forced to teach his men the need to groom their horses, pointing out the impossibility of the horses remaining healthy unless they were properly groomed. He was met with the reply that it was beneath his dignity for a warrior to clean his horse. Evelyn's response was that he insisted on every horse being cleaned either by a groom or by the 'warrior' who rode him and, taking off his own coat, set about grooming the 'Pig' in front of the assembled Regiment. When he completed the task Wood stated clearly that dismissal would be the fate of any 'warrior' who declined to follow his example. This approach had the desired effect and the horses were properly groomed after that display.[24]

Within a month of taking command, Evelyn had transformed the Regiment and, although he recognised much was still to be done, he could at least put several Squadrons into the field. This was timely, for in late December Wood received intelligence from the town of Sindhara that a band of rebels were in the vicinity. On reaching Sindhara, on 28 December 1859, Evelyn was informed by a local detachment that a robber chief named Madhoo Singh had been in the area only the day before and had kidnapped an influential landowner called Chemmun Singh, who had offered active support to the Government in the suppression of the Mutiny. Wood's intelligence was that Madhoo Singh had wanted to hang his kidnap victim, but had waited for instruction from a rebel of a higher rank. The reports conveyed to Evelyn that this senior rebel was due to meet with Madhoo Singh the following day, when Chemmun Singh's fate would be sealed. Wood knew he had to act quickly if the man's life was to be saved. Gaining information from the prisoner's wife, Evelyn was able to identify a local man who had previously been a member of Madhoo Singh's band and was able to lead Wood and his men to their hideout.

Evelyn's detachment consisted of sixty local police and thirty-five men from his own Regiment, but wary of the men's loyalty and aware that most were exhausted from the march to Sindhara, Wood elected to take only a sergeant, Burmadeen Singh, a corporal, and thirteen men on whom he felt he could rely. Intelligence reports put the rebel band at between twenty and twenty-five men, so Evelyn felt confident he could surprise them and free the kidnap victim.[25] The small party set out at around 9.00 pm, with the guide leading them steadily northwards over rough ground. The former rebel was extremely scared and Wood observed that he constantly took opium to calm his nerves. Evelyn was so concerned that the guide would soon become insensible that he had to bind his hands to stop him taking more and more doses. After three hours of scrabbling in the dark, the party saw the light of a camp fire. Evelyn decided to leave three men from his meagre detachment with the horses and he led the rest towards the flames. A slow and cautious approach got Wood within ten yards of the camp, only to discover that there were many more rebels than he had been led to believe. In fact his force of now just twelve men were facing a rebel band in the region of eighty strong. With such odds against him Evelyn considered retreat, but felt that this would not only discredit him, but also General Michel, who had placed such faith in him to command the 2nd Regiment. Wood also knew that if he did not attack, Chemmun Singh would surely be murdered. Finally, if his force did retire, their presence could well be detected by the rebel sentries and the small party overwhelmed. He thus resolved that a surprise attack was the only option.

In the action that followed Evelyn would receive another recommendation for the Victoria Cross, and this time he was to be successful. Yet compared to the many other acts of bravery Wood had shown in both India and the Crimea, this attack on a much larger force, although courageous, had an element of farce about it. His small party joined him and, before they could see the odds which they faced, Evelyn ordered them to get ready to charge. The click made by the hammer of one of his men's muskets startled a sentry, who cried out 'Who is that?' Evelyn replied, 'We are the Government', and shouted to his men to charge. Naturally, Wood led from the front, only to discover that two sleeping rebels were at his feet and he tripped over one of them and fell headlong into a hollow. He was joined there by his sergeant and a private, who had also fallen over the same man. In the noise and confusion, the rebels awoke, and the majority, thinking they were being assailed by a large force, fled without their arms; their rout was covered by the sentries and four or five of the braver rebels. Evelyn managed to raise himself off the ground, only to discover he was being attacked by a Brahman wearing a Sepoy's coat. The two foes cut and thrust at each other three or four times, but on each occasion the sword blows were deflected by the foliage surrounding them. Finally, by crouching down, Wood was able to wound the Brahman in the thigh; the wounded man staggered to his left into the path of Sergeant Burmadeen Singh, who cut at the rebel twice, but each time catching his sword in the trees. Wood ran after the two combatants, only to tumble into a drain into which the sergeant and rebel had just fallen. The three men scrabbled around in the mud for a few seconds until Burmadeen Singh managed to kill the Brahman.

Evelyn emerged breathless from the muddy, and now bloody, drain to discover that the remaining rebels had fled and that their prisoner, Chemmun Singh, was still alive, tied to a nearby tree. The remainder of the detachment, who had held back when Wood had ordered them to charge, made up for their lack of activity by shouting to the fleeing rebels 'Bring up the artillery, bring up the Cavalry,' and Evelyn later admitted that this action was perhaps more effective in dispersing the rebels than any bayonet charge might have been. The final act of farce was when Wood was forced to knock out, with a blow to the jaw, the private who had first joined him in the attack, when he became 'idiotic' at the sight of blood.[26]

Thus Evelyn Wood won his Victoria Cross. Although it is clear that Wood had already shown enough bravery to win the coveted award, the fact that it was won for this action perhaps requires some further explanation and consideration. News of Chemmun Singh's daring rescue was conveyed by the Political Agent in Bhopal, Captain Hutchinson,[27] to Colonel Sir Richmond Shakespear, Agent Governor General for Central India, who wrote a detailed report of the action to Cecil Beadon, Secretary to the Government of India, and concluded his letter with the comment, 'I feel sure that the conduct of Lieutenant Wood ... will be noticed and rewarded by His Excellency the Viceroy.'[28] Shakespear also wrote to Evelyn and stated that Wood had led a 'brilliant attack'.[29] It appears that not only the Political Agents in the area, Hutchinson and Shakespear, were keen for Wood's daring to be recognised, but also Lord Canning, the Viceroy of India. Canning ensured that the various reports of the rescue were brought before the Queen.[30] The reasons behind the concern of such overtly political agents can be understood when it is considered who Evelyn rescued, rather than how he achieved it. Chemmun Singh was influential in the area, loyal to the British, and one of the Indians who had actively supported them during the period of the Mutiny. If the rebels had succeeded in not only kidnapping Singh, but then murdering him, this would have sent a very unfortunate message to the populace: that the British might have crushed the Mutiny but that they could not maintain law and order, or even protect one of their own supporters. This may have been why so many were keen that Wood's daring should be recognised.

Evelyn himself stated that he believed he had won the Victoria Cross only because of a report from another officer, Lieutenant Bradford, which confirmed the rebel party to have been made up of eighty-three men in total. Wood had stated in his report of the action that there had been a mere sixty surrounding the campfire.[31] This whole episode was given another twist by a story that appeared in the book *A Century of Letters*, which claimed that Evelyn's eccentric sister, and champion, Anna Steele, managed to obtain entry to the London residence of Lord Clyde, who had responsibility for making award recommendations to the Queen. Anna confronted the dressing-gown-clad Lord over his breakfast with the various reports of the action. Clyde agreed with Anna that her brother should be recommended for the Victoria Cross and he promised to present his findings to Her Majesty. Whether his hasty decision was made so as to ensure he could still eat a warm breakfast, or to get rid of Mrs Steele, is not clear.[32] Whether there is any truth in this latter story, or whether it is a family myth, is not known, but what is sure is that on 4 September 1860 it was announced in the *London Gazette* that the Queen was 'graciously pleased to signify her intention to confer the decoration of the Victoria Cross on Lieutenant Henry Evelyn Wood'. Interestingly, the announcement stated that the award was made for gallantry shown in the rescue of Chemmun Singh and in the action at Sindwaho.[33] If there was a political angle to the award, or if indeed Anna had successfully lobbied on behalf of her brother, cannot now be established for certain, but it does seems clear that the award of the Victoria Cross to Evelyn was overdue and per-haps the authorities recognised this.

Having survived his latest exploit, Evelyn returned to his duties with the 2nd Regiment. Again, he concentrated on trying to improve the men's horsemanship and care for their mounts, whilst at the same time attempting to reduce the Regimental debts, including the Horse Insurance Fund, which was over £500 in the red. Wood introduced measures that financially penalised those of his men, particularly the officers, who neglected the care of their horses, by the removal of their mounts from the benefits of the Insurance whilst at the same time reducing the amount payable for the replacement of a horse from £20 to £15. Evelyn had discovered that some of his command were deliber-ately neglecting their horses so as to get the 400 Rupees payment from Regimental funds, buying a replacement mount for 150 Rupees and pocketing the difference.[34] By adopting these and other measures, Wood was able to reduce the debt by two-thirds within a period of four months, but by directly hitting the men in their pockets Wood's action began to cause disquiet.

By the end of March 1860, discontent over Wood's command prac-tices became evident. Knowing that the only other two British officers, the Medical Officer and the Adjutant, were away visiting an outpost, and therefore Wood was alone, all nineteen Native officers called on Wood. Seeing them approaching *en masse*, Evelyn feared for his well-being and called for his sword and pistol, which he left clearly on display on the table in front of him. The officers presented a petition to Evelyn, which demanded that the amount paid for replacement horses be returned to £20, as well as the removal of other financial penalties. Clearly the Native Officers had misread Evelyn's character, for he first gave them the opportunity to withdraw their demands and, when they refused to do so, pointed out that several of the words used by them in their petition were actually mutinous. Wood then promptly rose from his seat and suspended all nineteen Native Officers, ordering them back to their quarters and demanding that they leave their swords. The men meekly retired, but Evelyn felt so concerned for his own safety that he dispatched messengers to recall the Medical Officer and the Adjutant right away, as well as sending for Sergeant Burmadeen Singh, who was still at the Sindhara outpost. Wood realised that it would be several hours before he could expect relief.

Evelyn continued to work all day in the orderly room, trying to block from his mind his worst fears of mutiny. At five o'clock in the evening, it was with some misgivings that he went to inspect the men grooming their mounts. Evelyn was conscious of eyes following his every move and it was with relief that he returned to his quarters and armed himself. Later in the evening, Burmadeen Singh, having galloped from Sindhara on hearing of the threat, joined Evelyn, who explained to him the dangerous situation. Wood ordered his Sergeant to speak to the men and assess the likelihood of an attack. Singh returned several hours later with the worrying information that the two ringleaders, Ali Khan and Emam Khan, had attempted to incite the men to attack and kill Wood. Singh had done his best to dissuade the men from such action and had even managed to use his influence with the Hindu troops to place a loyal guard on the arsenal. Of course Evelyn had no idea whether these guards would resist any attempt to gain arms and ammunition and was forced to spend a long worrying night alert to every noise. Wood's groom stayed awake with him all night, with the 'Pig' saddled for a possible escape. At first light, to Evelyn's immense relief, Lieutenant Bradford and twenty men galloped in from Bhilsa in response to Wood's plea for support. Although still outnumbered, the presence of Bradford and his small detachment was enough to dispel any further thought of mutiny and the next day Wood was able to show his magnanimity by reinstating all but the two ringleaders, who were imprisoned on the base. Wood was to request the disgrace and dismissal of these two men and this was agreed by the Adjutant-General a few months later.[35]

Having survived this threat, Evelyn was now to experience what he considered to be injustice at the hands of the British authorities in India, which was to result in the end of his career on the subcontinent. Wood continued to work hard to improve the 2nd Regiment and, in the six months from December 1859 to June 1860, he transformed the abilities of his unit by a vigorous and ruthless expulsion of any man he felt did not meet his rigorous standards of horsemanship. In this time he dismissed 435 men of the original 535 he had inherited from Beatson, yet he was able to maintain the enlisted strength by recruiting what he described as 'high-class men'.[36] The message which was to indirectly lead to the termination of Evelyn's Indian Army career was received from the Major of Brigade, Lieutenant Mayne on 15th July 1860.[37] The note ordered Evelyn to proceed at once to Narsinghgarh, where it was reported that the rebels Baba Bhutt and Rustum Ali Khan were sheltering in the house of the Rajah's chief advisor, Bishund Dhutt. Unfortunately, Mayne also gave rather ambiguous instructions that Evelyn could apprehend the Rajah too if he did not cooperate.

Armed with his orders, Wood, in his youthful excited manner, summoned a troop from the 2nd Regiment and immediately galloped the forty miles to Narsinghgarh, arriving after an exhausting twelve-hour ride during the heat of the day. He placed his men to surround the fort and, accompanied by only one Native Officer and a Trumpeter, Wood entered. The Trumpeter was instructed to wait on the drawbridge and to alert the rest of the detachment if he saw that Evelyn and his companion were in difficulties. Wood requested a private audience with the Rajah and at this meeting asked the Prince for his assistance in apprehending the rebels. The Rajah at first denied all knowledge of the men Evelyn sought, but when Wood stated that he knew for certain that the rebels were in the palace, he was led to their quarters by the Rajah and there Evelyn arrested Rustum Ali Khan. The Prince informed Wood that the other rebel, Baba Bhutt, was sheltering in Bishund Dhutt's house, which was some distance away and a horse ride would be required to get there.

There then followed an incident which would place Evelyn in 'hot water' with the British political agents. It is clear that not only had Evelyn been poorly briefed by Lieutenant Mayne, but he was tired, probably hungry and was suffering from the intense heat. Furthermore, he was frustrated by the Prince's apparent lack of honesty and at his attempts at procrastination. The Rajah would not call for his own horse for some time and Evelyn grew increasingly impatient as he perceived that the Prince was deliberately trying to delay him. When a horse did arrive, the Rajah stated that it was not suitable and sent for another, declining Evelyn's offer that he could ride the 'Pig'. A second horse appeared, which was deemed suitable, but then the Prince further delayed the departure by requesting a succession of other items, such as a sword, cummerbund, pistol and dagger. At last, when the Rajah could delay no longer, he complained of a bowel complaint and fled into his palace. Evelyn was forced to ride to Bishund Dhutt's house without the 'ailing' Prince, and there he was able to arrest the owner; but the rebel Baba Bhutt had been informed of the much delayed approach and, dressed in women's clothing, he had made his escape.[38]

Throughout this frustrating meeting, Evelyn no doubt tried to maintain a respectful attitude towards the Rajah, but due to a combination of his tiredness, the heat and the lack of honesty displayed by the Prince, he was unable to control his frustration and temper, and this overspilt when he threatened to arrest the Rajah if he refused to accompany Wood to Bishund Dhutt's house. In his report to Mayne on his return, Wood expressed regret that he had used such words to the Prince, but stated that the threat was made only after an hour of delay and dishonesty on the part of the Rajah, which Evelyn knew was part of a plan to aid the escape of Baba Bhutt.[39] Mayne was clearly disappointed at Evelyn's behaviour towards the Rajah, and despite the fact that he had supplied Wood with the rather ambiguous order that he could apprehend the Rajah if required, Mayne verbally reprimanded Wood. Mayne then forwarded Wood's report to Colonel Sir Richmond Shakespear, Agent Governor General for Central India, who had been so instrumental in recommending Evelyn for the Victoria Cross.

Shakespear was clearly horrified and appalled to read of Evelyn's actions and threats towards the Rajah. Although Shakespear was quick to criticise Mayne for sending Wood to Narsinghgarh with such unclear instructions as to what actions he could take towards the Rajah, Shakespear centred his anger on Evelyn. It seems clear that the Agent Governor General felt that by the threat of arrest, Wood had not only antagonised the Rajah of Narsinghgarh, but that any of the Native rulers throughout Central India, hearing of Evelyn's actions, would be alarmed and view any officer approaching them with aversion. Shakespear went on to say that Wood's behaviour towards the Rajah, who was elderly and infirm, amounted to little less than 'actual cruelty'.[40]

Predictably, Wood, young and still inexperienced in the world of politics, reacted angrily to what he considered to be a censure from the Agent General. Writing to Mayne on 6 August 1860, he requested that he solicit permission from the Commanding Officer for him to resign his appointment in 'Mayne's Horse'. The reason Evelyn gave for such a request was the loss of confidence in him by Shakespear. Wood wrote, 'I am deeply concerned to learn that the Agent has such a low opinion of my Character as a Gentleman, as to consider that I treated the Rajah with either roughness, discourtesy, or actual cruelty ... I have therefore with feelings of the deepest regret determined in justice to myself to offer my resignation for the acceptance of His Excellency the Governor General of India.'[41] It is clear that Mayne was extremely upset to

51

receive Evelyn's resignation and remonstrated with him to persuade him to retract the decision, but with no success; Evelyn was clearly too discouraged to remain.

Mayne felt compelled to write a rather indignant, if not insubordinate, letter to Shakespear informing him of the loss of Wood to the Indian service. Mayne stated that 'Lieutenant Wood is an officer of most susceptible temperament ... and he feels your present censure most acutely.' Mayne went on to explain that he had already verbally reprimanded Wood for exceeding his authority, something Mayne claimed Evelyn was aware of, and this approach had been more effective than any written rebuke could ever be. Mayne went on to say that, 'Some men require such reprobation [written censure] but I hold it to be one of the great secrets of successful command to administer reproof with discrimination in regard to character.' Finally, after listing the essential services Evelyn had rendered whilst in command of the 2nd Regiment, which included 'His unwearied energy; his strict discipline; his close attention to detail; his admirable temper and his disregard of self and personal trouble', Mayne concluded that 'Lieutenant Wood is much loved in the brigade, and I consider his resignation as a loss to the public service.'[42]

No further correspondence survives between Shakespear, Mayne and Wood concerning the subject of Evelyn's resignation. It would seem apparent that Wood and Shakespear had boxed themselves into very separate corners with neither able to retract, apologise or, in Evelyn's case, forgive. It does appear that Wood, not yet twenty-three years of age, was extremely sensitive to criticism, especially in written form, and this had been the first serious rebuke he had received in his career. It is, perhaps, not surprising that Evelyn reacted as he did to such a heavy-handed reprimand. Although he was determined to leave the Irregular Cavalry, he had not at this stage turned his back on India. In October 1860, Evelyn received a letter from Colonel James Travers, Commander of the Central India Horse, in which it is clear that Wood had previously informed Travers that he would consider returning to India once Shakespear had left his position, and, for his part, Travers stated that he would always find a command for Evelyn in India.[43] Evelyn even received confirmation from the Viceroy, Lord Canning, that he would have no objection to Lieutenant Wood again being employed in India.[44]

This was not to be. In October 1860 Evelyn was ordered to Calcutta to appear before a Medical Board, where it was clear that his two and a half years in India, through three hot seasons and two monsoons, fighting, patrolling, resting when he could, had taken their toll on Wood's health. The Board concluded that he was suffering from exposure and modified sunstroke and was accordingly invalided back to England.[45] So Evelyn's brief, but very active, spell in India came to an end. He was to return to his homeland with the satisfaction of knowing he had done a superb job, his dedication recognised by his Commanding Officers, and his bravery symbolised in the award of the Victoria Cross. It is interesting to theorise what would have happened to Evelyn's career if he had remained in India. Certainly it seems clear that he would have had success. Perhaps even, in later years, he might have fought in the Second Afghan War and won fame, as General Roberts was to do, and might have ended his days as Commander of the Indian Army, or even Viceroy. This was not to be; instead, Evelyn returned to England for a period of home service, during which he was to find love and marriage, before embarking, once again, this time for Africa. It was to be on this continent that Wood was to spend many years on active service and here he was to be central to many of the famous, and infamous, colonial campaigns of the Victorian period.

Chapter Four

Love & Marriage

Leaving India in late November 1860, Wood arrived at his father's house in Essex three days after Christmas, after an absence of just over three years. It is not hard to imagine the relief his parents must have felt at the safe return of their son, as well as their pride at Evelyn having so distinguished himself. However, the sight of their sunburnt, lean son, fluent in Hindustani, must have seemed like having an exotic stranger in the house. There is no doubt Lady Wood fawned over her hero-son and that Evelyn's many brothers and sisters, even Katharine, must have been pleased and relieved to see their conquering brother. The New Year family celebrations must have been very welcome to Evelyn.

After a short period of rest and relaxation with his family, Wood was obliged to attend a Medical Board in London. Here, the state of Evelyn's hearing was found to be so poor that he was advised to see a Mr Toynbee, a renowned ear specialist. After numerous examinations, Toynbee informed his patient that rest from active service would lead to considerable improvement in his hearing, but that one ear would never fully recover as inflammation had caused the tympanum bone to adhere to the eardrum membrane. As a result, Toynbee advised that a return to India would be unwise for at least two years.[1] This diagnosis seemed not to have taken into account Wood's nine months duty with the Naval Brigade in the Crimea, where he had constantly exposed to the percussive effects of cannon fire, which surely must have been the cause of Evelyn's deafness.[2] Wood was to be afflicted with impaired hearing for the remainder of his life and, by the time he reached his fifties, contemporaries such as Wolseley and even Queen Victoria considered him totally deaf. Almost unbelievably, this affliction does not seem to have inhibited his career, whereas today he would have certainly been invalided out of the service.

Apart from his deafness, Evelyn was still suffering from another complaint acquired in the Crimea. His left arm had never really

54

recovered from his self-inflicted surgery to remove pieces of bone from it before he had begun his cavalry training. Furthermore, his constant toil in India had not allowed the arm to rest and recover. His left arm had now considerably shrunk but he endeavoured, successfully, to increase its strength by active exercise. Evelyn received tuition in the use of the foil and sabre, as well as boxing lessons, primarily using his left arm, and this illustrates his determination to regain his fitness. It seems clear that Wood used the first few months of 1861 to concentrate, for once, on his own health and well-being. He even found time in March to visit his old friend Viscount Southwell at Mortlake. It was here that he was again to met Southwell's younger sister the Honour-able Mary Paulina Southwell, and a distance love-affair began, which after some trials and tribulations, was to culminate in marriage six years later. In the meantime, Evelyn was once again determined to con-centrate on his career.

Evelyn decided to take the opportunity to improve his technical knowledge of the profession of soldiering by attempting to gain entry to the Staff College at Camberley, Surrey, which had been newly built in the grounds of the Royal Military College. He soon discovered that the College only accepted one officer from a regiment at a time, and as there was already a likely candidate from the 17th Lancers, he was forced, yet again, to transfer into another regiment, this time from the cavalry to the infantry. In April 1861, using money saved whilst in India, Wood purchased a captaincy in the 73rd Regiment, or Perthshire regiment, which was to become the Second Battalion of the Black Watch. In anticipation of taking the entrance examination, Wood used the summer of 1861 to improve his language skills, in both French and German, and he was later to receive 'cramming' instruction from a Captain Lendy on other aspects of the entrance exam, such as 'Military Drawing'.[3]

In July 1862, just before he was to sit the exam, Evelyn finally received his Victoria Cross. His rather sudden departure from India had meant that the medal had already been dispatched to the General Officer commanding the Troops in Madras, with instructions to present it to Evelyn there. However, the decoration had arrived after he had left for England and, of course, it then had to be returned to the War Office in London. The accompanying letter stated that 'Her Majesty desires me to say how deeply She regrets not being able to decorate you with it Herself.'[4] After all the trials and difficulties over both of Evelyn's recommendations for the Victoria Cross, to have re-ceived the medal in this manner, in an envelope with an attached letter, must have been extremely disappointing for him, yet perhaps the award boosted his confidence just as he was to sit the entrance examination. There is no doubt that Evelyn's confidence did need boosting as his tutor, Captain Lendy, had told him that he was so poor at the subject of Military Drawing that he would waste his time even attending the Examination Hall.

It was with some relief that, with the preparations finally over, Evelyn sat down to the first of many papers, spread over several days. He was to confound his critic, Captain Lendy, by gaining very high marks in the Military Drawing examination. Whether Lendy had misread, like many did, Evelyn's determination, self-belief and inner ability, or whether Lendy was simply trying to spur Wood on, is impossible to say; but what is clear is that Evelyn gained sufficient marks in this paper, as well as in the others, including German, to gain entry to the Staff College. Soon after sitting the various exams Evelyn received more encouraging news when he discovered that his former Commanding Officer in India, General Sir John Michel, had not given up his earlier attempts to obtain a Brevet promotion for Wood's service in the subcontinent and had finally succeeded in his quest. Thus the new young Captain suddenly found himself as an even younger Brevet-Major, of just twenty-four years of age.

Wood was not to begin his two-year course at the Staff College until January 1863 so he joined the rather relaxed atmosphere of his new regiment at Plymouth. Evelyn had not experienced life in an infantry regiment before and found his fellow officers very hospitable. The Colonel of the Regiment seems to have considered that it would be inappropriate for an officer of Evelyn's service record to receive instruction in infantry drill and would not order him to attend the basic instruction given to new Subalterns. Evelyn, however, thought otherwise and, for the period of the training, he reverted each week to the lowly rank of Subaltern in order to acquire the necessary proficiency in drill practice.[5] It seems clear that the vanity which was to be such a feature of Wood's character in later life had not yet established itself in the young Major, who clearly did not consider the basic drill instruction beneath him.

Evelyn did not stand out academically during his two years at the Staff College, although his natural ability with languages helped him through the course. At the time of Wood's entry, the College operated a system by which students had to obtain a minimum aggregate score across the numerous subjects taught in order to pass. Evelyn used this system to his advantage, for he seems to have struggled with Mathematics, particularly trigonometry, but was able to gain very high grades in the language exams, so as to ensure that he passed out from the College in the top ten per cent of the candidates.[6] There is no doubt that he enjoyed his time there, especially the many leisure opportunities that were presented to him, which included his favourite pastime of hunting. Evelyn was generally able to hunt two or three times a week during the two years of the course, although some of his Professors were concerned that Wood was neglecting his studies. Evelyn soon got into the habit of rising very early on hunting days so as to put in three hours of study before he went out, again showing his determination to both enjoy and succeed at life.

Once again the accident-prone Wood nearly ended not only his career, but his life, when he fell badly whilst out hunting at his brother-in-law's property of Belhus at the end of 1863. He fell from his mount as he jumped a fence and his head was kicked by the horse's rear legs as he hit the ground. He was carried into the house where his condition caused such concern that his mother was summoned at once. When she arrived, the look of horror on her face and the gasp of shock was such that Evelyn felt compelled to find a mirror to examine his face and head. Both his mother and the doctor refused to supply one so Wood was forced to crawl across the bedroom floor to the looking-glass. He discovered that the fall onto the crown of his head, and the blows from the horse's flying legs, had swollen his neck so badly that it protruded up beyond the cheekbones, giving the appearance of a large double goitre. Amazingly, after three weeks bed rest, and the wearing of a skullcap for protection, Evelyn was able, once again, to go hunting.[7]

Whilst at the Staff College Evelyn attempted to maintain his relationship with Paulina Southwell, and by the spring of 1863 he had declared the love that he felt for her. He also informed Paulina's brother, Viscount Southwell, who was the guardian of his orphaned sister. Although not in a strong financial position for such a match, Evelyn was unable to overcome an even larger hurdle, that of his religion. The Viscount clearly stated to Wood that the Southwell family would not consent to a marriage unless Evelyn converted to Catholicism. Despite his love for Paulina, Wood could not accept that he should abandon the Church in which he had been brought up and clearly he resented that such a condition should apply.[8] Over the next four years Evelyn and Paulina seldom met and never exchanged letters, until August 1867 when he wrote to ask her to marry him. Wood clearly felt that the Southwell family had imposed unfair conditions on a possible union, yet it was to be Evelyn's family which would place further obstacles to the marriage in 1867.

Although perhaps not impressive academically whilst at the Staff College, it is evident that Evelyn stood out enough to come to the notice of the College Commandant, Colonel William Napier. Wood's passing out from the College coincided with Napier's departure to assume command of a brigade in Dublin and he offered Evelyn the position of his aide-de-camp which he gratefully accepted, perhaps as a means of escape from the embarrassment of his rejection by the Southwell family. Passing out from the Staff College at the end of 1864, Wood took up his new position in Ireland in January 1865, but he was unable to distinguish himself in his new role, chiefly because he suffered from long periods of illness. For the next two years he spent his time alternating between Dublin and London, where he was to see a number of physicians. It seems clear that the Irish climate did not suit Wood, for every time he got wet he would suffer from recurring attacks of fever, which affected his ears, accompanied with neuralgia and swelling to his face; it appears that he spent more time in London receiving medical attention than on duty.

On top of his health problems Evelyn also suffered the loss of his father in February 1866, although he was able to journey from Ireland to Essex in time to be at his side when he died. By the summer of 1866 Napier was appointed Director-General of Military Education and Evelyn lost his position in Ireland. It was probably with some relief that he left Dublin to join his new Regiment at Aldershot, the 17th, the Leicestershires, into which he had been forced to 'exchange' when the 73rd Regiment were posted to Hong Kong.

Although this particular stay at Aldershot was relatively brief, in later life Aldershot was to become a second home to Evelyn. His reputation as an Army Reformer was gained whilst stationed there, and it is in Aldershot Military Cemetery that Wood decided to be buried alongside his wife and two of his children. However, his first experience of the base was not auspicious. On arrival he was given two positions, both of which he knew little or nothing about. The first was as Deputy Assistant Quartermaster-General, with responsibility for the Instructional Kitchen of Cookery. Since he had no knowledge of cooking this was indeed an alien environment for Evelyn, but he acquired the standard textbooks of the day and threw himself into learning his new vocation. Just as he was gaining some understanding of it, Wood discovered that he was also expected to instruct officers in Military Drawing and Field Sketching, which had been his worst subject at the Staff College. When he explained to his Commanding Officer that he had been the 'duffer' of his class at this subject and felt that he did not really understand it, let alone was able to teach it, Wood was told firmly that he had better learn quickly. To this end Evelyn managed to get a friend and private tutor to visit the base the weekend before lessons were to begin and, after forty-eight hours of cramming, the subject finally became clear in his mind. Perhaps fortunately for the officers he was due to teach, and the men he was supposed to feed, a vacancy for Brigade Major, under General Sir Alfred Horsford, soon became available and Evelyn's application was successful.[9]

In this more comprehensible role, and serving an officer whom he genuinely seems to have liked and respected, Evelyn flourished. This was to be his first staff role in England, and it was probably here that Wood really acquired the enquiring and questioning mind that would serve him so well in more senior positions. In the few months he was to remain at Aldershot under Horsford, Evelyn was encouraged to become involved in manoeuvres and he even found time to present a redesign of the standard knapsack and pouches, the latter being adopted through the Army.[10] This brief period came to an end when rumours of a Fenian outbreak saw Horsford ordered to proceed to Ireland to command a Division in December 1866. Evelyn followed a few weeks later. It appears that the rumours were somewhat exaggerated and despite the written encouragement of his uncle, Admiral Sir Frederick Michell, to 'give the Fenians no rest' there was little for Wood to do.[11] So after spending another wet winter in Ireland, Evelyn returned to Aldershot in the spring of 1867.

Wood's passion for riding saw him attend the Ascot week in June 1867 and it was here that his former commander, William Napier, who knew of Evelyn's love for Paulina, contrived an 'accidental' meeting between the two. Unfortunately, Viscount Southwell was also present and it appears that Evelyn may have behaved rather badly and refused to stay in the presence of both Paulina and brother, even though he was now back on friendly terms with the Viscount. Although this meeting may have been a disaster, it clearly sparked a desire within Evelyn to resume his pursuit of Paulina. This was the beginning of a whirlwind romance in which both his mother and sisters were influential. The possibility of a marriage proposal was the subject of discussion in the Wood family throughout the summer of 1867 and finally, with the encouragement of his mother, Evelyn wrote to Paulina in early August asking her to marry him. It appears that Wood was less than romantic in his proposal, in which he stated his poor financial position and particularly stressed that any marriage must be on the distinct understanding that Paulina should never, by word or even look, check his volunteering for any future War Service.[12]

After this pompous proposal, Wood was now forced to wait, impatiently, for Paulina's decision. It is clear that during the three weeks before Paulina gave her reply he was suffering. Evelyn's mother even wrote to Paulina asking her to 'decide at once ... the suspense is killing him ... I am sure your brother cannot wish that his friend should endure any needless suffering.'[13] Finally, on 25 August, Paulina wrote to Evelyn, 'I will no longer leave you in suspense as to my final answer to your proposal.' Paulina added, 'I do love you and have done so for a long time and too well to have the slightest fear in entrusting my future happiness to you.' She also explained why she had delayed her decision, claiming that, 'you must not think it was because I doubted your word in any way it was solely from affection to my brother who was most anxious I should not make a hasty decision.' She asked Wood to forgive the Viscount's behaviour and begged that Evelyn 'must for my sake forget his seeming want of courtesy to you in the affair for I can assure you he did not intend any thing of the kind, he has acted out of too great affection for me all through.' Evelyn must also have been relieved to read that Paulina considered that she would be 'the last person in the world to wish to deter you from rising in your profession – I marry you on your terms.'[14]

It was not only Evelyn who was delighted and relieved to read of Paulina's decision. Lady Emma Wood wrote to her future daughter-in-law as soon as she heard the news and was clearly ecstatic. 'May heaven bless you, my dear child, for the happiness you have given me this day, and for that which your letter must have conveyed to our boy – I hope he will get well now, with such bright hope to look forward to ... I long to give you the tenderness which brims over in my heart towards Evelyn ... I need not say how gladly I shall welcome you as a daughter.'[15] Evelyn, writing to Paulina on the same day, was able to express his own relief and happiness in a similar vein: 'Dearest Paulina, at last I may write to you without disguise, and I need not attempt to explain how happy I am however, I am so intensely happy that I can't write or talk in a coherent manner.' Wood was now keen to name the day and wrote, 'Now, dearest when will you marry me? Towards the end of the second week in September suits me best.'[16] These plans, however, were to be jeopardised and delayed, not this time by Viscount Southwell, but by objections from Evelyn's eccentric Aunt Ben.

Aunt Ben, the sister of Lady Emma Wood, had married John Page Wood's brother Benjamin Wood. Aunt Ben's real name was Maria, but she seems to have adopted a shorter version of her husband's christian name on his death. Benjamin had made a fortune in hops and became Member of Parliament for Southwark before his early death.[17] He left a very wealthy childless widow and verbal instructions that Maria, or Ben, should 'take care of Emma's children.' Aunt Ben appears to have become more eccentric as she aged, but she does seem always to have been generous to both her family and charities. For example, with the death of her husband in 1866, Lady Emma was left in financial difficulties, but her sister immediately offered support and provided Emma with a sizeable allowance.[18] Aunt Ben had followed her husband's wishes and had given £5,000 to each of her nieces and nephew when they married. However, despite the fact that she had not been inside a church for more than fifty years, the unpredictable Aunt took exception to Evelyn marrying an Irish Catholic and refused to bestow the now customary wedding gift.[19]

Evelyn had clearly been expecting to receive the monetary gift from his Aunt. He was already in a poor financial position to marry the sister of a Viscount and on an army salary he could not hope to maintain the expected style of household and, something Evelyn considered essential, stables, horses and a pack of hounds. Thus his Aunt's refusal to hand over the money caused consternation. Wood was shocked and wrote to Paulina of his disbelief at Aunt Ben's intransigence: 'I feel that Southwell might think I had deceived him [about his financial position], for I never for a moment doubted but that my Aunt would settle the money without any unwillingness.'[20] This letter also reveals that Evelyn's sister Emma had prompted her husband, Sir Thomas Barrett-Lennard, to advance her brother the £5,000 so that the marriage might take place. The understanding was that the money would be repaid on the death of Aunt Ben, when Evelyn could expect a generous inheritance, although no evidence has been found that Sir Thomas was ever repaid. However, Evelyn did certainly offer some repayment to his brother-in-law by successfully managing his Irish estate, Clones, for over twenty years, whilst still pursuing his Army career.[21] Wood appears to have been somewhat reluctant to accept the money from Sir Thomas and it was only after a reassuring letter from his mother, which stated that it was perfectly acceptable to take the financial offer, that Evelyn agreed to the advance.[22]

With the finances secured, the slightly delayed marriage could finally take place. On 19 September, Paulina's twenty-seventh birthday, the couple were married in Ryde Catholic Church.[23] Needless to say, Aunt Ben was not invited. Although Wood did take instruction in the Catholic faith, to allow for the wedding to take place in a Catholic church, he never became a practising Catholic. The couple were to spend twenty-four years together before Paulina's untimely death. In that time she bore Evelyn three sons and three daughters, and there is no doubt that Wood was devoted to her. Writing in 1892, Evelyn's biographer considered that Paulina 'made him'.[24] Whether this is true is hard to say, but what does seem clear is that the already ambitious Evelyn became more so and with ambition came increasing vanity. The later descriptions of Wood's character by his contemporaries bear little resemblance to the glowing testimonials he received when he served in the Crimea and India. Something had changed in the man and it is all too easy to place responsibility for this on Paulina and her relationship

61

with her husband. Evelyn seems to have had inherited from his father the ability to live beyond his means and, with marriage to the privileged Paulina, standards had to be further maintained. It is unclear whether the financial demands placed upon Wood by the union, and his subsequent large family, made him increasingly ambitious, or if Paulina pushed him to press for his own advancement.

What of Paulina's personality and character? She clearly displayed indecision in dealing with Evelyn's proposal and there is little doubt that her early adulthood was dominated by her brother and guardian, Viscount Southwell. She came from a sheltered and very privileged background and as a result of this may not have been able to cope as the wife of an army officer. It is claimed that Paulina was quite incapable of running an orderly household, and Wolseley once complained that Wood's house was as filthy as a railway refreshment room, with the disorganised and deaf Evelyn seemingly oblivious to the noise and chaos surrounding him.[25] The Commander-in-Chief, the Duke of Cambridge, once complained to Wolseley that he had never experienced such 'an infamous lunch' as he had been forced to suffer at Wood's.[26] On a subsequent occasion Cambridge instructed Wolseley to advise Wood to put his home in order.[27] Indeed it has been argued that one of Evelyn's many promotions, that of the Aldershot command in 1888, was only granted because the wife of his chief rival for the post had even more shortcomings than Paulina.[28]

Yet the state of the Wood household cannot all be placed upon Paulina's shoulders; Evelyn seems to have also inherited his father's lack of organisation and although his contemporaries viewed Evelyn as a very driven individual, his drive was as nothing compared to that of his mother. Lady Emma Wood's devotion to her son may have led her to smother and dominate Evelyn and there is some evidence that Paulina dominated him in a similar fashion. In one of her later novels, *Clove Pink*, Anna Steele, Wood's sister, has a character suspiciously like her brother Evelyn who when told by his sister-in-law, 'You are a VC man, why won't you insist on your wishes being carried out?', replies with a smile, 'You ought to know how helpless the boldest man is in his own house.'[29] If, as seems likely, Evelyn was rather dominated in his own home, this does not appear to have damaged the marriage in any way and there is not doubt the union was a happy and loving one.

Major and Mrs Evelyn Wood's ten-day honeymoon was abruptly ended when Evelyn was recalled by Horsford to attend an Army Review in Liverpool, and from there he returned with his General to Aldershot. The Woods now set up home in Aldershot and Paulina soon became pregnant. She decided to spend the summer of 1868 in

Brighton in the expectation that the sea air would be beneficial to her health. The baby, named Anna Paulina Mary, was born there, but unfortunately appears to have been in poor health; Evelyn described his new daughter as 'delicate'.[30] Paulina apparently suffered from postnatal depression, taking little interest in her new baby, and for the first few months the child's care was left to a nurse and to Evelyn.[31] With the baby poorly, it was decided that she and her mother should remain in Brighton and Evelyn was to travel daily between Aldershot and the South Coast to assist the nurse in the night-time care of his child. For a period of two months Wood alternated with the nurse in watching the baby through the night. Such a regime of travel, army work and nightly childcare soon took its toll on Evelyn's health. On several occasions he collapsed with exhaustion and he was forced to abandon the daily commuting. Fortunately, the baby grew stronger and Paulina's condition also improved enough for the Wood family to return to Aldershot.

Evelyn was to remain as Brigade-Major, under Horsford, until the end of 1869 when he was made Deputy Assistant Adjutant-General, under Sir James Yorke Scarlett, and moved to the South Camp at Aldershot. Wood seems to have again been fortunate to serve under an officer whom he not only liked but respected, and it appears Scarlett had a similar opinion of Evelyn. Scarlett was to later write to Wood to say how much he appreciated his services, 'especially in the field, where they have been so useful'.[32] Indeed, on one occasion Evelyn was able to rescue the reputation of his short-sighted commander when he was able delicately to point out, during a field excercise, that Scarlett had managed to detach himself from the forces he was supposed to be commanding and was in fact leading the opposition into battle![33]

Evelyn's continuing health problems, combined with ongoing financial concerns, led the Woods to consider his long-term future in the Army. In his position as Brigade-Major, Evelyn had acquired some interest in and knowledge of Military law, and this seems to have led him to consider becoming a barrister. Thus while serving at Aldershot throughout 1868 and into 1869 Wood studied to pass his entrance examinations to the Middle Temple. Somehow he managed to balance his responsibilities at Aldershot with study in London and an ever-growing family; the first son, Evelyn FitzGerald Michell, was born in November 1869. After years of study, in which Evelyn would rise at 4.00 am and work until 7.30 am, Wood passed his final exams in 1874 and became a barrister-at-law in that year. However, sudden army advancement from the middle of the 1870s ensured that he would never be obliged to earn his living at the Bar.

By 1871, still based at Aldershot, Evelyn was under the command of General Sir Hope Grant and throughout much of that year he was employed in surveying the surrounding area for suitable grounds for the General's planned, large-scale army manoeuvres. Evelyn must have surely enjoyed this role and the freedom it gave him to ride around the Hampshire and Surrey countryside. When the Army Commander-in-Chief, the Duke of Cambridge, visited Aldershot in September 1871, to handle an Army Corps in field exercises, Evelyn was fortunate to gain a temporary position as his Staff officer. This, of course, brought him in direct contact with the Commander-in-Chief. Wood found the Duke an amiable if hard task-master and was later to complain of the long hours he was forced to work. However, he gained valuable experience of Staff work and, crucially for his future prospects, his face, and not just his reputation, was becoming well known among the Army's top brass.[34]

After nearly five years at Aldershot, Evelyn once again joined a line regiment. Displaying his usual financial ineptitude, he managed to purchase an exchange into the 90th Light Infantry, which was later to become the Cameron Highlanders, just as the whole system of purchase was abolished as part of the Cardwell Army reforms. Before he joined his new regiment at Stirling Castle, Evelyn managed to find time for a tour of the recent battlefields of the Franco-Prussian war of 1870. However, the trip was slightly marred by his need to economise, having just spent £2,000 on the exchange, which saw him travel overnight in second-class railway carriages so as to avoid the price of a bed.[35]

Evelyn joined his new battalion at Stirling at the end of 1871, where, as a Junior Major, he assumed command of three companies. He soon established that his companies had enjoyed a rather 'easy-going' regime in the past, one which he was soon to radically alter. Evelyn focused on the fitness of the men after he discovered on his first route march with them that many struggled to complete the twelve mile walk. Wood's tactics centred on naming and shaming those men whose fitness was clearly not up to the required level. Although such an approach was sure to alienate those affected, it apparently worked, and Wood was able to state that within a few weeks his companies had no trouble in achieving distances of fifteen miles or more.[36] Evelyn also introduced a more rigorous training system. This saw his men regularly pitching and striking camps and drilling at one-pace intervals, and this approach was introduced at Aldershot the following year. His concern for the welfare of his men resulted in the introduction of straw matting in their tents whilst on exercise to ease their tired bones and ensure that they remained relatively dry.

At the end of July 1872 Evelyn accompanied his battalion to Aldershot, which was now becoming his second home. Within a fortnight Wood was able to take advantage of the presence of an old contact, his former commander in India, General Sir John Michel, to secure a place on the Staff of the Second Army Corps. With Evelyn's experience in the selection of suitable ground for field exercises, he was despatched to Blandford in Dorset to reconnoitre and prepare camps for the force under the command of Michel. Evelyn's success in this role was reflected in his confidential annual report, of 7 August 1872, which stated that he possessed 'a very high character in all particulars. He has a thorough knowledge of his profession in theory and practice.'[37]

Near disaster was to now strike the Wood household. Whilst renting a house in Aldershot, his two young children fell sick with the life threatening illness of diphtheria. Paulina, now pregnant with their third child, was out of the house when the children were struck down and, when she returned, Evelyn refused to let her back into the house, fearing for her own health and that of their unborn baby.[38] Wood now experience an anxious time in which he and a nurse cared for his two children through the worst of their illness. Again he was deprived of sleep as he stayed up most of the nights nursing his young son and daughter. Eventually, after three weeks, the children were well enough to be able to convalesce in a nearby hotel. However, after weeks of willing himself to remain awake Evelyn discovered he was suffering from insomnia. He was forced to seek the assistance of the Regiment's medical officer, who prescribed a dose of morphine and, in his haste to administer the syringe, accidentally injected Evelyn with an overdose. After some frantic remedial action, the doctor was able to ensure that Wood's life was not in any danger. Evelyn woke after nearly twenty-four hours sleep to be told that he had just missed the birth of his third child, Charles Michell Aloysius.[39]

Evelyn, who was now very conscious of his own standing and reputation, continued to ensure that his profile was raised amongst the Army's senior officers. To this end he was keen to advocate his views on the use of Mounted Infantry and circulated his beliefs to a number of prominent members of the armed forces. These included General Sir Hope Grant, General Sir Archibald Alison and General William Napier, at the War Office, to name just three. The responses of these and others to Evelyn's proposal were generally favourable.[40] There was further good news for Wood in January 1873 with the welcome decision that after ten years as a Brevet-Major he was to receive a pro-motion, based on seniority, to the rank of Brevet-Lieutenant-Colonel.

More encouraging news was received when Wood was asked to present his views on Mounted Infantry in the form of a paper at the United Service Institute in March 1873. Clearly, Wood's lobbying had been effective. His brother-in-law, Viscount Southwell, attended the evening presentation and later wrote to Paulina stating that, 'Evelyn's lecture ... was a brilliant success. I never saw the Institution fuller ... It was excellently well delivered in a colloquial tone that made you listen to him ... I had no idea he [Evelyn] had such a good delivery ... He got thunderous applause when he finished.'[41] After such a successful evening Evelyn had to wait three years for the Army to formally adopt some of his proposals regarding the use of Mounted Infantry and pioneers, men with specialist construction as well as sabotage skills, into the British cavalry. Wood was able to present his report to the Adjutant-General in 1876 and, before the end of the decade, Evelyn was to be in overall command of such a force in South Africa.[42] However, it was to take until the 1880s for detachments to be given formal mounted infantry training.[43]

Before Evelyn saw service in South Africa, he was involved in an expedition to another area of that continent. This was the Ashanti War of 1873–4, in which British forces were commanded by Sir Garnet Wolseley, who had recently achieved fame with his first independent command during the Red River campaign in Canada of 1870. It was while in Canada that Wolseley conceived the idea of compiling a list of the 'best and ablest soldiers'[44] whom he could second as 'special service officers' to be used on this and any future campaigns in which he might be in command. During the Red River campaign, the two officers of note who came to Wolseley's attention were Redvers Buller (1839-1908) and William Butler (1838-1910). Wolseley's patronage of such officers was to reach a pinnacle in the Ashanti war, so much so that the group of special service officers involved became known as the 'Ashanti Ring', or the 'Wolseley Ring', and they would follow Wolseley on many of his future expeditions, much to the dislike and jealousy of those less favoured.[45] Amongst this group were names such as Baker-Russell, Henry Brackenbury, Sir George Colley, and, of course, Evelyn Wood. These men would dominate the higher command positions in many of the African campaigns throughout the later nineteenth century, and Wolseley's patronage would ensure that they would gain some reflected glory from his successes.

Chapter Five

Into Africa

Ashantiland was to be found on the Gold Coast of West Africa, in modern-day Ghana. The British had had a trading station there from as early as 1618 but the territory itself was ill-defined and both the Dutch and the British staked some claim to it until an agreement was reached in 1868 by which Britain assumed the role of imperial master as well as policeman.[1] Like all of sub-Saharan Africa, the area was driven between tribal factions, and in this case the coastal areas were populated by the Fantis. The Ashanti's of the interior were well known for their warlike nature and enjoyment of human sacrifice, particularly of captured prisoners. Such behaviour could be tolerated when the responsibility for the area was shared between the Dutch and the British, but with sole imperial charge it was inevitable that, under pressure from the Press and public alike, the British Government would take issue with such goings-on.

In the past, local forces comprised of a few British officers, men raised from the coastal tribes and West Indian troops had kept some sort of order, but in June 1873 the aggressive Ashanti army of 12,000 men, under King Coffee Calcalli, invaded the British protectorate, leaving a wide swathe of death and destruction. The Ashantis even had the audacity to move on the British coastal fort at Elmina, in an attempt to drive the British into the sea, but were beaten back by a mixed force of marines, sailors and West Indian troops. It was clear that the British Government had to act to humble the aggressive Ashantis. Despite many newspapers advocating the dispatch of a force under the command of Charles 'Chinese' Gordon, the Government announced, on 13 August, that it had appointed Wolseley to be Administrator and Commander-in-Chief on the Gold Coast.[2]

According to Evelyn, he first became aware of the possibility of an expedition to the Gold Coast in the early spring of 1873 and, if his account is to be believed, it would seem that the Government were considering a campaign against the Ashantis even before they attacked

67

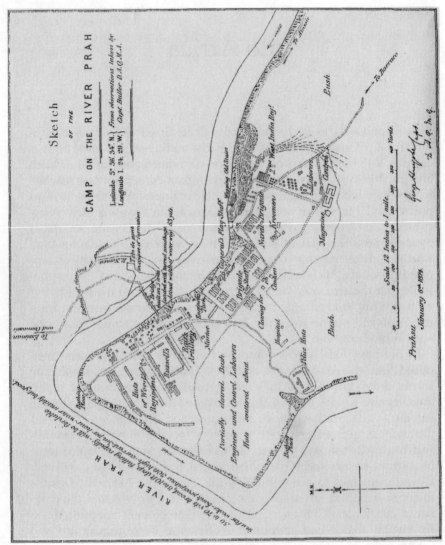

Sketch of the camp on the River Prah. From Henry Brackenbury, *The Ashanti War of 1873–4* (1874).

Elmina. In May, Wood visited Wolseley at the War Office, he claims by chance, and discovered Wolseley examining a Dutch map of Ashanti-land. Wolseley informed Evelyn that 'there was a King there who required a lesson to bring him to a sense of the power of England.'[3] A recent biographer of Wolseley also records that Wood visited Wolseley by chance when he was planning the campaign and was offered a position as a result.[4] However, it is perhaps somewhat naive to think that Evelyn, with all his contacts, would not have known that Wolseley was actively planning the campaign, and surely he would not have left his appointment to chance.

According to Evelyn, he joked with Wolseley that any campaign would involve the crossing of the Prah river and that with his naval experience Wood could steer any craft up the stream. Wolseley is alleged to have responded that if a force was to be dispatched, Evelyn would indeed accompany it. It appears that Wood took Wolseley at his word, for before it was announced that Wolseley would lead the campaign Evelyn was telling his family that he would join the expedition. At the end of July, Evelyn's Aunt Ben wrote to her sister, Lady Emma, to congratulate Wood on his decision to volunteer for service in Ashanti and she informed Emma that she felt it was right that Evelyn was leaving his position at Aldershot, 'because it would be unfair to others, who had a right to expect their turn.'[5]

On his appointment, Wolseley informed the Government of his wish to take two battalions, composed of hand-picked men from the most efficient units, one of which Evelyn was to command. However, this idea was vetoed by both the Commander-in-Chief and the Secretary of State, Cardwell. Instead Wolseley was instructed that he might make his choice of special service officers and with them enlist and train friendly natives for an advance on the Ashanti capital, Coomassie. If this was to prove impossible, the government would dispatch the first three battalions on the roster for overseas service. With these instructions, Wolseley informed the thirty-five officers he had personally selected that they would depart in September. Wood claims that he was instrumental in arranging for one of his officers from the 90th Regiment, Lieutenant Arthur Eyre, to be among the party by pleading for Eyre's selection to Wolseley on the grounds that the Lieutenant was 'the son of a good soldier, his mother is a Lady.' Such an endorsement apparently worked and Eyre joined the other picked men.[6]

Wolseley planned his campaign with the utmost detail. He was fully aware of the region's reputation as a 'white mans grave', the tropical climate being considered 'pestilent.' One officer scheduled to go asked a friend with experience of the Gold Coast what kit he should take and was told, 'A coffin. It is all you will require'. With this in mind,

Wolseley realised that the campaign must be of short duration, beginning at the start of the dry season in December and concluding by the end of February, before the return of the rains. Wolseley also believed that the campaign would only be successful if there was strict adherence to some of the 'minor' details of his planning. For example, the officers were instructed to wear loose-fitting outfits and were even told how much salt they should consume. All British troops would be given a daily dose of quinine, as well as instruction for well-lit tents, with fires inside or at the entrance, to aid ventilation. It was not known at the time that the bite of a mosquito was responsible for malaria, but the illumination of tents did have the added benefit of deterring the worst of the mosquitoes.

After all this planning, it was with a sense of acute disappointment that Wolseley, Wood and the other officers found themselves aboard the steamer *Ambriz* at Liverpool on 12 September 1873. The vessel was described by Wolseley as 'the most abominable and unhealthy craft I ever made a voyage in'.[7] Wood described her as hardly seaworthy and stated that on more than one occasion he thought the ship would capsize in the heavy seas.[8] Henry Brackenbury was to write that the cabin floor oozed with bilge-water, the whole ship reeked of foul smells and even that the discomforts suffered during the voyage in the Bay of Biscay exceeded any that the campaign itself inflicted.[9]

On 2 October, it was with huge relief that Wolseley, Wood and the rest of the 'Ashanti Ring' finally anchored off Cape Coast Castle. Evelyn was given the brief by Wolseley to try to recruit a regiment from the local tribes. To this end, he and Lieutenant Eyre set off at once along the coast to the fort at Elmina. In order to avoid being wholly dependent on the coastal Fantis, efforts were made to recruit from other parts of West Africa. Wolseley had already arranged for officers to be detached at Gambia and Sierra Leone to enlist likely recruits for the formation of Wood's regiment and that of the other irregular regiment to be commanded by Major Baker Russell.[10] At Elmina, Wood soon discovered that the Ashantis who had attacked the fort in July were still in the vicinity, at a place called Essaman, and that this force was receiving supplies from the coastal villages of Amquana and Ampenee. Evelyn, with his usual energy, set about trying to cobble together a force of sorts to advance on the Ashanti position. With a classically patronising Victorian generalisation Wood's biographer described the local Fantis as 'known to be among the most cowardly of mankind'.[11] With such unpromising material Evelyn tried to create an army.

One of Wood's first tasks was to summon those local chiefs who were known to have supported the earlier Ashanti attack to report to him at Elmina. Those nearest the coast obeyed the summons and were rewarded with the doubtful honour of supplying Evelyn's force with sufficient manpower for portage of all equipment and stores essential for an advance. Of those chiefs further inland, the Chief of Ampeene sent no answer, but beheaded a native loyal to the British and displayed the head for them to view, and another responded by saying that he had 'smallpox today, but will come tomorrow.' The Chief of Essaman wrote back with the invitation 'Come and fetch me if you dare. White man no dare go bush'. Evelyn was unable to resist such a challenge and, under the instruction of Wolseley, he began preparations for his force to advance on Essaman and then go on to burn the coastal villages which had been supplying the Ashanti force.[12]

Evelyn's decision to march his fledgling force on Essaman was fraught with danger. He was working with new conscripts untried in combat, whose reliability was unknown. He had little idea as to the numbers of Ashantis he might face, and the force would be travelling over miles of extremely difficult terrain. It was clear that success would be dependent on the drive and determination shown by the special service officers under his command, men such as Eyre and Buller, as well as his own fortitude. Evelyn was heartened by the arrival of the first men that who been recruited from along the coast, and over 120 Haussas joined his force on 10 October. Thus with a makeshift force comprised of Fanti labourers, Haussas, Royal Marines, naval volunteers and around 200 troops from the 2nd West Indian Regiment, he led his men towards Essaman, departing on 14 October.

Wood's advance was to be something of a side-show, but a very important one at that. Such was the control, based on fear, that the Ashantis exerted over the local tribes, that on arrival the British forces had been received with disdain and even insults from the coastal inhabitants. It was vital that the British should show they were capable of taking the fight to the Ashantis and that they could move through the bush and locate and defeat the enemy, thus shattering the local belief in Ashanti invincibility. Thus any sort of setback to Wood's force simply could not be countenanced and, as if this was not pressure enough for Evelyn, Wolseley was shortly to join the advance, although he promised Wood that he would not assume command or interfere in any arrangements.

It appears that Wolseley wanted to make it plain to the local tribes, as well as the Ashantis, that he did not see his role merely as an administrator for government, but 'as a general officer to command her Majesty's troops and personally to take part in all military operations.'[13] Perhaps Wolseley also felt that, as this was to be Evelyn's first time in command of such a large body of troops, it would be better if he was present to ease any concerns that Evelyn may have had. One of Wolseley's biographers described Wood at this time as 'constitutionally nervous.'[14] Whatever Wolseley may have said, Wood must have embarked on the advance with the fear that his commanding officer would supersede his authority at any moment.

The advance began soon after daylight on 14 October, and the Haussas were positioned at the front of the column. Unfortunately, in their enthusiasm, they set off too quickly and soon lost contact with the main body of troops. For over an hour, Wood and his command struggled to maintain contact with the Haussas as they waded through knee-deep swamps and then marched along a very narrow bush path, with dense jungle on either side. Eventually, just as Evelyn led the main force to the outskirts of Essaman, they found the Haussas engaged with Ashanti scouts. Apparently Wood's force had caught the Ashantis in the village completely by surprise and they had not had time to flee. The Haussas now began firing wildly in all directions, and it seems their excitement was infectious for the marines also started firing randomly into the surrounding jungle. A sharp rebuke from the commanding officer soon returned the marines to their senses, but the firing of the Haussas was only brought under control when they had exhausted their available ammunition.

The column, having regained some composure, was now ordered by Wood to be deployed for action. However, the moment he must have feared and anticipated now occurred when Wolseley, despite his earlier reassurances, began to issue commands over Evelyn's head. Wolseley ordered the marines to make a frontal attack on the village, whilst he sent his Chief of Staff, Colonel McNeil, to lead a party to the left of the settlement; finally he instructed the officer commanding the one artillery piece and rocket launcher, which had been manhandled through the bush, to commence firing on the village.[15]

Whatever Evelyn must have felt at this apparent snub to his command, he had little time to dwell on it, although it has been claimed that Wood viewed Wolseley's actions with 'dissatisfaction'.[16] The Ashantis now adopted their usual battlefield tactics and attempted to outflank their enemy. This placed them in direct contact with the West Indian troops and, at first, the Ashantis achieved local penetration. Three of the West Indians were hit and at this sight the others began to falter. It was now that Evelyn came into his own and, leading by example, he managed to rally the West Indians and was able to advance into the village with them. Now attacked on three sides, and having suffered some casualties, the Ashantis withdrew and melted into the jungle. British success had been at the cost of one dead and several wounded, including McNeil who was so badly hurt that he was forced to return to England. The British breakfasted in Essaman and then proceeded to burn the village to the ground. The advance continued on to the villages of Amquana, Akimfoo and Ampenee, and these settlements, which were known to have supplied the Ashanti army, were likewise razed to the ground. All were found to be deserted. News of the British victory had evidently spread quickly through the jungle, enabling the Ashantis to flee. After an exhausting day, Wood led his force back to Elmina in the early evening, having completed a march of 22 miles.[17]

This punitive raid had been a success, which provided a huge boost to morale throughout the area. More importantly, vital lessons had been learnt, perhaps the most obvious being the unreliability of native forces in battle. Wolseley was able to use the example of this first outing against the Ashantis to press forcibly for British troops and more special officers, for it was also clear that, due to the density of the jungle, a larger proportion of officers to men was required to maintain order and cohesion. He thus telegraphed Cardwell, to request more officers and two battalions of infantry with artillery and engineers.

Wolseley, Wood and all concerned realised that the task they faced in marching on the Ashanti capital of Coomassie was a formidable one. Not only could their foes fight in a disciplined and cohesive manner, but the elements were very much against a British advance. For example, the temperature and humidity experienced, along with the harsh terrain, had made covering the twenty-two miles on this first expedition extremely difficult. At one point, Wood's column could only achieve four miles in nearly three hours. Lieutenant Eyre dropped from exhaustion, and although the men had carried as much water as possible, this had been insufficient and some had been without any liquid for the last six hours of the march.[18] Clearly, the advance to the Ashanti capital was going to have to be well planned.

What of Evelyn's performance on this day? The decision, if it was his, to place the Haussas at the front of the column, was a strange and risky choice and could have resulted in far higher casualties, not only because these men advanced too rapidly and lost contact with the main body for over an hour, but because their random firing could have easily caused British deaths. Wolseley's usurping of Wood's authority at the crucial moment in the battle must have confused and hurt his pride, but it seems clear that Wood was able to hide his feelings and regain his composure so as to successfully lead the column for the rest of the day.

On the following day Wolseley wrote to Evelyn stating, 'I have to congratulate you upon the very able manner in which you did everything yesterday. I am very much obliged to you. The operations were well carried out, and all your previous arrangements were admirable.'[19] Furthermore, in his report to Cardwell Wolseley was to heap more praise on Evelyn when he told the Secretary of State of Evelyn's role in its success.[20] When Wood saw a copy of this report he was able to fawn over his commander when he wrote to him on 15 December, 'Having read Mr Cardwell's despatch I feel very grateful to you for the manner in which you heaped all the credit for the operations of the 14th October on my head, quite ignoring your own part ... I hope, please Heaven I may continue to earn your approbation and that you may continue as our chief.'[21] It is tempting to consider that Wolseley may have been somewhat overgenerous in his praise of Evelyn, knowing that Wood's vanity would respond positively to such an approach. Whether this is the case or not, what is clear is that Evelyn had become a most loyal supporter of his commander.

On his return from the Essaman raid, Evelyn set about conscripting and training what was to become known as 'Wood's Regiment' in preparation for the eventual march on the Ashanti capital. Such a move could not be considered by Wolseley until a route had been hacked out of the jungle as far as the Prah river and a base camp established there. Once the British contingent had arrived, the final advance could begin. In the meantime, the defence of the area and the logistical planning for future engagements was left to Wood and the other special service officers, particularly Buller who had responsibility for intelligence. This included not just establishing the location and size of the main Ashanti army, but also determining the location of what was termed 'good water' on the route of the British advance.

There is no doubt that Evelyn found the task of establishing his regiment of native troops extremely frustrating. He described No. 1 Company, composed of Fantis from the immediate coastal area, as 'a cowardly, useless lot of men'; No. 2 Company had some fighting value and were to be used for most of the scouting work during the campaign; No. 3 Company was made up of men recruited from Sierra Leone, known as the Kossoos, and it became clear that they treated captured prisoners very cruelly and had to be constantly reprimanded by the British officers. On one occasion, Wood and Eyre were unable to stop a group of these men literally cutting in half an Ashanti prisoner while he was still alive.[22] Finally, No. 4 Company contained men from the Bonny tribe, and the best that Evelyn could say about these men was that they were very clever at basket work, but had no aptitude for war![23] Wood was later to complain that throughout the war he never managed to convince the majority of his soldiers that shooting was more accurate if the butt of the rifle was put to the shoulder![24]

Wood was later to describe the difficulties of dealing with the natives and wrote that in his opinion there was a tendency to expect too much of these regiments: 'The native regiments were composed of four or five different races, no company understanding the language of that working near to it, and no men speaking the language of their Officers.'[25] Frustration with the inadequacies and ineptitude of many of the men's behaviour did result in some of the officers losing their composure. This, on occasions, resulted in the officers beating the men, a practice that Evelyn endeavoured to stamp out. Evelyn considered that such actions were due to the 'officers brimming over with energy' and having to 'deal with Races naturally indolent' as well as having to cope with the climate, which he described as 'very trying'.[26] In total, Wood would command sixteen British special service officers. Despite some evident shortcomings it was on them that the success of 'Wood's Regiment' would depend.

Wolseley received news from the War Office that the requested British battalions of the Royal Welch Fusiliers and the 42nd Royal Highland (the Black Watch) Regiment would arrive on the Gold Coast in early December. Knowing that the forces he currently had at his disposal were insufficient in both quantity and quality to mount any offensive action, Wolseley concentrated his efforts on establishing defensive positions against any surprise Ashanti attack, attempting to gather intelligence on the enemy, and clearing a route into the interior ready for the arrival of British troops. Wood's Regiment provided some of the manpower necessary to construct a road from the coast to a base camp on the banks of the Prah river. Evelyn worked along-side Major Home, the Commander of the Royal Engineers, not only to construct the road, but also to design and build the British camp. The construction of the roadway involved the building of nearly 240 bridges over the many rivers and streams on the route, as well as numerous causeways across areas of swamp. All was done with the expectation by Wolseley that his British troops would be able to reach the operational assembly area by the Prah river dry-shod and in first-class fighting condition.

Despite the harshness of the conditions, Evelyn, unlike many of his brother officers, did not succumb to illness during his time on the Gold Coast. Given his medical history this is perhaps surprising. Wood did suffer from a mild attack of malaria and he was later to tell of the 'sickening feeling of debility, which must be felt to be understood',[27] which malaria induced in him and others. However, he was to avoid the worst effects of sickness, diarrhoea and dehydration, that was to claim the lives of such officers as Captain Huyshe and Lieutenant Charteris. Wolseley himself was to fall dangerously ill throughout the month of November 1873. To improve his chances of recovery, he was moved to the hospital ship, *Simoon*. Evelyn went to visit his commander there and was clearly shocked by his condition, although Wood was not made aware that he saw Wolseley on one of his better days, for at least he was coherent. One of Wolseley's many biographers has claimed that the ambitious Wood, second in command to Wolseley, saw an opportunity to take over the expedition.[28] There seems little evidence to support this assertion, although Wood did later state that he considered that there was little chance of Wolseley recovering sufficiently to be able to join the advance to Coomassie, and if this had been the case, Evelyn would most probably have been given command.[29] By the first week of December, Wolseley had recovered sufficiently to return to active duty, and the question of command never arose.

It was while assisting the other force of irregulars, under the command of Major Baker Russell, that Wood's Regiment were engaged in a fire-fight with a larger Ashanti force, in which his men failed to distinguish themselves. Evelyn had been ordered to support Baker Russell's force at the village of Abrakampa, where, on 6 November, they had been attacked by the Ashantis. Evelyn led his force, now enlarged by the addition of 1,000 recently arrived men from the coastal tribes, on a gruelling march through the jungle, hampered by the unreliability of local guides, who led the force on a wide detour. Arriving on the morning of 7 November, Wood and his officers attempted to persuade the coastal men to advance on the village. Despite the Kossoos driving the local men forward with the flat of their swords and British officers resorting to more unorthodox methods (one broke his best umbrella whilst 'encouraging' the men to advance), the new recruits without exception simply lay down and refused to move.[30] Fortunately, the Ashanti commander, Amanquatia, considered that it would be prudent to withdraw, and the casualties of this engagement were limited to twenty Haussas killed when their companions began firing in panic at the Ashanti rearguard. This caused the remainder of the coastal men to flee the twenty miles back to the coast. Wolseley later wrote of their actions that, 'Their duplicity and cowardice surpasses all description.'[31]

Evelyn must have been both furious and concerned at the behaviour of his men. He surely feared for their future conduct in battle and also for his own reputation as a successful leader of men. Wood's Regiment were next engaged at the village of Faysowah, and the skirmish there was later to be magnified by some newspapers into something of a disaster. The Ashanti army were attempting to reach safety by crossing the Prah river, where, once across, they could choose good defensive positions in the hope of checking the British advance. Wolseley instructed Evelyn to follow the Ashantis and harass their rear. The Ashantis had shown that they were adept at rearguard actions, a lesson that Wood seemed to forget when he appeared to be less than prudent in his pursuit of them. On 27 November Wood's men captured an Ashanti prisoner, who informed Evelyn that Amanquatia and several of the more important chiefs, along with a large body of Ashantis, were at Faysowah. Here the Ashantis were celebrating an Adai day, or holy day, on which slaves would be sacrificed, and, once engrossed in such actions, nothing would make them move. Wood pressed on the ten miles to Faysowah, apparently ignoring the warning that the Ashantis would be likely to make a stand.

Initially the engagement went well. Both the Haussa and Sierra Leone troops advanced in open order and drove the enemy outposts back into the village. Here, however, they came up against the main Ashanti army who adopted their usual tactics and began to outflank Evelyn's men. Wood now thought it best to withdraw and ordered the remainder of the Cape Coast men to come up to facilitate an orderly retreat. However, these men suddenly ran off without even engaging the enemy and their panic spread to the Haussas and the Kossoos, who also bolted, throwing the whole force into confusion; and the retreat became a rout in which ammunition and baggage were lost. The men were only extricated when Wood, Eyre, Woodgate and other special service officers formed a sufficient rearguard so as to keep the Ashantis at bay as the force retreated over a distance of four miles.[32]

Although newspaper reaction at the time was somewhat critical, the low casualties, just one dead and eight wounded, meant that Wood was able to portray the retreat as a small force withdrawing from the presence of an overwhelming number of the enemy rather than a defeat.[33] This action seemed to convince Amanquatia that the Ashanti army should return across the banks of the Prah river and back into the heart of Ashantiland. Wood even received praise from his commander for the action when he stated that: 'This attack caused the whole of the Ashanti Army to retreat in the utmost haste and confusion.'[34] This, however, can be viewed as a piece of nineteenth century 'spin', on the part of Wolseley and Wood, to turn what had been a less than glorious action into an apparent success.

Wood's Regiment now set about constructing a base camp on the banks of the Prah river, which would be sufficiently large enough to accommodate the two British battalions when they arrived and would act as a staging post for their assault on the interior of Ashantiland. This was successfully achieved and the camp even offered a degree of comfort, if not luxury. The special correspondent of the *Daily Telegraph*,

Frank Boyle, who accompanied Wood's men, described how the camp for 5,000 men was constructed in a fortnight and how, during this period, the river bank resounded 'with the clang of axe and cutlass, the shouts of busy men, the thump of mallet.'[35] It is clear that Boyle and Wood enjoyed each other's company and they would frequently dine together. Evelyn seems to have actively pursued the relationship, perhaps hoping for favourable coverage from the correspondent. What is clear is that in future campaigns Wood was very much aware of the use and importance of newspapermen and was always keen to develop friendly relations with them, in complete contrast to the likes of Wolseley or Kitchener. Boyle highlighted one meal that he shared with Evelyn and described the evening as one of 'great cheerfulness and contentment,' but then stated that in the morning a poisonous snake was found asleep under the table, evidence of the dangers of jungle dining![36]

Wood spent Christmas Day assisting Major Home in the construction of a trestle bridge across the river and the following day received ambassadors sent by the Ashanti King to discuss possible peace terms. Wood had no authority to discuss such matters with them, but did arrange for the terms to be dispatched to Wolseley. Whilst they were waiting for the commander's response Evelyn endeavoured to make the envoys feel welcome. His idea of hospitality involved a demonstration of the new acquisition for the British army, the Gatling Gun. So effective was the display of British military might that one of the Ashantis used his blunderbuss to blow off his own head. Wolseley was furious with Evelyn for allowing such a thing to happen during a sensitive time in the peace negotiations and apologised to the Ashanti King, sending him a copy of the findings of Court of Inquiry he had convened. It seems that the king was uninterested and stated the matter was of no importance as the man was only a commoner. One of the surviving ambassadors even commented to Wood that, 'The man being a coward was afraid to live, that's all.'[37] Any censure Evelyn might have received was brushed aside by Ashanti indifference.

Wolseley's terms for peace, which included the payment of a large fine in gold and the surrender of members of the Royal family as hostages to ensure compliance with the treaty, were unacceptable to the Ashanti king, and both sides prepared themselves for further conflict. The British battalions had duly arrived from England and had journeyed to the Prah river. Scouting parties across the river, led by Wood and Baker Russell, had been active in the first weeks of January 1874 and their reports, combined with intelligence gathered by Buller, led the British to believe that the Ashanti forces would initially resist the British advance around the village of Amoaful, and again, if

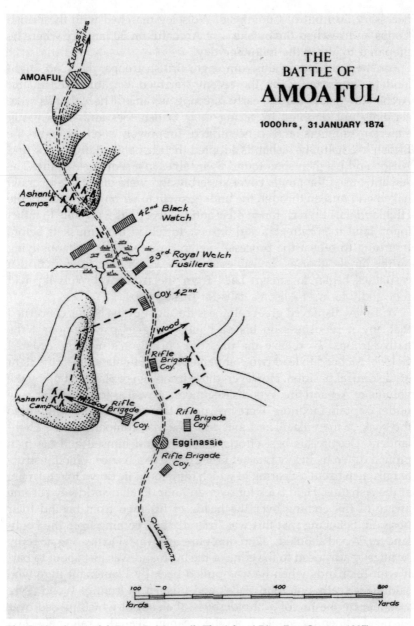

The Battle of Amoaful. From L. Maxwell, *The Ashanti Ring* (Leo Cooper, 1985).

necessary, in front of Coomassie. Wolseley marched with the British troops and reached the outskirts of Amoaful on 30 January where he prepared to attack the following day.

For the first time in this campaign, British troops, the 42nd Highlanders, commanded by the recently arrived Brigadier-General Sir Archibald Alison, led the early morning advance. The Ashantis were certainly not daunted by facing their British foes and, with vastly superior numbers and concentrated firepower, soon brought the British to a halt. The Ashantis adopted their usual flanking tactics, and Alison and his men soon found themselves in a semicircle of fire. The Ashantis used the jungle cover superbly and were often able to crawl naked and unseen through the undergrowth to within a few feet of the Highlanders, at which range their antique weapons were able to inflict injury, and then retreat, again unseen, to reload their muskets before returning to repeat the process. Evelyn described the Ashantis lying on the jungle floor as 'invisible as a hare ... till they fired.'[38] British casualties began to stream back from the front and Wolseley had repeatedly to meet Alison's calls for fresh troops.

Wolseley displayed great calmness throughout the battle, concerned that any nervousness on his part might trigger panic amongst the native troops. To relieve the pressure on Alison's men, he ordered Colonel McLeod to lead two companies of the Highlanders to the right of the central position. However, these troops were also held up by the volume of Ashanti fire. Wood's Regiment, as well as the Naval Brigade under Captain Luxmore, were instructed to move to the left, around to the back of the village, and join with the rear company of the Highlanders. Despite his best efforts, Evelyn found himself and his men pinned down by heavy musket fire. Unable to advance, Wood instructed his men to cut a clearing in which they could lie down to return fire at the Ashantis. Held back for over an hour, Evelyn suddenly became aware of fire coming over the heads of his men from behind their position. Believing that this was 'friendly fire' coming from the Highlanders, Wood shouted, '42nd don't fire this way'. On hearing no reply he angrily advanced to the edge of the bush and was just about to part it with his hands when he was pulled back by Lieutenant Eyre who said, 'It is really not your place', and pushed in front of Wood. Eyre was met by the fire of a blunderbuss, the shot of which passed over his head. When the smoke from the weapon cleared, a rather shocked Eyre returned to Evelyn's side to inform him, 'There are no 42nd men there; the fellow who fired at us is black, and quite naked.' Wood immediately ordered his men to fire a series of volleys into the bush and the threat passed.[39]

Wood's men were in an unenviable position. Unable to see the approach of the enemy through the thick bush, all they could do was maintain their own fire and ensure that they lay low to the ground. Concerned that his advance was stalled and conscious that he needed to set what Brackenbury was later to describe as a 'rare example' of bravery and fortitude to his men', Evelyn refused to seek cover, despite the protestations of Eyre.[40] As he turned to receive a Staff Officer, bringing fresh instructions from Wolseley, he was hit by a nail fired by an Ashanti only a few feet away. Knocked to the ground by the impact, Wood was aware of Eyre bending over him and asked him who hit him over the head. Eyre pointed out that it was not a head wound, but that Evelyn had been shot in the chest just above his heart and that blood was trickling through his shirt. Eyre helped Wood to his feet and attempted to carry him back to the aid station. Wood would not have this and insisted he could manage. However, Evelyn found that all he could do was walk in circles around the clearing, again exposing himself to enemy fire. It was with some reluctance that he finally agreed to be carried away from the fight, and command was handed over to Luxmore.[41]

On reaching the rear, the senior medical doctor, Mackinnon, examined Evelyn and expressed little hope for his survival, based on the weak action of Wood's heart. Mackinnon even invited Wolseley to say his last good-byes to Evelyn as he was dying. However, the ever-optimistic Wolseley refused to do so and declared that he would see Evelyn at the head of his men in a week! A second doctor, with whom Wood was on friendly terms, examined him and probed the wound but was unable to extract the head of the nail. Evelyn asked the doctor frankly if he was to die and was informed that as he had not already passed away it was likely that he would survive. With the surgeons unable to remove what was left of the nail, all that Evelyn was prescribed was rest, Brand's Essence of Beef and brandy.[42]

Meanwhile, the battle raged on. With fire on three sides, the Ashantis gave some ground, which allowed Wolseley to bring forward a seven-pounder gun. This weapon, firing over open sights at a mere fifty yards range, inflicted serious casualties on the Ashantis and after fifteen rounds of rapid fire they withdrew to another defensive position, allowing the Highlanders to charge forward and capture the village. Wolseley was keen that the Ashantis should not be allowed to again establish themselves in a defensive position. He deployed two companies of the Rifle Brigade to the north-east of the Ashantis' position and ordered two of Wood's companies, the Bonnys and the Kossoos to charge. Shouting war cries, they drove the Ashantis before them. The centre began to retreat and the flanks of the Ashantis gradually melted back into the bush. The British had carried the day, but Evelyn had been forced to miss the climax of the battle and had failed to lead his men in their successful charge. As Wood lay on a stretcher, he heard the victorious cheers of his men, and it must have been a bitter blow that he had missed the final moments of the battle.[43]

The battle had been hard-fought and lasted for twelve hours. The Ashantis proved to be skilled and determined fighters, who had kept the British infantry at bay and had only been dislodged by the introduction of artillery into the battle. Although the Highlanders had lost only two men, one in four of those engaged had been wounded and would play no further part in the campaign.[44] Wolseley, his force already depleted by sickness, knew that a rapid advance on Coomassie was vital if he was to achieve success. Naturally, Evelyn intended to part of this final march on the capital. On 3 February Wood received a worrying letter from Eyre which brought some bad news. It appeared that, despite earlier reassurances from Wolseley that Wood's Regiment would be represented during the final British advance on Coomassie, the men of the Regiment had been left to garrison a post and it looked unlikely that Evelyn's men would be present at the climax of the campaign.[45] Despite the fact that Wood had been lying on a stretcher for the past three days, he managed, somehow, to persuade his doctor that he was fit to return to service and within half an hour of receipt of the letter he was back on the trail in pursuit of Wolseley and his advancing force.

Marching through the night, in a 'deluge of rain which never ceased', Evelyn overtook Wolseley at 4.00 am the following day.[46] Wood sent an advance message to his commander, informing him that he was coming to rejoin the march on Coomassie and that he intended to lead his Regiment into the Ashanti capital in accordance with Wolseley's earlier promise. When Wood rejoined the main British force he was met with the news that Wolseley was delighted at his return and that he would indeed be granted the opportunity to lead his men in the advance. Any relief and excitement that Evelyn experienced at this news must have quickly disappeared when he attempted to get his troops, particularly the company of Bonny men, to advance on the village of Ordasu, where the Ashantis had massed to make a last stand before Coomassie. Evelyn spent over four hours attempting to persuade his men to attack. The situation was not helped by the Bonnys' complete inability to fire their rifles correctly; the lack of training they had received became very apparent, as they lay firing harmlessly into the air. Even their chief became exasperated at the reluctance of his tribe to advance, and Evelyn witnessed the chief kicking and buffeting the prone soldiers in an attempt to make them move forward.[47]

Evelyn was later to admit that it had been a mistake to place his men in the forefront of the advance, rather than the British regulars. Not only did he have to face the embarrassment of not being able to convince his Regiment to move forward, but they also sustained casualties, which perhaps the more disciplined British troops might not have done. Undoubtedly the greatest loss of the day was that of Lieutenant Arthur Eyre. Evelyn was, again, trying to set an example to his reluctant men by standing in full view of the enemy. However, he did order Eyre to kneel down, but just as he did so the young officer was shot in the stomach. Wood rushed over to him, but he at once realised, from the look on Eyre's face and the position of the wound, that there was no hope. The bullet had pierced Eyre's bladder and he suffered terribly, despite being given large doses of morphine. Wood was later to write that he was deeply distressed at the sight of Eyre's suffering, for he had grown extremely fond of the young man who had accompanied him on every patrol and skirmish and who had frequently positioned himself between Evelyn and any possible danger. It was with some relief that he saw Eyre finally pass away after two hours of agony.[48]

The reporter, Henry Stanley, who was later to gain fame as an African explorer and finder of David Livingstone, was with Wood's Regiment and claimed that Eyre's last word was 'Mother!'[49] On his return to England, Wood wrote to Lady Eyre and described the last moments of her son, clearly contradicting Stanley's report. Evelyn stated that Arthur's last words were, 'Give my love to my mother and say my last prayer is for her, tell her I was plucky to the last.' Wood also claimed that on Eyre's death he, 'fastened up the body, kissed his poor face once more for you, [Eyre's mother] and buried him, carefully covering his grave with dried leaves so that it might not be discovered.'[50] A volley was fired over his grave.[51] Evelyn was later to visit Lady Eyre and gave her Arthur's rings. Although Lady Eyre was later to write that she had found the visit 'painful' it is clear that she appreciated the time and trouble Wood had taken towards her.[52]

What of Evelyn's relationship with Eyre? The fact that Wood had many close relationships with his subordinates is clear. Not only did he express affection towards Eyre, who in death received a physical kiss from Evelyn, but he was also later to describe another of his men, Ronald Campbell, who died fighting with Wood during the Zulu war, as, 'soft, gentle and tender as a girl' and as 'my Ronald' in correspondence to Queen Victoria.[53] It is easy to consider such expressions somewhat odd, but they must be viewed in the historical context of Victorian colonial warfare. Wood and his officers would not only have spent a great deal of time together, travelling to the various campaigns in which they were engaged, they would also have endured and shared physical hardship as well as the dangers inherent in warfare, and this must have created a deep bond between them. There is also no doubt that Wood's 'managerial style', professionalism and his own example resulted in much devotion being shown to him by his men, a devotion which was returned by Evelyn. This was first apparent in the loyalty displayed by several of the Indian non-commissioned officers towards Wood during his time in India, but was seen in every campaign in which he was to serve. Such affection should not been seen as evidence of Evelyn's potential homosexuality, but as a reflection of hard-won friendship and comradeship.

The death of Eyre ended any attempts by Wood to muster his force for an advance. Brigadier Alison reported to Wolseley that, 'It is no use in sending Wood's and Russell's regiments to the front – the men won't go; but they can garrison this village [Ordasu], and keep up the communications with me.'[54] The Ashantis adopted their usual formation of attempting to envelop the British, and the flanks were heavily engaged. Wolseley cleverly used the Ashantis' tactics to his advantage and allowed them to encircle his force around the village. Then, using the Highlanders, he was able to effect the breakout of Alison's advance force onto the road to Coomassie. While Alison's men experienced little resistance, the remaining troops were heavily engaged in close combat fighting. Many of the Staff Officers surrounding Wolseley had to resort to their revolvers to keep the enemy at bay, whilst the commander himself was hit in the helmet; fortunately the bullet did not penetrate it. At 1.00 pm Alison sent news to Wolseley that his men had penetrated within a few miles of the capital and he confidently predicted that his force would be in Coomassie by nightfall. Wolseley ensured that this information was communicated to his troops and the natives wasted no time in shouting the news to the attacking Ashantis. Brackenbury later described the effect on the Ashantis: 'as by magic, the enemy's fire ceased, and not another shot was fired by him.'[55]

The battle, and the war, was won. Wolseley duly entered Coomassie on 4 February 1874. His force freed hostages and prisoners, but were unable to locate the King. The royal palace was looted and the following day, short of supplies, Wolseley ordered the destruction of the capital and his men began the march back to the coast. Evelyn and his men did not accompany Wolseley in his triumphant march into Coomassie, which must have been a bitter disappointment to them, having travelled so far and suffered so much in the jungle conditions. Instead, Wood's Regiment was given responsibility for a line of outposts covering the town.

The following day Evelyn was ordered back to Elmina, with a convoy of some seventy wounded and sick men, mostly Highlanders, although there were also men from his own Regiment. Wood himself should have joined the list of sick as he suffered from intestinal complaints throughout the journey, and he could only walk by resorting to frequent doses of laudanum and chlorodyne. It was probably the effects of this illness which led Evelyn to break his own rule about the beating of his men. The Bonny men, who had not distinguished themselves in the action, now tried Wood's patience further by refusing to carry their own wounded. They claimed that they would never care for sick and wounded men in their own country, but would leave them to die, and refused to care for them now. Evelyn's temper snapped and he ordered the Kossoos to flog one of the Bonny men as an example to the others. The Kossoos entered into their task with relish and Wood was to write that he 'was nearly sick from the sight'. He then had another Bonny man similarly treated, but after twenty-five lashes the flogged man gave in and he and the others agreed to carry the wounded for the rest of the trip.[56]

There must have been a number of reasons why Wood allowed such punishment. Undoubtedly, he was frustrated and annoyed by the performance of his Regiment, and the loss of Eyre surely affected his emotional state. These feelings, combined with his poor physical condition, must have led him to ignore his own rules and high standards. However, it must be remembered that flogging whilst on active service was still legal at this time, even for British troops. At the very least, such punishment did ensure that the wounded were returned safely to the coast and Wood was able to report that his orders had been successfully carried out.

Wolseley and his staff retired as far as the village of Fommanah and there awaited, with some nervousness, a response from the Ashanti King to the British offer of peace negotiations. It was feared that the King, remaining at liberty, would continue to be hostile. Finally, on 9 February, Wolseley received the King's acceptance of the peace terms, and the Treaty of Fommanah formally ended the war. Wood disbanded his Regiment at Elmina and all the men were transported back free of charge to where they had originally been recruited. Evelyn was able to fulfil his promise to the local chief of Elmina, Chief Essevie, with whom he had become friendly, when on his return to England he sent the chief a large black top hat, umbrella and walking stick as gifts to thank him for his good service.[57] Evelyn embarked with Wolseley on the *Manitoban* and returned to England. The expedition had been a great military success: not only had the might of the Ashantis been crushed, the capital destroyed and a peace treaty signed, but casualties and costs had been low. Wood was to write that the success was 'due primarily to Sir Garnet Wolseley', and that, 'every one acknowledged his superior Military Genius.'[58]

If it was clear that the success of the expedition rested on Wolseley's shoulders, what of Evelyn's performance during the campaign? There is no doubting Wood's bravery and determination throughout the campaign and, perhaps surprisingly, his constitution held up better than most of the 'special officers'. It was perhaps Wood's misfortune to have been given the responsibility of raising his own Regiment from native troops. It is clear that Wolseley viewed the appointment as an important and responsible one and he clearly had faith in Evelyn that he could rise to the challenge. However, it is also true that Wood was unable to find sufficient time to train his men in the crucial weeks leading up to the arrival of the British troops, since his men were being used by Wolseley for basic labouring work as well as reconnaissance. In retrospect, Wood, then Wolseley's deputy, should have insisted that he be granted some time to transform the abilities of his men. This lack of basic training, particularly with regards to rifle skills, was to cost Wood's Regiment dear when it was eventually given the opportunity to show its worth in battle. Wood was guilty of leading an ill-trained regiment into battle. For a man with high standards of professional soldiering, the performance of his Regiment must have caused Evelyn some pain and embarrassment, especially as he would have surely known that he had not given them sufficient opportunity to learn and improve.

However, it has been argued that Wood's and Baker Russell's men fulfilled a crucial role when, during the last phase of the campaign, they took all the weight off the British troops, leading the advance and carrying out all the fatigues in camp. The assistance that Wood's men gave to the construction of the Prah river base camp was exceptional. It is also argued that Wolseley was expecting too much of these native regiments if he thought they could show any fighting qualities after so little instruction.[59] The final judgement as to the success of Wood's Regiment can be left to Wolseley himself, who writing to the Secretary of State for War, stated: 'Both these officers [Wood & Baker-Russell] have, upon many occasions, been placed in very difficult positions requiring the exercise of high military qualities, and have invariably carried out their very arduous and trying duties most efficiently.'[60]

Any fears that Evelyn may have had about how his performance in the expedition would be viewed at home were soon dispelled on his return. Wolseley was rightly hailed as the 'conquering hero', and Evelyn certainly gained by reflected glory. He not only received a great reception at his brother-in-law's house at Belhus, where his mother was staying, but his brother officers in the 90th Light Infantry, stationed at Dover, turned out and carried him into the barracks amidst much celebration. More tangible rewards were soon to come Evelyn's way. At the end of March 1874 he was gazetted a Colonel in the 90th and received the honour of the Commandership of the Most Honourable Order of the Bath (CB). Within a month he was called to the Bar by the Honourable Society of the Middle Temple and then accepted an invitation to join the Livery of the Fishmongers' Company.[61] There were also a number of dinners to which Wood and many of the officers involved in the campaign were invited. These included an evening hosted by the Lord Mayor of London, as well as a night spent at Windsor Castle as a guest at the Royal table. This was to be the first occasion on which Evelyn met the Queen, although their deep friendship did not develop until after the Zulu war.

Wood was again given the privilege of speaking at the United Services Institution on his experiences in the Ashanti campaign, in June 1874. The lecture was again received well and was later transcribed in the Institution's journal for 1875. It is apparent that a strong bond existed between those officers who took part in the Ashanti expedition, which was above and beyond any 'ring' that may have been established between Wolseley and his favoured officers. Buller was to write to Evelyn, as well as the other officers involved in Ashantiland, in June 1874, to suggest that there should be a reunion dinner in 1875. Wood heartily agreed with this suggestion and replied, 'My dear Buller, Delighted to assist in paying for your annual dinner.'[62] For a man who constantly struggled to make ends meet, this was a generous gesture on Evelyn's part.

Wood's promotion to full Colonel caused some difficulties when he finally returned to his regiment after three months leave. The existing Colonel of the 90th was apparently not keen to have two full Colonels in his Regiment and made this very clear to Evelyn on his arrival, when he was told, 'Now Colonel [Wood], there is only enough work for one of us here, and I am fond of work.'[63] For the next two months the two men managed to avoid each other's company, until Evelyn, probably by design, returned to Aldershot. Given the atmosphere between the two Colonels, it was not beyond the realms of possibility that Evelyn used his old friends and contacts at Aldershot to obtain the position of Superintending Officer of Garrison Instruction for the United Kingdom and Ireland, and he began his new role in September 1874. Although based at Aldershot, Wood's new job required that he visit many of the garrisons and barracks across the land so as to ensure some consistency in officer training methods; so once again Evelyn was able to ensure his face, as well as his reputation, became more widely known throughout the Army. He was again to use his contacts the following year when his friend Major-General Arthur Herbert was able to appoint him to his Division for the Autumn Manoeuvres. Evelyn's previous experience at such exercises ensured he was noticed and in April 1876 he was given the title of Assistant Quartermaster-General at Aldershot, serving under another friend, Colonel George Harman.

In his new role at Aldershot, Evelyn was given much encouragement by Colonel Harman to arrange tactical schemes and exercises. Wood was able to introduce Minor Tactics operations for junior officers, in which they were able to gain experience of handling the three Arms of the Service (infantry, cavalry and artillery) in tactical operations during field exercises. Previous to this no officer under the rank of General had been allowed to gain such useful battleground experience. These were to be such a success that they were adopted across the Army for the next thirty years.[64] In August 1877, another of Wood's old friends, General Napier, Governor of Sandhurst, offered him the post of Commandant at the Military College. Although he was tempted by this offer, Evelyn was determined to command a battalion on active service and politely declined.

The expectation of war between Britain and Russia over the 'Eastern Question', the expansion of Russian power into areas of the Balkans under the control of Turkey, was very real throughout 1877, and Evelyn must have been expecting a possible posting to the region. However, despite much posturing, and shows of force by both sides, war was avoided by the Treaty of Berlin. The much sought after foreign service finally materialised when the 90th Regiment were instructed to sail to South Africa to help deal with a rising by the Gaika tribes. Even the posting of his Regiment did not ensure that Evelyn would join them as there still remained the intractable issue of two Colonels in the Regiment.

Although the original commander, Colonel Palmer, was nearing retirement, he still insisted on travelling with his men to the Cape, and they duly embarked, without Evelyn, on 11 January 1878. It is interesting to note that in his autobiography Evelyn at no time mentioned Palmer by name, but only described him as 'the Colonel'. Clearly, even after the passage of twenty-five years, Wood still felt discretion was required. Wood now pulled every string available to him and called in every favour from friends and foes alike; as a result received verbal guarantees from the Commander-in-Chief, the Adjutant-General, and the Military Secretary that he would succeed to the command of the 90th on 1 April 1878. With these promises, which had been conveyed in writing to General Thesiger, who was to be in overall command of operations in South Africa, Evelyn resigned his Staff appointment to follow his men as a 'Special Service Officer'.[65] Evelyn embarked for the Cape on 27 January and was delighted to find that he was to share the journey with his old friend Buller. The two men could not have known at the time that their destination was to provide both with moments of glory and infamy which would remain with them for the rest of their lives.

Chapter Six

Battalion Command

Evelyn used the opportunity presented by the long sea voyage to ensure Thesiger was made fully aware not only of his combat experience, but also of the issue of command of the 90th Regiment. Fortunately, this problem largely resolved itself when Colonel Palmer announced that he had become a Glasite, a member of a Christian sect with strong pacifist beliefs, and so had no desire to go on active service. Thesiger was thus free to use Wood as he saw fit and placed Palmer in charge of a few friendly Hottentots with the responsibility for supplies.[1] The ambiguity which still remained as to who was officially in command of the 90th was later to impact financially upon Wood, much to his frustration and annoyance.

The reasons behind the outbreak of what was to eventually become known as the 'Ninth Frontier War' are many and complex. The initial uprising of the Galekas tribe, of the Xhosa people, led by Chief Sarhili, began in September 1877. The primary cause for the conflict was one of white settlers encroaching into Xhosa tribal areas in the Eastern Province in search of farmland. This threat was combined with the enthusiasm of the recently appointed High Commissioner, Sir Bartle Frere, for the confederation of South Africa into the Empire. Frere firmly believed in a 'white' framed confederation and was convinced that the Xhosa people needed to understand that their salvation rested on a loss of their sovereignty. Sarhili refused to meet Frere, and an ever growing war-party amongst the Galekas ensured that border tensions increased. A clash of arms was inevitable and this finally occurred on 26 September 1877 at a place called Gwadana where a colonial force was driven from the field with the loss of six troopers. An escalation of the conflict resulted in a call for more Imperial troops and Wood became part of the second batch of reinforcements to be sent.[2]

On arriving in South Africa, General Thesiger and Colonel Wood were greeted by the retiring General, Cunynghame, with the news that his forces had defeated the rebellious Xhosa tribes in the Transkei

Sketch map of the Gaika Rebellion. From E. Wood, *From Midshipman to Field-Marshal* (1906).

region, at the battle of Centane on 7 February 1878. Once again, as with the Mutiny in India, Evelyn must have felt that he had missed an opportunity for active service. However, as in India, a fresh rebellion was to see a move away from set-piece battles into a war of bush fighting, characterised by tough marching in an unforgiving climate and terrain. In such circumstances, Wood's experiences in both India and Ashantiland would prove invaluable to Thesiger, who had no previous knowledge of active front-line fighting, having occupied a number of senior staff posts throughout his career. By the time the two men had travelled from East London to King William's Town, rebellion had broken out in the region of the Amatola Mountains.

What was to become known as the Ninth Frontier War began when Chief Sandilli, attempted to obtain independence from British control, as he had tried to do in previous Frontier wars in 1846, 1848, and again in 1850-53. Sandilli was by 1878 an elderly man, who could command respect and authority from his followers. Apart from being a great survivor, he also possessed a long memory. The humiliating terms imposed on him and his people at the end of the Eighth Frontier War had seen them forced from their Amatola home into a reservation, where they were made British subjects, and a white supervisor was imposed on their kraal. Such conditions still hurt the pride and dignity of the old leader and Sandilli continued to look for opportunities to break from his British yoke. Ever cautious, Sandilli had resisted initial urgings from Chief Sarhili, for the two tribes of Xhosa people to join forces against the British. However, Sandilli finally capitulated and both tribes were present at the decisive battle of Centane. From his position on the battlefield Sandilli was able to watch the defeat of the rebellion, at the hands of British marksmen. The rebels incurred high casualties and were thoroughly beaten but Sandilli and the survivors of the defeat were able to slip away and seek refuge in the Amatola Mountains.[3]

These men were soon joined in their mountain refuge by isolated groups from other Xhosa tribes, and it was to stop this concentration of potential rebels, as well as to isolate Sandilli, that Thesiger first took action. The General also received reports that in one of the numerous raids that Sandilli's followers had made into the Buffalo range, twelve miles north of King William's Town, three Europeans had been murdered. Thesiger had to act and he turned to Colonel Wood for help and support. Together the two men devised a simple plan of action to defeat and capture the remaining rebels. What men Thesiger had at his disposal, including several hundred friendly natives from the Fingoe tribe, would be used to beat through the dense bush of the Amatola Mountains, along the lines of a giant 'game drive', during which the rebels would be pushed from their sanctuary towards British forces covering the perimeter.

Such a plan of action clearly required detailed coordination of the available forces, which would only come from the skilled handling of troops and mutual trust between each officer. However, these requirements were sadly lacking at the start of operations. Thesiger ordered Colonel Wood to throw a cordon of troops around the eastern Amatoles and provided him with two companies of the 2/24th Regiment of Foot and 200 mounted colonials, mainly farmers from in and around Grahamstown and Cradock. Alongside this command where placed a mixed bag of colonials and natives, completing an arc-shaped line which was meant to cover the Buffalo ridge and squeeze the rebels out of their Amatoles hideout. The likely escape route for the rebels was towards the Pirie Bush area and here Thesiger placed five companies of the 2/24th as his final trap. In total, Thesiger had almost 3,000 men in his force, marginally more than Sandilli.

The date of 18 March 1878 was set for the start of the operation. However, any hopes that a coordinated movement of troops would be possible were soon dashed. Wood had received intelligence that over 1,000 warriors were aware of the planned march and had taken the Gwili Gwili Heights in an attempt to oppose his men. To reduce the risk of ambush, Evelyn decided to move out on the evening of 17 March; walking in single file, it took his men several hours to make the seven mile climb to the summit. Arriving at dawn, Wood found that the Heights had been vacated by the enemy and, despite the clear views provided by this position, he was unable to see any sign of either the rebels or other British formations. Indeed, unknown to Evelyn, Sandilli's men had already led a number of colonials into an ambush, and a detachment led by Frank Streatfield had been forced to abandon their advance to go to the aid of the colonials. Wood, with no supporting troops, was forced to sit it out on the Heights. Thesiger, waiting with his men, was no doubt puzzled by the lack of stampeding warriors, as well as any sighting of or news from his own men. By the evening it was clear that the day's operations had been an uncoordinated farce and, crucially, any surprise that British forces had been trying to achieve had been lost.

After such an inauspicious beginning, Thesiger had little option but to renew the drive the following day. Evelyn was soon placed in an awkward position when several of the colonial troops refused to enter the bush, claiming that 'it was not a fit place for Europeans.'[4] On hearing this Wood, in his usual style, led his young soldiers forward and, embarrassed by this demonstration, the older colonials soon followed. The next couple of days were ones of acute frustration for Thesiger as he tried to ascertain the whereabouts not only of his men but also of the enemy. Apart from the surrender of a large group of women and children, few warriors were killed and none captured, as they easily managed to evade the British in the thick bush. On one occasion the General was able to gain a vantage point and saw Wood's men break camp and continue the advance, only to witness the rebels then come out of the bush behind them and take possession of the deserted camp! The British experienced extreme weather conditions throughout the four days of operations: cold early morning mists, high daytime temperatures followed by driving rain and freezing night-time temperatures, combined with fear of attack from a cunning and elusive enemy, mentally and physically exhausted all those involved. Indeed Evelyn was later to state that 'the apparent result of our ... operations ... was not commensurate with the discomfort we underwent.'[5]

Thesiger, despite protestations from Wood that a repeat of the offensive would again result in failure, showed a singular lack of imagination in ordering a fresh advance. It seems clear that the General was very aware that the rapid departure and early retirement of his predecessor, Cunynghame, was as a result of dissatisfaction in the colony at the latter's reluctance to take action, and Thesiger did not want to be similarly charged.[6] This new offensive, which began on 28 March, followed the usual pattern, and although coordination between the various forces worked better the results were again disappointing. The rebels were again able to avoid confrontation, although the British could now claim that they held the highland plateau and the enemy were firmly corralled in the Pirie Bush. However, many of the colonial troops were not satisfied with their returns for eleven days of campaigning; only 200 cattle had been captured and three of their number had been killed. As a result many of the volunteers slipped away, depleting Thesiger's force of much needed local knowledge and support.

Thesiger's plans were then thrown into turmoil when he received news that one of Sandilli's old allies, a chief named Siyolo, had broken out of his reservation. Siyolo's intentions were to bring his 500 warriors to Sandilli and join him in the Lotutu Bush, close to the Pirie bush. These men had been spotted by a small patrol led by Captain Warren; in the resulting skirmish Warren's men had killed twenty warriors, and the remaining rebels had scattered into the nearby bush. Thesiger acted quickly and ordered all available troops to the Lotutu Bush. Wood's detachment was increased by the addition of two companies of his own regiment, the 90th, as well as the arrival of two squadrons of the Frontier Light Horse (FLH), a mainly colonial unit commanded by Wood's old comrade Redvers Buller. With these forces Evelyn had sufficient troops to place a thin line of men on the northern and western boundary of the Lotutu Bush. Thesiger placed units of the 2/24th to guard the southern and eastern sectors.

The subsequent operation clearly demonstrated the folly of a hastily assembled force venturing into an unfamiliar area, held by an enemy who knew the terrain intimately and was able to exploit it. The native troops proved reluctant to advance and when they did were easily

94

beaten back. To add to their troubles, men of the 2/24th mistook them for the enemy and unleashed both rifle and artillery fire, causing some casualties. When the British advanced, they soon discovered that they were too thin on the ground, with the gaps so large between each trooper that the rebels could easily evade detection. It was during this operation that Evelyn again had a fortunate escape when he was fired on by sentries when he did not respond to their challenge.[7] This was not to be the only occasion during his time in South Africa that Wood's increasing deafness was to cause him problems. Thesiger now wisely decided to suspend operations until his men were fully rested and, leaving three companies of the 2/24th to guard the Pirie Bush, he returned to King William's Town with Evelyn.

Thesiger was now compelled to take stock, and no further operations took place for three weeks. This was some relief for Wood, who through overwork was suffering from a return of neuralgic pains. The time spent in King William's Town allowed both men to consider alternative tactics to trap the rebels. It soon became clear that any plan would require additional manpower and the British were fortunate that a force of 300 mounted colonials, under the command of Commandant von Linsingen, fresh from putting down a small rising nearby, joined the General's command. In addition, more native warriors were recruited, this time from areas that had felt the full force of the rebel rising, in the hope that this would make them more likely to fight.

As was becoming all too apparent, Thesiger showed a deep reluctance to accept advice, particularly from colonials. Instead of adopting the strategy that was being advanced by his colonial commanders – that of dividing the rebel area into military districts in which mounted forces could be stationed to continually harass the enemy into submission – the General persisted in the belief that Sandilli and his followers could be driven from their hideout. Criticism can also perhaps be levelled at Wood, who, as second in command, might have taken greater consideration of the colonial plan and been ready to advocate it actively to his General.

Thesiger's new plan of operations was to ring the Lotutu Bush with large forces, which were to converge on it from four separate directions. These movements were designed to drive the enemy to the west where Wood, with the largest force, would be waiting. In total nearly 4,000 British troops were to be employed in an area of less than sixteen square miles. The General confidently predicted success. The advance began at dawn on 30 April and soon scattered the token resistance made by Siyolo's men. The use of artillery was particularly effective, and Siyolo ordered his men to attempt a breakout in the direction of Wood's command. Evelyn's men had the greatest distance to cover and were late in getting started that day, with the consequence that his troops and Siyolo's men clashed in the thick bush. The rebels saw Wood's troops, who were forced to advance in single file, first and poured fire into them from all sides. Evelyn must have thought he was back fighting the Ashantis. As the enemy closed in, men and officers began to fall, others stumbled into trees and collided into each other in the now smoke-filled thicket. Panic was averted when Wood ordered up the two seven-pounder artillery pieces. Loaded with case shot, the artillery tore into the bush and caused Siyolo's men to break and run in attempt to find another escape route.

Elsewhere the British were constantly skirmishing with an unseen foe until, at one point in the north, a line of unarmed women emerged from the bush. The astonished troopers stopped in their tracks and a number of warriors were able to make their escape. By the end of the day, Wood and the other commanders were able to report to Thesiger that 100 rebel dead had been counted. This was to be the most successful of the numerous operations, but it can perhaps be considered a poor military outcome for such a large coordinated advance. The next day, further sweeps by the British discovered that, under cover of darkness, their elusive foe had manage to make their way stealthily past the troops and were now safely back in the Pirie Bush.

Thesiger, perhaps blinded by frustration, devised another offensive into the Pirie Bush. Again, it could be considered than Evelyn should have offered his General some cautionary counsel. Whether he did or not is unknown, but what is clear is that this last offensive was a disaster. Wood and Buller combined to drag the two artillery pieces to a high point in a night march in the driving rain. This was in the hope that such a move would surprise the enemy, but after enduring a terribly difficult advance, daybreak revealed that the element of surprise had been lost and once again the rebels had fled. The other contingents were unable to coordinate their infantry advance and in one of the few engagements of the day, Sandilli's men managed to ambush a detachment of the FLH, killing several including the commander, Captain McNaghten. Thesiger had had enough and finally he adopted the strategy of his colonial commands and divided the remaining area of the Amatola Mountains into eleven districts, each patrolled by cavalry units. The rebels were continuously harassed and within weeks Sandilli sought peace terms. The British reply was that only unconditional surrender would be acceptable.

As the month of May progressed, the British gained more successes against the rebels. Siyolo finally bolted from the Amatola region and was killed in a chance encounter with a colonial patrol, while Sandilli and his ever shrinking band of followers remained confined to a diminishing area, where they remained despite the probing of Buller and the FLH. Finally, at the end of May, Sandilli fled from his stronghold and was pursued and eventually brought to battle in the Sidenge Hills. Outnumbered, Sandilli and his men stood their ground until half of their number lay dead. Their leader, mortally wounded, managed to escape, only for his dead body to be discovered a week later. With the capture of Sandilli's sons in early July, the rebellion was over.

Wood had led his detachment effectively throughout the three months of operations. He had coordinated the movements of his troops better than most and had performed well during the few direct contacts with the enemy. Thesiger was later to report to the War Office that, 'I cannot speak too highly of the good service rendered by this officer [Wood]. He has exercised his command with marked ability and great tact. I am of opinion that his indefatigable exertions and personal influence have been mainly instrumental in bringing the war to a speedy close.'[8] Thesiger later informed Wood that he had written to the Commander-in-Chief, the Duke of Cambridge, that he [Thesiger], 'could not have succeeded if it had not been for your active and energetic aid.'[9]

It seems clear that Wood drove both himself and his men to great efforts during the numerous operations, often at the expense of his own health, and that his determination alone ensured that the various drives did achieve some limited success. Indeed, it seems to have been generally appreciated that Evelyn's energy had enthused all under his direct command . Writing to his mother in June 1878, Lieutenant Henry Curling reported, 'Col. Wood who commands the column is the most energetic, plucky man I ever met, in fact his energy almost amounts to a mania as he wears himself out and everybody under him.' Curling concluded with words of warning, which can be seen as somewhat prophetic, when he stated, 'He is so plucky that he imagines that everyone is like him and would lead us into trouble if there was any serious fighting.'[10]

These operations in which Evelyn was so actively engaged involved his first contact with colonial officers and volunteers. From the outset, Wood seems to have acquired a low opinion of their dedication and motivation. Indeed, there exists direct evidence of his disdain for their abilities and judgement. In early June 1878 one of Wood's colonial officers, Captain Haynes, wrote to him to criticise Evelyn's decision to place a small force of natives, under the command of two European officers, to occupy the area around Murray's Krans in the Buffalo Range. Haynes considered the force to be inadequate and was concerned that if any rebels returned to the area, his small force would face 'disaster' and that 'any blame would be your own [Woods'].' Haynes concluded, 'I beg most firmly, yet most respectfully to protest against my small force being placed in such a dangerous position.'[11] Wood's response can best be described as direct, 'I am in command of ... the Buffalo Range. I propose to place Fingoes [natives] permanently on Murray's Krans. If Capt. Haynes fears a disaster, we can dispense with the services of his men. I can ensure that 100 Fingoes will stay on Krans if I order them.'[12] Wood's evident disdain for such colonial officers as Haynes is perhaps indicative of the strain which this hard campaign had placed upon him.

With an end to the rebellion, the volunteers were disbanded and sent home. Evelyn was ordered by Thesiger to proceed with his new command of the 90th Regiment, now fully assembled, and the FLH to Pietermaritzburg in Natal, where there was growing concern as to the military intentions of the Zulu nation; although, as will be shown, any immediate threat from the Zulus was contrived by the British High Commissioner Sir Bartle Frere for his own political motives. In his action, Frere was actively supported by the Commander of British forces, Thesiger, who on the death of his father had become Lord Chelmsford. There is no evidence that Wood was aware of the plotting for war between Frere and Chelmsford, indeed it seems clear that Evelyn was convinced by Frere's propaganda machine, which painted the Zulus as a warlike race, ready to cross the border into Natal and attack settlers at will. With such a belief, Wood no doubt considered it right and proper for a professional soldier to prepare his force for the likelihood of war and set about this task with great gusto.

The 500-mile march from King William's Town to Pietermaritzburg, although arduous, was without incident. Evelyn clearly believed that it was his responsibility to impress upon the colonials, and the various tribal leaders he encountered, the sense of British power that his force was attempting to convey. To achieve such an aim was not without difficulty as Evelyn was much concerned with the shortcomings of the Regiment's equipment, particularly uniforms, which did not help to present the imagine to the locals that he would have wished. For example, from experiences in the Amatoles Mountain, it became evident that the men's regulation shirts were totally unsuitable for the huge variations in temperature. Also it was clear that the soldiers' boots would not last the hundreds of miles they would be forced to march across the veldt. Evelyn set about finding solutions to these clothing problems with his usual enthusiasm.[13]

However, perhaps the most important lesson learnt from this long march was the difficulty of transporting wagons across the terrain. The importance of acquiring suitable wagons to carry food and equipment, as well as securing the sixteen to eighteen oxen and their fodder, which each wagon required, became paramount to Wood's planning of any offensive against the Zulus. He was under no illusions as he realized that no matter how good the transport arrangements were much would still depend on the terrain and the hard work of his men. He described how the passage of the river Kei, which was only ninety yards wide and four feet deep, took five hours with much manual labour required to assist the oxen through the crossing.[14] When Wood reached Pietermaritzburg he immediately impressed upon Chelmsford the urgent need to acquire sufficient and suitable wagons and oxen for any likely advance against the Zulus.[15] In gaining Chelmsford's support for such a scheme of purchase Wood made a decisive contribution to the eventual logistical solution to the problem of invading Zululand.

After spending only one week in Pietermaritzburg, during which time he formulated a scheme for regimental transport, Wood left with his battalion to march north to Utrecht. Here Evelyn set about improving the town's defences against any likely Zulu attack. He then moved on to the other German immigrant settler town in the region, Luneberg, where he again formalised defence arrangements. In both towns Wood purchased as many wagons and oxen, mealies and other supplies as he could find. At first he expressed his delight at the straightforward manner in which the Germans did business with the British. However, this was to change as the likelihood of war increased. For example, one seller of mealies held back supplies from Wood in the expectation that there would be a significant price increase once war broke out.[16]

Evelyn, from his experiences in Ashanti, realised the vital importance of developing an intelligence network, which needed to be in place before any likely invasion. To this end he instructed Captain Woodgate, one of his staff officers, to acquire as much information about Zulu tactics and fighting formations as possible, as well as ordering him to develop a network of Zulu spies and informants. Thus whilst Wood was attempting to acquire wagons and oxen in Wessel-stroom in September 1878, Woodgate secretly visited the homestead, or kraal, of Chief Tonga, who was the half-brother of the Zulu king, Cetchwayo. Tonga supplied important information as to the likely Zulu battle tactics. Woodgate also gained promises of intelligence as to Zulu troop movements, once hostilities were to begin. The Zulus' respect for Wood's column stemmed as much from its ability to gain intelligence as its fighting skills.[17]

In October both Chelmsford and Frere wrote to Evelyn to encourage him in his efforts to ensure that the German settlers did not leave their farms, despite apparent Zulu intimidation and threat of hostilities. Frere was particularly keen that troops should be sent from the Utrecht garrison to support the settlers in Luneberg, and in this he was supported on the ground by Mr Rudolph, the district magistrate of Utrecht. Rudolph informed Wood that unless he offered military support to Luneberg the farmers would be certain to leave. Evelyn convinced himself that in purely military terms it would be vital to keep the communication lines open between Utrecht and Derby via Luneberg, and he therefore dispatched two companies of the 90th to Luneberg. Wood had been unable to discuss this troop movement with Chelmsford, and when the General finally learnt that the garrison at Utrecht had been reduced, for what he considered political expediency, he was not best pleased with Wood. Indeed Chelmsford wrote to Evelyn stating that, 'you have taken a serious responsibility upon yourself, and I doubt very much if you have acted wisely.'[18]

Wood's reaction was true to form. He was clearly hurt to have earnt some displeasure from his General and he was never one to take criticism lightly. However, he was able to respond forcefully to Chelmsford; firstly he thanked the General for his continued support and secondly he emphasised that he was his own man, although loyal to his commander, by stating, 'A "safe man" would not have run the risk, but I did what I believe you would have told me to do if you had been there.'[19] No doubt much of Chelmsford's annoyance was due to the fact that he had clearly envisaged that the 90th would remain a complete battalion and he wrote to Evelyn later in the month stating, 'I want the 90th L.I. to be all together ... one complete battalion will not be one man too many when we enter Zululand.'[20] This statement would seem to be an admission by Chelmsford that conflict with the Zulus had already been decided upon, for it was made weeks before the British High Commissioner was to present Cetchwayo with an ultimatum for the disbandment of the Zulu army, the eventual refusal of which would lead to war.

With the Army High Command apparently set on war with the Zulus, preparations for invasion, in which Evelyn was to play a prominent part, continued. Major Crealock, Lord Chelmsford's secretary, wrote to Wood at the end of October to outline the preparations for war the Headquarters Staff were making, as well as informing Evelyn of all the troops' movements towards the border.[21] Evelyn had already been in correspondence with Crealock concerning the fact that as he had been forced to sail to South Africa as a Special Service Officer, he had been drawing the pay of only a captain on active service.[22] Wood found himself in the ridiculous situation of earning less than many of his subordinates. It would take several more letters both to Crealock and Horse Guards before the matter was favourably resolved, but Evelyn's sense of injustice was to remain with him for months.

In November Chelmsford instructed Wood to travel to the northern town of Wesselstroom, in an attempt to attract the Boers to fight alongside the British in an advance into Zululand. To assist him in this new role, Frere appointed Wood as political agent for North Zululand and Swaziland, in the hope that this official title would aid him in his attempts to gain the respect and support of the locals, yet Evelyn was to receive an extremely chilly reception. The British had recently annexed, into a confederation of South African states, the bankrupt Boer region of the Transvaal, much to the displeasure of many of the Boer residents. However, Chelmsford hoped that Evelyn could bring his charm to bear on the Boer leadership, which included Andries Pretorius, to persuade them to fight. It was hoped that with the agreement and support of prominent Boers other might follow their lead.

Wood's journey north was accompanied by the most appalling weather, with torrential rainstorms washing away many of the already poor roads. Again, Evelyn's accident-prone nature was evident when he was almost killed by a runaway wagon. In the pouring rain one of the wagons in Wood's small convey turned over. Despite the conditions, Evelyn insisted that all his available men help their Colonel to right the wagon. It took several hours not only to set the vehicle back on its wheels and push it back onto the road, but also to unload and then reload its contents. When this had been done, Wood, for reasons perhaps only he knew, considered that both the driver and the mules were too shaken by their collective experiences to pull the wagon down the slope on which it was now resting. Evelyn thus decided that the wagon should be run down the hill by hand and he joked with his men that, 'If anyone is to be killed over this job, it had better be an officer.'[23] Thus with one of his men, Maude, he tied himself to the wagon by the wrist, and all in the detachment began to push. It did not take long for the loaded wagon to accelerate down the slope; and Evelyn realised in horror that he had lost control of it; digging in his heels he tried in vain to regain some control as he feared that, 'I should soon be like a pancake'.[24] In a massive surge of energy the Colonel managed to vault onto the wagon, free both himself and Maude and jump clear just before wagon and load disappeared over a cliff. Wood escaped with a few cuts and bruises but Maude had been slightly crushed in the accident, although he returned to duty two weeks later.

Evelyn later wrote to Chelmsford to describe the incident and admitted, 'I did not anticipate so bad an accident.'[25] Wood had been guilty once again of placing himself too close to the action; the Regiment's commander should never have been involved in such an enterprise and his actions could easily have resulted in the loss of his own life as well as that of Maude. His energy, and the desire to get things done, had again seen Wood put himself in unnecessary danger. There is no record of what Chelmsford thought of Wood's actions, but he is unlikely to have been happy to read of such recklessness.

When Wood and his small party finally reached the home of Andries Pretorius the anticipated frosty reception was indeed evident. Despite it being the custom in that region for the host and his family to come out and assist in unharnessing a guest's horses, only a rather embarrassed Pretorius ventured out of his house to help. He explained to Evelyn that his kindred and followers 'detested the sight of an Englishman'.[26] A two hour meeting ensued in which Pretorius and Wood discussed many issues, including the annexation of the Transvaal and of course the possibility of the Boers fighting with the British against the Zulus. Even Evelyn's charm and persuasive skills failed to work on these Dutchmen, and at the conclusion of the meeting the Boers refused their military support. Evelyn had, however, gained their grudging respect, and all the Dutchmen came out of the house to express to Wood their hope that he might safely survive any conflict with the Zulus. The lessons learnt from this encounter with the truculent Dutch would come in very useful in Evelyn's later negotiations with the Boer leadership following the first Boer war of 1881.

Although Wood had failed to win over Pretorius and his followers, he did achieve some success at a meeting in Utrecht on 4 December, where he gained promises of support from the Boers in the vicinity. However, such promises were hastily withdrawn when news of the British decision to find in favour of the Zulus over the Boers in a land dispute became known.[27] The one Boer who remained loyal to Wood was Piet Uys, whose father and younger brother had been killed fighting the Zulus in 1838. Evelyn wrote to Lieutenant-Colonel Crealock stating that, 'though a frank opponent of our late Imperial policy [the annexation of the Transvaal] he [Uys] has rendered me great assistance in influencing his numerous friends and relatives to their duties.'[28] Indeed Piet had little time for the British and, as he saw them, their imperial designs, but he hated the Zulus more and saw the British as a means by which the region could be rid of the threat they presented to the Boers. The forty friends and family that Piet Uys brought to Wood's command were most welcome. This was to be Wood's only success in bringing the Boers under British command, yet, conscious of the difficulties he had faced in his negotiations with the Boers, both Chelmsford and Frere thanked him for his persistence.

Whether Frere saw the removal of the Zulus as vital for the British to gain the respect and trust of the Boers, than allowing for an easier transition to imperial Confederation across South Africa, or whether he sincerely considered that there was a real threat of an uprising of black tribes across southern Africa is unclear. However, both Frere and Chelmsford felt sure that war was justified, and to this end an ultimatum was issued to the Zulus on 11 December 1878, listing many demands with which they would have to comply if war was to be avoided.[29] Central to the British dictates was the requirement that the Zulu army would have to be disbanded. Cetchwayo could not possibly countenance this, as the army was central to his political hold on his nation, and this Frere knew. With such conditions applied to the ultimatum, the war Frere and Chelmsford wanted was inevitable.

Furthermore, Frere knew that the Home Government, under the Premiership of Disraeli, Lord Beaconsfield, would not sanction a war. Therefore, Frere cleverly used the fact that, with no direct telegraphic link between South Africa and London at this time, all communications took three weeks to travel each way. He informed London of the issuing of the ultimatum, and thus the likelihood of war, knowing that any response would be received weeks after British troops had entered Zululand. Frere and Chelmsford were banking on an easy initial victory and thus a rapid end to the forthcoming conflict.

With the pressing need for a quick victory Chelmsford entered the conflict with a serious shortage of men and, in particular, of cavalry. He decided that he needed to engage the Zulu army in a set-piece battle, crush them and then advance to destroy the Zulu capital at Ulundi. Thanks to the foresight of Wood, Chelmsford had sufficient transport to be able to divide his force into three separate columns, each of which was to converge on Ulundi. Chelmsford hoped that at least one of these columns would be able to find and destroy the Zulu army. Number 4 Column was to converge on Ulundi from the north, and command of this detachment was given to Wood. His command consisted of his own 90th Regiment, the 1st Battalion of the 13th Light Somerset Infantry, Buller's FLH, six seven-pounder artillery pieces and 'Wood's Irregulars', a poorly armed unit of Zulus friendly to the British. In total the column comprised 1,565 men. Number 3 column, to which Chelmsford attached himself, was the largest, composed mainly of the 24th Regiment of Foot and amounting to over 4,700 men. The final column to enter Zululand in the initial advance was Number 1, commanded by Colonel Pearson and made up of a number of colonial volunteer units and six companies of the 99th Regiment of Foot.[30]

Although Wood's was the smallest of the columns, Chelmsford saw its role as vital to the success of the advance of his own column. The Commander of British forces was certain that the reliable Wood was the perfect man to protect the open left flank of his own column, as well as being the most able of his Colonels to begin the pacification of the mountainous country north of Utrecht, controlled by the abaQulusi tribe, who were loyal to the Zulu king.[31] In order to provide cover for his left flank, Chelmsford ordered Wood to cross the Blood River into Zululand on 6 January 1879, four days before the British ultimatum to the Zulus was to expire and five days before Chelmsford himself was to advance. In true gentlemanly style, Evelyn had forewarned the local Zulus of his intention to invade early and, although the warriors in the area had long since departed to join their regiments at Ulundi, the speed of Wood's advance caught many of the remaining Zulus by surprise; their cows, central to the economy of the Zulu nation, were tempting targets for the roving bands of Buller's FLH, who were able to benefit from the prize money they gained from the sale of the raided cattle.

Evelyn led his men ten miles into Zululand to a flat-topped hill named Bemba's Kop where, with advice from Piet Uys, he built a fortified camp. With fresh orders from Chelmsford to travel south for a meeting, Wood set out on 10 January with a small detachment of the FLH for support. The meeting, just north of Rorke's Drift, lasted three hours and was called mainly in order to discuss the advance. Chelmsford ordered Wood to slow his column in order that the other columns, with greater distances to travel, could catch up. So confident was Chelmsford of success that he even offered Evelyn, with the approval of Frere, the office of Resident of Zululand. Although flattered, Wood declined the position, stating he favoured soldiering to any political appointment.[32] Chelmsford orally instructed Evelyn now to concentrate his forces on those Zulus to his left flank and in front. This fateful instruction was to expose the whole area north of the central column and was to allow the main Zulu army to slip between Wood's and Chelmsford's scouts and venture unseen to within five miles of Chelmsford's position.[33]

In the next few days, Wood followed the new orders with his usual energy and directed several operations in the north-east, with the intention of clearing the Ityenteka Range and the Hlobane mountain of Zulus. The FLH were heavily engaged at this time and, in one demonstration against several hundred Zulus in the region of the Zunguin mountain, were able to force the Zulus to retire to the safety of the mountain. Evelyn followed up this initial success by marching the 90th through the night, and at dawn on 21 January he was able to lead his regiment up the Zunguin mountain. Here they caught the Zulus by surprise, drove them off the mountain and captured several head of cattle. The Zulus sought refuge on the connecting Hlobane mountain and it was from here that they were later able to launch attacks against the British. Both Wood and Buller were able, from their new position on Zunguin mountain, to look eastwards and there they saw the magnificent sight of 4,000 Zulus drilling. Evelyn was later to describe how the Zulus formed a succession of circular, triangular and square formations and how highly disciplined they were in their movements. Realising that his force was now outnumbered, Wood broke off the action and returned to camp. In the evening, Evelyn and his men clearly heard the distant sound of artillery fire and, when asked by a senior officer what such firing could mean, he responded that such fire at night could only be unfavourable.[34]

Evelyn was indeed correct in his judgement as to the reason for the night-time artillery fire. What he and his men heard was the British firing into their own camp at Isandlwana, which had been taken by the Zulus. By clever deception, perhaps assisted by Chelmsford's disdain for his foe, the Zulus had enticed part of Number 3 column, with Chelmsford at its head, away from the British camp, in a futile hunt for elusive Zulus in the Hlazakazi hills, on the road to Ulundi. Undetected, the main Zulu army had got within five miles of Isandlwana before being discovered by chance in the late morning of 22 January. The Zulus now boldly advanced in a highly disciplined regimental attack on the British. The 1,700 men left in camp, including the battalion of 1/24th, were unable to concentrate their fire sufficiently to stem the rush of 20,000 Zulus and, although substantial casualties were inflicted on the attackers, the camp was overwhelmed and only fifty-five of the European defenders were able to make their escape. Isandlwana was to be the most serious defeat the British army was to endure at the hands of a 'savage foe'. The artillery fire heard by Wood was caused by the return of Chelmsford's force to the camp and was directed at the few remaining Zulus still scavenging amongst the ruins of the British position.

The defeat at Isandlwana had a devastating effect on British plans. Chelmsford, with the remains of Number 3 column, retired back into Natal to refit and await the arrival of reinforcements from England. Colonel Pearson, commander of Number 1 column, had beaten a smaller Zulu force at the battle of Nyezane river on the same day as the defeat at Isandlwana. On hearing the shocking news of the large British losses, Pearson decided to press on to the town of Eshowe, which he fortified, and where he and his men were effectively besieged by the Zulus. News reached London of the dreadful defeat on 10 February and caused a tremendous shock, not only in Britain, where few even knew that British forces were engaged in South Africa, but across the empire. This sense of disbelief was to ensure that there was a huge amount of newspaper coverage of events in Zululand, and this in turn led to much focus on the individuals involved in the conflict. Evelyn Wood was soon to become a household name.

Wood and his command first knew of the shocking defeat at Isandlwana on the morning of 24 January. Whilst engaged against a force of 4,000 Zulus below the Hlobane mountain, a messenger arrived with news of the loss. Wood did not immediately order his men to break off the action, but he watched as his young infantrymen held firm and fired into the Zulus, who were later driven from the field by the FLH, which pursued the fleeing warriors back to their sanctuary on top of the Hlobane mountain. Evelyn then called a halt to the operation and ordered the column to fall in. It seems clear that the news of the earlier defeat seriously shook many of Wood's officers, who, like newspaper readers across the empire, could not believe that over a thousand British soldiers, armed with modern rifles, could have been beaten by savages who advanced against them armed only with spears. The officers' sense of shock was no doubt compounded by the fact that so many of them had lost good friends. Some of Evelyn's more senior officers advised him to keep the news of the defeat from his men for fear that they might panic. Typically, Wood would not hear of such a deception, preferring to take his men into his confidence, and he himself read out the note to his column. The news was heard with a deathly hush.[35]

Wood and his men returned to camp and it was here that he received a brief account of Isandlwana from a clearly traumatised Chelmsford. His commander informed Evelyn that he now had a free hand to use his column as he thought fit to harass the Zulus. Chelmsford ended by warning Wood that, 'You must now be prepared to have the whole of the Zulu Army on your hands any day.'[36] Realising that the present camp was inadequate for defence against a large Zulu attack and that his right flank was now dangerously exposed, Evelyn risked the chance of being caught out in the open by the Zulu army and decided to move his position to one which was more defensible. The situation Wood now chose was fifteen miles further west on the slopes of Kambula Hill. Here water was plentiful and Evelyn set about preparing a strong entrenched camp.

At Kambula Wood really came into his own. Realising that his young infantrymen must have been extremely fearful of a Zulu attack, Evelyn concentrated on improving their morale and confidence and, once again, he threw himself into his work. Alfred Davies, a private in the 90th, was to complain that, with the expectation of a Zulu attack, the men were not allowed to take their clothes off, only to unlace their boots. Furthermore, according to Davies, Wood insisted that every man sleep with his rifle by his side and 100 rounds of ammunition round his waist.[37] Evelyn was tireless in ensuring that every precaution for the camp's defence was taken. This even included posting loyal Zulus 200 yards outside the camp at night where their acute sense of hearing, which was far better than any of the British troops, could warn of an approaching attack.[38] Wood constantly patrolled the camp and was always ready with a smile or word of encouragement to his men. Such an active, hands-on approach no doubt won Evelyn the loyalty of his officers and men. He later claimed that he never slept for more than two or three hours at a time from mid-January to the end of March 1879, as he was constantly patrolling the camp to ensure that the night sentries were doing their duty.[39] Wood's most senior staff officer, Captain Ronald Campbell, would discreetly follow on these nightly patrols, as he was particularly concerned that his Colonel's growing deafness would result in his not hearing the challenge of a nervous sentry and could result in an accident.[40]

Over the next weeks, Wood's command was swelled by the addition of a number of reinforcements, mostly mounted men. These included a number of colonial outfits with exotic names such as Schermbrucker's Corps of Kaffrarian Rifles, the Border Horse, a unit raised by its commander, Lieutenant-Colonel Weatherley and No.1 Squadron Mounted Infantry under the command of Lieutenant-Colonel Russell of the 12th Lancers. These additions forced Evelyn to shift camp to accommodate the extra men, although another move would have probably been forced on Wood due to the unhealthy conditions prevailing in the old camp. Wood's Irregulars could not be prevailed upon to practise any form of hygiene, with the result that they and the cattle so fouled the ground that a move was needed to avoid disease. Even Piet Uys' Boers could not be persuaded to use the latrines that had been specially dug for them.[41]

Wood sited the new camp on a ridge running east-west across the Kambula spur. At the eastern end a redoubt was constructed in which Evelyn placed two of his seven-pounder artillery pieces. Close by was the main laager, roughly in the shape of a heptagon, 250 yards wide. The outer defences were entrenched and a second line was added by lashing wagons together. South-west of the redoubt was a cattle-laager, again defended by entrenchment and wagons. A plank palisade linked the redoubt with the cattle laager. Unlike Chelmsford at Isandlwana, Wood was quite capable of learning from the Boers, who had such long experience of fighting the Zulus, and his choice of camp and construction of the laagers clearly owed much to their advice.[42]

Evelyn did not seem to mind that the camp had to be moved. He believed that the work this entailed gave the men plenty to do and was good for morale. Wood particularly focused on the need for officers and men to get plenty of exercise. For the officers a tennis court and polo ground were constructed, and Evelyn especially enjoyed an evening game of tennis with his staff officers, such as Lieutenant Lyson. For the men there was tug-of-war. Wood was proud that his own regiment, the 90th, had been regimental champions in Britain, and frequent matches were organised. However, Evelyn was to be dismayed when Piet Uys' Boers proved to be more than a match for his best teams. The Boers' tactics were simply to hold their ground until the men of the 90th became exhausted and then the Dutchmen easily pulled the British over. Wood even established sporting activities for the natives of Wood's Irregulars. These included spear throwing, at which the Zulus showed no great aptitude, having only been trained to close and stab their opponent. Ever conscious of the need to provide for his men's spiritual needs, voluntary Divine Service was introduced. This proved to be very popular, especially as it excused those attending from work parties.[43] Finally, Evelyn, probably as a result of the hardship and hunger he had experienced in the Crimea, ensured that a bakery was set up and the men received a daily ration of fresh bread. However, Private Alfred Davies claimed that the bread was made of Indian corn and mealies and that half of it was sand![44] Wood also endeavoured to include a daily meat ration for his men and this led to the Commissariat complaining that he had heavily overdrawn his meat ration allocation. With a typically direct response, Evelyn ordered Buller and the FLH to raid into Zululand to 'acquire' more cattle, which more than made up for the deficit.[45]

As both military and civil representative, Evelyn had more than just the protection of his own men to worry about. There existed the real fear that the Zulus might simply by-pass his defences and raid towards Utrecht and Luneberg. Sir Theophilius Shepstone, Secretary for Native Affairs in Natal, ensured that Evelyn was made aware of his responsibilities for the defence of the border towns. Shepstone was evidently critical of Wood's choice of Kambula for his camp, fearing that from there the British forces could not offer protection to the border. Evelyn was clearly angered both by Shepstone's encroachment into his area of responsibility, and by the fact that his military judgement was being questioned. Writing to Shepstone, Wood protested, 'I consider that the choice of position for the camp of the forces under my command is one for my consideration alone.'[46] The very next day a clearly indignant Wood again wrote to Shepstone, this time concerning Shepstone's criticism of his preparation for the defence of Utrecht, 'The Utrecht people have for twelve months enjoyed the pecuniary advantage of a border village occupied by Imperial troops, they must now accept some of the disadvantages, we can only die once, but I see no probability for any one dying at the hands of the Zulus in Utrecht so long as its inhabitants bear themselves like men.'[47] Some of the mental and physical strain that Evelyn must have been under can be seen in this far from diplomatic response. It also perhaps reflects his frustration at having to deal with panicking civilians for whom he had little time.

Shepstone was not going to let matters rest with Wood's last response. He was a man used to getting his own way and he expected his authority to be both respected and recognised. He thus wrote to Chelmsford to complain of the treatment he had received from Evelyn. In an apparent effort to avoid a confrontation, and to reassure himself that the necessary defensive measures had indeed been put in place, the General sent Lieutenant-Colonel Russell to Utrecht to report back to him on the state of defences. Of course it was not long before Evelyn learnt of Russell's mission. Wood was clearly livid with Chelmsford's actions and his pride was undoubtedly hurt. Evelyn wrote to his General complaining, 'Dear Lord Chelmsford, Lt. Col. Russell has been to Utrecht to report on the defences of the place on an order supplied in your name by Major Clery. I have written to Colonel Bellairs [District Adjutant General (DAG)] officially on the subject as I cannot believe your Grace ordered one of my very juniors to report on my arrangements.'[48] Again this letter indicates Evelyn's state of mind and the pressure he was clearly under, for Wood was never one to show such indignation to a superior officer. Indeed, throughout his career he always ensured that when writing and reporting to his superiors he was appropriately deferential.

Writing to Chelmsford on the same day, Evelyn candidly described how the pressures of work had affected his health and admitted to the General that he had been so ill over the last thirty-six hours that he had been unable to read any correspondence. Wood also took the opportunity to inform Chelmsford of his opinion of one of his other officers: 'Russell is the most unsatisfactory man I've ever tried to work with.'[49] This blunt comment on the character and abilities of Russell was to prove a remarkably accurate assessment in the following month.

Despite the obvious strain Wood was under, it did not stop him taking the initiative against the Zulus. The war was now to enter a much more brutal phase, in which Wood's men focused on the need to destroy the Zulus' homes and economy in an effort to wear down their resistance. Wood ordered Buller to conduct a number of harrying raids and reconnaissance missions towards the Hlobane mountain. On 1 February Buller rode thirty miles east of the British camp to the further end of the Hlobane range to attack a Zulu homestead which was a rallying point for the northern Zulus. Buller's men captured 300 head of cattle and killed a number of Zulus for no British losses. The

Zulu response was twofold: firstly, they further fortified their sanctuary on the Hlobane mountain by the construction of stone walls and moved their vast herds of cattle to graze on the plateau of the mountain. Secondly, Prince Mbilini, the local Zulu commander who loyally supported Cetchwayo, led a series of marauding parties into the neighbourhood of Luneberg. The white settlers had long since evacuated the area for the safety of such towns as Utrecht but the local tribesmen who had worked for the settlers remained. These were brutally attacked by Mbilini's warriors, with men, women and children falling either to Zulu spears or suffering a horrible death by being burnt alive in their huts. The empty white properties were also razed to the ground.

Wood's response centred on a retaliatory raid by Buller and the FLH, during which the British succeeded in driving the Zulus out of the Ntombi river valley and back towards Hlobane. In the same raids, five of Mbilini's strongholds were attacked and over thirty Zulus were slain. These and other raids soon earned Evelyn the fear and respect of the Zulus. Indeed, he learned that the Zulus named him Lakuni, which was the native word for the particularly hard wood used to make the Zulus smashing weapon, the knobkerrie.[50]

Evelyn's successful raiding tactics, along with the network of spies and informers that he had developed amongst the Zulus, finally paid great dividends in March 1879, when a local chief, Prince Hamu, Cetchwayo's eldest brother, agreed to come over to Wood with all his followers. Although this was a great coup for Wood, it was also a logistical nightmare for him, not least because Hamu insisted that his wives join him, all 300 of them! Whilst Hamu was safely ensconced at the Kambula camp, Evelyn, Buller and 360 mounted men, along with 200 of Hamu's warriors, set out to bring the remainder of Hamu's people from their kraal back to the safety of Kambula. There is no doubt that this was a dangerous undertaking. Cetchwayo was angered by his brother's defection, and it has been argued that it was this act that firmly convinced the Zulu king to launch his largest impi (regiment) against Wood. In the meantime, the local Zulus were ordered to try to stop the remainder of Hamu's people from joining the British.[51]

Realizing that the defectors faced certain death if his mounted troops could not offer them protection, Wood decided to risk a short-cut which would bring his force close to the Zulus entrenched on the Zunguin Mountain. This brought his force within rifle range of the warriors and shots were exchanged. Evelyn himself joined his men in returning fire into the Mountain, which silenced the Zulus' fire. It took all day, on 14 March, to reach Hamu's settlement and in the heat of the day Wood suffered from sunstroke. By the evening he was unable to ride his horse and had to let it negotiate for itself the path through the rocky terrain surrounding the kraal. With Evelyn indisposed, Buller had to assume effective command and it was he who spent the sleepless night worried about the precariousness of their position. Buller had to react quickly to protect his accident-prone commander when a troop of the FLH almost walked over him in the dark.[52]

At daybreak Wood was sufficiently recovered to reassume command and led what he described as 'a long stream of humanity' of 1,000 refugees, men, women and children, the thirty miles back to Kambula. The unlikely party were constantly harassed by Zulu warriors, and Evelyn and Buller were forced to form a rearguard. Even so, two stragglers were speared within their sight. The day was as hot as the preceding one and both troopers and the refugees suffered in the heat. Wood was astonished to see that their predicament brought out a softer side to Buller, who carried six Zulu children on his mount. After thirteen hours of marching it became evident that the party was not going to reach the safety of the British camp that night, and they were forced to spend another worrying night out in the open. However, after another long day's march, during which one of the Zulu refugees gave birth and was back on the trail within half an hour, the column finally made it to safety.[53] It seems clear the Zulus' fear of cavalry and their respect for 'Lakuni' had been sufficient to keep them at bay.

Praise was lavished on Evelyn for this successful act. Both Frere and Chelmsford realised the political importance of the defection and each knew that it was Wood's careful management of the Zulus in his area, combined with his intelligence network, that made the defection possible. Frere wrote, 'I have ... expressed my sense of the importance of Uhamu's [Hamu] defection from Cetewayo [Cetchwayo], which ... is mainly due to the judicious management of Colonel Wood.' Likewise, Chelmsford declared to Evelyn, 'I congratulate you upon Uhamu's surrender – the whole credit I consider lies with you.'[54] As a consequence of Wood's success, Chelmsford requested that the local rank of Brigadier-General be conferred on him. This was duly granted by the High Commissioner on 3 April 1879. A further reward was to be granted to Evelyn in June, when the Queen conferred upon him the appointment of Knight Commander of the Bath. Before Evelyn was to receive either honour, he was to undertake the two most desperate engagements of his career from which his reputation and fame were to emerge enhanced. Yet one of these battles was to be a crushing defeat and would reveal a side to Evelyn's character, that of the political survivor, that had not yet been seen.

Chapter Seven

Hlobane & Kambula –
Defeat & Victory

British reinforcements had been pouring into Natal and initially the arrivals had been directed towards Lord Chelmsford, who was busily preparing to advance on Eshowe, so as to relieve Colonel Pearson and his besieged men. There is no doubt that at this moment in the campaign Evelyn still felt respect and loyalty towards his General, although this was to diminish as Wood worked more directly with Chelmsford in the latter stages of the war. Soon after Isandlwana, when the British commander was in the depths of depression, Wood had received a letter from Chelmsford which stated, 'I feel confident that you two [Wood and Buller] are going to pull me out of my difficulties.' A few days later the General was to write in a similar tone to the two men, 'you two will have to pull me out of the mire.'[1] There is no doubt that such pleas inspired Wood's and Buller's successful raids of February and March, which can be seen as an expression of their desire to help Chelmsford. Wood's appointment as Brigadier-General was as a result of Chelmsford's appreciation of his actions. Thus when Chelmsford informed Evelyn that he was to march to the relief of Eshowe, and requested Wood's support in the form of a diversionary attack, Evelyn did not hesitate to offer his immediate assistance.

Chelmsford's intelligence led him to believe that Cetchwayo intended to oppose the relief column with all the forces available to him. Wood's network of spies provided him with contrary information since they suggested that Chelmsford would only meet resistance from the local Zulu tribes and that the main Zulu army would attack Evelyn's troops. Despite the fact that Wood informed his General of this intelligence, Chelmsford was still convinced that the main blow would fall on his force and he therefore made a plea to Evelyn that, 'if you are in a position to make any forward movement about the 27th

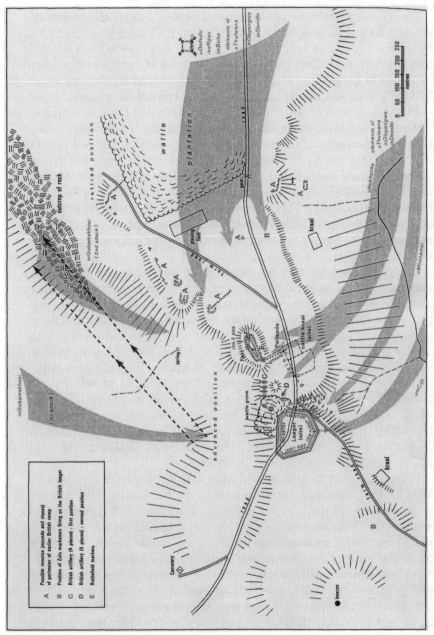

The Battle of Kambula. From J. Laband & P. Thompson, *Field Guide to the War in Zululand and the Defence of Natal 1879* (University of KwaZulu Natal Press).

[March], so that the news of it may reach the neighbourhood of Eshowe about the 29th, I think it might have a good effect.'[2]

For Wood there was an obvious choice of target: the mountain stronghold of Hlobane, home to the resourceful Prince Mbilini and his followers. From this sanctuary Mbilini had not only launched raids into the Ntombi valley, but had also harassed Wood's forces as they had gone to the relief of Hamu's followers. The final insult came when Mbilini's warriors managed to surprise a convoy of wagons, along with a detachment of the 80th Regiment, at Ntombi Drift, killing over 100 men. The 80th Regiment had been sent into the Ntombi river valley following the earlier Zulu raids and were technically part of Evelyn's command. He would certainly have been keen to avenge the British defeat. Hlobane also offered the tempting prize of thousands of Zulu cattle, which had been driven up on to the plateau to be out of the reach of Buller's marauding FLH.[3] Wood was aware that any attack would be difficult, for he told Chelmsford that he was, 'not very sanguine of success', yet he clearly considered that it was his duty to support his General.[4]

Evelyn wasted no time in drawing up his plans for the attack, although, strangely for a man who prided himself on his intelligence sources, he would go into battle with little idea of either the opposition he was likely to face or the terrain over which he was to fight. The same sources that had informed Wood that the main Zulu army was destined to attack his command also told him that this army was to depart the Zulu capital on either 26 or 27 March. It would thus arrive in the vicinity of Hlobane on or around the 30 or 31 March. Evelyn decided to make his move against Hlobane on 27 March. Unfortunately, however, Wood's usually reliable intelligence was incorrect in this instance, and the main Zulu army had actually left Ulundi on 24 March. This placed the main Zulu force on a collision course with Evelyn's men raiding Hlobane on 28 March.[5]

Evelyn decided that he would only take horsemen, supported by Wood's Irregulars and Hamu warriors, for his assault. His infantry was to remain behind to guard the camp. Wood clearly felt that his foot soldiers would unnecessarily slow the advance and his mounted men would be useful in rounding up the Zulu cattle. The fact that the broken ground of the plateau was unsuitable for rapid cavalry movement was unknown to Evelyn, yet even a cursory glance at the slopes of the Mountain, which Evelyn had passed on at least two earlier occasions, would have indicated that any ascent on horseback would be at best extremely difficult and at worst impossible. The attacking force was divided into two separate columns, one under the command of Buller and the other led by Colonel Russell. Wood's plan was that

Officers of the 90th Regiment, 1873, including Lt.Eyre, seated on the right. *Killie Campbell Collection*

British Officers in the Egyptian Army, 1884. *Killie Campbell Collection*

Evelyn Wood writing at home, 1918. *Killie Campbell Collection*

Lady Wood, 1880.
The Royal Collection

Brigadier-General Sir
Evelyn Wood, 1880.
The Royal Collection

Wood winning the Victoria Cross for his rescue of Chemmum Singh, 28 December 1859. *National Army Musuem*

Wood's personal escort at Hlobane, 28 March 1879. *Ian Knight*

Evelyn Wood dressed for fox-hunting, 1917. *Author's collection*

Evelyn Wood at the end of the Zulu Campaign, July 1879. Note Wood's tired and haggard look. *Ian Knight*

Evelyn Wood aged three. A pen and ink drawing by Lady Wood. *Author's Collection*

Field-Marshal and Lady Wood's Grave in the Aldershot Military Museum. *Author's Collection*

Wood in action at the Battle of Sindwaha, 19 October, 1858. *From E.Wood, 'From Midshipman to Field Marshal'*

Battle of Comassie, 4 February 1874. Wood stayed beside the fatally wounded Lt.Eyre until he passed away. *From E.Wood, 'From Midshipman to Field Marshal'*

Battle of Kambula, 29 March 1879. Wood is standing behind his men directing their fire. *From Leigh Maxwell, 'The Ashanti Ring'*

the two columns were to simultaneously assault the eastern (Buller) and western (Russell) slopes of Hlobane. Buller's force left Kambula in the early morning of 27 March and, after lighting deception fires designed to convince the Zulus watching from the heights of Hlobane that they were still encamped, they advanced under cover of darkness to the base of the Mountain. Russell's force rode as far as the base of the nearby Zunguin mountain, where it bivouacked. Evelyn, with an escort of three staff officers and eight mounted men of the 90th, joined Russell's force for the night. Wood had decided, once the assault was in motion, to play the part of roving observer in an attempt to co-ordinate the movements of the two separate columns. This was to prove an impossible task, for the Mountain plateau was over four miles long and a mile and half wide.[6]

The Zulus had not been deceived by Buller's fires and, throughout the night of 27/28 March, a series of beacons were seen from the top of Hlobane signalling to the approaching Zulu army the presence of Wood and his men. Evelyn appears not to have realised the significance of these fires. He always insisted that mounted scouts were placed at least six miles out from his Kambula camp to give notice of any impending Zulu attack, yet on the morning of 28 March no such precautions were taken, despite the fact that he was aware that the Zulu army was on the move. It seems that as Evelyn's intelligence sources had been so reliable in the past he did not consider that they might be wrong on this occasion, and the fact that he did not dispatch scouts in the direction of an advance from Ulundi must be considered a serious command failing. At dawn, with some difficulty, Buller's force assaulted the eastern slopes, incurring several casualties from the rifle fire of Mbilini's warriors. At the western end it soon became apparent to Russell that his mounted men would not be able to reach the top plateau, due to the very rough terrain, and he used his force to assist Hamu's warriors and Wood's Irregulars in rounding up the herds of cattle found on the lower plateau. On the upper plateau, Buller's men were now engaged in heavy skirmishing and Buller began prudently to examine and secure possible lines of retreat down the precipitous slopes.

Wood, in his role as a roving observer with his small escort, had reached the southern slopes of Hlobane, where, riding east, he met part of Buller's command, Colonel Weatherley and his Border Horse, who were riding west. Weatherley had not kept up with Buller's advance and had been struggling to locate his Colonel. Earlier, two of Wood's escorts, Mr Lloyd, Assistant Political Agent and Interpreter, and Lieutenant Lysons, 90th Regiment, had noticed that Evelyn was much quieter than usual and asked what he was thinking. Wood responded rather morbidly that he had been thinking which of them might be writing to his wife with bad news or whether he would be writing to their families with ill tidings. The day's events were to show that it would be Evelyn who was to write such letters.[7]

Weatherley had seen the approaching Zulu army and told Evelyn of its presence, although due to the undulating terrain the army could still not yet be seen. It is thought that Wood replied to Weatherley, 'Nonsense, I have had my men out yesterday, there is no Zulu impi about.' Dennison, Weatherley's deputy, replied that he had got within 'touching distance' and judged them to be 'a strong force'.[8] Wood is said to have retorted that Dennison must be mistaken.[9] Dennison was to write his memoirs in 1904 and the chapter concerning the events of Hlobane was withdrawn, presumably at the behest of the publisher. By that time Evelyn was a Field-Marshal, and the controversy and potential legal action that would no doubt have ensued from Dennison's claims seems to have been a consideration. Evelyn made no mention of any such conversation in his memoirs, but focused instead on what happened next. It does seem strange that, if Weatherley had considered Dennison's account to have been accurate, a senior officer such as he, a veteran of the Crimea and the Indian Mutiny, did not support his Deputy's' report, and this must throw some doubt on Dennison's claims.

Wood's party now came under fire from Zulu marksmen hiding in a cave on the lower slopes. Weatherley's men immediately sought cover, and a rather indignant Evelyn rode past them with his escort up the slope. The ground became impossible for the horses and Wood and his men were forced to dismount. Soon after, Lloyd was mortally wounded in the back and although Evelyn tried to lift him on to his horse, the weight was too much. Captain Campbell intervened and carried Lloyd back down the slope to the shelter of a nearby stone kraal.

In what must have been a blind fury, Evelyn continued his ascent until his horse was shot and killed, knocking him to the ground as it fell. Although unhurt he was clearly shaken and returned to find Lloyd and Campbell. Collecting his thoughts, Evelyn ordered Weatherley's men to storm the cave. Although the order was issued three times, none would advance. In disgust, Campbell shouted at the colonials that he considered them cowards and declared he himself would turn the Zulus out. This action does not seem to have been initiated by Wood, for Lyson asked his permission to join Campbell. Evelyn replied, 'Yes! Forward the Personal Escort.' Even so, only four men responded. These men reached the entrance to the cave unhurt, but on entering, Campbell was shot at point-blank range, his head was 'half blown off and death was instantaneous'. The remainder of the party cleared the cave of Zulus and carried Campbell's body back down to the kraal.[10]

Wood had lost two of his best officers and closest friends within minutes of each other. The death of Campbell was a particularly hard blow; Evelyn later told both Campbell's widow and the Queen that he had loved him like a son.[11] There now followed an act for which Evelyn was later to receive much praise from the families of the two dead officers, and that would be portrayed by the newspapers, in true Victorian style, as a noble and gallant act.[12] Wood insisted that the two officers be buried and he even ordered his bugler, Walkinshaw, to return up the mountain to retrieve a prayer book from the saddle bag of his dead horse. Walkinshaw was to be awarded the Distinguished Conduct Medal for his actions. For Wood to have so lightly ordered one of his men to risk his life for a prayer book indicates how the death of Campbell had affected his judgement. Walkinshaw, despite Zulu sniping, retrieved the book and the 'funeral' commenced. It seems clear from this action and subsequent decisions taken on this day, that the death of Campbell seriously affected Evelyn and he may even have suffered some sort of mental breakdown on the slopes of Hlobane. He subsequently showed a disregard for the fate of his command, and for a large part of the rest of the day his movements are shrouded in mystery.

With only the assegais of his native escort available, the digging of the grave was a laborious task. In fact the whole process, including the reading of an abridged form of the Burial Service by Wood, took over an hour. Even when the Zulus advanced from the slopes to within 600 yards of the burial party, Wood did not falter from his task and even insisted that the grave be made longer so that the dead men's legs did not have to be doubled up. During this hour, the Zulus constantly sniped at Wood and his escort. Miraculously no more men from the escort party were hit, thanks in part to covering fire from Buller's men on the plateau and support from Weatherley and his Border Horse. Yet Evelyn's decision to bury his beloved officers would cost the Border Horse six men dead with seven more receiving wounds, a fact which Evelyn rather callously mentions in an almost throwaway line in his autobiography.[13] Wood must have felt that history was repeating itself as he stood over the grave of yet another of his staff officers. The loss of Eyre in the Ashanti war and now Campbell must have made him consider how responsible he was for their deaths, and almost certainly threw a cloud of depression and inertia over him, which was to affect his judgement for the rest of the day.

With the burials complete, Wood now ordered Weatherley and his men up the slopes to support Buller on the plateau, and by doing so sent the vast majority of them to their deaths, including Weatherley and his young son. Evelyn and his reduced escort then cantered on around the base of the Mountain on a direct collision course with the main Zulu impi of 20,000 warriors. Fortunately, Evelyn had at last decided to send one of Hamu's warriors in advance of his party and it was this man who first spotted the Zulu army at around 10.30 am. Buller and his men had already seen the advancing hordes of Zulus from their position on the mountain and they were now frantically trying to extract themselves before the advancing impi cut off all hope of escape, whilst at the same time attempting to keep at bay Mbilini's warriors on the plateau. Wood, on seeing the Zulu army assume its attack formation, immediately dispatched his remaining staff officer, Lysons, to Colonel Russell with the following order: 'There is a large army coming this way from the South, get into position on the Zunguin Nek.'[14] It was apparently Evelyn's intention that Russell's force assume a defensive position on the neck of land between the lower plateau of Hlobane and the Zungwini Mountain from where he would be able to support Buller's retreat.

Russell had seen the approaching Zulu army, and his men had already withdrawn off the mountain to the position where Wood had intended them to be. However, when giving his order Wood had confused the place names; he had actually wanted Russell to move to the Zunguin range, where he was now located, not the Zunguin Nek, which was to be found six miles to the north-west. It is thought that Russell consulted with his officers as to where exactly Wood wished his force to be and he was perhaps influenced by some of the survivors of Isandlwana, who had seen first hand what the Zulu army was capable of. He decided to accept Evelyn's instruction without question and moved his force the six miles to where it could be of no conceivable help to Buller and his men, whose retreat was soon to become a rout. The move also left Hamu's warriors and Wood's Irregulars, who were still herding the rustled cattle, to their fate, as the Zulu impi rapidly overtook them.

Wood made no further contribution to the defeat at Hlobane. In his official report, written two days later, he stated that he and his escort had assumed a position on Zunguin Nek – that being his incorrect interpretation of the nek's location. However, it is now considered that he occupied an elevated position at the south-eastern end of the range, about two and a half miles from the bottom of the plateau.[15] From here he could view the dramatic life-and-death struggles of Buller and his men as they tried to make their escape down the slopes of Hlobane, via what was to become known as the 'Devil's Pass'. Evelyn did state that on seeing Russell assume the incorrect position, he sent a further message to him ordering his return to support the retreating Irregulars and Hamu's warriors. This order was complied with, but Russell returned too late to save very many. Wood claimed that he remained in his position until 7.00 pm, and then returned to Kambula, where he had earlier sent an urgent message to the officer commanding the camp to prepare its defences for an immediate attack.[16]

This view was contradicted by Private Edmond Fowler of Wood's escort, whose letter to his mother, written two weeks after the battle, was printed in a magazine called *British Battles on Land and Sea*, published in 1914. Fowler, who on Wood's recommendation was awarded the Victoria Cross for his part in the action which saw the death of Campbell, wrote, 'After we had ridden three miles we saw on our right front the whole of the Zulu army. The old man [Wood] says "Gallop for your lives men" which we did, and a hard run we had of it for twenty-five miles ... We had a lucky escape,and when we reached camp [Kambula] and told the news it caused a great sensation.'[17] This account of Wood's actions runs contrary to the manner in which he had behaved in all his previous engagements. Evelyn was considered to be a resolute and courageous officer and, of course, he held the Victoria Cross. To have fled the battlefield and returned to Kambula would have been completely out of character, but, as has been shown, his behaviour at Hlobane was indeed unusual. Wood was later to write that Buller, having made his escape and returned to Kambula, found that Evelyn was not there and immediately set out again and located him, much to Buller's evident relief, on the Zunguin range.[18] Rather than flee, it is more likely that, due to the loss of Campbell and Lloyd, Wood was overwhelmed by depression and remorse, which resulted in at best inertia and at worst a breakdown, and which meant that he played no part in the events on the battlefield.

Hlobane was a disaster for Wood. Ten officers were dead and a further eighty men out of a total European force of 404 were killed. Further losses included well over 100 of Hamu's warriors and Wood's Irregulars.[19] Much to the regret of both Buller and Wood, Piet Uys was amongst the fallen. Despite the chaos and carnage, there had been several acts of bravery which would see the Victoria Cross awarded to four individuals, including Buller, who won his award for assisting many of his men in their escape down 'Devil's Pass', during which he repeatedly risked his own life. There was one positive outcome from the defeat: the fight had delayed the main Zulu army's attack on Kambula, and the rapid final advance of the impi towards Hlobane had tired many of the warriors, already exhausted from the march from Ulundi and from lack of food. Evelyn had been given a vital opportunity to prepare his defences for the imminent attack. Kambula was to provide Wood with the opportunity not only to redeem his failures at Hlobane, but also conveniently to hide the true scale of the defeat in the euphoria of subsequent victory.

It is quite astonishing to compare Evelyn's inertia at Hlobane to his active, inspired command at Kambula on the following day. If he had in fact suffered a breakdown his recovery was remarkable. No doubt the new threat to an entrenched position inspired him, and certainly the energy that deserted him at Hlobane had returned by the time he had reached the camp. Even with his renewed vigour, Wood was unable to stop the desertion of most of the black auxiliaries, whose comrades had been left to their fate by Russell's hasty departure, and all of the remaining Boers, who with the death of their leader, Piet Uys, felt no loyalty to the British. Even with these losses, and despite the fact that his infantry was to be outnumbered ten to one by the Zulus, there is no doubt that the British position, well planned by Evelyn, was a strong one. The early morning mist of 29 March hung around the camp and added an extra chill to the already nervous young troopers of the 90th and 13th Light Infantry. Wood was determined that today he would inspire these men with his own confidence and to that end he endeavoured to make the preparations for the forthcoming battle seem to be as normal as one of his many rehearsed exercises. A party of men were even sent out to collect sufficient firewood to prepare an early lunch for all, and the bakery ensured that each man would receive his bread ration.

The Zulus had spent the night just ten miles from Kambula and in the morning they marched steadily in five separate columns towards the camp. Around midday the whole army underwent their pre-battle purification rituals, and at this time the Zulu commander, Chief Munyamana, reminded his warriors of the King's instruction not to attack the British behind their entrenched position, but to seize the camp cattle, which, it was hoped, would lure the soldiers out from their defences. The attack began at around 1.00 pm and Wood viewed the classic 'horns of the buffalo' formation across a front of ten miles as it quickly advanced on the camp. The Zulu plan was for the right and left horns of the army to surround the camp and join forces to raid the cattle kraal. However, the advance of the left horn was stalled by the need to cross swampy ground and, as the right horn stopped within 800 yards of the British position to regroup, Wood made a brave and inspired tactical decision to provoke the right horn into an attack before the left horn could join them.

Evelyn ordered Buller and his mounted men to ride out from the protection of the camp to within 100 yards of the right horn and pour volleys into the packed mass of warriors, before retreating back to the safety of their laager. This action had the desired result, and the right horn lost its discipline and charged forward into a killing ground of rifle and artillery fire. Evelyn had earlier ensured that range-markers had been positioned around the camp and, as a result, the British fire was particularly effective. Even so, several Zulus did manage to reach the perimeter of the wagons, where they were beaten back. The bravery of the Zulus was later to be acknowledged by Wood.[20]

Before the left horn could launch its attack, the survivors of the right horn were in retreat. However, the left horn managed to mass within 100 yards of the cattle laager and it was now the turn of the British to keep their heads down as Zulu snipers, using British rifles captured at Isandlwana, began to pour a persistent if somewhat inaccurate fire into the camp. It was at this crucial moment that Private Banks of the 90th saw Evelyn amongst his men. Banks was later to write, 'I do not think there are many like him in the army. He is as cool and collected in action as if he were in a drawing room. Walking down from the fort to the laager under a heavy fire, swinging a stick and whistling, then going past the wagons he has a pleasant look and a smile of encouragement for every one he meets, let him be private or officer, it matters not. The men here I am sure would follow him anywhere, they are so fond of him.'[21] Wood himself recalled several near misses as he exposed himself to enemy fire whilst encouraging his troops, just as he had done during the Ashanti campaign; 'I . . . lost all sense of danger, except momentarily, when, as on five occasions, a plank of the hoarding on which I leant was struck. This jarred my head.'[22] Under the cover of sniper fire, the left horn advanced, but now Wood ordered his young infantrymen to fire volley after volley into the warriors. His men responded and Evelyn had now blunted the attack.

Zulu riflemen now sought cover behind anthills, in ravines and in any 'dead' ground which would provide some cover from the British fire. Wood was later to estimate that around forty Zulus were able to use such cover to fire at the British troops, who were occupying the cattle laager. The Zulu fire was so intense that Evelyn decided to withdraw a company of the 13th, posted at the right side of the laager. This movement encouraged a large body of warriors, who had sought refuge in a nearby ravine, to make the 100 yards dash to occupy the laager. The remaining British troopers in the cattle kraal were forced to depart hastily in the face of this Zulu advance. Four soldiers fell at the hands of the charging warriors and a further seven were wounded. Wood, with his usual impetuousness, rushed forward to try to save one British infantryman who had fallen in front of the advancing Zulus. He was physically restrained by three of his officers, including Lieutenant Lysons, who told his commanding officer, 'Really it isn't your place to pick up single men!'[23] The soldier was saved, although one of the rescuing officers was severely wounded during the sortie. Wood saw that he could not let the Zulus maintain a hold on the cattle laager. Within a few moments, the number of Zulus there could have swelled to thousands, and from the laager and it was only a fifty yard rush to the main British redoubt.

Evelyn selected Major Hackett, whom he had commanded in operations against the Gaika tribes, with two companies of the 90th, to charge the Zulus in the laager at bayonet point. In bitter fighting the British drove the Zulus back to the ravine. Wood now became actively engaged in supporting the 90th. One Zulu chief, holding a red flag, was standing at the top of the ravine trying to encourage his warriors forward. With encouragement from Private Fowler, who handed Evelyn his own carbine, Wood began to take aim at the chief. As a result of the barrel of the rifle being hot, Evelyn fired before he had brought the weapon fully into his shoulder and in consequence hit the ground at the Zulu's feet. However, with his second shot Wood hit the Zulu chief in the stomach and he fell back into the ravine. On three further occasions a Zulu warrior picked up the red flag and waved it in defiance and encouragement, only to be shot by Evelyn.[24] Hackett's advance and Wood's marksmanship ensured that the Zulus were forced back to the ravine, but from there they were able to return fire at the now exposed men of the 90th. Soon casualties began to mount, including Hackett, who was shot in the side of the head resulting in permanent blindness, and Evelyn realised their position was untenable and ordered their withdrawal.

Wood knew that the Zulu snipers must be nullified and ordered his gunners to pour shells into the ravine. This action silenced the Zulu riflemen at a vital moment in the battle, as the warriors at the head and centre of the Zulu attack had massed for a direct attack on the main laager. Evelyn again used the tactic of the bayonet charge in an attempt to break the Zulu advance before it had a chance to gain momentum. A company of the 13th were sent out to engage the enemy, only to be beaten back by the rushing warriors. However, the retreat of the 13th brought the Zulus under the British artillery and, loaded with case-shot, they carved swathes through the mass of warriors, who retreated back down the hill. The battle had been raging for nearly four hours and still the Zulus had strength and reserve for two more charges, both of which were stopped by rapid and accurate infantry fire.[25]

Wood had gained a complete and thorough victory, but the day's slaughter was not yet over. At around 5.30 pm the Zulu army seemed, individually, to decide to retreat, and Evelyn used this opportunity to unleash his mounted troops, who were determined to avenge their comrades lost the day before. By this act Wood ensured that the Zulu retreat became a bloody rout. Buller's men gave no quarter as they pursued the enemy for over an hour, until darkness ended the mayhem. As if the battle itself was not a complete enough victory, over 800 dead Zulus were found within 800 yards of the camp, and the pursuit is estimated to have taken a further 1,500 lives. British casualties, killed and wounded, numbered eighty-three.[26] The viciousness and vengefulness shown by Wood's men at this moment was later to have serious repercussions for Evelyn, when news of the events reached Britain.

While Wood was gaining his most complete and famous victory, Lord Chelmsford had encountered and beaten a smaller Zulu army at Gingindlovu and gone on to relieve Colonel Pearson's besieged forces at Eshowe. All that now remained to await the arrival of the final British reinforcements, obtain sufficient supplies and wagons and then march on the Zulu capital, Ulundi. Evelyn was to play a prominent part in this finale, but first he had his own reputation to save. His performance at Hlobane had been far from perfect. Not only could questions be asked about his decision to attack the mountain top in the first place, but clear errors had been made in reconnaissance, and Evelyn's whereabouts for most of the day were shrouded in mystery. However, most important was the fact that over 100 of his mounted troops had been lost, and while it may have been possible to hide his mistakes in the euphoria of the victory at Kambula, the loss of such a number was not going to be so easy to explain.

Wood sat down in his tent in Kambula to write his official report of the events at Hlobane and Kambula at 9.00 pm on the evening of 29 March. Edited copies of this report were to appear in the newspapers of Britain from around 17 April. This timing was of great benefit to Evelyn as it coincided with news that Chelmsford had relieved Eshowe and, as the British public had been waiting anxiously to read of this, the reports of Wood's two engagements were rather lost in the coverage of the relief. Evelyn's report, as published in such papers as *The Times* and the *Daily News*, and many provincial newspapers read:

DESPATCH FROM COLONEL WOOD. Kambula Camp. March 29th 9.00 pm. We assaulted the Kholobana [Hlobane] successfully yesterday and took some thousands of cattle but while on top about 20,000 Zulus coming from Ulundi attacked us, and we suffered considerable losses, the enemy retaking the captured cattle.

Our natives deserted. Our camp was attacked today from 1.30 pm to 5.30 pm in the most courageous manner by about 20,000 men. We have lost about seven officers and seventy killed and wounded, but we have entirely defeated the enemy who were pursued for a considerable distance.

What Wood did not make clear in this initial report was that the casualty figures referred only to those that occurred at the battle of Hlobane. This ambiguity continued in the press reporting of the events surrounding the two battles. For example, both *The Times* and the *Daily News* of 17 April listed Captain Campbell, Mr Lloyd and Piet Uys as among seven officers and seventy men killed at Kambula. Such losses could be accepted if they were linked with a crushing victory.

It was not only the British Press that was initially confused as to the events and casualities associated with the two battles. An examination of the numerous Natal Government telegrams, which can be found in the letters and correspondence of Lord Chelmsford held at the National Army Museum, does seem to indicate that, firstly, Wood's initial report of 28 March was delayed in reaching Pietermaritzburg and secondly, that Wood's report was superseded as earlier as 2 April by an official communiqué correcting the earlier report. A telegram sent from Bellairs in Durban to Chelmsford on 1 April clearly shows that news of the battle of Hlobane on 28 March, presumably Wood's report, was not received in Pietermaritzburg until 1 April.[27] Strangely, however, Norris-Newman, special correspondent of the *Standard*, claimed that news of the defeat was reported in Ladysmith on 29 March.[28] If this was the case then either the news was severely delayed in reaching Pietermaritzburg, or the military authorities there were extremely slow in forwarding the news to Chelmsford, and presumably the Government. A second telegram, also from Bellairs to Chelmsford, dated 2 April, requests that the telegram of the previous day, presumably Wood's initial report, be superseded by this second telegram, which outlines the extent of the casualties from Hlobane.[29] With such apparent delay and confusion in the telegraphic correspondence concerning the battle of Hlobane between the British forces on the ground in South Africa, it is understandable that the casualties and events of this battle were initially reported incorrectly in the papers of Britain. It is, of course, now open to conjecture as to whether the delays and ambiguities were deliberate or caused by the 'fog of war'.

It would also appear that the Prime Minister himself was only made aware of the scale of the British reversal at Hlobane on 24 April. Writing to Lady Bradford, from Downing Street, Disraeli appears to suggest that Wood's initial report had even hidden the scale of the defeat from the Government: 'Pearson's relief was a great relief to us and to all – but nothing else seems very good. It is quite clear that Evelyn Wood has had another "Disaster", though partly veiled by the subsequent repulse of the Zulus; but we lost many men and quite a massacre of officers. He was surprised riding at the head of his staff!'[30]

Curiously, the editor of the *Devon Evening Express*, of Exeter, thought there had been a cover-up, or a deliberate attempt to confuse, and made the following claims in the edition of 2 May 1879:

> It seems that we might have had the news of Colonel Wood's engagement a week earlier, but that it was purposely held back, at least, so says the correspondent of the *Argus*, telegraphing from Maritzburg on April 2nd. This is the message: Further particulars of Wood's affair leaked out through officers who have seen despatches, which are not yet published [presumably Wood's detailed report]. Seems, as I suspected, to have been the narrowest escape from most appalling disaster. Two hundred and fifty men (Buller's Horse) were killed in cutting their way out of the Zulu army. Have best grounds for knowing that full extent of disaster was known yesterday, but was kept back until steamer left the Cape for England.

Despite extensive research, these claims cannot be found to have been repeated in any other British newspaper. Indeed, although the *Devon Evening Express* made such strong initial claims, they are not seen again in its pages. Apart from some general criticism of Wood's actions, the newspapers of London do not make any comment on Wood's ambiguous initial report and certainly do not imply that Wood deliberately tried to confuse and deceive.

It was only with the receipt of details of the two battles, via both the colonial press and Wood's more detailed official report, that the confusion as to the casualties and the events of the two battles was resolved. The returning mail steamer, the *Dublin Castle*, brought these sources to Plymouth on 1 May and the British press wasted no time in printing articles from the colonial newspapers. Once this fresh information had been received, it did not take long for some criticism to be directed at Colonel Wood. The *Devon Evening Express* of 2 May supplied full details surrounding the events of Hlobane and this led the editor to questions Wood's abilities:

> We have regarded Colonel Wood as the one competent general engaged in this war on our side. But the occurrences of the 28th of March [Hlobane] have shaken our faith in his skill and judgement as a commander.

An editorial in the *South Molton Gazette* of 10 May, which commented on the events surrounding the battle of Hlobane, was able to review the latest information concerning the reversal, and its conclusion gives an indication of the likely furore that would have resulted had this defeat not been followed by the victory at Kambula:

> Further details respecting Colonel Wood's daring raid on Umbellini's stronghold [Hlobane] show that it resulted in a disastrous rout of the English troops, which might have been averted by more caution, and about which there would be a far louder outcry had it not been retrieved by the repulse of the Zulus from the camp next day.

This passage is an accurate summary, and indeed Wood's victory at Kambula did allow him to survive the criticisms of his failings at Hlobane. However, the military historian Charles Rathbone Low, writing in 1880, did not hesitate to point out to his readers that Wood himself had written to Chelmsford before Hlobane to instruct the Commander-in-Chief that his spies had informed Wood of the likely approach of the whole Zulu army from Ulundi. In these circumstances, Rathbone Low commented that, 'it is somewhat singular that he had not taken precautions to guard against surprise.'[31] Certainly, despite a number of errors at Hlobane, it is Wood's lack of intelligence gathering before the battle for which he can chiefly be blamed.

Evelyn was additionally fortunate in that he had a ready scapegoat for the Hlobane defeat in the form of Colonel Russell. There is no doubt that Russell was suffering from some sort of trauma, as a result of the scenes he had witnessed in the aftermath of Isandlwana, and should have been withdrawn earlier from active service. His decision at Hlobane to take Wood's incorrect directions at face value undoubtedly cost the lives of many of Buller's fugitives as well as native allies. Buller stated to Wood that he would never serve with Russell again in any form of joint operation, and Evelyn now saw his opportunity to rid himself of Russell and shift some blame. In his full official report on the events of the day, Wood firmly asserted that Russell was at fault: 'Colonel Russell reports that he moved from the Hlobane to the Zungui nek, but this is incorrect, the contrary, he went away six miles to the west.'[32] Evelyn wrote to Chelmsford, listing Russell's errors and requesting that Russell by removed from his command, saying, 'As I have already written to you there is no want of personal courage on Colonel Russell's part, but I firmly believe his presence in command is detrimental to the public service.'[33]

Evelyn recommended that Russell be given a non-combatant role commanding a remount depot at Pietermaritzburg. Chelmsford quickly sanctioned the move and Russell left Wood's command under a cloud. Evelyn was also fortunate in that Chelmsford himself was willing to accept his share of the blame for the Hlobane defeat. The General was to write to the Duke of Cambridge that, 'I am quite sure that General Wood would never have allowed the attack to be made had I not asked him to make a diversion in favour of the column moving forward to relieve Eshowe.'[34] Wood had survived any backlash for his failings at Hlobane.

With reinforcements in place, Chelmsford could now concentrate on the task of redeeming his own military reputation, shattered after the debacle of Isandlwana, and to that end nothing less was required than the destruction of both the Zulu army and their capital. Thus, despite the fact that Cetchwayo actively sought peace terms, Chelmsford prepared his second invasion of Zululand, determined that he would beat the Zulus in open battle. He again decided upon an advance by separate columns. With the arrival of numerous senior officers, Chelmsford was spoilt for choice as to which of his many Generals should command these columns. His plan was for two divisions, Major-General Crealock's in the south and Major-General Newdigate's in the north, to converge on Ulundi. However, while Newdigate was given command of an area which included the Utrecht District, Chelmsford was adamant that Evelyn's command was not to be broken up. Wood was to retain his independence and his command was now christened 'Wood's Flying Column.' As all three columns advanced, the 'Flying Column' was to link with Newdigate's command for the final battle outside Ulundi.

It is clear that Chelmsford had a high regard for Evelyn's fighting abilities, as well as appreciating his apparent loyalty and friendship. Chelmsford not only ensured that Wood kept his independent command, but also gave him a field-promotion to Brigadier-General. Wood was able to write gratefully to Chelmsford, 'to thank you for your kind intention of keeping me in an Independent position as long as possible.'[35] Regard for Wood's fighting ability was not restricted to his commanding officer. Lieutenant Curling, who had served with Wood in the Gaika wars and was now with Chelmsford in Newdigate's column, wrote, 'We leave this place on Thursday for a camp nearer Colonel Wood. Our column will form one brigade of a force while Col. Wood will command the other brigade. He is far the best soldier out here and I wish we were joining with him.'[36] As the advance towards Ulundi continued, Curling's good opinion of Evelyn increased, at the expense of Chelmsford and other senior officers: 'Col. Wood's column marches a few miles ahead of us. It is a pity we are not organised like him but we consist of Generals with large staffs: too many cooks spoil the pudding and we have no less than five generals (including two Brigadiers) with us.'[37]

The second invasion was to receive much criticism, in both Britain and South Africa, for the slowness of its advance. This was due in part to Chelmsford's timidity, caused no doubt by his desire to avoid another Isandlwana, and the lack of transport wagons to meet the needs of three separate and large columns. The presence of a horde of 'special correspondents' from the British newspapers, who had arrived en masse to cover what had become the news story of the year, fuelled the criticism, as they were more than willing to report on any delay or reversal. Evelyn's forward planning had allowed for a surplus of wagons in his command and he was able to transfer thirty-seven to Newdigate's column. However, the poor state of the roads, if any existed, and the numerous rivers to cross, ensured that even the 'Flying Column' struggled to progress towards Ulundi. Wood was to recall how on one occasion he had cursed and raged at an officer who he considered was not properly supervising a difficult river crossing. Not only was Evelyn embarrassed to have lost his temper and to have used foul language in front of his men, but his embarrassment was compounded when his cursing echoed seven times down the river valley for all to hear. Wood was to blame this outburst on the fact that he had almost reached his physical limit. He had not had a unbroken night's sleep for nearly six months, nor had he had an opportunity to change his clothes in all this time. At one point in the advance he was so crippled by pain and exhaustion that he was forced to have his face tied up for a week, 'suffering from continuous neuralgic pains in the eyes, coupled with gastric neuralgia.'[38]

By a strange quirk of fate, Louis Napoleon, the Prince Imperial, son of the exiled Napoleon III and great-nephew of Napoleon Bonaparte had, whilst exiled in Britain, passed through the Royal Artillery training school at Woolwich. While it is apparent that Louis had enjoyed his military life, his nationality and the political situation made it impossible for him to continue in the British Army. He did, however, maintain close links with the Army, and even managed to attend manoeuvres. With news of Isandlwana, the Prince was desperate to see active service and, after lobbying from his mother, the Empress Eugenie, and Queen Victoria, the Prime Minister, Disraeli, bowed to mounting pressure and very reluctantly agreed that Louis could proceed to South Africa to serve on Chelmsford's staff.

It was thus that Evelyn met the Prince when the latter accompanied Chelmsford to Wood's camp in early May. Louis returned a fortnight later and impressed Evelyn with, 'his soldier-like ideas and habits, and was unwearied in endeavouring to acquire knowledge and Military experience.'[39] Wood even allowed the Prince to accompany Buller on some of his reconnaissance patrols, although after Louis's behaviour on 21 May, when he charged off alone in pursuit of several distant Zulus, Buller refused to take the Prince out again. Louis returned to Chelmsford's staff and, after some persuasion, managed to convince his commanding officer that he should join a small reconnaissance party on 1 June. It was during this operation that Louis and his party, nominally led by Captain Carey, were surprised by a group of Zulus and the Prince was slain. It was Wood and Buller who first met the fleeing Carey, as they advanced with the Flying Column, and the next day it was Wood's men who located the Prince's body. This incident was to have an impact on Evelyn's future as he would later return to South Africa on a pilgrimage with the Prince's mother to the spot where her son fell.

The slowness of the British advance towards Ulundi can be understood when even Evelyn complained of difficulty in actually mobilising the huge train of wagons which formed the core of each column. On the same day as the Prince was killed, Wood stated that it had taken the Flying Column over two and a half hours just to organize itself into a moving force, due to the inexperience of the wagon drivers; and this was despite the fact that Evelyn had ensured that a number of friendly Zulus had received training from the more experienced wagon masters. It was not just that the drivers were inexperienced, but many of the reinforcements who joined Newdigate's and Crealock's columns were very young and had never seen active service before. This made them very nervous of possible surprise attack, particularly at night, and there were numerous occasions when sentries were guilty of firing at shadows or even their comrades. The worst example of this occurred on 6 June, when a battalion manning the defences of the Newdigate column opened fire on its own outposts and on a company of sappers. Amazingly, despite the expenditure of a huge amount of ammunition, no casualties resulted. Wood was so incensed by this incident that four days later he paraded the whole of the Flying Column and informed his men that such an incident would not be tolerated in his command.[40]

Chelmsford wisely placed Evelyn's command ahead of Newdigate's column of inexperienced soldiers in the advance. This combined forward movement began on 18 June, and Wood placed Buller and his mounted men in front of his own advance and ordered them to gather what information they could about the movements of the Zulu army. Evelyn's intelligence led him to believe the Cetchwayo had ordered his army not to attack the British behind prepared defences, but, if an opportunity arose, to fight them whilst they marched in column order.

On hearing this, Wood initiated a drill for forming a laager and discovered that this could, after practice, be achieved in thirty-five minutes. For once he was satisfied with his men's preparedness.[41] A Mr Streatfield, an author, who accompanied the Flying Column at this time left a vivid description of Evelyn and his work ethic: 'I feel grateful to him for many an arduous duty and weary march made light by the kindly tone in which the order was given that they should be done ... Let not the reader imagine that a duty slurred over, or ineffectually carried out would meet with but a gentle rebuke from Colonel Wood. Far from it. On duty he is to others as to himself, hard as adamant; and woe betide the careless, slovenly soldier who happens to serve under him.'[42]

Similarly, an unnamed officer from Wood's Flying Column recalled that he had overheard a conversation between two sentries one night whilst he, the officer, was trying to get to sleep in his tent. This story again illustrates the grudging respect Wood's men had for him. The first sentry was heard to say, 'I say Bill, there is one comfort that we have got a general now who won't ask a man to go where he won't go himself.' Bill supposedly replied, 'Yes, that is a comfort, but the worst of it is that the bugger will go anywhere!'[43]

On 17 June, Chelmsford learned that he was to be superseded by Wood's old commander from the Ashanti campaign, Sir Garnet Wolseley. The news seemed to spur the timid Chelmsford on and there was indeed a renewed urgency to move towards Ulundi. The commander was now more determined than ever to achieve a crushing victory to regain some of his military reputation before Wolseley could arrive from England. To this end, and despite urgings from Evelyn that he should face the Zulus behind a prepared defensive position, Chelmsford insisted on meeting the Zulu army out in the open, and he ignored the increasingly desperate peace overtures from the Zulu king. Finally, the morning of 4 July saw Chelmsford's combined force of Wood's and Newdigate's columns just three miles from Ulundi and opposed by a force of Zulus later estimated to be 20,000 strong. Wood himself was not over confident of success and he later admitted that, 'all were not confident how our men would face a horde of Zulus in the open', though he stated that he, 'could not contemplate the possibility of any man in the Flying Column quailing.' Chelmsford clearly shared Wood's view as to the ability of the experienced men of the Flying Column, for as he advanced towards the Zulu capital in a square formation, two sides were composed of soldiers from Wood's command, whilst Buller and his mounted men protected the British flanks.

Throughout this final battle of Ulundi, Evelyn stayed by the side of Lord Chelmsford, as both mounted men exposed themselves to Zulu fire. Archibald Forbes, the special correspondent of the *Daily News*, was to write of Wood at Ulundi, 'Evelyn Wood's face was radiant with the rapture of the fray as he rode up and down behind his regiment exposed to a storm of missiles.'[44] Despite repeated Zulu attacks, the square remained firm and the combined artillery and infantry fire, along with the Gatling guns of the British, ensured that no Zulu got within thirty yards of the British position. As the Zulus wavered under such fire, Chelmsford repeated Wood's tactic at Kambula and unleashed the 17th Lancers, and then Buller's mounted troops, on the fleeing warriors. The slaughter of Kambula was repeated.[45]

In Wood's official report of the battle of Ulundi he was to write, 'The Zulu attack was conducted in a hurried disorderly manner contrasting severely with the methodical system pursued at Kambula.' Evelyn also claimed that the Zulus displayed a 'want of resolution'.[46] This was perhaps a little harsh, as other witnesses to the battle marvelled at the way the Zulus advanced in perfect order, and the fact that some managed to get so close to the British wall of fire certainly displayed no lack of bravery on their part.[47] In attempting to be dismissive of the Zulus' performance at Ulundi perhaps Wood was attempting to enhance the importance of his victory at Kambula. A week after Ulundi, Evelyn wrote to one of his old commanding officers, General Horsford, that he, 'was rather disgusted that the Zulus made such a feeble attempt', and that a captured Zulu who had fought at Kambula had told Wood that, 'our hearts were broken at Kambula.'[48] If Ulundi ended the war it seems that Kambula had been the war's decisive battle.

Chelmsford had finally achieved his victory and he now resigned his command to the recently arrived Wolseley. For Wood, exhausted by over eighteen months of continuous active service, there remained just a few loose ends to tie up before he could join Chelmsford on the ship back to England. One of these was to repudiate claims made by a Private Snook of the 13th Light Infantry, who claimed in a letter to his uncle back in Tiverton, Devon, that over 500 wounded Zulus had been slain by Wood's men after the battle of Kambula. Snook's uncle sent the letter to his local newspaper and eventually Snook's claims were pursued by the Aborigine Protection Society, and Mr O'Donnell MP raised the issue in the House of Commons. Under mounting pressure, the War Office were forced to initiate an enquiry into Snook's claims, and it was one of Wolseley's first duties to instruct Evelyn to investigate the accusations.

In his letter, Snook had stated that the supposed massacre had taken place on 30 March and Wood was able to report that:

The whole of the infantry were employed all day on the 30th except when at divine service, in burying 785 Zulus close to the camp ... The horses being exhausted by six days hard work, only one patrol of the men was out. They saw no Zulus; and I, passing over the ground covered by the patrol two days later, did not see a body. I believe no Zulus have been killed by white men except in action, and as I rewarded Wood's Irregulars for every live Zulu brought in, I had many saved.[49]

This response was printed in the British press on 1 September and was seen as an official denial by Wolseley and Wood of Snook's claims. However, the controversy surrounding Snook's allegations continues today and it has been asserted that Snook either exaggerated his claims or that he made a mistake by citing 30 March, when his allegations referred to the pursuit of the Zulus by Buller's men on 29 March.[50]

Whether wounded Zulus were murdered by Wood's forces, and with his knowledge, remains a mystery, but what is clear is that both Wood and Buller pursued a policy of 'total war' against the Zulus, in which Zulu civilians and property were targeted, and it is certain that many Zulus were killed in their flight from Kambula. Whether Wood could have stopped, or would have wanted to stop, this slaughter, is open to doubt. Snook's claims were among many made during and after the war concerning British atrocities, and all added weight to the arguments of those who maintained that the war was cruel and unjust, including William Gladstone, who was to use such material to denounce the Disraeli Premiership.

Wood's active pursuit of total war against the Zulus can, in retrospect, be considered cruel and even vindictive. Certainly, by today's standards, the actions taken by many of his men would be considered war crimes, for which, if such events occurred today, he would be held ultimately responsible. On the field of battle Evelyn was a determined and clear-sighted professional soldier of his age, sure of what needed to be done to overwhelm and defeat the enemy. It is certain that he would have viewed the slaughter of fleeing Zulus as a necessary measure that would bring about the defeat of the enemy and the end of the war. It is perhaps in this context that Snook's claims should be viewed and although, if Snook was indeed telling the truth, such acts cannot be forgiven, there exists no concrete evidence that Evelyn knew of or actively encouraged the slaughter of wounded Zulus.

After the battle of Ulundi, Chelmsford, to the disbelief of both Wood and Buller, decided to withdraw his force away from the capital, claiming that supplies were short. It seemed a strange final act by the General, especially after so many men, none more than Evelyn, had worked so hard in the advance. On meeting their old friend and new commander, Wolseley, both Buller and Wood expressed to him the oppinion that they considered Chelmsford, 'not fit to be a Corporal.'[51] Although it seems clear that both men personally liked Chelmsford, they had become exasperated by his timidity in command, and the withdrawal from Ulundi was the last straw for them. Wood was later to tell the Queen that he found, 'Lord Chelmsford ... the kindest and most loveable of men, but he is not hard enough for a soldier.'[52]

Wolseley soon discovered that many in the army in South Africa considered that Evelyn was *the* man of the moment and that many believed that Lord Chelmsford would never have progressed to Ulundi if it had not been for Wood's energy and determination. Wolseley delighted in writing to his friends in England with a riddle that was current in the British camp: 'Why is it that the men of Lord Chelmsford's column cannot be regarded as Christians? Answer: Because they make an idol of Wood and did not believe in the Lord.'[53] Wolseley was no doubt pleased that he still had Buller and Wood by his side, for the Zulu king was now a fugitive who had to be hunted down, and Chief Sekhukhune of the Pedi region, north of Zululand, was displaying a lack of loyalty to the British authorities. There was also the issue of growing unrest amongst the Boers of the Transvaal. Wolseley, however, was to be disappointed; both Evelyn and Buller were physically exhausted and unwell. Buller, for example, was suffering from open sores on his legs and hands, the latter permanently affecting his handwriting. Wolseley bowed to the inevitable, and allowed the men to return home. In grateful thanks, Wolseley issued the following order: 'Sir Garnet Wolseley desires to place on record his high appreciation of the services they have rendered during the war ... The success which has attended the operations of the Flying Column is largely due to General Wood's genius for war, to the admirable system he has established in his command, and to the zeal and energy with which his ably conceived plans have been carried out by Colonel Buller.'[54] Privately, Wolseley informed Evelyn that, 'you and Buller have been the bright spots in this miserable war, and all through I have felt proud that I numbered you among my friends and companions in arms.'[55]

Wolseley also wrote to the Duke of Cambridge to recommend Evelyn for the permanent rank of Major-General: 'I most humbly and respectfully urge ... that an officer who had proved himself fit for command in the crucial test of active service before an enemy, should in the interest of the nation be given permanently the position in the Army which he has been now so long holding temporarily in the field.'[56] Evelyn would have to wait until his return to England to learn whether Wolseley's urgings had secured his promotion. In the meantime, Evelyn was honoured to learn that the Queen, 'had been graciously pleased to confer upon Colonel Evelyn Wood the dignity of a Knight Commander of the Bath'.[57]

There remained one ceremony for Evelyn to organize before he could say goodbye to his command and return home. This was to be a march past of his Flying Column in front of their new General, Wolseley. Evelyn was insistent that his men look their best and to this end, the night before, he had them all mending ripped uniforms, washing their white belts and cleaning their rifles so that when they marched past, although their uniforms were ragged, the men's belts and rifles were as, 'clean as if they had been parading in Hyde Park.'[58] All their handiwork was evidently noticed, as Wolseley wrote to the Duke of Cambridge that, 'all things considered the men marched past remarkably well. I never desire to command better soldiers than those comprising the three regiments of that Column.'[59]

On 18 July, Wood and Buller, with Evelyn's personal escort, rode to Pietermaritzburg. As the party departed, the men of the Flying Column gave a collective shout of 'God speed you', which brought tears to Wood's eyes. He was later to write:

We had served together, one battalion eight months, and the other for eighteen months. Much of the time had been fraught with anxiety; the goodbyes of these men, of whom it was commonly said in South Africa, 'I worked their souls out,' and whom I had necessarily treated with the sternest discipline was such that I have never forgotten.[60]

The stamp of authority that Evelyn had imposed on his command, as well as the force of his own personality, was clearly recognised by his intelligence officer, Captain Woodgate, who, when writing to Wood, stated, 'A general makes his own army Napoleon is said to have stated, and I suppose no army has been more its General's creation than the Flying Column.'[61] Wolseley was to write one last letter to Wood before the latter departed for England and in it Sir Garnet stated that he had sent confidential letters to both the Duke of Cambridge and Colonel Stanley, the Army Minister, recommending Wood for promotion. Wolseley ended his letter to Evelyn, 'if they don't make you a General they should all be hanged at the Horse Guards.'[62]

In recognition of the bravery and loyalty displayed by his personal escort, Evelyn, before departing for the coast, treated them and Buller to a dinner in Pietermaritzburg's principal hotel. Fortunately, Wood had received his share from the sale of plundered Zulu cattle and was well able to afford the meal, for he described it as, 'costly, and the variety of the liquids which my guests ordered was astonishing, for they drank beer and every sort of wine to be found in a hotel cellar.'[63] Even Wood, who usually drank only moderately, awoke with something of a hangover, although he was later to learn that most of his guests had to be transported to their beds in wheelbarrows and carts. The men's exuberance was certainly a reflection of the strain and anxiety that they had all endured. Chelmsford, Buller and Wood shared a passage from Cape Town to Plymouth, where they arrived on 26 August 1879. For Evelyn, his return was to mark months in which he was to be showered with honours for his service, but it was to be a brief stay for he was soon to be called upon to return to South Africa.

Chapter Eight

Honours & Dishonour

On Evelyn's arrival in Plymouth, his wife, brother and sisters were there to greet him. He had returned as a 'conquering hero,' and now began several months in which he was to be wined and dined, and would meet the great and the good, including the Prime Minister, Lord Beaconsfield (Benjamin Disraeli) and Her Majesty the Queen. Wood first journeyed to his brother-in-law's property at Belhus in Essex, where his mother, who was now quite poorly, was residing. Here he received a great reception; the local inhabitants had decorated their houses and the horses were removed from Wood's carriage and it was pulled up the drive to Belhus by the villagers.[1] There was also in attendance a guard of honour of the 2nd Essex Artillery and the 1st and 15th Essex Rifles.[2] Evelyn's wife and mother had both been very concerned for his safety throughout the Zulu conflict, but now shared in his joy at his safe return and his success. Frederick Greenwood, former editor of the *Pall Mall Gazette*, had earlier reassured Lady Wood that Evelyn would survive unscathed and he was able to write, 'did not I tell you that he would come safe home, with a load of new honours ... and is there a prouder and happier mother in England than you are now?'[3]

Although there is little doubt that Evelyn was happy to be back among his family and friends, and that he revelled in the praise and honours directed towards him, it was also a period of sad reflection. Wood was to write to Rear Admiral Whyte, an old colleague from the Crimea, that he had been 'much occupied since my return to England and not altogether with pleasures for I have been visiting the friends of those I lost in Africa.'[4] One of these visits was to Lord Cawdor, father of Wood's aide and friend Ronald Campbell; Evelyn planned to call on him at Nairn following his visit to Balmoral as a guest of the Queen. However, Wood was placed in a difficult position when Her Majesty informed him that he should extend his stay at the royal residence from one night to three. Evelyn had evidently impressed the monarch.

136

Writing in her journal, Victoria recorded that, 'Sir Evelyn is wonderfully lively and hardly ceases talking, which no doubt comes from his deafness and inability to hear general conversation. He is clever and amusing, and all he says is very interesting.' The Queen also recorded that, 'Sir Evelyn said he was very tired, that it had been a terrible war, and they had lost so many friends. Poor young R. Campbell he specially grieved over.'[5] The proposed extension to his stay now placed Evelyn in an embarrassing and sensitive position, for he did not wish to disappoint Lord Cawdor. Wood was firmly told that he could not raise this issue with Her Majesty and that it would also not be etiquette for her staff to do so. Evelyn expressed his view firmly to the Royal staff that as the Queen had been so gracious in receiving him he could not possibly imagine that she would wish to inconvenience him or disappoint Lord Cawdor. This statement had the desired effect and the following day it was the Queen who raised the issue and insisted that Evelyn depart to visit Cawdor.[6]

The Queen impressed upon her Prime Minister that he too should meet Evelyn. Victoria had written to Disraeli, now Lord Beaconsfield, that she had found Wood a remarkable man and an admirable General with, 'plenty of dash as well as prudence', and a man of, 'Imperial views, loyal and devoted to Sovereign and country.'[7] Wood duly received an invitation to join Lord Beaconsfield at his home, Hughenden Manor. It is evident that Beaconsfield was very keen to ascertain Evelyn's first-hand experience of the war. The Prime Minster particularly wished to quiz Wood as to whether he believed that Sir Bartle Frere had initiated the Zulu conflict for his own purposes, and he also wanted to know Evelyn's opinion of Lord Chelmsford's abilities to command. Evelyn foresaw that the visit could be a trap and was reluctant to go, but had no alternative. He spent the first two days of the visit trying to avoid the Prime Minister, but by the end of the second day Wood realised that, if he stayed, a searching inquisition as to Frere's actions could not be avoided. Evelyn thus declared that he must leave early the following morning, but Beaconsfield stated that he too would rise early so that they could have a conversation over breakfast. Wood would not bow to the inevitable and asked his butler to serve breakfast in his room, but the following morning he discovered that the meal had been laid out in a nearby anteroom and that the Prime Minister was waiting for him. Many searching questions were asked of Evelyn which centred on whether he considered that war with the Zulus could have been avoided, to which Evelyn replied in the negative, although he did confirm that he felt the war could have been postponed for a month. Beaconsfield stated that even this would have aided the Government in their negotiations with the Russians, which were taking place at San Stefano at the time, and that the defeat at Isandlwana had weakened the British position. The Prime Minister left Evelyn with a warning that if he was ever to command abroad in the future he should, 'carry out , not only the letter of the Cabinet's orders, but also the spirit of its instructions.'[8] These words were to haunt Evelyn within two years, when he was placed in a position of choosing between obeying such orders or doing what he knew to be right.

Despite Wood's rather unnerving experience with the Prime Minister, Beaconsfield was able to tell the Queen that he had been 'delighted' by Evelyn's visit.[9] He was probably not so delighted with Wood when, just a week later, he made a very public defence of Sir Bartle Frere at a dinner held in his honour by the Fishmongers' Company. Wood later claimed that he had simply tried to redress the balance as to how Frere's actions should be viewed and he spoke of the High Commissioner's 'unflinching courage and rectitude of purpose'.[10] Evelyn also used the opportunity presented by the dinner to remember publicly many of his fallen comrades and he specifically praised the courage of the Prince Imperial. Although Evelyn received some criticism in the Press for his defence of Frere, he also enjoyed some favourable comment. The publisher John Murray wrote to Evelyn's uncle, Lord Hatherley, stating that he was, 'delighted with the speech of Sir Evelyn Wood especially by his defence of the absent and maligned Sir Bartle Frere.'[11]

Frere himself, on reading a copy of the speech, wrote to Wood and thanked him for his defence, which he described as 'noble' and claimed that it had 'done more to set people right than a ship full of despatches'. In this letter Frere also expressed his disappointment with the settlement that Wolseley had imposed on the Zulus and claimed that it was 'very different from any you would have made had it been left, as Chelmsford and I hoped it would be, in your hands.'[12] Thus it is clear that both Frere and Chelmsford had felt that Evelyn would have been more than able to handle any political settlement of Zululand after the war, or at least that he would have been more their man than Wolseley was ever likely to be. Evelyn did not exactly stand alone in his defence of Frere, but he was certainly in the minority. His attitude towards the High Commissioner was certainly based on friendship and loyalty, and it seems clear that Frere had pandered to Evelyn's vanity. However, it is perhaps somewhat surprising that Evelyn did not see, like so many of his contemporaries, including the Prime Minister, that Frere had indeed manipulated events so as to cause war between Britain and the Zulu nation. Perhaps Wood had been captivated by Frere's charm and was simply too close to the situation to see the wider picture. Evelyn's apparent political naivety was to re-surface again and again throughout the remainder of his career, but on this particular occasion it did not harm his prospects of advancement.

Evelyn was now a famous man and as such he was to receive many invitations and offers of employment outside of his army career. In October 1879 he was invited to become Vice-President of the Society for the Protection of Animals liable to Vivisection[13] and during the following year he was approached by both William Saunders, pro-prietor of the Central News, and Frederick Greenwood of the *St James Gazette*, to provide material for their columns.[14] However, Wood was disappointed to learn that he was not to receive the promotion to Major-General that Wolseley had pressed for. The Duke of Cambridge is said to have considered such an advancement as 'too early'.[15] Evelyn even tried to use the influence of his new champion, the Queen, to try to persuade the Duke, but he learned in December 1879 that even this attempt had failed. The Queen's secretary, Sir Henry Ponsonby, wrote to Wood: 'The answer I have received is that you have received the K.C.B. for the Zulu War – a G.P. Pension and the command at Belfast – a higher authority [Duke of Cambridge] replied also to the highest authority [the Queen] that Sir Evelyn Wood's name was sufficiently renowned to make it difficult to increase that renown.'[16]

Evelyn was to be involved in further controversy over honours when he was asked by Ponsonby whether he thought Russell should receive a decoration for his services in Zululand, a proposal which was then being advocated by Russell's friend, the Prince of Wales. Evelyn would not have wished for any award to be granted to Russell, as this might have exposed Evelyn's own performance at the battle of Hlobane. Apparently Wood produced a letter sent to him by Lieutenant Browne, second in command to Russell at Hlobane, which stated that he would never serve under Russell again and, without saying so in plain terms, reported Russell for cowardice.[17] This action seemed to convince the Queen to refuse any award to Russell, and the matter was dropped.

Early in December, the health of Evelyn's mother caused concern, and on 13 December, whilst Wood was in London entertaining the Attorney-General, Sir John Holker, and members of the Bar, she began to fade. When Lady Wood was asked whether she wished to see Evelyn she replied that she did, but insisted that the telegram asking for his recall should only be delivered after 11.00 pm so as not to spoil the party. On receiving the news, Evelyn managed to catch an early morning mail train back to Belhus and was at his mother's bedside when she died peacefully the following day. Wood had had a very close relationship with his mother and was naturally devastated at her loss. He threw himself into his new army appointments, first spending a few weeks in command of the Belfast District before taking over the Chatham command in January 1880. Both commands were two of the sixty-six infantry units devised in 1871 by Edward Cardwell, Secretary of State for War. Each had a regimental depot, which it was thought would appeal to the local patriotism of recruits, and where they underwent their basic training. By adopting this system, Cardwell was attempting to replicate a similar system within the army of Prussia, which had proved successful.[18] He was not to remain long here either, as his speech of September 1879 at the Fishmongers' Company, in which he had praised the courage of the Prince Imperial, had been brought to the attention of the Prince's grieving mother, the Empress Eugenie, who was planning a pilgrimage to her son's grave in Zululand.

After several interviews with the Empress, Wood was summoned to Windsor, where he received instructions from the Queen that he was to take charge of Eugenie and convey her to South Africa. Evelyn had little choice but to comply, but did insist that the Empress must follow his instructions 'as if she were a soldier in my command.'[19] Evelyn also requested that he be allowed to take his wife with him. The party was also joined by the Honourable Mrs. Ronald Campbell, who, like the Empress, was also on a pilgrimage, in this case to her husband's grave. It is not clear whether Mrs Campbell joined the group on her own initiative or whether she was invited by Evelyn, but what does seem clear is that Wood himself was still grieving for Campbell, no doubt felt some guilt and responsibility for his death, and it was hoped that the proposed journey would also assist him to overcome these feelings.

The party reached Cape Town in April 1880 and here the Woods and the Empress spent a few days as guests at Government House of Sir Bartle Frere, who apparently was rather over attentive to Eugenie. Wolseley was also present and recorded events in his journal of 23 April: 'One could see all day that the poor Empress was trying to be cheerful, but the tears kept constantly filling her eyes. Wood and Barrow and Lady Wood all tell me the same story about mother Frere's conduct: the Frere family proved themselves utter snobs and bored the Empress out of her life, never leaving her alone for a moment ... Dear Evelyn and Lady Wood speak what they believe to be French to the Empress ... and the effect is most amusing.'[20] If the Woods and the Empress did have a slight communication problem, it did not stop them developing a real friendship during the visit, a friendship which continued for the rest of their lives.

Whilst in Cape Town, Evelyn was able to call on the Zulu king, Cetchwayo, who was then held captive in the castle. During two visits the men were able to discuss aspects of the war. The king confirmed to

140

Wood that the Zulus had really feared the mounted troops under Evelyn's command and the king himself thought that they might mount a raid on Ulundi in an attempt to kidnap him. Such an attack had never been contemplated, but it indicated the level of anxiety that Wood's command excited in the minds of the Zulus. On his second visit, Evelyn brought Cetchwayo a blanket, which the king had requested. However, it was found to be too small to cover the sovereign's large bulk and Wood had to purchase another. During the party's stay in Cape Town, Evelyn also learnt of the tensions between the British and the Boers of the Transvaal over the restoration of Boer independence in that region; he did not yet know that he was to play a prominent part in the forthcoming conflict.

In the meantime, the party journeyed to Natal. True to his earlier statement, Evelyn viewed his task as a military command and each day's progress was regimentally calculated, with distances worked out in advance. For example, on 25 June the party was to cover twenty miles to the battlefield of Kambula and on 26 June remain there for the day; on 30 June the group would advance the sixteen miles to Hlobane, where again it would rest the following day and explore the site. In total, from 29 April to 27 June, the party would cover 503 miles to view all the major battlefields of the war, including Isandlwana, as well as the site at which the Prince Imperial was slain.[21] Wood even calculated the itinerary so that the party would arrive at this last site on the anniversary of the Prince's death.

Wood was also able to use the journey as his own pilgrimage. In the region of Hlobane he spent some time searching in vain for the remains of one of his officers, Captain Robert Barton, and Evelyn was able to join Mrs Campbell in erecting a tombstone on her husband's grave at the base of the Hlobane mountain. This was undoubtedly a moving, and perhaps healing, process for both of them. At the site where the Prince had been killed, Wood joined the Empress in prayer, and a tree was planted to mark the spot. The aftermath of the Prince's death had been marked by controversy. The officer in charge of the party, Captain Carey, who had fled the scene and made no attempt to discover the fate of the Prince, had claimed at his court-martial that in reality the Prince had assumed command and that it was he who had selected the poor and dangerous site at which they had stopped for lunch and were so easily ambushed. Carey also stated that he had thought that the Prince had fled the ambush like himself and that he was following close behind him. When he discovered that the Prince had fallen there was nothing Carey could do to save him.

During his visit on 21 June, Evelyn was able to interview a man named Grubb, who had been a trooper in the Prince's party on the day of his death. Grubb contradicted Carey's testimony and claimed that after he saw the Prince become separated from his horse he had tried to encourage Carey to go to his aid. Grubb stated, 'I waved my hat to Lieutenant Carey, who was then about 300 yards ahead of me, to stop – he turned his head and beckoned me to come on, which I did, thinking he must see something. We never walked our horses until we had gone at least three miles.' On his return to England, Carey was considered to be something of a scapegoat for the general failings in command, but Queen Victoria quashed the findings of the court-martial and Carey's promotion to Captain was confirmed, although his career was forever tainted by the incident. Evelyn's interview with Grubb apparently confirmed Carey's guilt and when Wood reported his findings to Her Majesty at Osborne House in late July 1880, the Queen was clearly shocked that she had been so taken in by Carey. She ordered Evelyn that the report should be kept secret and that he was to write on the bottom of it, in his own hand: 'Her Majesty commanded that all the above so far as it regards Captain Carey be regarded as confidential.'[22]

The pilgrimage had been a success, and on 1 July, much to his relief, Evelyn was able to place his royal charge on a train just outside Pietermaritzburg, knowing that he had done a good job in escorting the Empress and returning her safely. Sir Evelyn and Lady Wood now returned to England. He received the Queen's personal thanks and there is no doubt that a real friendship was growing between them, a relationship which would naturally benefit Wood in his future career. However, he had one substantial regret from his latest trip to South Africa, that being that the War Office, wary of criticism in Parliament, refused even to allow Evelyn to draw half pay for the months he was absent with the Empress. Evelyn, never particularly well off, was seriously financially disadvantaged by obeying the command of his Queen.

Wood now returned to his new home and command at Chatham. Again, he was not to be there for very long as events in South Africa moved towards war between the Boers and the British over the issue of independence for the Transvaal. The British had annexed a financially bankrupt Transvaal into the empire in 1877, as part of Lord Carnarvon's attempts to form a confederation of South Africa. The Boers resented the British presence and a section of them, under the command of such individuals as Kruger and Joubert, were prepared for armed intervention to restore their Republic. Via the Queen's Speech at the opening of Parliament, the new Prime Minister Gladstone confirmed the British aim of maintaining supremacy over the Transvaal. The Boers expressed their bitter disappointment at this stance and continued to make preparations for armed resistance. In this atmosphere of tension, Evelyn received notice that he was once more required for service in South Africa. His old colleague from the Ashanti war, Sir George Pomeroy-Colley, had, following the return of Wolseley to England, been appointed High Commissioner for all of South-East Africa. The decision to send Wood and reinforcements to the colony was as a direct result of Boer attacks on various British outposts, such as the one at Rustenburg, and the massacre of British troops under the command of Colonel Anstruther. Evelyn's appointment left the War Office and the government with something of a dilemma, for Evelyn was both more experienced than and one degree senior to Colley. In Parliament the Secretary of State for War, Hugh Childers, was bluntly asked who was to take command, Colley or Wood. Childers deferred his answer, but it was later announced in the Press that Evelyn would be subordinate.

Evelyn has recently been described as 'a canny political soldier who knew how to keep his options open'[23], and he had no qualms in accepting the approach from the Duke of Cambridge to go to South Africa and buttress Colley's position. His desire for active service outweighed any reservations he might have had in serving under an officer technically junior to him. Evelyn learned from his previous mistake when escorting the Empress, and only accepted the position on the grounds that he would maintain the rank and salary that he currently enjoyed with the Chatham command. With the rank of Brigadier-General secured and with command of the reinforcements in his hands, he had an audience with the Foreign Secretary, Lord Kimberley, who candidly informed him that he favoured the retrocession of the Transvaal.[24] Evelyn was now entering the dangerous and confusing world of politics, where reputations could be won or lost. On hearing the news of Wood's appointment, Colley was able to write to his old friend: 'My dear Wood, I was right glad to hear that you were coming out here, and think it very generous of you to be ready to serve under a junior and less experienced officer. However, you can afford to be generous with your reputation.'[25]

The decision to send Evelyn to South Africa was welcomed in both Britain and South Africa. In the colony, he was seen as the hero of the Zulu war and had gained the respect of the Boers for his political and military skills. In Britain, the *Graphic* summed up the prevailing thinking when the newspaper stated: 'If the war is to go on, we have reason to congratulate ourselves that it henceforth be partly conducted by Sir Evelyn Wood. General Colley may be an excellent commander in some respects, but he has not the important secret of success, whereas General Wood has a way of carrying to a triumphant conclusion every enterprise he undertakes.'[26] On hearing that Evelyn was to leave for

South Africa, the officers of the 92nd Highlanders, then serving in India, devised a plan whereby their senior subaltern, Ian Hamilton, telegraphed directly to Wood: 'Personal. From subalterns 92nd Highlanders. Splendid battalion eager service much nearer Natal than England do send.'[27] Such a cheeky gesture would have raised eyebrows at the War Office, and many other senior officers would have taken the request as an affront, but Evelyn was delighted by such an eager, direct approach; he rewarded the subaltern's impudence and the battalion promptly received orders to sail to Natal. Wood himself left Plymouth on 14 January, and he indicated his initial lack of understanding of the political and military situation he was to face when he wrote to his friend and family doctor, Norman Moore, from aboard the SS *Nubian*: 'I scarcely expect to see a fight this time and anticipate the rebellion will collapse as soon as the British reinforcements arrive, if not sooner.'[28]

Evelyn arrived in Durban on 9 February 1881, to discover a colony which was thoroughly demoralised after two successive British defeats at the hands of the Boers. Colley had tried to force the strong enemy position at Laing's Nek on 28 January, only to see his troops repulsed. The British suffered casualties amounting to sixteen per cent of their total force, a loss which has recently been described as, 'a casualty rate indicative of a thoroughgoing defeat'.[29] Later, on 8 February, an armed force, again under the command of Colley, which was escorting ambulance wagons back to Newcastle, was ambushed by a smaller Boer contingent at a place named Schuinshoogte. Once more the British suffered high casualties and Colley had to endure the indignity of a night-time retreat to save what was left of his force, leaving the many wounded to face either death or captivity. Colley had singularly failed to distinguish himself in the field: almost twenty-five per cent of his men lay dead or wounded and he had lost many close comrades on his staff.[30] All Colley wished for, as he described in a letter to his sister, was a quick end to 'this hateful war',[31] and he must have hoped that Evelyn would prove to be the means to that end.

It was believed by many that now the military side of operations would be placed in the charge of Wood, and that Colley, who had shown little aptitude in battle, would attend to his duties as Governor. Evelyn certainly threw himself into his new enterprise with the energy and drive he had displayed in his earlier forays in South Africa. On landing in Durban, he did not wait for a public reception but immediately boarded a mail-cart and arrived early the next morning in Pietermaritzburg, perched on a sack and looking anything but the distinguished Brigadier-General.[32] However, once in Government House, he was able to change into uniform to attend a ball given in his honour, and even shared the first dance with Lady Colley. Away from the battlefield and the severe demands he placed on his subordinates, Wood was charming in a social setting, and the correspondent Archibald Forbes described the 'sweetness of his smile' which 'goes to the heart and stays there'.[33] Another correspondent, Melton Prior, described Wood as a 'soldier to the backbone, dapper, smart, brisk and full of energy.'[34] After this brief social interlude, Evelyn returned to the job in hand.

He led the column of reinforcements to Newcastle where he met Colley on 17 February. He managed to persuade Colley to let him reconnoitre the left flank and rear of the enemy position, and then led 100 Hussars on a sixty-mile dash into enemy territory, during which he ascertained that there were no major concentrations of Boers in the vicinity. The Press seized upon this daring raid and exaggerated its military significance out of all proportion to its achievements. Evelyn had correctly judged that the raid would improve the morale of the soldiers and colonists, whilst at the same time giving a firm message to the Boers that the businesslike General Wood had returned to the scene of his greatest triumphs, and this would hopefully disconcert the Boers.

On his return, Evelyn agreed with Colley that no further advance should be made until more reinforcements were brought from Pieter-maritzburg. Wood went south to bring up the extra troops. On his journey, he met the war correspondent and illustrator, Melton Prior, and informed him that he need not hurry north as, 'I have just left Colley, who has given me his word of honour that he will not move out of camp until I return.'[35]

Whilst British military preparations were progressing, attempts at peace negotiations stalled. On 12 February the Boers had submitted an overture for peace, which included the terms that the Boers would withdraw their forces, currently in Natal at Laing's Nek, and allow safe passage for the British troops besieged in the Transvaal. Crucially, however, the Boers stated that if the British upheld the annexation, they would continue the fight. The Boer message was discussed by the cabinet in London three days later, and although Kimberley considered that the terms were inadmissible, he felt that it was incumbent on the Government to explore the situation to see if a settlement was possible. The Government instructed Colley to tell the Boers that if armed opposition ceased, the British Government would dispatch commissioners to arrange a settlement. Colley clearly found this approach confusing and ambiguous, as it implied to him that the Boers would maintain their position on Laing's Nek, and this would give them a military advantage and hence imply a tacit recognition of their political demands for independence. Colley sought clarification from Kimberley, whilst explaining his concerns to him. A rather indignant reply was received, in which Kimberley stated that the Government had not committed itself to any scheme, but that the appointed commissioners would find a means to establish a permanent settlement. Thus the armistice offer was despatched to the Boers on 21 February.

Whether planned or not, the offer coincided with the departure of one of the key Boer players, Kruger, to a remote part of the Transvaal to deal with some local unrest, and thus a response to the British offer was delayed. Colley's terms reached Kruger on 28 February, and within an hour Kruger had signed his acceptance of them. However, news of this would not reach Natal until 7 March, long after the British had suffered another defeat at the hands of the Boers.[36]

Whilst Colley waited impatiently for the Boer response, he became aware that the Boers still continued to fortify Laing's Nek and he became obsessed with the idea that, if the British offer was accepted with Laing's Nek still in Boer hands, this would inflict a deep injury on Britain's reputation and power in South Africa. Certainly, he was aware of his own earlier failings and must have wanted to repair his reputation with one last success. Whatever his motive, after several days planning and intelligence gathering, Colley resolved to lead a night-time attack on 27 February to occupy the extinct volcano of Majuba, which looked down upon the Boers at Laing's Nek. Once in place, Colley thought the British occupation of Majuba would make the Boer position untenable and force their retreat.

From the start, the advance up the 2,000-foot slopes of Majuba encountered delays and difficulties, and it was not until nearly dawn on 27 February that a disorganized force finally reached the summit. British confidence in the apparent strength of their position was misplaced, for what Colley's reconnaissance had failed to establish was the size of the area he now had to defend, and it soon become clear that the 400 British troops would be too thinly spread to offer a concentrated defence. The reconnaissance had also failed to note the significance of the dead ground below the summit, which would allow the Boers to approach the British unseen.

After the initial shock of realizing that the British now held the high ground had lessened, the Boer leader, Joubert, called for volunteers to drive the British off Majuba, and around 450 men joined in an assault. The Boers, cleverly using the dead ground, managed to get within forty yards of the British, and it was not long before enemy fire was claiming the lives of British soldiers. As more and more Boers infiltrated the thinly spread British lines, panic, and the hopelessness of the British position, forced a retreat, which became a rout in which, bravely trying to stand his ground, Colley was shot dead. In total, 87 British soldiers were killed, 123 wounded and 50 were taken prisoner. The British had been thoroughly beaten.[37]

In his autobiography, written in 1906, Evelyn was very kind to the memory of his old friend Colley. He stated that, 'Sir George's long and valuable life is unappreciated, and forgotten in its culminating and dramatic disaster.' Furthermore, Wood went on to claim that, 'Colley was justified, in a military sense, in moving on the 26th [on Majuba].'[38] However, this is not what Evelyn believed in 1881. Writing to the Duke of Cambridge, Wood said: 'I gather your Royal Highness inclines to Herbert Stewart's [one of Colley's staff officers] story that the Majuba disaster is due to a panic. I start by saying the men did not behave well. They failed to do what our soldiers have so often done, retrieve the bad handling of the officers by indomitable courage ... the movement [to Majuba] was unnecessary and too wide had we been ready to march up the Nek by the road. As we could not possibly be ready for days, the movement was silly.'[39]

Additionally, when writing to William Napier, Evelyn said: 'You would probably prefer I should write to you something on the actions fought by Colley. I cannot – if I did I should in order to be honest with you, criticise the "intention" and "execution" of two out of three, and the "execution" of all three. I have not mentioned this to any one military man, and I do not think I should mention it now, were it not for the fact that some – at least one – of the officers [Stewart] who was on the Majuba is explaining the disaster as being entirely to the cowardice of the men is absurd. I tell you privately, and pray tear up this. I ascribe the bad behaviour of the men to the insufficient way in which they were handled.'[40] Furthermore, in response to a question from Queen Victoria as to how Colley could have failed at Majuba, Wood wrote: 'He [Wood] writes now For Her Only. In his [Wood's] opinion the attack on Majuba was ill-timed, precipitate, badly organised – the men badly handled and indeed the only redeeming front is the heroic conduct of the General [Colley]'.[41] There is no doubt that, although defending his old friend publicly, in private he considered Colley to have been at fault. Furthermore, Wood probably resented the fact that Colley had broken his word and advanced on the Boers' position, when he had earlier reassured Evelyn that he would undertake no further action until he had returned with the reinforcements.

In a letter to his wife, Evelyn described how he had first received reports that the action on Majuba was taking place, and that the fighting was not going as expected. He wrote: 'About 3 o'clock we had an unpleasant telegram. This was followed by a succession of telegrams, one or two so nervously written as to excite my wrath – I have after full enquiry removed a staff officer who wrote one of them. When the news came Colonel Mitchell [Deputy Governor of Natal] became very fussy – you never saw anyone so upset. I desired Colonel Mitchell to send for the Chief of Justice and at 8.00 pm I was sworn in as Administrator.'[42] Clearly, news of the defeat and the death of Colley produced upset, if not panic, among some of the senior staff, although Evelyn was apparently very level-headed and clear as to what needed to be done. His decision to be sworn in at once as Acting Governor of Natal and Administrator of the Transvaal sent a sign to the Army, the colony and the Boers, that he was a man of action, ready to accept the responsibilities of office. Throughout the night, telegrams arrived for the new Governor on such a regular basis that sleep was impossible, and at 5.30 am on 28 February he set off north to join the remains of the British forces at Mount Prospect, opposing the Boer position at Laing's Nek.

In the weeks that were to follow, both Natal and the Transvaal were to experience constant rain, which hampered both troop movements and peace negotiations. Delegates were delayed in their attempts to attend the various meetings between the British and the Boers, which were hastily called to try to establish a peace settlement, and this all added to an air of uncertainty. The rains delayed Evelyn as he tried to hasten to the front; on one occasion it took his party five hours to travel a mere twenty miles and, of course, reinforcements were similarly hindered. A reporter for the *Cape Argus* wrote, 'If any person is ambitious to see mud in perfection let him come here.'[43] Wood finally arrived at Mount Prospect on 4 March, to find the troops thoroughly demoralised as a result of three successive defeats. He ordered the issue of an extra ration of grog to boost morale, and set instructions for the strengthening of the camp. Evelyn at once realised that no further British advance could be contemplated until reinforcements arrived, but with the rain and the resultant poor state of the roads, he had no firm idea as to when the extra troops could be expected. Back in Britain, a now heavily pregnant Lady Wood heard rumours that, like Colley, Evelyn had fallen in battle with the Boers. It was not until she was sent written confirmation from one of her husband's secretaries that he was alive and well that her fears were allayed.[44]

Given the precarious British military position, Evelyn felt that he needed to buy some time, so as to allow for the arrival of reinforcements. To this end, and with the encouragement of Brand, President of the Orange Free State, who was to act in the role of peacemaker and arbiter, Evelyn decided to enter again into negotiations with the Boers. Although it appears that Wood had initially viewed such an approach as a means by which he could buy time so as to accumulate sufficient troops to be able to defeat the Boers entrenched at Laing's Nek, this was an error on Wood's part. Once negotiations began again, the Boers were probably shrewder than Evelyn, for they realised that it would be difficult for the British to renew hostilities, having once initiated the peace talks. To suddenly break off discussions, without sufficient cause, would give the impression that Wood had entered into them solely for military expediency, and that he, and by association the British Government, had acted in bad faith. Evelyn's military brain had overruled his political consciousness, and this suggests an element of naivety on his part.

On 5 March, the day before he met Joubert in peace talks, Evelyn telegraphed Kimberley and stated: 'My constant endeavour shall be to carry out the spirit of your orders but considering the disasters we have sustained I think the happiest result will be that after a successful action which I hope to fight in about 14 days, the Boers should disperse without any guarantees, and the many now undoubtedly coerced will readily settle down.'[45] Evelyn also confirmed to the Queen that his intention had been to fight before entering into peace negotiations.[46]

If Evelyn had been solely responsible for agreeing to a resumption of the peace talks, the negotiations were rapidly taken out of his hands by the Foreign Secretary, Lord Kimberley, and other members of Gladstone's Government. Now raised to the local rank of Major-General, Wood, with Brand's encouragement, suggested to Joubert a venue of O'Neill's cottage, which was halfway between the British camp at Mount Prospect and the Boer entrenchments at Laing's Nek, for a meeting. On 6 March Wood and Joubert agreed to an eight-day armistice, which would allow for a response to be received from Kruger to Colley's earlier terms. Additionally, the Boers permitted Evelyn to dispatch eight days supply of food to the besieged British garrisons in the Transvaal, the position of which was causing some concern, particularly the troops at Potchefstroom, where it was felt that food was running very short.

Wood was delighted with this first meeting. He telegraphed his apparent success to both Childers, the Secretary for War, and Kimberley. He indicated to the Government that the armistice would allow him time to bring up sufficient troops to launch a possible attack on Laing's Nek. In the meantime, Evelyn learnt that the British Government had appointed Sir Frederick Roberts, hero of the Second Afghan War, to succeed Colley in South East Africa, and that he would supersede Evelyn on his arrival. This appointment should not be considered as a slight on Wood, or an indication that the Government had any lack of faith in his abilities; it was simply that Roberts possessed the headline-grabbing profile that a Government, reeling from three successive military defeats, needed to reassure the public and the Boers that it was serious in its prosecution of the war. Roberts sailed for Cape Town on 5 March, and at Madeira learnt of Evelyn's negotiated armistice. When he eventually landed in Cape Town on 28 March, Roberts was greeted with the news that a peace settlement had been reached. In disgust, he returned to England on the next available boat, not wanting to be associated in any way with what one of his secretaries described as Wood's 'abject surrender' to the Boers.[47]

On 7 March Wood received Kruger's positive response to Colley's earlier offer, and five days later Evelyn was sent the British Government's view as to how peace negotiations could proceed. The telegram declared a British willingness to name Commissioners to discuss a peace settlement, which would consider self government for the Transvaal under British suzerainty, with a British Resident at Pretoria, as long as the Boers first dispersed their forces at Laing's Nek. At a stroke, Evelyn had had his plans for a military occupation of Laing's Nek, before the agreement of a peace deal, taken away as an option by the stance of the British Government. Wood, who must have been disheartened by the lack of firmness in the government's response, conferred with Joubert, and both men agreed to an extension of the armistice until 18 March, so as to allow Kruger to attend the negotiations.

Kruger finally arrived at Laing's Nek on 14 March, and when he heard the terms of the armistice he expressed his unease to Joubert. Kruger was convinced that Wood was simply using the time bought by the armistice to prepare sufficient forces to attack the Boer position, as Evelyn seems to have been planning. Yet Joubert felt sure that the British Government was sincere in its desire for peace, and would recognise the Republic and not sanction any military move. However, even Joubert must have been nervous when he heard of the arrival of Redvers Buller at the front to assume responsibility for military affairs, leaving Wood to focus on the pressures of civil administration and the peace settlement. After Buller's exploits in the Zulu war, the Boers had a huge respect for his strength and determination and must have feared his presence.

On 16 March, the British delegation, led by Wood, met the Boer party at O'Neill's cottage to discuss the response of the British government. The meeting lasted eight hours, during which Evelyn led the exchanges in a lively and bustling fashion. Although confined by Kimberley's instructions, Wood was determined to stand his ground; if any concessions were to be made, it would have to be for the Boers to do so, for certainly Evelyn was confident, as was Buller, that if there were further military engagements, the British would be victorious.

One moment Evelyn was at his most charming, affable and persuasive, the next he would switch to display extreme stubbornness. He seems to have been the ideal candidate to negotiate with the Boers; not only had he won their respect during the Zulu war, but they appreciated his plain speaking. Additionally, there seems little doubt that his legally trained mind, combined with his often convenient deafness, made him quite formidable in any debate.

At the end of the marathon session, the Boers agreed to the general proposals from the British government, although they, particularly Kruger, were unhappy with the composition and powers of the Commissioners. The Boers wanted to see at least five members of the Commission, two of whom they wished to nominate. Wood countered that he had no power to adopt a different course of action, and when Kruger requested that the Transvaal garrisons be withdrawn, Evelyn angrily responded that if the Boers insisted on this point, it would not only be refused, but hostilities would be resumed. The meeting ended with handshakes all round and a commitment to reassemble once a response had been received from the British government. Wood telegraphed to Kimberley news of the general acceptance of the terms by the Boers, and reiterated that he still considered the best option was to throw back the Boers from Laing's Nek and then dictate terms to them.[48] Of course such an approach had been taken out of Evelyn's hands, and he must now have realised that, unless the Boers broke off peace talks, the military option was no longer viable. Due to the fact that he had initiated the armistice, Evelyn had moved from the realms of military command, where he had gained such fame and glory, into the quagmire of politics, in which he had become the instrument of government policy and a likely fall-guy.

Kimberley informed Evelyn on 17 March that there would be no agreement on the withdrawal of garrisons from the Transvaal, although later events were to show that this was little more than a symbolic stand by the government. The Foreign Secretary also reaffirmed that the Commission would only consist of three members, all appointed by the British. Wood reported these points to Joubert on 18 March, but due to the illness of several members of the Boer delegation, including Kruger, Joubert was forced to defer any decision until all the Boers were fit enough to attend another meeting. When this stand by the British was reported by Joubert, it caused much anger in the Boer camp and, with the genuine suspicion that Wood was planning an attack, both Kruger and Smit spoke of fresh military measures. President Brand arrived on 20 March, determined to find a way for both parties to agree a peace settlement. After a brief meeting with Wood, he spoke with Kruger for three hours and urged a more conciliatory attitude. However, Kruger was adamant and he had the support of many of the Boers, who decided that if an acceptable result was not achieved at the next meeting then they would attack Mount Prospect. Joubert, however, agreed with Brand that the terms on offer were liberal and should be accepted.

The final negotiations began at 8.00 am on 21 March, and continued until 9.00 pm that day. Wood managed to get the Boers to withdraw their demands as to the composition of the Commission and the withdrawal of the British garrisons. In return, Evelyn promised that the British would not occupy the Boer positions on the Nek, once the Boers had withdrawn, nor send additional troops into the Transvaal. The meeting came close to breaking up when Evelyn raised the issue of the British retaining the eastern Transvaal. Both parties stood firm and both Wood and Kruger insisted that each party would resume the fight over this issue. Kruger was close to leaving the room when Evelyn seized him by the arm and asked him not to be so hasty. If Wood had not physically stopped Kruger, there is little doubt hostilities would have been resumed. Thus it is perhaps surprising that Evelyn intervened, for Kruger's departure from the meeting would have brought the conflict, for which Wood had so earnestly hoped, much closer. Yet peace prevailed, and furthermore Kruger agreed that the separation of any territory would be left to the decision of the Commission. With this last issue left to the Commission, the parties agreed that the peace agreement could be ratified, awaiting sanction from London, and Wood duly received Kimberley's approval on 22 March.[49]

Evelyn was to receive the thanks of the Gladstone government, as well as some support from the London press. The *Pall Mall Gazette* was able to report that, 'President Brand himself told me that with any other man except General Wood, whom the Boers know and respect, an arrangement would have been impossible.'[50] Likewise, the *Daily News* stated, 'Sir Evelyn Wood, to whose patience and tact in dealing with the points raised ... there can be little doubt that the satisfactory result of the negotiations is largely owing.'[51] The *Illustrated London News* also praised Evelyn; 'The negotiations carried out by General Sir Evelyn Wood, have most happily resulted in the mutual acceptance of terms of peace which are equally convenient and honourable to the British Imperial Government and to the Dutch Community.'[52] However, there was also to be much criticism of his actions.

The *Daily Telegraph* of 28 March openly criticised Evelyn, claiming that he had negotiated with armed rebels. Furthermore, two days later, the same paper, under the headline 'Sir Evelyn Wood's Disastrous and Unwelcome News' stated 'the arrangement concluded with "armed opposition" on Natal soil, will no doubt make her Majesty's gallant soldiers in South Africa and elsewhere more than ever "dejected and indignant" and the people of this country will bitterly share their natural feeling.' The *Daily News* reported that, 'the feeling throughout Natal is intense. People regard the peace terms as humiliating. The idea that the settlement is a noble and gracious act of the British Government has few advocates at present.' However, one of Evelyn's sternest critics was Her Majesty The Queen.

Queen Victoria had been suspicious of her Government's intentions as to the future of the Transvaal and was not pleased that even an armistice had been negotiated. She wrote in her journal that, 'I do not like peace before we have retrieved our honour.'[53] When she was informed that Evelyn had signed peace terms with the Boers, she was furious. She expressed her feelings to Wood in an extremely direct letter:

> Oh! Why have you made peace after them [the three British defeats] and a peace giving up the Transvaal? It is so unlike Sir E.Wood's character that the Queen looks for some explanation to what (she is bound to tell him) has produced a very painful impression here and we hear at the Cape too. To give up the Transvaal when the Government maintained they would retain it is very humiliating. The Queen has such faith in Sir E.Wood that she trusts he can explain that this is not so – but she feels anxious and unhappy about it all.[54]

Evelyn was stunned by his sovereign's response and wasted no time in writing back to her in an attempt to offer some explanation for his actions. Wood stated that he was sending some of the telegrams which had passed between him and Kimberley to his wife and he, 'begs the Queen to peruse some which are 'noted' that she may see he has consistently urged that he should for the future welfare of the country be allowed to beat the Boers once ere peace was made. If Please God Sir Evelyn has once more the honour of waiting on his Queen he will tell her all. Sir Evelyn is thoroughly flattered by Her Majesty's confidence in him. He trusts he may be pardoned for asking her to destroy this sheet.'[55]

It appears that Evelyn's letter did not completely reassure the Queen, for the following month he was again forced to write to her so as to further attempt to justify his action. He wrote:

> Sir Evelyn Wood is unfortunate in being the instrument of a policy which is condemned as he anticipated it would be by a great majority of the educated classes in England. He is unfortunate in that his proceedings have made his Sovereign anxious and unhappy but he would consider himself as still more unfortunate if

the Queen should cease to trust him. As regards the Treaty of Peace, Her Majesty will perceive from the publication of the telegrams that Sir Evelyn being in daily communication with the Ministry had no discretion left to him, and that his only duty was to obey orders. Sir Evelyn humbly represents to Her Majesty, that in his judgement the armistice was absolutely necessary to give the garrison of Potchestroom a chance of holding out, and that it was most desirable to postpone hostilities for a few days in order to avoid further disasters to our troops.[56]

In this letter Evelyn clearly outlined his thinking behind the decision to arrange the initial armistice; that being the welfare of the troops at Potchefstroom. Yet the fate of the men of this small garrison, who would later be forced to surrender by Boer deception, clearly blurred Evelyn's grasp of the wider military and political picture. By arranging the armistice Wood lost the initiative to both the Boers and Kimberley, and this mistake would blight his career for the next few years.

In the same letter, Evelyn was able to inform Her Majesty of his view concerning the cession of the Transvaal, and he wrote that he had:

the best grounds for believing that this step was virtually decided on in January, before Sir George Colley left Maritzburg for the front. Sir Evelyn did not, nor does he approve of it but in his opinion the first duty of a soldier is to carry out loyally the instructions of his superiors. He regrets that his efforts to carry out the orders he received have not gained the approval of Her Majesty. This is, and always must be, a source of the deepest regret to him, but he is not conscious of having failed in his duty.

Clearly Evelyn thought he had had no alternative but to obey the instruction received from Kimberley, but he was also conscious that in doing so he had alienated many, including the monarch.

In June, Victoria was able to congratulate Wood on the birth of his third daughter, and by doing so she clearly again bestowed her confidence upon him. She wished, 'to congratulate him on Lady Wood's safety and the birth of a third daughter which The Queen is anxious should bear the joint names of Victoria Eugenie, which she hopes he will approve.' Furthermore, Victoria went on to say, 'The Queen is so sorry that her letter of 31 March gave Sir Evelyn pain, for she has such a very high opinion of him and so much confidence in him that she grieves to think that anything she has written could add to his great difficulties and trials at this time.'[57]

In addition to the criticism from the Queen, Evelyn was also to be vilified by certain sections of the Army. Officers in South Africa openly denounced the 'abject surrender', and even one of Wood's own Colonels offered his resignation, so disgusted was he by the peace agreement. Evelyn refused to accept it. Even Wood's old comrade, Wolseley, bitterly claimed that if Colley had had 10,000 men at his command, as Evelyn had, he would never have made such a peace, and he furiously declared that by signing the peace treaty Wood 'has injured our national renown most seriously abroad'.[58] Wolseley could not bring himself to forgive Wood for not driving the Boers out of Natal before agreeing a settlement, and his patronage was reduced for a number of years.

Wood's argument that he had been forced to obey the orders of the British Government, and was thus chained by telegrams from London, was not accepted by a large majority of the Army. The call went out, 'Why didn't he [Wood] cut the [telegraph] wires and fight?'[59] Evelyn was even more wounded by criticism from the Army than that from the Queen. He later explained to the Duke of Cambridge that, as a mere soldier, it had been his first duty to obey the instructions of the Government; but in reply, the Duke correctly pointed out that it had been Evelyn's decision to call for a ceasefire, and that it was this very thing that the Government had 'needed to carry out the peaceful policy in contemplation.'[60] Personal attacks, in the newspapers of both the colony and London, increased in the immediate weeks following the settlement, and all went unanswered by Evelyn, who clearly thought it best not to enter into a public dialogue; indeed, he refrained from any public comment until the publication of his autobiography twenty-five years later.

At the end of March, after witnessing the promised retirement of the Boers from Laing's Nek back into the Transvaal, Wood visited Pretoria, under instruction from Kimberley, to explain the terms of the agreement and to arrange the provisional administration with the Boers. On route he stopped at Heidelburg and found to his intense anger that the Republic's Flag was flying over the courthouse. At once Evelyn tried to haul it down, but a sentry intervened and threatened to shoot him. Wood summoned Smit and Pretorius, pointed out that there could not be two governments in the Transvaal at the same time, and demanded that the flag be taken down. This request was refused and Wood issued the burghers with an ultimatum; if the flag was not down by 6.00 am the next day, he would personally pull it down. If he was shot in that act, Evelyn informed Smit and Pretorius, this would be 'unpleasant for my family, but honestly speaking I think it will be a gain for England. Even Gladstone will not be able to give you back your country if you are so foolish as to shoot a Governor, who dies insisting on your carrying out the terms under which you dispersed

155

from Laing's Nek.' The next morning the flag was still flying and at 6.00 am Wood duly marched towards the pole; as he did so the sentry hauled the flag down. Smit even admitted the Boers had committed an error and apologised to Evelyn.[61] Wood's three days in Pretoria were decidedly uncomfortable ones, for he faced much protest from the British residents about the manner in which they believed the Gladstone Government had abandoned them. Evelyn was even heckled whilst addressing army volunteers.

The Government informed Evelyn, much to his frustration, that he was to be a member of the Commission tasked with drawing up the final peace settlement; the other two members were the newly-appointed High Commissioner at the Cape, Sir Hercules Robinson, who was to be chairman, and Sir Henry de Villiers, Chief Justice of the Cape, who had something of an affinity with the Boer position. It appears that Evelyn was determined to voice openly his opposition to many of the proposals of the Commission, and he was particularly concerned to defend the British military position in any potential future conflict between the British and the Boers. This was evident when Evelyn attempted, during the negotiations, to push hard for the British annexation of 6,000 square miles of south-eastern Transvaal so as to gain control of the passes into the high veldt, which would then lessen the Boers' ability to interfere in the affairs of Swaziland and Zululand. Wood certainly believed that any peace settlement agreed in 1881 would not be long lasting, and he clearly saw the strategic significance of the British holding this area. Indeed, it has been argued that if Evelyn had succeeded in his demands, the British possession of this area would have made the Boers' Natal offensive in the Second Boer War impossible, and might even have deterred them from war at all.[62] However, he was not supported by the other Commissioners, who reported to Kimberley that to insist on Wood's demands would be political folly. Kimberley concurred and Evelyn's plan was dropped, despite his several protests.

Major Grenfell, one of Evelyn's staff officers, wrote to his family in May 1881, and recalled Wood's reaction to Kimberley's decision regarding this area of south-eastern Transvaal: 'Wood is perfectly disgusted ... at the first threats of the Boers Lord Kimberley threw Wood over, and took the view of the other members of the Commission who wished to give up everything, settle the question for the moment and get away ... Poor Wood, left to Buller and me, had a conversation on his situation – Buller strongly recommended resignation, he is anxious for it: I as strongly recommended against it, firstly, because once having begun to carry out a distasteful policy, I thought he ought to go on with it, insisting that all his objections could be noted on the

156

Minutes of the Commission, but particularly if he left the Commission, loyalists and natives would be entirely thrown over, and though he is unsupported from home, still he is able to do much good.'[63] For the moment, Evelyn accepted Grenfell's advice, for he still thought he might achieve some success on the Commission.

Throughout the deliberations of the Commission, it appears that it was largely a case of Wood pitted against the others. He was opposed not only on his views of a border-buffer in the south-east Transvaal, but also on his insistence on the establishment of a special tribunal to try parties accused of usage's contrary to civilised warfare. The other Commissioners claimed that there were already sufficient courts in place to try such cases, yet Wood was proved to be correct when none of the Boers charged with the murder of British troops were convicted in the Transvaal courts. With every opportunity, Evelyn expressed his views 'with a fierceness and a vigour that was quite astonishing'[64] and the Boers soon grew to dislike his confrontational attitude. Such an approach was not simply directed towards the Boers, but on more than one occasion at his fellow Commissioner, de Villiers. The chairman, Robinson, even had to take Evelyn to one side and ask him to try to get along with de Villiers. Wood expressed to Queen Victoria his frustration, as well as his view of the other Commissioners: 'The Work of the Royal Commission has been most distasteful to him [Wood] – Sir Hercules Robinson was very anxious Sir Evelyn should remain as a counterpoise to Sir Henry de Villiers, who is devoted to the Boer cause and advocates their case as Sir Evelyn thinks without having any regards to the interests of the population, white and coloured, who have been loyal to Her Majesty.'[65]

So frustrated had he become that Evelyn finally felt he had to offer his resignation from the Commission, specifically over the south-east Transvaal border issue, and to this end he telegraphed Lord Kimberly in June 1881: 'for your [Kimberley's] consideration and decision whether your policy might not be better carried out by withdrawing me from the Commission.'[66] Evelyn received Kimberley's response three days later, which stated that the Government 'appreciate your motives in suggesting your retirement from Commission, but cannot accept your offer. We attach much importance to the retention of your services on Commission, your retirement from which cannot fail to have prejudicial effect on prospects of peaceful settlement. Our agreement with majority on Boundary question does not imply any diminution of our confidence in you.'[67] Unable to resign, Evelyn had to look to other means to register his opposition.

By July Evelyn began to despair of his position, and clearly was looking for a way home, or at least out of South Africa. Despite

157

Wolseley's privately held views as to Wood's actions over the peace settlement, he was able to reassure Evelyn that if he took to the field again 'you may always depend upon joining with me'.[68] Later in the year, Wolseley, in a letter to Wood's sister Anna Steele, with whom he was on friendly terms, wrote, 'I wish Evelyn was out of that horrid South Africa, for he has no chance of gaining any honour there, and he may miss some worthy employment in Egypt or somewhere nearer home.'[69]

Meanwhile, the work of the Commission was finally completed, and the Pretoria Convention was signed on 3 August. This was a complex document, which substantially conceded Transvaal independence, while apparently retaining final imperial control. A British Resident was placed in Pretoria to represent the Queen's suzerainty, or supremacy, and borders were defined. Suzerainty, which was to cause further difficulties amongst the Boer leadership, was a rather nebulous term, but referred to the placement of restrictions on the Transvaal's ability to make treaties, and thus have an independent foreign policy. It also offered some protection of African rights, which would in the future be largely ignored.

Evelyn, unable to resign and reluctant to push this matter further, was able, at last, to formally record his Dissent to the Convention, which appeared in the *Blue Book, Transvaal Royal Commission Report*, issued in 1882. A subsequently published edition mysteriously omitted this Dissent, and thus Evelyn felt justified in reprinting it in his 1906 autobiography. Wood's objections covered six separate issues, and included the border, the trial of alleged offenders by special tribunal and compensation paid to loyalists by the Boers for damage inflicted upon them. This Dissent was not made public until the publication of the *Blue Book* in 1882 and at the time of the Convention, Evelyn's opposition was not generally known; thus, once again, many considered him a party to the surrender of British territory to the Boers. Why didn't Wood make more of his dissatisfaction at the time? His 1892 biographer, Charles Williams, considered that this can be viewed as an act of self-sacrifice and suggested that: 'He [Wood] would not abandon his post though he totally disagreed with the policy of those who begged him to continue to represent not his, but their, views and purposes.'[70] The Duke of Cambridge wrote to Wood to commiserate with him: 'I can well imagine that the duties you have been engaged upon are not agreeable ones to you, and that you are glad they are over.'[71]

Wood's experience of the world of politics had left him exhausted and had affected his health, particularly his nerves and stomach. In August he was to write to Godfrey Lagden, Secretary to the Administrator, that he was 'old and unwell' and that his diet consisted of 'milk and water.'[72] Evelyn returned to his duties as Acting Governor of Natal at Pietermaritzburg. Here he was able to regain his strength and enjoyed entertaining at Government House. His guests included Bishop Colenso, who had been such a critic of Evelyn's actions during the Zulu War, and Lady Florence Dixie, a young reporter who had covered the events of the Boer conflict. His relaxation was disturbed in October, when it appeared that the Boers' Parliament, the Raad, sitting in Pretoria, would not ratify the Convention, with some burghers fervently objecting to the issue of the Queen's suzerainty. In this instance Gladstone's Government stood firm, and on 3 October the Secretary of War contacted Evelyn to ask whether he considered the forces already at his disposal were sufficient, in the event of the Boers failing to ratify the Convention, to renew hostilities.[73] Evelyn asked for additional cavalry and horse artillery from India. Kimberley informed the Boer leadership that no further concessions would be considered and, unless the Convention was signed by 3 November, British forces would enter the Transvaal. Evelyn made elaborate plans for invasion, but the Boers backed down and he was never to get his longed-for military action against them.

By November the tension had cooled sufficiently for Wood and Buller to embark on a tour of the Zulu War battlefields. Both found Isandlwana of particular interest, and they were able to talk to survivors of the battle, both Zulus and members of the Natal Police who had fought there. Evelyn was then able to honour a promise he had made to the Empress Eugenie to travel once again to the site where her son had fallen. Here he was able to check on the condition of the tree that he and the Empress had planted the previous year and arrange for a photograph to be taken of the spot. Evelyn turned down a secret offer from Kimberley to accept, permanently, the position of Governor of Natal,[74] and in doing so he accepted the advice of Lady Dixie, who had earlier told him to 'come home soon and hunt, and don't let Gladstone or Kimberley turn you into a musty old Governor of Natal. It's not good enough do you think and you ought to be reserved for better things.'[75] At the end of December, Wood finally left South Africa to return to his command at Chatham. It was to be the last time that he would see the colony. However, the future Boer war, which he had predicted, would later involve him in more difficult decisions.

159

Chapter Nine

Egyptian Command &
the Race to Khartoum

Despite the fact that Evelyn was yet to hold his baby daughter Victoria, who was born whilst he was serving in South Africa, he did not rush home to England, but instead used the return trip for sightseeing. Rather than follow the usual route via Madeira, he travelled instead to Mozambique and Zanzibar and then through the Suez Canal. This route probably allowed him to gauge the political turmoil in Egypt, which would soon be calling upon his services. From Egypt Evelyn sailed to Naples and then journeyed briefly to Rome to view the highlights of the city. He resumed command at Chatham in February 1882.

There is no doubt that Evelyn was happy to return to both Army and home life and he was able to use the next months to renew old friendships, as well as enjoy some leisure pursuits. However, one of his first tasks was to chair an Army committee of enquiry into the condition of barrack hospitals, of which Florence Nightingale was also a member.[1] There is no record as to whether Wood reminded Ms Nightingale of the last time the two had met, when her nurses had almost killed Evelyn, nor whether Wood recalled how his mother had clashed with Florence over the quality of nursing he was receiving. In any case, the two now shared a common purpose. Both firmly believed not only that army patients would benefit from a feminine approach to their care, but that the presence of female nurses in the barrack hospitals would improve the morale of the infirm, and would speed recovery.[2] Although the widespread use of female nurses throughout the army was later adopted, the provision of modern ventilated barrack hospitals, also advocated by the committee, would not be addressed for a number of years, and again it was to be Evelyn who was at the forefront of innovation in this area.

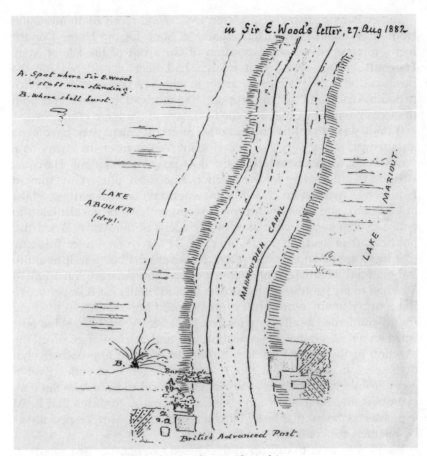

in Sir E. Wood's letter, 27. Aug 1882.

A. Spot where Sir E. Wood
    a staff were standing.
B. Where shell burst.

LAKE
ABOUKIR
(dry).

MAHMOUDIEH CANAL

LAKE MARIOUT

B.

Barricade

British Advanced Post.

Sketch map by Evelyn Wood of an incident at Alexandria.

On 20 February 1882 Sir Evelyn and Lady Wood were once again in the presence of Queen Victoria, when the monarch presented Evelyn with the Knight Grand Cross of St Michael and St George, the highest position in the Order.[3] This honour was apparently in recognition of his services in South Africa during 1881. The issue of why Evelyn had initially agreed to a truce with the Boers clearly still troubled the Queen, as she recorded in her daily journal that, 'He [Wood] said he could not have attacked, before he made the truce, as the men were too exhausted.'[4] This was indicative of the rumblings of discontent that Evelyn was to experience in the Army for a number of years over his decision to negotiate with the Boers. Although he felt obliged to justify his action to his Queen, he resolutely refused to enter into the controversy until after he had finally retired.

161

Somewhat surprisingly, in March 1882 Wood received an invitation from Sir William Harcourt, Secretary of State for the Home Department, to accept the vacant position of Governor of the Isle of Man. Harcourt's letter stated that Evelyn had been considered for the position due to the esteemed manner in which he had rendered service in South Africa, and that the proposal had received the sanction of both the Commander-in-Chief and the Secretary of State for War.[5]

It does seem that this curious offer of employment may have been an attempt, at the very least, to sideline Wood from the Army as a punishment for his handling of the Boer peace negotiations. Harcourt stressed that the salary for the position, £1,800 p.a. plus a Government House, was twice as much as Major-General Wood was earning whilst at Chatham, and such an approach seems to have been calculated to entice Evelyn away from the upper echelons of the Army. Wood did not hesitate in his reply to the offer. On 24 March he wrote; 'It is true that there are personal reasons which prevent my being indifferent to the material advantages of such a post as you suggest, but I am so attached to my profession that unless I could render especial service to the country in any other profession, or could hope to save something for my numerous family, I prefer doing soldier's work'[6] That Harcourt acted on his own initiative seems unlikely, and that he had received the sanction of the highest military authorities even to approach Evelyn does seem to suggest that this offer was designed to entice Evelyn away from any future army career. That Wood did not take the bait, even with the promise of a huge salary increase, confirms that he at least was confident that he still had a career in the Army, especially as he retained the confidence of the Queen.

Wood was soon to call upon the Queen's support, when events in Egypt required the dispatch of a British Expedition, which naturally Evelyn wished to be part of. It may have been that Wood had realised he could no longer rely on the patronage of Wolseley, who was to command the force; indeed, future events would confirm Evelyn's suspicions that Wolseley's favour towards him had cooled. However, Evelyn could still turn to Victoria for informal support. This he did on 4 July, when at lunch with the Queen he impressed upon her his 'great anxiety to serve'[7] in Egypt. It appears that Evelyn thought he might be passed over for service in Egypt and was using all means possible to ensure that he was appointed to the expedition. British intervention was as a direct response to the increasingly vocal and violent nature of the nationalist movement in Egypt, under the leadership of Arabi Pasha, the minister of war. The movement focused on hostility towards European control of the Egyptian Government of Khedive Tewfik, and its finances, and it reached a crescendo when riots broke out in

Alexandria in June 1882. Gladstone's Government felt compelled to send a military force not only to protect its financial assets in Egypt, which included a share in the Suez Canal, but also its citizens resident there.

Evelyn was to receive the much sought after news that he was destined to command the 2nd Brigade, 2nd Division, in the Egyptian expedition, on 21 July 1882.[8] Before his departure from Portsmouth, Victoria herself joined Evelyn on board the SS *Catalonia* to say her personal goodbyes. *The Times* reported that Wood was, 'easily recognisable by [his] numerous decorations'[9], and, indeed, Evelyn's vanity was becoming something of a trademark. It was rumoured that he even wore his decorations on his pyjamas![10] Although this last tale was no doubt fanciful, there is evidence that he did place a small black border around each of his many ribbons so that the contrast would make them stand out more, and perhaps also add to the length of the rows on his chest. On one occasion, Wolseley could not resist chaffing Evelyn over the use of the black border and he shouted, 'Hullo! Evelyn you seem to have got some more medals lately. Where did you get them? From the Mahdi [his forces were besieging Khartoum]?'[11] It appears that Wood conveniently used his renowned deafness to pretend not to hear Wolseley's comment, and the moment passed.

On arriving in Alexandria on 15 August, Evelyn's vanity must have taken a severe dent when he discovered that he was to remain with the 2nd Brigade, 2nd Division to guard the lines around Alexandria, and act as a diversionary force for the movements of Wolseley's army. This main British force was to advance on Cairo, via the Sweetwater Canal, from Ismailia. Wood was particularly upset that Major-General Graham, who was junior to him, was to accompany Wolseley with the 1st Brigade. Graham would later see action at the battles of Magfar, Kassassin and Tel-el-Kebir, which must have further angered the ambitious Wood. Wolseley sold his decision to Evelyn by explaining that he needed someone in charge of the forces around Alexandria on whom he could depend; he also stressed to Wood the importance of his role in maintaining a vital supply line and, if need be, an escape route. However, there can be little doubt that for Graham to be given precedence in field command over Wood was a slight to the latter. Whether this was a deliberate act on Wolseley's part, or an unconscious one, is open to debate, but the animosity that Wolseley showed towards Evelyn during the later attempts to rescue Gordon, and the clear disgust Sir Garnet expressed at Wood's handling of the events following Majuba, suggest that Wolseley's decision may have been motivated by bitterness.

Evelyn was later to express to Queen Victoria how 'aggrieved' he was that he had been overlooked and that Graham had been favoured.[12] Yet even the monarch could not influence Wolseley's decisions in Egypt, and Evelyn found consolation in work and a little pleasure. On 14 September he was the guest of honour at a dinner hosted by the Khedive[13], and two weeks later *The Times* reported that he was suffering from sunstroke as a result of a sightseeing trip to the Pyramids.[14] However, Wood's time was not spent simply in the pursuit of pleasure, as there was some serious soldiering to do. Evelyn was now under the direct command of the Divisional General, Lieutenant-General Sir Edward Hamley, who ordered him to lead a reconnaissance with two battalions towards the enemy's lines at Kafr Dowar on 19 August. During this action, the Egyptians directed several artillery shells at the parading British and Colonel Maurice, who wrote the official history of the campaign, incorrectly stated that one infantryman was killed.[15] It was left to Evelyn in his autobiography to clarify that the lone casualty suffered no more than slight burns when an Egyptian shell landed between his legs and the upward explosion, which was reduced by the sand, threw the soldier into the air, resulting in his only loss being all the clothing, including underwear, from his back. Evelyn recorded that the infantryman was in more pain from embarrassment than from his wounds![16]

Evelyn also experienced a near miss when leading another reconnaissance a few days later. Once again the Egyptian artillery opened fire and Wood was in advance of the British forces with his staff officers. One shell landed nearby and failed to explode. Evelyn claimed this as a souvenir and took it back to England. However, another did explode just forty yards in front of Wood and his party. In a letter to Queen Victoria, which was accompanied by a sketch of the incident, Evelyn stated that fortunately the shell landed in mud and the force of the explosion, 'merely covered those near it with mud and debris.'[17] Following instructions from Wolseley, Hamley continued to harass the enemy positions at Kafr-Dowar in an attempt to convince the Egyptians that this was to be the direction of the main British attack. On both 20 and 21 August Evelyn was involved in demonstrations against the enemy lines, which were met by a heavy concentration of artillery and rocket fire and led to the deployment of the Egyptian troops. Having achieved their objective the British fell back, and the enemy loudly claimed that they had been victorious. It was only in the following year that the captured rebel leader, Arabi Pasha, admitted that he had no idea that Wolseley had already taken the majority of his force towards Ismailia and that he firmly believed that these British demonstrations were a prelude to a major attack, forcing him to maintain 15,000 troops in the area throughout the campaign.[18]

With the deception complete, Wolseley now planned his final push towards the Egyptian forces at Tel-el-Kebir and on 26 August ordered Hamley to join him with four battalions. Wolseley instructed Hamley that Wood was to remain outside Alexandria with three battalions to maintain the deceit. Once again, Evelyn was to remain largely inactive and, greatly disappointed, he expressed his feelings to the Queen's Private Secretary, Ponsonby, in early September: 'We are as you may suppose wretched at this enforced inaction and fearful lest Sir G. Wolseley may strike his blow ere we arrive. Tis all the harder on me as I am senior to Graham and should have had the 2nd Brigade.'[19] Wolseley himself is said to have stated that the absence of Wood and his men was a 'sad weakening' of his own force, but that he dared not leave Alexandria unprotected.[20] Wolseley wrote to Wood on 5 September, in an obvious attempt to reassure his old comrade, 'You being detained at Alexandria is a sad blow to me, and I know it will be to you.'[21]

As Wolseley advanced towards Tel-el Kebir, he encountered enemy opposition at Magfar and Kassassin, and Arabi Pasha was finally forced to weaken his troop concentration facing Wood at Kafr Dowar. Evelyn had not been idle and, despite Hamley taking all the cavalry reconnaissance troops with him, he instructed Smith-Dorrien to cobble together a mounted force. Smith-Dorrien was one of the few survivors of the British defeat of Isandlwana and a future World War One General. The force he created had its origins in the Khedive's own stables, and within a day he had a complement of cavalry thirty strong, although many of the men had little riding experience. They were to be extremely useful in impeding the enemy's own reconnaissance, as well as supplying Wood with the news that the Egyptians were now especially weak in the area surrounding Mandora. Never one to miss an opportunity, Evelyn conveyed this information to Wolseley and asked his permission to lead an attack on the enemy there. This was briskly denied by Wolseley: 'You must act on the defensive and risk nothing until after my action, when I may be in a position to let you act, but make no forward movement without orders from me.'[22]

It seems likely that Wolseley did not want anything to disrupt his own plans, and Evelyn's sideshow attack might have been a risk that Wolseley was not prepared to take. Wood was left in Alexandria to 'eat his heart out'[23], and there is no doubt that he felt aggrieved and abandoned by Wolseley. The final battle of the campaign, at Tel-el-Kebir, took place on 13 September and the crushing British victory, which effectively ended the war, was masterfully planned by

Wolseley. Yet, for all his success, Wolseley was to write to Anna Steele, Wood's sister, of his worries and anxieties during the night-time advance on the Egyptian position and of his desire that Evelyn could have been with him.

Wolseley was to write in an open and candid fashion to Anna that Evelyn's absence, 'was just the drop wanting in the bowl to make the contents perfect. I [Wood] missed for other reasons which I shall not put on paper, but which I will when we meet. I am sure Evelyn feels his absence from Tel-el-Kebir as keenly as I felt it that night, but he feels it in a different way; he feels like a man thrown out, that he has lost the best run of the season; but my feelings were more personal, and they made me a little anxious. In the early morning before daylight I was out with Redvers Buller reconnoitring the enemy's position, and when returning to camp I poured into his ears my sorrow and anxiety occasioned by the retention of Wood's brigade at Alexandria.'[24] Within two years, Wolseley would privately write of his contempt for his old friend as once again they soldiered together in Egypt. Several years would pass before Wolseley's true feelings towards Wood were made known and they would clearly indicate that Wolseley's words to Anna Steele had been nothing more than lies.

The battle won, the war over, there remained little for Evelyn to do but to accept the surrender of the remaining Egyptian forces outside Alexandria and to attend numerous victory dinners and parades. Despite his clear disappointment at the role he had played in the campaign he threw himself into these last tasks with his usual energy. *The Times* correspondent described how he accompanied Evelyn in the days following Wolseley's victory: 'At an hour which Sir Evelyn Wood's energetic aide-de-camp calls morning, but other people call the dead of the night, I was again permitted to accompany him to the lines of our amiable enemy. The object of his mission was to bring in Yakoob Pasha Sani and a Bey who had arrived from Cairo, who desired to surrender themselves.'[25] Such a story seems typical of Evelyn's routine throughout his army career, for he was renowned for his early-morning starts and he expected that his staff officers would also make themselves available at an early hour. Although there is no doubt that Wood was a demanding taskmaster, who was always frank in his views, he did possess a delightful sense of humour and a 'kindness and chivalry that were unique'[26] and which earned the respect and loyalty of both his officers and men, whether in India, South Africa or the trying environment of Egypt. The relative inactivity of his command during the summer of 1882 must, surely, have tried both his humour and temper, yet he was able to maintain the morale of his men by his usual display of energy and hard work.

By the time of the British victory parade in Cairo, the strain and frustration was beginning to take a toll on Evelyn's health. *The Times* commented on this and also reflected on the important role that Wood and his men had played during the campaign: 'Next [in the parade] came Sir Evelyn Wood looking thin and worn, with, perhaps, the least conspicuous, but not the least trying part of the campaign.'[27] On 18 October Wood returned to England, where he was expected to resume his command at Chatham. Little could he have realised that he was destined to return to Egypt within two months to take up the challenge of creating a new, modern, Egyptian Army.

Before Evelyn could face this new Egyptian challenge he had once again to ask the Queen to intercede on his behalf, when he discovered that, although he was to receive the thanks of both Houses of Parliament for his contribution to the recent campaign, he would not be rewarded with any decoration or medal. Wolseley wrote to Wood to thank him for 'the energy and gallantry with which you have executed the services you have been called upon to perform,'[28] but it seems that because the War Office were under the impression that Evelyn had not been under fire, he was not entitled to any Egyptian decoration. Apparently, with Evelyn's encouragement, Victoria instructed her private secretary, Ponsonby, to write to the Secretary for War to express her concern at this apparent oversight. Ponsonby wrote that the omission of medals for Evelyn and his staff was considered by them as an implication that 'they were wanting in their duty'[29], and the Queen pointed out that Wood and his staff had been under artillery fire, as Evelyn had outlined in his earlier letter to her. This correspondence had the desired result and Evelyn and his staff officers were awarded the Egyptian Medjidie medal, although he must have been perturbed to discover that his rival, Major-General Graham, had received the additional honour of having a clasp added to his award.[30]

Intriguingly, just two weeks before officially receiving the offer of command of the newly established Egyptian army, Evelyn was approached by the Liberal Chief Whip, Lord Grosvenor, to consider a career in politics. Writing on 13 November, Grosvenor asked Evelyn, 'Has it ever entered into your mind to have a seat in the House of Commons? If you are the least anxious for that honour I think that there is a very fair opening at Preston just now'.[31] Grosvenor stated that the local party had already been approached to see if they would consider a 'good Liberal Egyptian General' and that the feedback had been positive. The Chief Whip followed up his letter with a further note to Evelyn on 14 November, which expressed the hope that Wood would meet him in the lobby of the House of Commons, 'on most important and immediate business.'[32] There remains no record of

Evelyn's response to Grosvenor's political overtures, but it is clear that he was not enticed and that he remained committed to an army career. It is perhaps surprising that the ruling Liberal Party considered it possible to approach a serving British General with such an offer and that Grosvenor had the confidence in Evelyn's political loyalties to approach him in the first place. It is fair to say that the majority of senior serving Army officers, such as Buller and Wolseley, would have had more sympathy with the views of the Tory party and Evelyn's Liberal sympathies would have been in the minority amongst his army contemporaries.

There remains some ambiguity as to who recommended Evelyn for the position of head, or Sirdar, of the re-commissioned Egyptian Army, which had been disbanded after the battle of Tel-el-Kebir. The most likely candidate was Wolseley, although it has recently been suggested that Gordon first mentioned Evelyn as a suitable candidate to Lord Granville.[33] Whether Wolseley, aware of Wood's tireless energy, attention to detail and skill in training men, considered Evelyn best suited to the role, or whether he saw the position as an opportunity to sideline Wood is not clear, but future events suggest that it could have been the latter. The British Government saw an urgent need to develop an Egyptian army along British lines with British officers, not only to ensure that Egypt did not fall into anarchy, but also to make provision against the army being used as an instrument by a future nationalist movement. The pressing need to reduce the number of British troops stationed in Egypt was also an important financial and logistical concern.

Evelyn first received an offer of the Egyptian post in a letter from Lord Granville in late November 1882. Granville resorted to flattery to attract Wood by stating, 'It is most important to get the best possible man to be the first of the English officers in the Egyptian service. Everything depends upon it.'[34] This approach worked, and after numerous telegrams between Wood and Lord Dufferin, High Commissioner in Cairo, over the likely salary for the position, Evelyn finally negotiated twice what Dufferin had initially offered. Despite this, it seems Wood was far from enthusiastic over his new role. On 2 December he had an audience with the Queen, in which he told her that he was not particularly happy to accept the post, but that he would do so for two years. He also expressed an awareness of the many difficulties he would likely face.

With his eyes clearly open to his new challenge, Evelyn once again sailed for Egypt, arriving just before Christmas 1882. Although it was apparent that both the British High Commissioner and the Khedive were pleased with Wood's appointment, Lord Grenfell, who served as a Major in the new force, clearly thought otherwise. He was later to write in his memoirs that he was doubtful, 'whether Evelyn Wood was the best officer who could have been selected at this time as Sirdar of the Egyptian Army, as his strong military instincts caused him to despise the Orientals whose Army he was commencing to reorganise.'[35] Although Grenfell's opinion cannot be discounted, for he was to serve alongside Wood for a number of years, his claim does not seem to be supported by other sources. Indeed, as will be shown, Evelyn apparently displayed a great deal of patience in the training of the new force, and although he was quick to discipline and remove officers and men who failed, for whatever reason, to live up to his high standards, there is no additional evidence that his actions were prompted by any racist beliefs or any consideration that the Egyptians were inferior. He was, however, always realistic as to their limitations as a fighting force.

Evelyn spent his first week in Cairo in conferences with the Khedive, Lord Dufferin and Sir Auckland Colvin, the British Government's financial adviser to the Egyptian Government. From these various meetings Wood emerged with a free hand to train and equip a 6,000-strong Egyptian army, provided he did not spend more than £200,000. This sum was to include the salaries of twenty-five British officers, who were to be the backbone for the training of this force. Wood was to be dependent on the help and support of the Duke of Cambridge who, from the War Office in London, supplied Evelyn with the names of likely officer candidates. Wood set extremely high standards for his new officer corps: every successful applicant had to have an impeccable military record which displayed high standards of both horsemanship and musketry. Evelyn placed a great emphasis on linguistic ability. Every officer had to be capable of carrying on official correspondence in French and all had to pass an exam in colloquial Arabic. Such high demands were rewarded with far better pay than could be expected at home and all officers stepped up in rank, with none holding a rank lower than Major. Leave was generous and with rapid transport links between Cairo and London an officer could be back in England within a matter of days, which was of great appeal to those officers based in India, who had to spend much of their leave allocation travelling between the subcontinent and home.

In his memoirs Grenfell did admit that the officers Evelyn collected were of 'the very best,'[36] and there is no doubt that the initial success in recreating the Egyptian Army owed as much to the hard work and dedication of his officers as to Wood's own drive and determination. Thirteen of Wood's officers would later rise to the rank of at least Major-General in the British Army, and many, such as Lord Kitchener,

Smith-Dorrien and Sir Archibald Hunter would become the more enlightened leaders of men in future conflicts. These facts clearly support Grenfell's claim that Evelyn's officers were of a particularly high standard. The Khedive insisted that the British officers wore a fez and a resplendent uniform, with gold buttons embossed with the crescent and star. Evelyn himself declined the fez, but instead adopted traditional Bedouin headgear, with a circlet of black goat wool and gold thread to keep it in position, thus again displaying his tendency to theatrical vanity.[37]

Within two weeks of his return to Egypt, Wood was accepting recruits into his new Army. Under firm but fair management they speedily showed an aptitude for barrack yard drill and bayonet exercise. However, the difficulties Evelyn experienced in the Ashanti campaign, when he had attempted to instructed his men in the skills of musketry, were repeated in Egypt. Major Wingate, recalled that the use of the rifle, 'the manner of holding it, the use of the sight, the importance of the trigger, were but constantly recurring novelties to them [the recruits] for a long period. When it came to intricate calculations as to the allowance necessary for a side wind, the question was summarily decided by the officer in command moving his firing party six yards up wind!'[38] Overall, however, Evelyn was pleasantly surprised by the progress of his new army. Towards the end of January Wood wrote to the Duke of Cambridge that his Egyptian officers had tried to convince him that, 'a Recruit won't learn unless he is thrashed but so far as we can judge they are entirely wrong, and the Egyptian is very attentive and quick in learning.'[39] Similarly, when writing to the Queen in February 1883 he was able to report that, 'Sir Evelyn has never seen any men learn drill so quickly – Recruits caught only 28 days ago are now drilling their newer comrades better than the English officers.'[40]

Despite this promising start, Evelyn was to experience some difficulties with his men, particularly the Egyptian officers. Again writing to Cambridge, Wood reported that he 'had to punish another Egyptian officer for thrashing two non-commissioned officers on parade – unfortunately the officer was one of our best and speaks English well.'[41] Later in the year Evelyn informed the Duke that he had been forced to dismiss about twenty-five of the most inefficient Egyptian officers and stated that these men had 'clung desperately to the Service being as useless for other work as they are for our business.'[42] Discipline among his Egyptian officers was to be a recurring problem throughout the year as Evelyn tried to impose his own high standards upon them. As late as December 1883 Wood was still being forced to remove senior Egyptian officers. He described to Cambridge how one

Colonel had been proved to have pulled the ears of a Captain on parade and had ordered him to brush a private soldier's boots.[43] Evelyn was even forced to dismiss one of his English officers who had not paid his tailor's bill and was found to have 'pecuniary troubles.'[44]

However, for all these problems the recruits progressed so well under the stewardship of Wood that he felt confident enough, at the end of March, to parade them in front of Lord Dufferin and the Khedive. Although Evelyn admitted that the cavalry in the parade 'were not fit to do more than "keep the ground",' he was able to show eight battalions and four batteries after just six weeks' instruction. He recorded that they, 'marched past in the stereotyped Aldershot fashion'.[45] Wood wrote candidly to the Queen that, 'The soldiers none of whom joined before the 10th of February, and some since the 1st of March marched past in a manner which astonished everyone but none perhaps more than Sir Evelyn himself!'[46] When Lord Dufferin ended his spell as High Commissioner, to be replaced by Sir Evelyn Baring in May 1883, he wrote to Wood to express his thanks to the Sirdar for all his efforts in developing the new Egyptian force. Dufferin went on to say:

> I am sure it will be a satisfaction to you to know that the success of your efforts is recognised by everyone, by the Khedive, by his Ministers, and by the Egyptian colony, as well as by Her Majesty's Government. The justice, the humanity, and the consideration with which you have treated your men have already changed the point of view from which the Native regards Military service, and all your countrymen are proud to think of the effect your character and conduct have produced upon all who have come into contact with you.[47]

One of Evelyn's biggest difficulties was attempting to train men in a multi-lingual country, such as Egypt was at this time, as well as providing suitable translations of both the drill book and the code for military court-martial from English into Arabic. British officers were forced to speak French to Egyptian officers and Arabic to the ranks. Words of command were given in Turkish. Adding to this confusion was the fact that only one British officer, Lieutenant Mantle, had sufficient linguistic skill to attempt translations into Arabic. Wood was forced to seek assistance from his Egyptian aide-de-camp, Colonel Bey, who spoke only French and Arabic, and he instructed Bey to translate the British Army Court Martial Oath into Arabic. After some delay Bey produced a somewhat comical translation which Evelyn described to the Duke of Cambridge as: 'an elaborate affair epitomising all the

171

denominations in our communion service – when it was translated back again for my information I thought it was too late to change it, so I let it go.'[48]

On the eve of his return to England on leave in July 1883, Wood was able to report to the Khedive, with some satisfaction, of the progress the Army had made. He wrote that his duty had been, 'one of the most pleasing nature for the progress made far exceeds my expectations.' He was able to confirm that the cavalry had rapidly improved and would be fully trained by December, and the artillery by October. Evelyn expressed his delight at the advancement of the two infantry brigades and concluded that all the English officers had, 'worked with zeal and perseverance, which I have never seen equalled in 30 years service.'[49] This happy state was soon to be shattered by an outbreak of cholera in Cairo.

Just twenty-four hours after leaving Cairo, for his return to London, Evelyn's ship was intercepted by a special launch sent for him, and he was brought the sad news that cholera had broken out amongst his men. The horrors of this disease were especially real to him after his experiences in the Crimea. Evelyn must have returned to Cairo with dread in his heart at what he would find there. Fortunately, the number of cases amongst the Army were not as high as at first feared, although the disease did take a heavy toll on the civilian population. Both the Khedive and his Ministers fled Cairo for Alexandria, and Wood, Sir Edward Malet and Valentine Baker virtually ran the country in their absence and were thus free and able to take the harsh measures necessary to control the disease.

The care of those Egyptian troops that did succumb to cholera was left, primarily, to Evelyn and his English officers, as neither the senior Egyptian officers nor the Egyptian medical staff would approach the Army hospital. Not only did the British officers nurse the stricken patients day and night, performing all menial duties, but they even washed the corpses of the unfortunates prior to their burial. Such devotion to their men won the praise of Sir Edward Malet, who stated that Wood and his officers had given an example of selfless devotion, 'which may have lasting consequences for good on the promotion of the respect and regard of the men towards the officers.'[50] When the outbreak had died out in August Evelyn resumed his two months leave and returned to England.

Whilst on leave, Evelyn visited the Queen at Balmoral who expressed great interest in his work with the Egyptian Army. Wood also visited Lord Granville, the Foreign Secretary, and there is little doubt that the worsening situation in the Sudan and the future role of the Egyptian force would have been high on their list for discussion. The

172

Gladstone Government had adopted a policy of non-intervention in the affairs of Sudan, but this was all to change as the military success of the Mahdi and his forces became a real threat to the security of Egypt proper.

In the spring of 1881, Mohamed Ahmed, who had a local reputation as a *faqir*, or holy man, sent emissaries to all provincial Governors and tribal heads throughout Muslim Sudan announcing that he was the Mahdi, or chosen one, who would guide his people along the right religious path. Initially, the Egyptian Governor of the Sudan underestimated the Mahdi's following and, when a force was sent to apprehend him, his loyal supporters heavily defeated the Egyptian troops. From this victory, and by appealing to religious fanaticism, the Mahdi recruited a large and committed army, which was able to defy Egyptian authority, and the Mahdi defeated two Egyptian armies that were sent to quash him. The events of 1882 in which the British intervened directly in Egyptian affairs, and defeated and disbanded its army, effectively meant that the Sudan, technically under Egyptian rule, was left to its own devices. The Mahdi used this opportunity to recruit tribal leaders from north and south of Khartoum and the revolt spread ever closer to the Egyptian border proper.

After Wolseley's crushing victory at Tel-al-Kebir the Khedive was restored to power by the British. However, Lord Dufferin, Sir Edward Malet, and later Sir Evelyn Wood as Sirdar, had enormous powers to influence and run the country. Thus a British response to the growing crisis in the Sudan had to be considered. Sir Charles Wilson, Military Adviser to the British Agency in Egypt, turned his attention to the Sudanese question and it was he who first suggested that Gordon should be reappointed as Governor-General and sent to Khartoum; but by November 1882 the British Government was of the opinion that the crisis had been exaggerated and the matter was dropped.

By the time Evelyn Wood was beginning his work of recreating an Egyptian Army, the Egyptian Government was calling upon Britain to supply British officers to lead its remaining forces in the Sudan. Whilst the British Government objected to the secondment of serving officers, it had no objection to the employment of British officers from the retirement list to serve in the Sudan. To this end, Colonel Hicks, an ex-Indian Army officer, was employed by the Egyptians and left for the Sudan. Although Hicks gained some initial victories against the Mahdist forces, this failed to stop the spread of the rebellion. Eventually, after months of toiling in the deserts, Hicks's army of 10,000 were overwhelmed by the 70,000 strong Mahdist army at the battle of Kasghil on 5 November 1883. The death of Hicks caused a sensation in London and the Government was unable to convince the British public that it was not a British force that had been defeated. There was a general call for revenge and an expectation that the Gladstone Government would have to intervene.

By the time the news of Hicks's defeat reached Cairo, Wood had returned from leave and was once again busily trying to transform his 6,000 new recruits. The defeat of Hicks now made the British Government's policy of trying to disassociate itself from events in the Sudan impracticable, and naturally it turned for advice to the newly appointed British Agent in Egypt, Sir Evelyn Baring, who in turn approached Wood. Both men considered that it was no longer possible to hold the city of Khartoum from the advancing Mahdist army, and the evacuation of the garrison and the civilians there would be extremely difficult, if not impossible. It is clear that Wood believed Gordon to be the only man who might actually be able to effect the evacuation and settle the situation in the Sudan. As early as the first week of December 1883, Wood wrote to the Queen stating that Her Majesty should read *Colonel Gordon in Central Africa, 1874–79*, by G. Birkbeck, so as to obtain an understanding of what Gordon might possibly achieve by returning to the Sudan. Wood went on to say, 'Sir Evelyn has never met Gordon – but after allowing for all his peculiar views about religion, Sir Evelyn believes his account of Egyptian caused misery in the Sudan is accurate, and that he is the only man who could do anything up there at this moment without a good army.'[51]

It appears that Wood had used his friendly correspondence with the Queen to try to convince her that Gordon was the immediate solution to the Sudan crisis. He must have considered that the monarch was then likely to try to use her influence on her Government to approach Gordon. There is no direct evidence that the Queen tried to press for Gordon's appointment, but it is clear from later letters between Wood and Victoria that Evelyn had at least convinced the Queen of Gordon's desirability.

In early December 1883 Evelyn secretly dispatched Colonel Fraser, Adjutant-General of the Egyptian Army, to Upper Egypt to report on the likely defence requirements in the event of the Mahdi and his forces moving on Egypt proper. In a letter to Baring, Wood outlined Fraser's findings and his own recommendations as to the required defence arrangements if the Sudan was to be abandoned. Wood stated, 'it will be necessary for strategical and political reasons to garrison Apouau, and later to push forward posts for observations to Korosko and possibly Wadi Halfa, this should, if feasible, be done before the intention of leaving Khartoum is made known.' Evelyn went further by firmly stating that he did not believe his own Egyptian Army was yet ready to face the Mahdists in battle and that, 'The Field Force mentioned should, I think, be composed of British Troops ... and the reserve at the capital, should, in my opinion, be composed of British Troops.'[52] It seems clear that Evelyn did not yet have sufficient faith in his own Egyptian troops to employ them to garrison Cairo, let alone be part of a Field Force on the border with Sudan. Wood ensured that a copy of this report was sent to the Duke of Cambridge in London.

For all his outward show of confidence in the abilities of his new Egyptian Army, it is clear that in private Evelyn was far from confident and must have secretly feared that they would not distinguish themselves if pitched into battle with the Mahdi's forces. In a frank letter to the Duke of Cambridge, in December 1883, Wood admitted, 'these four battalions are as good as Egyptians can be made in ten months and I think will stand up well until their English officers are knocked down, when they would become sheep. I regard the other four battalions as practically useless for Field work.'[53] Yet, within a few months, Evelyn was actively campaigning for the inclusion of his Egyptian troops in the force sent to relieve Khartoum from the Mahdi's men.

Talk in London was still focused on the need to decide whether to attempt an evacuation of Khartoum. If this was considered necessary, the immense logistical difficulties would be compounded by the fact that the likely escape path was across the Suakin-Berber desert. All discussion foundered on the British Government's firm position that it would not authorise the use of British or Indian troops, despite the calls of Baring and Wood from Cairo and Wolseley in London, who felt that troops should be sent to reinforce and hold Khartoum. Charles Gordon's name came more and more to the fore as a possible solution to the problem, and he himself made his own case for being sent to Khartoum in a celebrated interview he gave to the *Pall Mall Gazette* of 9 January 1884, in which he firmly stated the impracticability of evacuating Khartoum and the need for it to be held at all cost. Gordon stated that it would be possible for, 'a man whose word was truth to come to terms with Sudan'[54], and implicit in the newspaper interview was the suggestion that he was the man for the job. Although the interview did provoke an enormous amount of public agitation for Gordon to be sent, it was probable that the Government was tempted to send Gordon because by handing the problem to him the Government was extricating itself from an awkward situation.

After several days of discussion between Gordon, the Cabinet and Wolseley, it was finally agreed on 18 January that Gordon would be dispatched to the Sudan. For various reasons, including the need for haste, the reluctance of the Government to face up to the dangerousness of the situation, and Gordon's own limited understanding of the actual mission, the task given to Gordon was rather unclear. Whilst he was instructed to brief the Government as to the seriousness of the situation on the ground, the need to prepare for an evacuation of Khartoum was also impressed upon him, as was the firm certainty that he would not receive any British military assistance. An agreement reached, the London Press gleefully announced that Gordon would soon be leaving for Egypt.

Wood was initially pleased to hear of Gordon's pending arrival. In a letter to the Duke of Cambridge he stated, 'We are very pleased Gordon is on his way. I thought it my duty to offer to go up to Khartoum, but neither I nor any other man could do what Gordon can.'[55] In a similar vein, Evelyn also wrote to the Queen. 'Sir Evelyn is delighted to learn that Chinese Gordon is coming ... Gordon is a man of heroic frame – one in a thousand, and it will be a happy day for Egypt if he reaches Khartoum in time.' However, Wood did express some concern as to the appointment, which later events would prove to be somewhat prophetic: 'the only anxiety now is to get him to start and keep in the same mind e.g. to carry out a settled policy, whatever it may be. His best friends cannot deny that he often changes his opinions, but nevertheless the state of the Sudan is so bad that Gordon's coming must improve matters.'[56]

Gordon telegraphed to Sir Evelyn Baring that he had no intention of going to Cairo on his arrival in Egypt, but was keen to travel straight to Khartoum via the Suakin-Berber desert route. On Gordon's arrival at Port Said, Wood was dispatched by Baring to meet Gordon and inform him that his proposed route was now impracticable; he was to per-suade him to go first to Cairo to see Baring and the Khedive, and from there travel to Khartoum via the Nile. On boarding Gordon's steamer, Wood was greeted by its captain, who wagered that Evelyn would be unable to persuade Gordon to alter his travel plans. However, using his immense charm and skill at flattery, Wood was able to entice Gordon to Cairo and so won his bet with the ship's captain. Gordon spent just a few days in Cairo, during which he stayed with Evelyn and Lady Wood. Wood, Gordon and Baring held numerous confer-ences in an attempt to clarify Gordon's mission, although his instruc-tions were given in the broadest terms and were centred on the need for the evacuation of the Egyptian garrisons and personnel from the Sudan.

During this brief time, Evelyn was to see at first-hand Gordon's tendency to rapidly change his mind and alter his position, as well as to experience his temper. Before arriving in Egypt, Gordon had tele-graphed Baring and requested that a former slave-trader, Zobeir Pasha, with whom Gordon had various encounters whilst previously serving in the Sudan, should be exiled. Gordon feared if Zobeir was allowed to remain in Cairo he would plot against him and prejudice his mission. On meeting Zobeir in Cairo, Gordon claimed that he had experienced a 'mystic feeling', which led him to believe that Zobeir should now accompany him to Khartoum. Baring and Wood were naturally shocked at such a change of heart and both combined to block Zobeir's appointment. Matters came to a head on the night of Gordon's farewell dinner, before his departure to Khartoum, which Evelyn hosted. On hearing of Wood's involvement in resisting Zobeir's employment, Gordon refused to eat at the same table as Evelyn and dined in his room alone. It was announced to the arriving guests that Gordon had suddenly been taken ill.[57]

Gordon's erratic behaviour continued the next day, as he departed on his mission. On leaving Wood's residence, Gordon gave his evening coat to Walkinshaw, Evelyn's devoted valet and bugler, claiming, rather fatalistically, that he would never have cause to wear it again. However, within a month of arriving in Khartoum, Gordon was to write, 'There is no chance of any danger being now incurred in Khartoum – a place as safe as Kensington Park.'[58] Finally, as his carriage was about to depart, Gordon shouted out that he had packed neither soap nor towels and Lady Wood had to fling these items from her bedroom window as Gordon left for the train station on the first part of his final journey to Khartoum.[59]

The early good opinion Wood had had of Gordon was clearly shattered by the few days Gordon spent under his roof and by Gordon's later decision not to attempt an evacuation of Khartoum. However, at the end of January 1885 Evelyn wrote, rather diplomatically, to the Duke of Cambridge that Gordon's presence had been, 'a great help, and if any one man can effect the safe withdrawal of the Khartoum garrison, it is Gordon Pacha.'[60] Gordon's subsequent decisions no doubt angered and frustrated Wood, for he was to write to his physician and friend, Dr Norman Moore, that he was, 'now devoured by anxiety to go to Khartoum to extricate that chivalrous (but uncertain) hero Gordon.'[61]

The situation worsened in Egypt in February, when a force of 3,500 Egyptian Gendarmerie, under the command of the Englishman Valentine Baker, were defeated by Mahdist supporters near the Red Sea port of Suakin. The British Government finally reacted, having decided that the Red Sea coast area was too strategically important to remain in rebel hands. Evelyn's expectations that he, and perhaps some of his Egyptian army, would be involved in this operations were soon crushed when it was announced that the force was to be led by his old rival, Major-General Sir Gerald Graham, with Evelyn's old comrade and number two, Sir Redvers Buller in command of an Infantry Brigade. To add insult to injury, Evelyn was compelled to hand over some of his own cavalry horses and camels to Graham's command. One of Wood's staff officers, Wingate, wrote that, 'Nothing could be more crushing to the Egyptian Army ... The General [Wood] feels the insult very much: it is harder on him than many of us, for he has worked might and main to do all in his power.'[62]

Hard-fought British victories at El Teb and Tamai restored the region to British/Egyptian control, but clearly demonstrated that any British advance on Khartoum would be bloody and difficult. By May, matters in Sudan had worsened. The fall of Berber in this month to Mahdist forces, as part of their campaign northwards up the Nile, effectively cut off Khartoum from the outside world. Gordon's position began to look perilous indeed and it seemed, given the political authority from Gladstone's Government, that British troops would be forced to march to the relief of Khartoum.

Months before the fall of Berber, plans were being considered as to the best way to relieve Khartoum, if the situation required it. Wood had been at the centre of planning in Egypt. He was in regular correspondence with the Duke of Cambridge, in which he stressed the need for British troops to work alongside his own Egyptian forces in any relief operation.[63] In London, Wolseley was doing his utmost to make the British Government aware of the growing crisis and was actively working on his own proposal to send a British relief force via the Nile. This route was opposed by Evelyn and General Sir Frederick Stephenson, commander of the British army of occupation in Cairo, mainly because of the potential difficulties of sending men and supplies through the six cataracts along the way. Both men favoured the Suakin-Berber option, although this plan would require the laying of a railway line, at great expense. The various arguments and discussions became known as the 'Battle of the Routes.' Government procrastination and the fall of Berber to the Mahdi effectively ended the debate; the Nile route was now the only choice.

In June 1884 Wolseley wrote to Evelyn of his plans for the relief of Khartoum and stated that he hoped to use 2,000 men of Wood's Egyptian army along the lines of communication. Wolseley also raised the issue of whether the Khedive would spare Evelyn if Wolseley was to call upon his services. Although Wolseley thought the Khedive might resist such an appointment as, 'you [Wood] are virtually his military advisor and his Minister for War,' he also expressed the hope that, 'if a large expedition is sent to Khartoum I hope your services could be lent for a few months.'[64] Evelyn would have been delighted to receive such news and must have been relieved that his old patron had not forgotten him; he now began to plan how he could extricate himself from the Egyptian army.

At the end of August the British Government finally approved the dispatch of a relief expedition under the command of Wolseley. Although Evelyn must have been delighted that his friend and patron would now be in a position to use his services, Wolseley himself confided his contempt for Wood to his private journal. On 22 August, Wolseley wrote that Wood was, 'the vainest but by no means the ablest of men ... he has a depth of cunning that I could not have believed it possible for any brave man – such as he most undoubtedly is – to possess.'[65]

As the two men spent time together on the campaign, Wolseley's feelings towards Wood, as expressed in his journal, became more virulent. Writing on 5 October, Wolseley recorded, 'Wood's vanity and self seeking and belittlement of everyone but himself would be positively disgusting if one did not view it from the ridiculous side, and laugh at it and him instead of being angry over it. He is now anxious to make everyone believe that [General] Earle is a fool and an old woman, this because he, Wood, is the junior and therefore Earle being in his way, must be got rid of. When I look back and remember my estimate of Wood's character as it was presented to me ten years ago ... I begin to think I can be no judge of character, for Wood's cunning completely took me in ... All this ridiculous Egyptian Army has been worked by him for purposes of self-glorification.'[66]

There is no doubt that Evelyn was vain, but Wolseley's claims that he was cunning and manipulative are only the opinion of one man, whereas much testimony survives from Evelyn's subordinates that he was supportive and loyal towards them and their careers. This patronage by Evelyn could, of course, be considered to be a form of reflected glory, for, if his protégés advanced within the army, Evelyn would maintain his own influence and prestige. This seems to have been the case with Kitchener, Haig and Smith-Dorrien in later years. However, some of the true reason behind Wolseley's outbursts can perhaps be found in his journal of 26 January 1885, when he wrote, 'I am sure it is wrong, but whenever I meet Evelyn Wood now he reminds me of the disgraceful peace he made with the Boers in 1881.'[67] When at a low point after the news of the fall of Khartoum, it appears that Wolseley considered his own resignation and again in his journal he reflected upon Evelyn's actions of 1881: 'Had I been Evelyn Wood I should have resigned everything, aye, even my commission in the Army, before I had consented to the arrangements with the Boers, which he carried out to prevent General Roberts from superseding him, but I have not yet been asked to do anything which I think is derogatory to England.'[68] Wolseley's opinion of Wood as a cunning man, ready to undermine his contemporaries for the sake of his own advancement, cannot be discounted, but the extent to which this was realistic needs to be considered alongside Wolseley's continued anger and resentment towards Wood over the peace terms he agreed with the Boers.

Whatever Wolseley thought of Evelyn, he must have known that he would have to use his services, and that of the Egyptian army, in some form. Wood's friendship with the Queen and his position as Sirdar made it impossible for Wolseley not to consider Evelyn for some role. As in the Egyptian campaign of 1882, in which Wood had been rather sidelined, Wolseley again found a less than glamorous position for him. On 6 September Wolseley wrote to Wood and offered him the position of 'General of the Lines of Communication', which would extend over 1,400 miles, and Wolseley used his knowledge of Evelyn's vanity to sell the role to him by stating that it would be, 'a most difficult, arduous, and responsible one, but its duties are those which I also know you could discharge with credit to yourself and great advantage to the public service.'[69] Evelyn could not resist such flattery and gratefully accepted.

Wood had in fact, on his own initiative, already been at Wadi Halfa, just above the Second Cataract on the Nile, for nearly a month, and had used the time to begin to collect stores, purchase camels and arrange some river transport. Again Evelyn's drive and determination ensured that the relief campaign got off to a good start. The use of men from the Egyptian army in the role of porters and the availability of Arabic-speaking British officers most certainly aided the expedition. What did not help was Wolseley's insistence that Canadian flat-bottomed boats and Canadian crews, rather than the local craft, should be used to negotiate the cataracts. This is not to say that Evelyn did not also make some errors. For example, against Wolseley's advice he purchased Egyptian camel equipment, saddles and bridles, which was soon discovered to be inferior to that which could have been bought from India. Also, Wood refused to pay the increasing prices for sound camels and instead bought inferior animals which could not cope with the demands placed upon them.[70]

There was also some criticism that Wood's personal baggage added to the delays of transporting the British force for it was said to contain ninety-six cases of stores, of which forty contained wines of various types including champagnes.[71] However, there is no doubt that it was chiefly the existence of the cataracts which hampered the progress of the relief expedition. In December Wood wrote to the Queen and described the difficulties he was facing: 'Just where the sharp bends of the Nile occur, there are so many rocks, that it was found to be nearly impossible to back or pull the whalers up and they were therefore pulled out of the water and carried to avoid the bends – a distance of one and a half miles. The whalers have on the whole done fairly well, but the Nile is not suited to them, and the force of the current is so great in the shallow places that the boats give way when the crews struggle against the stream.'[72] Later in the month Evelyn informed the Queen that when the whalers approach a cataract, 'everything is taken out – 2½ tons in weight in each boat, and is carried on camels, on the heads of Egyptian soldiers, and Dongolese labourers for three miles.'[73]

The harsh conditions, combined with the need for haste, resulted in some disagreements between Evelyn and other officers as to the best means to make progress. On more than one occasion Wood had to assert his authority over the Naval officers in command of the various steamers attempting to negotiate the cataracts, as they feared for the safety of their vessels and were reluctant to risk the dangerous passages. Wood even clashed with his old friend, Buller. Their main dispute was over whether priority should be given to men or supplies on the river. In late September, Buller wrote to Wolseley: 'There is just at present a great difference of opinion between me and Wood. Wood … has made up his mind that we have not got enough supplies up to warrant him in getting up more troops, and I am of opinion that we have enough.'[74] This disagreement came to a head over a dinner at the end of October, where Buller who, according to Wolseley, 'had a little too much liquor on board,'[75] entered into a noisy altercation with Wood. This row must have had its funny moments as the drunken Buller, who had a lisp, shouted at the deaf Wood. It seems that the pressure of work had seriously affected Wood's health; he suffered badly from conjunctivitis and his hearing became worse than ever. Wolseley was to complain that any conversation with Evelyn had to be conducted at a roar.[76] The tiring and tense conditions in which all men were forced to work must have tried the patience of many.

As the weeks progressed, and the level of the Nile fell, it became clear to Wolseley that Khartoum would not be reached in time via the river. He thus decided to send a force of camels and infantry across the desert from Korti to Metemmeh, where it was reported steamers were available to transport the force to Khartoum. This plan was not without risk, as the British contingent would be heavily outnumbered and vulnerable to the harsh desert climate, but such a detour would avoid two of the cataracts. Evelyn was again to be frustrated as command of the force was given to Sir Herbert Stewart, who set out from Korti on 8 January. The Dervishes, as the Mahdi's followers were known, had of course observed Wolseley's slow advance and had ample warning of Stewart's dash across the desert. As a result, the British met stubborn resistance, and at the battle of Abu Klea (17 January 1885) the British square was broken and over seventy troops killed. Although the battle ended in a crushing British victory, the Dervishes failed to disperse and continued to harass Stewart's men; on 19 January, just outside Metemmeh, Stewart was mortally wounded in another engagement. When news of Abu Klea reached Wood, he wrote rather dejectedly to Victoria that, 'soldiers should be happy in doing their duty whether it is fighting or providing and forwarding supplies but Sir Evelyn must admit feeling somewhat envious of his more fortunate comrades who were at Abu Klea.'[77]

With Stewart's death, command fell to Sir Charles Wilson, the Intelligence Officer of the column, and it was he who, after more skirmishes and much hardship, managed to make contact with the four steamers Gordon had sent from Khartoum. Wilson then took a small party of troops with him on board two of the steamers and arrived off Khartoum on 28 January, only to find that the city had fallen to the Mahdists on 26 January. It was left to Wilson to return with the devastating news that, despite all the efforts of Wood, Wolseley, Buller and all in the relief expedition, Gordon was dead.

Before news of the fall of Khartoum, Evelyn had already been considering his position as Sirdar and, by October 1884, he had decided to resign in early 1885. He wrote in bitter terms to Victoria, informing her of his decision: 'Sir Evelyn ... intends to retire from the Khedivial service as soon as he can after Christmas ... Sir Evelyn hopes to leave and forget Egypt, where he has been assigned an unsatisfactory role for two years.'[78] Undoubtedly, Wood felt that he had done as much as he could to create a modern Egyptian army and he must have been annoyed and frustrated at the use of so many of his men in the role of mere porters in the expedition. Likewise, he was upset at continued interference by the British Government, particularly by Lord Northbrook, in limiting the size of the Egyptian army. However, he was probably most annoyed that, by holding the position of Sirdar he had been prevented from taking command of British forces in their liberation of the Suakin region from the Mahdi's supporters, and thus had again missed front-line service in Egypt.

Wolseley sent Buller to ensure that the desert force that had reached Metemmeh could be safely brought back to Korti. To Evelyn's delight, Wolseley appointed him as his Chief of Staff to replace Buller. When news of Gordon's death was received Wolseley dispatched Evelyn to Metemmeh to consult with Buller as to whether the British troops should be withdrawn. Wood was in terrible pain from an injury to one

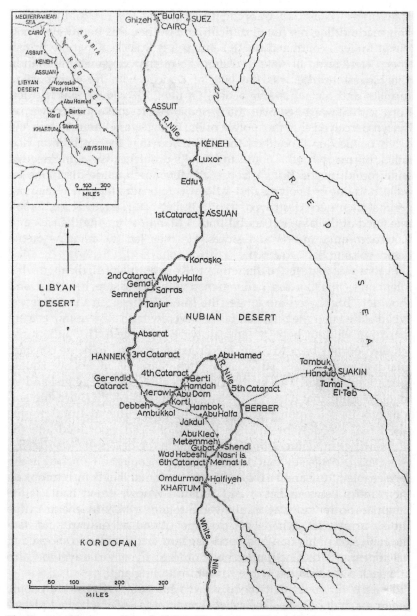

The Route to Khartoum. From *In Relief of Gordon: Lord Wolseley's Campaign Journal of the Khartoum Relief Expedition*, ed. Adrian Preston (reprinted by permission of The Random House Group Ltd).

of his fingers, caused by trapping it between the legs of a fold-up chair. This made riding his camel difficult, but despite this handicap Wood joined Buller's command on 18 February. It was clear that the British troops were in no fit state to resume an offensive against the Mahdi. The biggest hurdle was the lack of camels, both for transporting supplies and for aggressive action. Of the 2,200 camels that had left Korti with Stewart just over thirty remained. To make matters worse, Evelyn perceived that the morale of the troops was extremely low; the death of Gordon, and thus the realisation that the expedition had failed, hit many hard. To add to Wood's problems, the abundance of wine found by the British troops at Metemmeh made discipline an issue, and one of Evelyn's first tasks was to ensure that the remaining wine stocks were destroyed. While Buller returned to Korti, Wood remained at the base in Gakdul until 3 March, removing the sick and wounded, ammunition and stores. He then led the remains of the desert column back to Korti.

Evelyn was to describe the return to Korti as, 'painful; the men who, intent on saving Gordon, had marched with elastic step, heads up, and shoulders back, were no longer the same soldiers.' In their defence, Wood stated that the men had been, 'severely tried ... two-thirds were marching without boots,'[79] and all were exhausted. Throughout the ten-day journey back to Korti, the British forces had to be on constant guard against enemy attack and often marched in hollow square formation. Evelyn was everywhere, encouraging stragglers and at night ensuring that the sentries remained awake. All this hardship and toil took its toll upon his body and he now suffered from chronic diarrhoea, probably brought on by lack of sleep, poor food and the huge swings in temperature experienced in the desert. By May 1885 it was clear to Wolseley that no new offensive could be launched in the foreseeable future and he offered Evelyn command of British troops on the frontier between Egypt and Sudan. By now, Wood had left the Egyptian army and was fulfilling the role of a Major-General in the British army. Yet, when Wolseley met Wood at Assuan, and saw the condition of his thin body and haggard face, he was so shocked at his appearance that he immediately ordered Evelyn to travel to Cairo and seek a medical discharge for return to England.

There is no doubt that Wood viewed his time in Egypt with some bitterness. Not only had the relief expedition, in which he had played an important role, failed, but he felt that his time and energy spent reforming the Egyptian army had not been recognised in London. In addition, he had not seen the front-line service which he craved. The private hostility that Wolseley felt for Wood no doubt hindered his appointments in both 1882 and 1884. Furthermore, at the end of his period in Egypt, Evelyn returned to England still a Major-General and he was to see no official recognition, in terms of honours or appointments, for his services. Yet, in retrospect, his time spent as Sirdar stood him in good stead for the next role he was to play within the British army; that of reformer and trainer of men, in which he was to show great inherent ability.

Chapter Ten

A Skeleton in the Cupboard

Evelyn returned to England still suffering the effects of ill health. This time he was not met with a hero's welcome, but returned rather unnoticed to army life. The remainder of his career was now to be spent in England and it was here that his talent for the training, motivation and management of men, and his questioning mind, really came to the fore. Indeed, Wood's 1892 biographer and friend, Charles Williams, claimed his work in the area of army reform was to have more far-reaching and longer lasting effects, 'than any he achieved in the field'.[1] He was also soon to be at the very heart of a family scandal, which would see him appear at the High Court in one of the most sensational divorce cases of the nineteenth century.

Although it is possible to list many of Evelyn's admirable characteristics, such as his renowned bravery and his ability to motivate and train men, his approach to paperwork cannot be considered one of his best features. Whilst in charge of the Lines of Communication along the Nile, he was under the watchful and critical eye of Wolseley. In this role, Wolseley described him as, 'dear puzzle-head Evelyn Wood,' and expressed, in his journal, the wish that he had appointed General Earle to this job rather than Wood.[2] Wolseley even wrote to Buller to express his frustration at Evelyn's lack of personal organization when serving under him on the Nile. Wolseley complained: 'Wood never shows any of the telegrams or letters he receives to anyone – but generally stuffs them into his pocket and apparently drops them down the "rear", for many can never be found.'[3] Whether Evelyn was aware of this failing is not known, but he at least had the sense to surround himself with more than competent aides who took some of the administrative burden off his shoulders and thus allowed him time to consider the issues of army reform.

Within a few months of his return from Egypt, Evelyn was invited to join a House of Commons Committee to draw up 'Regulations for the Organisation of the Lines of Communications for an Army in the

Field'. One of the many lessons learnt from the two Egyptian campaigns was that the Supply Department had been ill prepared and, as a result, extra costs and delays had been caused to procurement. Wood was a natural choice for the committee, for not only had he seen at first hand the effects of supply failings on the Nile expedition, but he was also close to Wolseley and Buller and was thus able to approach both men for their input. The findings of the committee were thought to be a success and Evelyn's work on it can be considered his first practical step in army reform. Wolseley's attitude towards Wood seems to have been mollified and, rather than trying to secure placements in which Evelyn might have been marginalised, he actively sought positions in which his talent for training could be best used. It was in his role as Adjutant-General that Wolseley helped secure for Evelyn the command of the Eastern District, based at Colchester, Essex. However, despite his interest in reform, Wood was still in search of active field service and even sought Wolseley's help to obtain a role during the Second Burmese War at the end of 1885. He wrote to Wolseley, 'I imagine all who go will be sent from India, but if any one goes from England I hope you will remember me. I am now as fit as ever I was ... I would gladly go anywhere for a fight.'[4]

Both Wolseley and Wood were to be disappointed; indeed neither was to be called upon again to serve abroad on active service. Wolseley would rise to become Commander-in-Chief, replacing the elderly Duke of Cambridge in 1895. He was renowned for his attempts at army reform, in which he was often at loggerheads with Cambridge, and he naturally wished for allies and supporters in important positions to help and influence the cause of reform. Whilst Wolseley may have disapproved completely of Evelyn's peace with the Boers, which clearly caused him to resent his fellow General, and though he may have thought Evelyn a 'little too flighty'[5] for independent command, he clearly recognised that he had a talent for reform and training. Furthermore, Wolseley needed all the support he could get in his attempts at army reform and was therefore keen to promote Evelyn's claims and initiatives. As the years of Home Service went by, and the two comrades supported each other's reforms, there seems little doubt that the friendship Wolseley once felt for Evelyn did return, and Wood's feelings of respect for Wolseley remained strong.

Evelyn arrived at his new command in Colchester in April 1886 with his head full of ideas, and he wasted no time in implementing his thoughts on training. Amazingly, the British Army had never undertaken any formal instruction on night-time manoeuvres, and this was to be Wood's first challenge. He concentrated initially on training officers and sergeants in the skills of night-time map reading and compass navigation and, once this group had acquired sufficient ability, he let them loose on the men. In a series of exercises from August 1886, the Eastern District gained proficiency in night-time operations, and Evelyn drew up procedures for such operations which were later adopted across the Army. He next turned his attention to long-distance rides by cavalry troops, by both day and night, so that the men acquired the necessary ability to navigate across wide areas, as they would have to do in the field. This method with the cavalry was also later adopted by the Army as a whole, although he did encounter severe opposition from the Duke of Cambridge, who claimed that night work interfered with horses' rest![6]

Perhaps Wood's greatest asset was his ability to question existing procedures, and this gave his men the confidence to use their own initiative and likewise question the current systems in place. Evelyn loathed waste, in whatever form. One of his pet projects was to reduce the numbers of sentries, and time spent on sentry duty, across the British Army. When he assumed command at Colchester, he discovered on his first day that a sentry was detailed to be outside his office. He dismissed the man, stating that he did not require a sentry, but found, much to his annoyance, that he returned on the two subsequent days, on the grounds that a sentry had always been posted outside the commander's office. It took his staff three days before they seriously encountered Wood's temper, but from that day on the sentry did not reappear. Likewise, when on a tour of the camp hospital, Evelyn discovered a sentry standing outside the prisoners' ward. He soon ascertained that there were no prisoners receiving treatment and that in fact this ward had last had an inmate three months before!

It was by first removing such petty regulations that Evelyn gained the support and confidence of his men, and it is clear they responded. For example, on night exercises the artillerymen, without instruction, covered the wheels of their gun carriages with straw to deaden any noise they might make. Naturally, Evelyn was delighted to see such initiative. Wolseley was to write to Wood that he fully supported the reforms at Colchester and, in particular, Evelyn's efforts to raise the tone of the 'Rank and File' by trusting them.[7]

Evelyn also possessed a keen business brain. He discovered that the canteen at Colchester hardly made a profit and, from October 1886, set about trying to improve both the fare and the amenities. Wood turned to the men for inspiration and even involved them in the choice of beer. He encouraged the men to help choose the decor and fittings of the bar and the area was soon transformed into a 'respectable music saloon, allowing free choice of music ... with armchairs and marble-topped tables.' The result was a dramatic increase in profits, from £340 in 1885 to £1,540 in 1887. Once again, the improvements that he had initiated, both in the canteen food and the facilities for recreation, were drawn up by Wood into 'Canteen Regulations' and were adopted across the British Army.[8]

Wolseley seems to have fully realised and appreciated Wood's dedication to reform, for he ensured that Evelyn was placed on numerous War Office Committees looking at reform of all kinds. One of the most important concerned the decision to replace the infantry rifle, and here the crucial choice was whether to adopt one with a permanent or detachable magazine, with both Wolseley and Wood favouring the latter. Although, Wood's voice was the only one on the committee which favoured the detachable option, his fervent argument eventually won enough of the committee over so that the detachable magazine was adopted. Wood now entered a period in which his opinion was readily sought on all areas of change within the Army. His training as a barrister was no doubt of benefit when he was directed to rewrite the sections on 'Outpost Duties' and 'Musketry Fire Tactics' in the Field Exercise Manual. In addition, he was asked to draft instructions for the resupply of ammunition to infantry engaged with the enemy. In August 1887 he was appointed president of a committee to look at ways to provide suitable ranges for the Volunteer Corps, and this was to begin an association with the volunteer movement which was to continue until his death. All this work was in addition to his role as Commander of the Eastern District and meant that Wood's working day would often begin at 4.00 am.[9]

Evelyn was asked to report on the new Drill Book, which had formed the subject of numerous heated discussions between Wolseley and what Wood described as the 'Old School', who favoured rather antiquated drill movements. Although Evelyn saw himself as something of an arbiter between the two camps on many issues, he still felt he had to express his opinion forcefully. He wrote to Cambridge in August 1887, 'I hope ... we may recognise now, all our Drill is for the more ready destruction of our enemies, with a minimum loss to ourselves, and that we prescribe formations accordingly.'[10]

In the space of just two years Evelyn had transformed the Eastern Command. Even the Duke of Cambridge had to admit, after an inspection, that the troops' general appearance and efficiency were, 'all that could be desired', and Wolseley was to write to Evelyn that, 'Yours is our model District in every respect'.[11] After such a success, it was natural that Evelyn should be considered for the vacant position of commander at Aldershot. This post was one of the top appointments available in England in peacetime, for Aldershot was the Army's main training centre. For Wood there was the extra incentive that the post carried with it the local rank of Lieutenant-General. However, Evelyn was to encounter some severe opposition to his appointment.

Writing in August 1888 to Lady Wood, Wolseley could not hide his eagerness that Evelyn should get the Aldershot command: 'As soon as it was settled that Alison was to be given the India Command, I at once urged Evelyn's appointment to Aldershot as really the only fit man for it ... I told the Queen last Monday when she spoke to me about Alison's successor that Evelyn was out and away the best man for the post. I look upon the matter as so certain that if I was a betting man I would lay ten to one on it. I cannot tell you anything more definite, but I think you may regard the matter as settled'.[12] Wolseley's certainty was misplaced as there was strong opposition to Wood's appointment from the Duke of Cambridge; even the Queen had her own favoured candidate, her third son, Prince Arthur, Duke of Connaught. However, with memories of the controversy that had been caused when the Queen had appointed her cousin Cambridge as Commander-in-Chief back in 1856, the suggestion of another royal appointment was soon dropped. Evelyn was no doubt aware of the opposition, for he wrote to his friend Dr Norman Moore, 'There is a fierce struggle going on about my going to Aldershot – Lord Wolseley is urging it hotley, HRH [Cambridge] wants to reserve it for some one in his declining years instead of using it as a Training ground for Generals!'[13]

Cambridge's opposition to Evelyn's candidature was very real and in November 1888 the lobbying for Wood's appointment became frantic. Wolseley approached the Queen and the Secretary of State for War, Edward Stanhope, to try to obtain their support for his candidate. In a letter to Victoria's Private Secretary, Ponsonby, Wolseley wrote: 'I hope Evelyn Wood may get Aldershot. We want a really good military schoolmaster there, who has had plenty of war experience and who is well read in all the most recent works at home and abroad on the practice of war.'[14] By the end of the month it seems that the decision had been made in Evelyn's favour, for the Queen wrote to Stanhope to say that she, 'has a high opinion of Sir E. Wood and trusts that his relocation will justify the recommendations which have been put forward on his behalf.'[15] While this does not imply that Victoria had been actively supporting Evelyn's candidature, it does seem to confirm that Evelyn had received much lobbying on his behalf. The following day, Arthur Bigge, one of Evelyn's former aides in South Africa and now one of the Queen's secretaries, wrote to Ponsonby that Wood felt somewhat aggrieved that Victoria had not given him more support in trying to obtain the Aldershot post. Bigge went on to say, 'Of course I did not discuss the matter except to say that the Queen could not act in opposition to the Duke who Wood knows is dead against him. This he quite saw.'[16]

Once the news of Evelyn's appointment became generally known, Bigge again wrote to Ponsonby, and his letter touched on some of the reasons behind the Duke's original opposition to Evelyn, as well as stating that the Queen had perhaps been rather more supportive of Wood than indicated earlier. It appears that Wood's personality, his vanity and even the perceived poor housekeeping of his wife had all damaged his chances. It has even been argued that Wood was successful because the wife of Evelyn's principal rival, John Ross, had even greater shortcomings than Lady Wood.[17] Bigge wrote: 'Wood would, I know, be gratified to feel that the Queen had stood by him so much as you say she has done in this struggle. Of course, poor fellow, he doesn't realise that the personal objections are so admitted even by Wolseley and those who are supposed to be his friends but who recognise his merits as a soldier. With the Duke and Prince of Wales against him he ought if he gets the appointment to be careful how he plays his cards at Aldershot.'[18] With his appointment confirmed in early December,[19] Wood looked forward to beginning his new job at Aldershot in the New Year, unaware of how close he had been to missing out on the sought after post.

Surprisingly, one factor that did not seem to affect Evelyn's appointment was the existence of a pending lawsuit between members of his family and his youngest sister Kitty, who on her marriage had become Mrs Kitty O'Shea. The dispute centred on the will of their wealthy, and now very elderly, Aunt Ben. For a number of years Kitty had lived near to her Aunt in Eltham, south London, in a house bought for her by Aunt Ben. The two had become very close and Aunt Ben called Kitty affectionately her 'Dear Swan'. Kitty would spend many hours with her Aunt as a companion and carer. Wood and his brothers and sisters watched the relationship between Aunt Ben and Kitty strengthen and began to fear for their own inheritances. Evelyn, like his mother and father, never had much success managing his own household budget, despite the fact that he was so deft when dealing with army finances. His large family, his love of fox-hunting, his expensive lifestyle and the need to support his eccentric sister, Anna Steele, all combined to make the importance of securing his inheritance even more crucial.

Anna was a particular worry for Evelyn, as her behaviour had grown more extreme. After the death of their mother, Anna remained alone at Rivenhall Place, the maintenance of which drained Evelyn's resources. Furthermore, Anna would buy old decrepit cab-horses and turn them out in the park attached to Rivenhall, where they would stay until they died. She became well known for paying large sums for worthless animals, and less than scrupulous individuals would travel from London to take advantage of her generosity. She also began to collect stray dogs and cats, and the numbers grew so large that Anna planned to purchase a Mediterranean island for her collection to live on. Evelyn managed to persuade Anna of the impracticality of such a plan.[20] Although Anna's behaviour must have concerned him, at least Evelyn knew that he would be able to count on her support for any action he might have to take against Kitty.

By the end of 1887, Evelyn, Anna and Charles Wood were becoming more and more concerned at the extent of Kitty's influence over Aunt Ben. They were aware that their Aunt had altered her will twice in favour of Kitty, each time leaving a larger share to their youngest sister. Furthermore, Kitty had become, in their eyes at least, something of an untrustworthy and sinister character, for she had begun a secret affair with the Irish Nationalist leader, Charles Stewart Parnell, whilst still giving the pretence to the world, and Aunt Ben, that she was happily married. The Woods probably also feared that Kitty had become dominated by Parnell and that he had his own designs upon Aunt Ben's fortune, perhaps to further the cause of Nationalism in Ireland. What attitude Evelyn took towards Kitty is uncertain; he makes no mention of her in his autobiography, nor does his biographer comment on the scandal and court cases. What is clear is that the Woods combined in an attempt to secure their inheritance and that Evelyn and his brother Charles led the campaign against Kitty, a campaign that was to become more and more ruthless in its prosecution and would eventually end in the High Court.

At the end of 1887, Evelyn, Charles and Anna embarked on a strategy to persuade Aunt Ben to change her will back to its original form, in which the surviving Wood children had equal shares. To do this, the Woods decided upon the tactic of trying subtly to blacken Kitty's character, but without resorting to outright attacks; there appears to be no evidence that they even hinted to Aunt Ben of Kitty's infidelity. It is, perhaps, surprising that the Woods considered they could attempt to dictate to their Aunt, and their tactics proved disastrous; their infuriated Aunt did indeed alter her will, but this time she left her entire estate of nearly £150,000, plus considerable property, to Kitty, completely cutting out Evelyn, Charles and Anna from their inheritance.[21]

The Woods closed ranks and decided on their next course of action. It appears that Evelyn now led the campaign, perhaps because his legal training made him the natural choice, and he suggested that there now remained two possible courses of action. They could wait until Aunt Ben died and then contest the will on the grounds that their Aunt had been unduly influenced by Kitty in drawing it up. However, this process could be a lengthy one and it seems clear that all wanted to get access to the fortune sooner rather than later. Alternatively, they could try to prove that Aunt Ben was of unsound mind; if this were established, she could be declared legally insane and the prospects of then having the will invalidated would be good. There is no doubt that Aunt Ben was rather eccentric, she also possessed a hard edge and Evelyn frequently felt the sharp side of her tongue. In her last years he acted as her almoner, for she donated large sums to charity and she often criticised his choice of beneficiaries. On one occasion she was particularly angry with Evelyn for he had given a sum to a hospice, which she considered a waste because the residents; 'do but cumber the earth and are useless.'[22] The Woods agreed to adopt Evelyn's second plan and they now entered into a callous proceeding from which none would emerge with any credit.

There has been some uncertainty as to how the Woods were able to secure sufficient medical documentation of Aunt Ben's supposed insanity, in order to present their petition to the Masters in Lunacy, the first stage in their attempts to get their Aunt declared insane. However, it would appear that it was Evelyn who orchestrated the collection of evidence. His doctor and friend, Dr Norman Moore, had been visiting Aunt Ben for a number of years in both a professional and private capacity. Moore frequently called on Aunt Ben for Sunday lunch and it is clear from the tone of letters between the two that Aunt Ben considered Moore a friend and trusted him. Evelyn seems to have used his friendship with the Doctor to persuade him to visit his Aunt and assemble the required evidence. That Moore was implicated can be established by the fact that in his private papers can be found letters between him and the Woods' lawyers, one of which indicates that, at the end of the case, material was returned to Moore with the thanks of the lawyers for his help.[23] There is no evidence to suggest that the Woods stopped for one moment to consider the effects of their actions upon their Aunt's well-being, and their Petition was duly presented to the Masters in Lunacy by Sir Evelyn Wood and Charles Page Wood Esq.

When notification of the Petition was served on Aunt Ben, Kitty naturally reacted with anger. She realized that if the Petition was not fought, her Aunt would be forced to leave her beloved home and would spend the rest of her days at best in some private home, or at worst in a lunatic asylum. Of course she also realized her own future fortune was now threatened and she turned to Parnell for support and advice. He too must have feared the loss of Kitty's inheritance and he approached the Prime Minister, William Gladstone, to obtain his assistance in putting pressure on his own doctor, Sir Andrew Clark, to produce a report on the state of Aunt Ben's mental health. After some persuasion, Clark eventually agreed to call on Aunt Ben at her home on 7 April 1888. Kitty and Parnell clearly hoped that with a favourable report from such an illustrious doctor as Clark, the Woods would be forced to withdraw their Petition.

It appears that Kitty managed to keep the fact that Evelyn and other members of the family were trying to get Aunt Ben certified away from her ailing Aunt, for prior to her death Aunt Ben was still sending money to Evelyn. Writing in 1902, Wood stated that his Aunt 'left rather over two millions sterling behind her. I am sorry to say I did not get much, but she sent me £1,000 just before she died as a little keep-sake – I am not so certain about the "keep" '. This correspondence does suggest that his Aunt was unaware of Evelyn's legal actions against her and that, even in 1902, he was still aggrieved at the amount he received from his Aunt's estate.[24]

Clark seemed somewhat reluctant to produce a report, and it was only after a personal plea from Parnell to Gladstone that the Prime Minister put sufficient pressure on Clark to deliver his findings. The fact that such a proud man as Parnell resorted to begging a favour from Gladstone serves to illustrate what was at stake for Kitty and Parnell. Clark's findings stated that he had found Aunt Ben to be 'attentive, capable of apprehension and reflection, to reply coherent and logical, free from illusions, delusions and hallucinations.'[25] In other words, Clark considered Aunt Ben to be sane. Even Clark's findings were not sufficient for the Woods to withdraw and the case was duly heard on 7 May 1888. Kitty, determined not to be beaten, again called upon Gladstone's help to acquire the services of a famous barrister, Sir Charles Russell. Whether good won over evil or whether the combination of Clark, Russell and Gladstone won the day is uncertain, but the Inquiry into Aunt Ben's alleged lunacy was dismissed. The Woods were now in a disastrous position.

There must have been a series of crisis meetings throughout the summer of 1888 between the Woods to discuss what their next course of action was to be. Evelyn would have known that legally they now had to wait until Aunt Ben's death before they could contest the will. However, he must have known that their position was not a strong one. Kitty had devoted over fourteen years of her life to the care of her Aunt, and the Woods had somewhat boxed themselves into a corner by failing in their attempts to have their Aunt declared insane; it would now appear that Aunt Ben was more than mentally competent when she altered her will to exclude all but Kitty. To contest the will, the Woods would therefore need strong evidence that Kitty had been an undesirable influence on their Aunt and for this they would need to blacken Kitty's character. Of course Kitty was very vulnerable because of her affair with Parnell, and now the Woods turned their attention to their younger sister's character. If it could be shown that she was the kind of woman to pursue an illicit affair, surely it would not take much effort to convince a probate judge that she was also the kind of woman who had exerted undue influence on a vulnerable old lady.

Whilst nothing could be done until Aunt Ben's death, the Woods must have felt that they at least had a trump card still to play. It was Evelyn who had first brought Captain William O'Shea into the Wood family in the early 1860s. Both men shared a passion for horses and Evelyn frequently invited O'Shea to stay at his brother-in-law's property at Belhus. It was here in 1862 that Kitty met her future husband, who Evelyn introduced as, 'the only man who sat properly over the fences at the Aldershot races'.[26] It appears that the marriage was a loveless one, and after O'Shea left the Army he was engaged in a number of failed business ventures, including one in Spain, which took him away from his wife for long periods. According to Kitty, her relationship with Parnell began in 1881[27] and it seems likely that O'Shea was aware of the affair from around 1884. There is little doubt that he himself engaged in numerous liaisons, although Kitty's later claim that her husband had had relations with her sister Anna seem preposterous. If the Woods were to use their trump card they would need the support of O'Shea and this was not, as yet, forthcoming.

It seems clear that O'Shea was initially happy to maintain the status quo. Not only was his wife, via Aunt Ben, financing his life style, but he had an interest in the expected legacy from the old lady's death. This was a strong motive to induce him to remain silent about the relations between his wife and Parnell. Furthermore, O'Shea had benefited from his association with Parnell, who had actively sought an Irish Parliamentary seat for O'Shea in Galway, at great personal cost to his own authority and credibility within the Nationalist move-ment.[28] Yet, on Aunt Ben's death in May 1889, O'Shea was to learn that his expecations had been in vain, for the will had been worded in such a manner that the money left to Kitty would be considered to be outside of the marriage settlement. O'Shea must have been frustrated and confused and he was now to take several months to consider his next course of action.

On Aunt Ben's death, the Woods predictably returned to the attack and contested the will, claiming that Kitty had exerted an unfair influ-ence over her Aunt. The inheritance was, therefore, tied up in probate until the matter was resolved and this seriously reduced Kitty's and thus her husband's own income. It took until Christmas 1889 for

O'Shea to decide to act. It has been argued that the delay can be explained by the fact that O'Shea was simply trying to establish which was to be his most profitable course of action.[29] Indeed, Kitty believed that O'Shea could have been paid off with £20,000, but with the will held up in probate she did not have access to that amount of money.[30] However, O'Shea's final choice was prompted as much by revenge and spitefulness as financial gain, and there is little doubt that the Woods were the catalyst for his action.

The Woods had, by their attempts to prove their Aunt's insanity, shown that they were prepared to stoop low in an effort to secure their inheritance. Indeed, William O'Shea stated in a letter to Joseph Chamberlain that, 'Evelyn Wood and the rest of Mrs O'Shea's relations would use any weapon to change her [Aunt Ben's] will.'[31] With Aunt Ben having ensured that O'Shea was not to share in his wife's inheritance, it seems that the Woods now put pressure on O'Shea to finally take action against his adulterous wife. The fact that the Woods were now contesting that will in the Court of Probate seems to have convinced O'Shea that his best course of action, if he wanted to secure a share of the inheritance, was to side with them. There can be little doubt that Evelyn, with his legal training, would have explained to O'Shea that the best tactic was to blacken his wife's name and the best way to do this was to divorce Kitty, citing her adultery with Parnell as the grounds for bringing the action.

O'Shea filed for divorce on Christmas Eve 1889; his hatred for Parnell and his own self-interest finally made him decide to accept Evelyn's advice. It was not until Saturday 15 November 1890 that the case was heard in Divorce Court Number One, the High Court, London. The proceedings became one of the most scandalous trials of the period and aroused intense public interest. Kitty denied the claims of her husband and presented a counter-petition against O'Shea and her sister, Anna Steele, on similar grounds of adultery. Thus the action appeared on the official list as 'O'Shea, K. O'Shea and Parnell (Steele intervening).' According to the *Pall Mall Gazette*, 'the approaches to the court and the corridors outside were crowded with persons anxious at least to catch a glimpse of the parties, if not to hear some portions of the evidence.'[32] The scenes were repeated on Monday 17 November, when the hearing continued. *Reynolds Newspaper* reported that, 'The Court was again crowded long before the proceedings commenced, and the same difficulty was experienced as on Saturday in obtaining seats, the accommodation being quite inadequate for those whose duty it was to be present.'[33] William O'Shea was of course present on both days. He was joined by his son, Gerald, who clearly supported his father against his mother. Evelyn Wood and Anna Steele made a last minute entrance into the Court on both days. Just why Evelyn felt he had to attend the proceedings is a mystery. He had no evidence to give; perhaps he was simply offering support to Anna, or he might have wished to revel in Kitty's discomfort and disgrace. Whatever his reasons for attending, his presence, and the absence of his brother Charles, do seem to confirm that he was the leading player in the Woods' attempts to secure their inheritance.

For those in Court, and for the newspaper readers of the day, the case provided juicy titbits of scandal to prove that Kitty and Parnell were indeed lovers. O'Shea's lawyer presented numerous witnesses, including a servant at Kitty's Eltham home, who testified that the pair had shared a bedroom, and staff from the Brighton house, which Kitty had rented so that she and Parnell could share some privacy. After two days of damming and scandalous evidence, Judge Butt asked the jury to consider whether adultery had been committed and stated, 'unless you are prepared, for some reason or other which I cannot imagine, to say that almost every one of the witnesses examined have been telling a false story, there can be no doubt as to the adultery.'[34] It took the jurors only one minute of deliberation to reach a verdict: both counts, including the counterclaim against Anna Steele, went against Kitty and Parnell. Custody of the two youngest children, one of which, at least, was Parnell's, went to O'Shea.[35]

O'Shea had his divorce and Kitty's reputation had been dragged through a scandalous court case. Kitty and Parnell were free to marry and they duly did in June 1891. Parnell's political career was severely damaged by the revelations, and his energetic attempts to rebuild his career undoubtedly took a toll upon his already poor health, resulting in his death on 6 October 1891, at the age of only forty-five. Despite all the consequences of the divorce case, the matter of the will remained unsettled. With the will still contested, Kitty had been unable to obtain any funds, and after the death of Parnell she was in a difficult financial position. She was finally forced to settle the dispute out of court in 1892, and the Woods obtained fifty per cent of the estate. Evelyn's share would have been in the region of £20,000. There is no record as to whether O'Shea received any money from Kitty or a pay-off from the Woods for his assistance, but the latter must be considered a real possibility. Anna Steele used her share to continue her life as a recluse and she surrounded herself with yet more animals, including a favourite monkey which she fed on anchovy paste sandwiches.[36]

There is no evidence that the scandal caused by the court case and the various attempts to contest the will hindered Evelyn's career. However, there does exist a letter that Evelyn wrote from Aldershot in October 1890 to the War Office, in which he states that: 'After careful consideration of my position I feel I ought not to be "considered" even for Bombay ... I have a lawsuit in progress which not only involves a large monetary stake but necessitates my presence in England.'[37] Thus the disputed inheritance did at least cause some obstacles to Evelyn's army career, if only in his own mind. When Evelyn's conduct is considered throughout the whole episode, it can be said that he acted in a determined and ruthless manner and that his actions, particularly with regard to his attempts to get Aunt Ben certified as insane, were heartless and callous. Whilst his vanity and ambition have been well illustrated, this darker side of his character might be considered surprising. Yet, in his defence, it is clear that he felt that he was being tricked out of his inheritance and he was thus forced to react aggressively. However, it was perhaps his love of money, and urgent need for it to maintain his high standard of living, that made him act as he did. Not one of the parties emerged from the legal tussle with much credit, but Evelyn emerged with less than most and thus it is somewhat surprising that his standing in the Army and with the Queen was not affected.

During the period 1887–92, in which Evelyn was heavily engaged in the legal tussle over Aunt Ben's will and his sister's divorce case, he was also at the forefront of army reform, both at Colchester and Aldershot. The demands of the various court hearings must have impinged upon the time and energy he could give to his career, yet it did not appear to be hampered by the additional pressures placed on him. Once in position at Aldershot, from January 1889, Evelyn continued to be the leading light in Army reform and he was now in the perfect place to realise some of his plans.

Wood had served many times at Aldershot and was fully aware of the camp's shortcomings in terms of facilities. By 1889, the old accommodation huts, which had been built in 1855, were wretched and Evelyn could vouch from his own experience that they were neither wind nor rain-proof. Furthermore, the annual expenditure needed just to keep the huts from collapsing amounted to several thousands of pounds, money which Evelyn considered to be wasted. With the assistance of the Secretary of State, Edward Stanhope, whom Evelyn seems to have considered a friend and ally, he presented his plans to transform the barracks at Aldershot. These included the reconstruction of the South Camp and the replacement of huts in the North Camp with brick-built units in Company-sized blocks. This latter suggestion, along with Evelyn's idea that each new barrack should be named to commemorate a British victory, encountered surprisingly severe opposition in the War Office from the Duke of Cambridge, and it was only with the support of both the Adjutant-General, Lord Wolseley, and Stanhope, that Wood's plans were approved.

Throughout his four years at Aldershot, Evelyn supervised the new construction, even going so far as to draw up the tenders and examine the quality of the bricks being used, and his work can still be seen today at Aldershot. The Military Museum can be found in 'Evelyn Wood Way' and it is housed in one of Wood's former brick barracks, although the vast majority of his buildings were replaced in the 1960s. The building programme was not confined just to accommodation, since Evelyn was also able to demonstrate his concern for the care of the sick by designing a new hospital at Aldershot. He had earlier shown his interest in this area when he had worked alongside Florence Nightingale in 1882. Now he was able to design and build a modern facility, and he turned to his friend, Dr Norman Moore, for help and advice. In August 1890 Wood was able to tell Moore of his plans to increase the number of available beds at Aldershot from 300 to over 1,000, and he asked Moore his opinion on such matters as the space between beds and the ventilation of the wards.[38] All this was yet another demonstration of Evelyn's forward thinking and of his concern for the welfare of the troops under his command.

Many of Evelyn's early reforms at Aldershot centred on the welfare of both troops and animals. Again, from his own previous experience of Aldershot, he was aware of the need to focus on improvements in the fare offered to the men, and he set about improving not only the quantity and quality of the food, but also the education of those who prepared it, via the Cookery School. Throughout his career, Evelyn endeavoured to read the latest thinking in any area of army reform, and this would frequently lead him to correspond with, or meet, those who were promoting specific improvements. To this end he invited Colonel Burnett, who had been working hard to improve the food offered to his own battalion, to Aldershot to lecture about food purchasing and economy. One of the brigades at Aldershot adopted many of Burnett's suggestions and became pioneers of the introduction of improved fare across the Army. Evelyn also focused on the supply and quality of forage and oats fed to the horses and ensured that, by purchasing further away from Aldershot, the costs were reduced and the quality improved, as the local suppliers had clearly been overcharging. Wood even arranged for cavalry officers to be taught how to judge the quality of different oats, so as to ensure that due economy was being exercised, and sent two men to the London Corn Exchange so that they could pass on the knowledge gained there to their brother officers.[39]

Evelyn continued to pursue at Aldershot his belief in the decentralisation of training, as well as his conviction that the quality of troops could be raised simply by trusting them. This went against two accepted beliefs at the time. The first was that instruction was the business of only the commanding officer of a battalion and the sergeant-major. Evelyn laid down that training at Aldershot should follow the model of the German Army, whereby it was the Captain of a company who was responsible not only for discipline but also for training. The men looked to their Captain for everything they required in the way of knowledge in how to conduct themselves in the field, and Wood ensured that the Captains were aware of their responsibility to their men. Secondly, Evelyn also departed from the received wisdom of contemporary military writers, whose dominant image of the soldier was that of a child who had to be led by the more mature and experienced.[40] Wood's ability to engage with all ranks and to show that he trusted their abilities, whilst still maintaining discipline, earned him an enormous amount of respect and affection from officers and men alike. However, it is in the matter of manoeuvres that Evelyn left his mark not only on Aldershot but on the Army as a whole.

Wood began his ambitious plans for field exercises on a small scale in 1890, when he utilised Government ground at Woolmer Forest for infantry work; later the same year he took six cavalry regiments to the west of Berkshire, where in a series of exercises he clearly demonstrated that large scale cavalry manoeuvres were very necessary. Although he was pleased that he had been able to mount these operations, Evelyn was determined to expand the manoeuvres so that all forces in the army, the infantry, cavalry and artillery, gained an understanding of how each functioned and how best all three could be utilised and coordinated so as to achieve battlefield success. He realized, long before the barrages of World War One, that artillery would frequently determine the fate of future battles and he prided himself on keeping up to date with current military thinking so as to aid his attempts at reform. He had been impressed by the writings of a young artillery officer, Edward May, who had produced a series of papers for the Royal Artillery Institution under the heading of 'Achievements of Field Artillery'. Evelyn was to begin a correspondence with May in which he admitted that May's views on the use of artillery had been a 'revelation' to him.[41] Eventually, Wood would ensure that May was present at all his future manoeuvres, as he began to build a team of bright, young, forward-thinking officers around him.

From the summer of 1890 Lady Wood's health began to give Evelyn some concern; she was frequently out of breath and spent long periods confined to bed. However, in early 1891, the Empress Eugenie, who had remained a good friend of the Woods ever since their pilgrimage to South Africa in 1880, persuaded Lady Wood to accompany her to

St Remo for a change of air. It appears that Evelyn was unaware of the gravity of his wife's state of health, for he admitted that he was ignorant of her condition until he received an urgent telegram from the Empress, which urged Evelyn to journey to the Riviera, for Paulina's heart was causing grave concern. The local doctor feared that Lady Wood would not survive the journey to Paris, let alone to Aldershot, but after a week's rest in the French capital, the party were able to continue home.

The couple did not have long together at Aldershot. Paulina's heart condition worsened, yet Evelyn's dedication to his Army life led him to leave his wife's side during her last week, when he surveyed an area around West Meon in Hampshire, which he was to use for field training in the August of 1891. Paulina finally passed away on 11 May 1891. The Woods had enjoyed twenty-four years of 'uninterrupted happiness' and he described her not only as an affectionate wife, but also as his adviser and confidential secretary.[42] From a letter Evelyn wrote to Norman Moore, it is clear that Wood was devastated by his wife's death: 'No doubt time will soften what now appears to be inconsolable grief. When in the saddle or in my office I experience merely a dull depressing sensation, but as I return to this house [Government House, Farnborough] the sense of loneliness is most painful. I had loved her since May 1861. For 24 years she had increased yearly in my estimations.'[43] Queen Victoria, writing in her journal, described Evelyn's 'great distress' and his 'terrible loss,'[44] yet Wood was able to throw himself into his work, to hide and relieve some of his grief. Within a day of the funeral, he was back at Aldershot to supervise the training of an Infantry Brigade, and, on the following day, the Cavalry. He was still working to revise the Drill Book, which frequently took him to London, and when at Aldershot he spent much time in the saddle, so as to avoid the loneliness of Government House.

It does seem clear that Paulina had been a great friend and adviser to her husband and there is little doubt that his renowned ambition came as much from his wife's prompting as from his own designs. There is no record as to whether Paulina had advised her husband during the dispute over Aunt Ben's will, but she was the daughter of a Viscount who would have expected a high standard of living, and it is inconceivable that Paulina would not have influenced Evelyn in his battle to obtain some of the inheritance. Evelyn was now left with the immediate issue of the care of his youngest daughter, Victoria, aged ten, and it is clear that he was forced to rely on a Governess, Miss Telford, as he threw himself more and more into his plans for training and reform. That is not to say that he was not close to Victoria; many letters survive between them which clearly illustrate their mutual love and friendship, and Evelyn was always ready to offer her his fatherly advice.

Evelyn now turned his attention to the large manoeuvres he planned for September 1891. The biggest hurdle to overcome was finding suitable land for the exercises, and the frustrations he experienced during his search made Evelyn into a firm advocate of the passing of a Manoeuvre Act, to give the power to the military authorities to take what ground they wanted for such purposes; he was to see some success in this regard later in the decade. In the meantime, Evelyn trawled the countryside of Berkshire and Hampshire trying to find a suitable tract of land. Finally, he found an area around West Meon in Hampshire which, after pacifying the local clergy, who initially opposed the idea of field exercises in their parishes, was consider fit for purpose, although rather small. This was to be the first time that infantry, cavalry and artillery had combined on a manoeuvre, and it was to be something of a revelation.

The fact that no large-scale manoeuvres had taken place before, in which all branches of the armed forces were actively engaged, was as much a factor of space as of lack of willingness to undertake such operations. However, it must be considered surprising that it was not until 1891, under Evelyn's initiative, that such an exercise was undertaken. In his official report to the War Office on the lessons learnt from the various exercises, Evelyn clearly outlined that the three arms had demonstrated a clear lack of understanding of each other. He reported: 'The failing most apparent is that of officers considering only the branch of the service to which they belong. Many officers have not sufficient confidence to give decided orders to the other arms of the service: thus officers of the same force were observed working in the immediate vicinity but independently of each other. Commanders of units neither asked for nor gave information to other units operating near them.'[45] On the plus side, Evelyn did remark that tactical skill had improved, but he chose to focus on the improvement in, 'military spirit, in eagerness to learn, and to submit cheerfully to great physical discomfort, is even more remarkable, and this spirit reacts naturally on the lower ranks.'[46] Progress had been made, but Evelyn surely realised he had a long way to go.

Wolseley had now accepted command of British forces in Ireland, from where he maintained his interest in army reform and kept in constant contact with Evelyn, who likewise was keen to inform Wolseley of all the reforms he was attempting. Wolseley also now introduced manoeuvres in Ireland and turned to Wood for his knowledge and experience, or what Wolseley was to describe as Wood's 'tips'. In October 1891 Wolseley went so far as to write to Evelyn to offer praise: 'No man has in my time effected more useful military work than you, and the Army is beginning to realise that as fully as I do.'[47] In February 1892 Wolseley again wrote to Wood to congratulate him on his syllabus for annual training, which he described as 'very good.'[48] Certainly, in some circles of the Army, Wood was now clearly viewed as an authority on reform.

His reputation was to be enhanced by the success of the 1892 manoeuvres. He was able to mount tactical training days for infantry, moving as flying columns on Government ground in the vicinity of Aldershot, as well as an operation for a Cavalry Division. What was also pleasing for Evelyn was the enthusiasm shown by the Auxiliary Forces. A Division of the 13th and 14th Militia Brigades joined an exercise in July, and in August 16,000 men from the Volunteer Corps joined regular troops for the largest manoeuvres yet held. Wood even found time to host an exercise for 600 young men from the Public School Volunteer Cadet Companies, who slept in two large marquees on the lawns of his residence at Government House. Lord Methuen, who took part in these summer exercises as Commander of the Home District, which included the Metropolitan Volunteers, wrote to Wood to express his delight at how well they had gone: 'You have given us the best five weeks soldiering we have ever had and your work must do us permanent good. I had no chance of saying goodbye and of thanking you from my heart for your kindness and instruction to the Guards and myself.'[49] Similarly, Evelyn must have been delighted to have received a letter from his old comrade, Arthur Bigge, which told him that, 'On all sides I hear praise of this year's manoeuvres. I was immensely gratified at reading a letter from Albert Williams to Gardiner in which he spoke in loud praise of your work at Aldershot.'[50]

Evelyn also received praise from General Sir George Higginson, who had spent a week at the manoeuvres in August. He wrote to Wood in early September: 'My recent opportunity of seeing your work has convinced me that the changes you and your colleagues have made are not only justified, but imperatively called for by the altered circumstances of modern welfare.'[51] Support came too from the Duke of Connaught, who particularly favoured Evelyn's approach of delegating control to section commanders or captains. However, not all were so full of praise and support for Wood's work. In response to some criticism of the summer manoeuvres from Lord Roberts, a future Commander-in Chief of the British Army, Wood felt obliged to say, 'I have not seen all your remarks. Those I did see disappointed me, touching on trivial points such as position of officers' gloves.'[52] Clearly, Evelyn still had to convince some of the senior ranks.

Certainly, in Evelyn's eyes the manoeuvres had been a great success. Not only had they been held for nearly £800 less than the authorised budget of £4,543, but Evelyn was able to report on real progress. He was delighted to inform Lord Roberts that, 'perhaps the most remarkable advance shown in 1892 has been the appreciation shown by all ranks of the tactical value of the arms of the service other than that to which they belong. The Ordnance and Supply and Transport branches worked with unfailing spirit and zeal.' Evelyn was also able to state that he had been, 'urging the study of artillery tactics on Cavalry and Infantry Officers for we find the importance of concentration of fire is not being recognised at brigade division.'[53] Wood soon decided that the manoeuvres of 1893 should focus strongly on the need to equip all arms of the services with a firm understanding of the capabilities of artillery on the battlefield, and he turned to Edward May and others for help and support.

Evelyn made a point, after each of his manoeuvres, of reflecting on and analysing the most common mistakes, so as to avoid their repetition. At the end of 1892 he received frank criticism from Colonel James Alleyne of the Royal Artillery as to some of the decisions he had made during the exercises in the use of artillery. As a result of this criticism, Evelyn decided to call upon Edward May to be his artillery adviser at the 1893 summer manoeuvres. Evelyn was able to gain the permission of the Earl of Craven to use downland between Swindon and the river Kennet. On this larger area Wood was able to hold useful manoeuvres for up to 15,000 troops. May was joined by other 'bright young things' at the manoeuvres: he and Major Frederick Wing reported for the artillery, Lysons supported the infantry, whilst Hew Fanshawe of the 19th Hussars, a future son-in-law to Wood, represented the cavalry. All these men would accompany Evelyn during the exercises, and May described how, 'Sir Evelyn rode very fast, no matter how hard the road might be, and it was as exhilarating as a day's hunting to leather along with him through the fresh morning air.'[54] May reported that Evelyn kept all these officers very busy; they would start off at 6.00 am and not return to Government House until late in the evening. Here, Wood would insist that each then write a criticism of the day's manoeuvres, which, wherever possible, should be illustrated with reference to specific military history.

May also wrote of occasions when the exercise had been a complete failure; for example, in one incident, a Colonel commanding a Brigade of Field Artillery was instructed to march his batteries out of Aldershot along three different routes and then re-assemble all three at a specific crossroads at noon. Only one battery reach the desired spot on time, one got completly lost, and the third, led by the Colonel, went astray when the Colonel was knocked insensible after falling from his horse. On 4 September 1893 May joined a camp at Idstone for another exercise, and here he was introduced to the likes of Lord Methuen, Smith-Dorrien, French (the future Lord Ypres), and many other officers who were later to hold senior commands in both the Boer war and on the Western Front. Although these men may have impressed, May recalls that the exercises themselves presented a colourful spectacle, as no khaki uniforms were worn. The troops were dressed in red and blue and, to distinguish the two sides, one side had to wear full-dress head-gear. May described how, 'Guardsmen and Fusiliers were to be seen skirmishing and endeavouring to hide themselves in red coats and huge busbies,'[55] and he went on to tell of the impressive sight of the Greys in red tunics and immense busbies charging a line of guns, reminiscent of Waterloo. Yet within a few years these colourfully dressed soldiers would be facing an unseen enemy on the South African veldt, where the shock tactics of the cavalry charge would be impossible to repeat.

Although it is perhaps now easy to ridicule Evelyn's efforts in holding such manoeuvres, they did serve a purpose greater than that of allowing men in red tunics to hide in bushes or charge guns wearing huge busbies. Wood himself, in describing the success of the 1893 exercises, focused on the fact that, 'such manoeuvres induce officers to study their profession more keenly than they otherwise would do.' Evelyn had turned Aldershot into the premier military training station and he continued to receive praise from many, including Wolseley. Support from Wolseley was again central to Evelyn gaining his next appointment, that of Quartermaster-General, in October 1893. On leaving Aldershot, Wolseley wrote to Wood, 'You have not only taught men a great deal, but have managed to popularise the acquisition of military knowledge.'[56]

Perhaps the highest praise that Evelyn was to receive was to be found in the pages of *The Times*, which commented that before Wood's arrival Aldershot had become 'somewhat stagnant.' The paper went on to claim that, 'Along with an impatience of pedantry and a habit of casting about for novel departures, the new chief brought to his work that infinite capacity for "taking pains" which is hardly distinguishable from genius. From the highest tactics to the humble details of catering and cookery, nothing escaped his vigilance.' In conclusion, *The Times* stated that Wood:

struck a blow – a mortal blow, we may be allowed to hope – at that system of interminable parades, which disgusted the soldier, filled up his time and squandered his energies. In compensation, field-training, which is, after all, the best substitute and preparation we can give the soldiers for his ultimate business of fighting the enemy, has been invested with actuality, and brought to a pitch of excellence hitherto unknown in the British Army in time of peace ... Sir Evelyn Wood will be remembered as the originator of the cavalry manoeuvres. What is still more important, he has taught the three arms to work together as they have never worked before ... To sum up, the intelligence and interest of all ranks have been spurred, and troops quartered at Aldershot are far in advance of others in field training. Aldershot has become what it ought to be, the exemplar to which all other camps of exercise look for light and leading. Sir Evelyn Wood has breathed into it a new spirit. It would not be too much to say that he has founded a new system.'[57]

Whilst Evelyn had succeeded in turning the name of Aldershot into a shining example of all that was best and brightest in military thinking, events during the Boer war were to suggest that the lessons learnt, and the experience gained, on the manoeuvres around Aldershot, were not always applicable on the field of battle. This is not to say that the reforms and innovations that he instituted at Aldershot were wasted, but they were not always more generally adopted across the Army as a whole. By his appointment as Quartermaster-General, Evelyn moved into the War Office in London, where he was to spend the remaining years of his career. It was during these years that Boer rifles were to roughly emphasise the general failings of British tactics and training and he, along with others, would be forced to explain why the senior Army hierarchy had allowed these failings to happen.

Chapter Eleven

The War Office, Army Reform &
Personal Survival

Evelyn was to enter the War Office with a reputation as *the* senior army officer who was dedicated to reform and the enhanced training of all ranks. He was to remain as Quartermaster-General for four years, in which position he was again able to demonstrate his ability as a cost-cutter; yet, at the same time, he was quite prepared to advocate significant expenditure if he felt that it would improve the welfare of the rank and file and, by doing so, attract new recruits. However, in retrospect, this appointment was probably not the best use of Wood's talents at this time. His appointment had been advocated by both Buller and Wolseley and criticism can be levelled at both these senior officers for it, as well as at Evelyn for accepting the position.

All should perhaps have realized that, although Wood had made a significant contribution to training and improvements in manoeuvres, his changes had been made from a very low base. Progress had been made, but there was still much work to do before Wood's reformist attitude spread throughout the Army. In these circumstances it can be argued that the Army as a whole might have benefited if Evelyn had remained at Aldershot for a few more years, where he could have continued to pursue his innovative approach and possibly widen thinking about the tactics required in future warfare.

It can be safely postulated that if Wood had remained at Aldershot there would have been more officers and men better prepared and better able to adapt to the challenges that future conflict would present. That men such as French, Smith-Dorrien and even Hamilton, who had all successfully passed through Aldershot under Evelyn's regime, became some of the more successful British commanders in the Boer war is testament to Wood's training skills and his ability to broaden military thinking. How other officers destined for South Africa might have benefited from a period at Aldershot under Evelyn Wood, can only be guessed at.

As Quartermaster-General Evelyn was responsibility for army transport, quarters, clothing and so on. In his first year he succeeded in visiting every barracks in the United Kingdom as well as a number of possible sites for future Artillery practice grounds. It seems that he did not like being stuck behind a desk for too long. His position allowed him to focus on the welfare of the rank and file and in this regard he introduced two changes that significantly improved their lot. The first was a complete overhaul of the means by which troops could travel to and from barracks, when going on and returning from leave, or on manoeuvres. Wood discovered that the Army used a combination of rail and coastal steamer, in an effort to reduce costs. He learnt of the farcical situation whereby 'parties both large and small were sent by sea and by land, even where it was possible to make the entire journey by rail, if the mixed journey was any cheaper than the direct route; thus, soldiers were sent from York by rail to Hull, then thence by sea to London, then by rail to Aldershot.'[1] In order to help the men, who often experienced great discomfort and long delays, Evelyn approached the various railway companies, and after some negotiation managed eventually to obtain an agreement that troops were able to purchase a return ticket for the cost of a single; this not only put some savings in the soldier's pocket, but also initiated reductions in the Army Estimates by removing the need for contracts with the coastal steamer companies, as well as saving on the cost of moving troops for army manoeuvres. Evelyn was then able to turn his attention to the condition of troopships and, much to Wolseley's delight, was able to send the oldest and least suitable to the breakers' yard, relying on commercial hire for future requirements.

Evelyn did not concentrate on savings alone and he would often press for increased expenditure if he saw that the troops would benefit by it. For example, he fought hard to ensure that all barracks had sufficient electric lighting. This was opposed by the Accountant-General on the grounds that the initial outlay would run to several thousands of pounds. Wood, from personal experience, impressed upon the Secretary of State, Lord Lansdowne, the fact that troops were expected to find their way to latrine blocks in the dark and stressed the inconvenience, rather than the convenience, this caused. Lansdowne enjoyed Evelyn's pun and sided with him for the necessary expenditure.

By 1895, after nearly forty years service as Commander-in-Chief of the British Army, the Duke of Cambridge's tenure of office was drawing to a close. Evelyn, in his new role at the War Office, was ideally placed to view all the intrigue and politics behind the appointment of a successor and he became something of a confidant to Wolseley, who was desperate to secure the ultimate Army prize.[2] After months of speculation, Wolseley was duly appointed to succeed Cambridge. The Secretary of State used the opportunity presented by Cambridge's departure to reduce the concentration of power at the War Office in the hands of the C-in-C. By the effect of an Order of Council there were now to be five senior military offices. Wolseley, as C-in-C, became chief adviser to the Government with general command of all the forces; the Adjutant-General was now responsible for recruiting, discipline, training and military education; the Quartermaster-General for food, forage, quartering, fuel, transport and pay; the Inspector-General of Fortifications for barracks, store-buildings, fortifications and lands; and finally, the Inspector-General of Ordnance for the design and the holding of military stores.

Wolseley's new function was to supervise the other four branches and to focus opinion, but the reality was that all five were responsible to the Secretary of State. Thus Wolseley felt that he had been given general responsibility with little effective control and he was to state that he was merely 'the fifth wheel of the coach.'[3] In theory, this meant that Evelyn was now in a stronger position with access to the Secretary of State, yet, after the Boer War, Wood was to argue that he alone could not approach the Secretary of State unless invited to by either the Secretary or the Commander-in-Chief and that in reality his access to his superiors was limited.[4]

Writing in his 1906 autobiography, Evelyn makes mention of his own attempts to make provision for a war with the Boers, which he had predicted as early as 1881. His assertions were clearly an attempt to deflect some of the criticism which had been directed towards the five senior army officers for the Army's apparent failings in South Africa. Wood claimed that as early as January 1896 he was giving serious thought to the provision of an additional Division, and a Brigade of Cavalry, for South Africa. He also stated that he attempted to secure transport contracts in South Africa for the swift mobilisation of troops and, when this was refused on grounds of economy, tried to secure a reserve of two months' supplies of food for the Ladysmith garrison, so concerned was he for their immobility. This was also refused by the Secretary of State. Similarly, he advocated the provision of Regimental transport for all units in South Africa to facilitate the carriage of ammunition, tents, baggage and two days' rations. This suggestion was likewise rejected, as was Evelyn's desire to fit out suitable vessels for the transportation of cavalry and mounted infantry horses to South Africa.[5]

It seems that Wood was battling against a culture, in both the War Office and the Government, which focused on the need for economy; at the same time, it does appear there was a reluctance to make any preparations for war in case this aggravated the Boers. There seems little doubt that Evelyn, with his unique knowledge of the Boer mentality gleaned in 1881, did press for such preparations, for perhaps he alone was convinced about the inevitability of war with the Boers. Yet this does not absolve him from the blame which was heaped on the Army Command for their unpreparedness for war. If he felt so strongly that such preparations should have been put in hand, it can be argued that he sould have been more vocal and more demanding, particularly of the Secretary of State; if need be, he might have considered his position and perhaps even resigned. However, he did not do so and consequently would have to answer his critics both during and after the conflict.

As Quartermaster-General, Evelyn maintained his interest in field exercises and continued to attend, if now not initiate and organize, them. In 1895 he attended a cavalry manoeuvre on Haywards Heath, in which John French played a prominent part. Here Wood was to meet one of French's staff officers, Captain Haig, the future Earl Haig and Commander of British forces on the Western Front in the First World War. Haig made a great impression on Evelyn and in later years both men were to benefit from their association and friendship. Also in 1895 Wood joined his old friend Buller in the directing of staff on the first manoeuvres based on the large-scale German system. Edward May, who played an important part in organising infantry attacks with artillery support during this particular exercise, described the manoeuvres as, 'the best means ever invented of teaching officers their duties in the field.'[6]

Yet, for all Evelyn's hard work in training and reform he was partly responsible for the material to be found in the last pre-Boer war Drill Book, which was issued in 1896. This version confirmed, 'the value of quarter-column formations, frontal attacks, and a virtual disdain for cover.'[7] Although it can be argued that Evelyn did not advocate such tactics, and that he can be applauded for supporting the kind of measures and thinking which would eventually secure victory in South Africa, again, perhaps, he can be criticised for not being more vocal in his condemnation of the old forms, which were to claim the lives of so many British soldiers in the opening months of the war.

Evelyn was rewarded in October 1897, when he received promotion to Adjutant-General. Whether he would have achieved this if he had been more vocal in his desire to prepare for the Boer War is now a matter of conjecture. What is clear is that, despite his commitment to change, he was still of the establishment and displayed almost a reverence towards men such as Wolseley and the Secretary of State, which seems to indicate a sycophantic approach to his superiors. Although he believed in reform, he also did not consider that 'rocking the boat' was the best way to advance or achieve it.

Once again, however, Wood found that his position was not assured. As with his appointment to Aldershot, it was Wolseley who was his chief advocate for the post of Adjutant-General. The Queen was the most prominent objector for she argued that Wood was a better commander than administrator, but after a lengthy campaign by Wolseley she finally gave way.[8] In a candid letter to Arthur Bigge, the Queen's secretary, Wolseley again demonstrated that he did not advance Evelyn for the vacancy because of friendship or favouritism, but solely on the grounds of suitability. Wolseley wrote: 'Wood's besetting sin through life has been vanity, but his foolish, his wicked conduct at Majuba drew down upon him so hostile a feeling, that his eyes were somewhat opened. I could not myself bear the sight of him, and left him behind at Alexandria because I did not care to have him with me at Tel-el-Kebir, one who it seemed to me had for personal reasons played into the hands of that traitor Gladstone at Majuba. In fact, it was a long time before I could be cordial to him after that event. I mention this to convince you that in naming Wood as the best man, all round to succeed Redvers Buller I did not name a man from any personal feelings towards him, but that I had done so on public grounds alone.'[9] This admission by Wolseley of the disgust he felt towards Evelyn over Majuba, and that this had influenced his decisions in Egypt in 1882, is clear evidence that Majuba had certainly affected Wood's career in the short term.

In a letter to his old friend, Lieutenant-General William Napier, Evelyn displayed a very mercenary attitude to his new appointment. He wrote: 'I prefer to be Adjutant General rather than any other staff officer, for many reasons it is better than being Q.M.G. and amongst other reasons there is £300 p.a. more pay. I should have liked India 5 years ago, but now prefer to be A.G.'[10] Money was again a pressing concern for Evelyn; he even claimed at this time that he could not afford to buy his youngest daughter, Victoria, a bicycle.

Evelyn received many letters of congratulations on his new appointment. The Duke of Connaught wrote, 'I am heartily glad to see your appointment, and rejoice that we now shall make progress in our War training.'[11] Clearly, the Duke considered that Wood was now in the right place to utilize his skills, for his new position saw him responsible for the 'discipline, military education, and training of the Officers, Warrant Officers, non-commissioned officers and men of the Regular and Reserve Forces and Militia of the United Kingdom, and of the Yeomanry and Volunteer Force'.[12] Evelyn was to be greatly aided in this new role by the passing of the Manoeuvres Act of 1898, which he had earlier advocated, since this allowed greater access to land for exercises. Also, the Government purchased 41,000 acres of Salisbury Plain. Here the army was able to assemble two army corps for field manoeuvres. In the months before the mobilization of forces for South Africa, Wood ensured that this land was utilized for both cavalry and artillery exercises.

Although Evelyn's response to Napier may have indicated a less than enthusiastic desire for his new appointment, Wood's actions on his first day in his new position clearly indicate otherwise and demonstrate clearly that Evelyn had been considering what action he needed to first undertake. He submitted a pre-printed memorandum to Wolseley which highlighted the absolute inadequacy of British forces to meet the needs of an ever increasing Empire. Evelyn suggested that an additional 9,000 men be added, but, although Wolseley agreed with Wood's general premise he felt that 13,000 more troops were required and he advocated this to the Secretary of State. Evelyn did have some success in recruiting additional troops to the British colours when he managed to secure permission from the Secretary of State to recruit a battalion of Yoas tribesmen for British Central Africa and a Chinese battalion to be based at the Wei-hai-wei coaling station. This latter force comprised 27 British officers and 10 British NCOs who commanded 1,000 Chinese troops.[13] One of Evelyn's sons served in this battalion for a short time.

Evelyn's ability to identify not only friends and allies, but also those with the skills and knowledge to improve the British Army, saw him promote and seek the advice of a number of young officers. One such man was Ian Hamilton, in whom Evelyn recognised an inherent ability as a trainer of men. Wood was pleased to offer him the position of Commandant of the School of Musketry at Hythe, Kent in March 1898. The two men had first met in 1881 and subsequently in Egypt and on numerous training exercises, and Wood clearly felt that Hamilton was the man to improve the Army's then woeful training of musketry skills. The position came with a salary of £800 p.a. and, on the very day that Evelyn made his offer, Hamilton was also invited to become the Quartermaster-General in India on £3,000 p.a., a spectacular salary. Hamilton, respectful of what Evelyn was trying to achieve, accepted the Hythe post and the two men set about writing new musketry regulations. Wood even managed to obtain more money for firing practice so that by the early 1900s, 'a British soldier fired seven times more ammunition on the ranges of Hythe than any conscript in any other European army.'[14] Together, Hamilton and Wood laid the foundation for future success on the battlefields of 1914.

That the increasing likelihood of war with the Boers did not completely dominate military thinking at this time was due to the fact that British forces were heavily engaged elsewhere, both in the Sudan and on the North West Frontier in the Tirah campaign. As Adjutant-General, Evelyn had a role to play in both theatres. Ever since the main British force had left Egypt, after the failed effort to save Gordon in Khartoum, there had remained a supposition that, eventually, British forces would enter the Sudanese capital to avenge Gordon and destroy the followers of the Mahdi. The Mahdi himself had died shortly after his forces had taken Khartoum in 1885, but his beliefs remained and the Dervish followers of Mahdism were a constant thorn in the side of both British and Egyptian forces. Kitchener was given the responsibility of leading British and Egyptian troops into Khartoum.

As a former Sirdar of the Egyptian army, Evelyn naturally had a great interest in the progress of Kitchener's forces. As a former Major in the Egyptian army, serving under Wood, Kitchener clearly felt no reluctance in turning to him for help and support. Throughout 1896-8 Evelyn and Kitchener were in regular correspondence, in which Wood was eager to give advice on such matters as the men's diet and general welfare, and Kitchener was happy to receive it.[15] As early as January 1898 Kitchener sought the help of the Adjutant-General in obtaining three officers, newly graduated from the Staff College, for service in his campaign. Kitchener had made a request to the War Office in 1896 for Special Service officers, which had been denied, and Kitchener clearly felt that his old commanding officer might be more persuasive.[16] Wood had no hesitation in recommending Captain Haig as one of those three and by the end of the month Haig was in Egypt. An inspection of Evelyn's motivation in recommending Haig shows that there was no doubt some self-interest on Wood's part. For all his kind words of help and support, it does appear that Evelyn had some doubts as to Kitchener's abilities, which he would voice during the Boer war, and it seems that Wood was keen to have his own man on the spot to report back to him. Haig, for his part, recognised that his advancement so far had owed a great deal to Evelyn's patronage and he assured Wood that he was, 'ever mindful of how much I am indebted to you.'[17] Evelyn was keen to stress to Haig that he should, 'write to me as frankly as you will, you may be sure I shall not quote you to anyone.'[18] Although not a direct order, Haig gratefully responded as if it was one.

Haig supplied Wood with his own opinions on Kitchener's military exploits. Evelyn would have had to sift through the criticism supplied by Haig, as much was clearly inflated by Haig's own ego and frustrations. Wood's motivation for using Haig as a 'mole' was probably driven by a number of factors. Certainly, Evelyn would have been keen to have another point of view from which to draw his own conclusions and he was sure to have wanted to know of any likely criticism that might be directed towards him personally, so as to prepare his defence; for the structure then in place at the War Office almost certainly created a blame culture, in Evelyn's mind at least. The fact that five senior officers had, supposedly, direct influence over the Secretary of State, or at least access to him, would have appealed to Wood's vain and competitive nature and he probably saw the information that Haig might supply as potentially vital for him to maintain and even enhance his influence.

In a similar fashion, Evelyn directed Smith-Dorrien to write privately to him from the Tirah campaign on the North West Frontier. While, on this occasion, Wood did not direct Smith-Dorrien to offer his opinion on the commanders, he was keen that his informant share his views on opportunities for any improvements in operational matters. Thus, for example, Smith-Dorrien informed Evelyn that it was not possible to follow the regulations of the new Drill Book when retreating or retiring from a position, and also reported that there had been difficulties in identifying Regimental ammunition carriers during battle.[19] Of course it could be considered that such information would naturally have been of interest to the reformist Wood, but it would also have been a way for Evelyn again to attempt to nullify any likely criticism before it became an issue.

Evelyn clashed with Kitchener over the latter's attempts to 'vet' and restrict the officers who were keen to join the advance on Khartoum, one of whom was a young man named Winston Churchill. Kitchener, quite rightly, considered that Churchill would use the opportunity of joining the campaign to write critically of Kitchener and he was also unimpressed by Churchill's use of connections to try to force his appointment. Furthermore, Kitchener objected to Churchill using the chance of action as, 'a public convenience on his path to politics and journalism.'[20] Lobbying by both Churchill and his mother successfully obtained the backing of the Prime Minister, Lord Salisbury, but even his intervention failed to move Kitchener's stance. Churchill would not give in and he turned to Evelyn and succeeded in persuading the Adjutant-General to insist upon the War Office having the last word on appointments. Wood then, 'seconded Churchill to the 21st Lancers, despite Kitchener's expressed wish and intention.'[21] Churchill was not to forget Evelyn's help and he was to become another of Wood's 'moles' when he served in the Boer War. On Kitchener's triumphant return to England, after the reconquest of the Sudan, he was met and welcomed by Roberts, Wolseley and Evelyn at Charing Cross station. However, there is no doubt that a wedge had been driven between Wood and Kitchener and neither man would trust each other in quite the same way again.

The discovery of gold in the Boer-dominated Transvaal region of South Africa in 1885 resulted in tens of thousands of British settlers streaming into the region. The Boers came to resent these foreigners, or *uitlanders*, as they called them, denied them voting rights and taxed the gold industry heavily. With the apparent political persecution of British residents in the Transvaal and the Orange Free State, several important British colonial leaders, such as Sir Alfred Milner, and a number of mine owners, such as Alfred Beit and Lionel Phillips, saw the chance to press for annexation of the Boer republics. The British Government issued an ultimatum to the Boers, demanding full equality for British residents in the Transvaal, and likewise the Boers, led by Paul Kruger, simultaneously proclaimed their own ultimatum that all British troops should withdraw from the borders of the Transvaal. Both parties, by their uncompromising stance, had boxed themselves into a situation where renewed conflict between British troops and the Boers became inevitable.[22]

Evelyn received instructions from the Secretary of State for the mobilization and dispatch of troops to South Africa in the early autumn of 1899. Although the scheme for sending an expeditionary force was developed by Wolseley, following an initiative by the then Secretary of State, the successful implementation was due to Wood and his department. The findings of the Royal Commission on the War, published in 1903, concluded with regard to mobilization that, 'mobilization was effected smoothly and with remarkable despatch.'[23] Furthermore, the Commission went on to report that if the same care and forethought that Wood had applied to the mobilization of forces and their dispatch had been seen throughout the war, 'there would have been little criticism to make.'[24] Writing in 1900, Arnold-Forster praised the work of the Adjutant-General and described how, between 7 October 1899 and April 1900, 'the whole of the regiments and battalions serving in the United Kingdom were raised to a war footing by means of drafts from the Reserve; in six months a force of 146,000 men were raised.'[25]

Yet, despite this praise, Evelyn was bitterly disappointed that he was destined not to see active service in South Africa. He later claimed at the Royal Commission hearings that the first he knew of Redvers Buller's appointment as the commanding General was when Buller walked into his rooms at the War Office and informed him of his appointment. That Buller had been given the position over Wood, who

215

was effectively senior to him, and, of course, had been his commanding officer during the conflicts of 1879 and 1881, would have been viewed as a slight to Evelyn. If Wood knew nothing of Buller's appointment, as he claimed, then this fact illustrates that the workings of the War Office at this time were very much centred on the Secretary of State and the Commander-in-Chief. Evelyn was later to state in his defence, at the Royal Commission, that the structure in place in the War Office meant that, although he was supposedly the second most senior man in the Army, he was not involved in any operational military decisions.

When war seemed inevitable, Wood approached Wolseley to express his willingness to command an expedition to South Africa. Wolseley was blunt in his response when he informed Wood that, 'This Ministry will never employ you in South Africa with the remembrance of the Laing's Nek Treaty [1881 Peace Treaty].'[26] In desperation, Wood wrote to the Secretary of State, Lord Lansdowne, hoping that this direct approach might have more success. Evelyn stated that he was prepared to serve under Buller and claimed that, 'My greatest wish is to fight those I was forbidden to fight in 1881.'[27] Clearly Wood felt that he still had a stain to remove from his reputation and a score to settle. To his credit, Buller was to write, 'I have always looked upon this as Evelyn's journey ... so it was a surprise when I was told I was the man. I think he would have done it better than I shall, but I shall try my best.'[28] Events were to prove that Buller's best was not good enough.

Although Evelyn had received general praise for his handling of the mobilization of British troops, there were other areas where criticism was not slow in coming, and despite that fact that much negative comment was directed at the Quartermaster-General's [QMG] department, a good deal of it stuck to Wood, as a member the Senior Staff and a former QMG. It soon became evident that the Army was critically short of artillery pieces and, despite hurried orders and supply and the forming of new artillery battalions, the Army was open to criticism for lack of foresight. Similarly, criticism was raised over the issue of a lack of reserve of ammunition, which had meant that volunteer munitions and supplies from the Curragh Camp in Ireland had to be given to the departing troops[29] All this would have been no doubt forgotten if not for the disasters of 'Black Week'.

The success of the British mobilization meant that substantial forces were able to be put into the field in South Africa by December 1899. However, by then the Boers had reacted and the towns of Ladysmith (as Evelyn had foreseen), Mafeking and Kimberley were placed under siege. Straight away the initiative had been lost by the British, and Buller's policy now was centred on the relief of these towns. The British public and the military at home were shocked by these early reversals, but they were also reassured that the troops were now in place to redeem British honour.

However, this was not to be, for British troops suffered three crushing defeats during what became known as 'Black Week' (10–15 December 1899). Gatacre was the first British General to experience humiliation when he sent his troops against a prepared Boer position at Stormberg. Over 130 men were killed and 600 captured. The following day, 11 December, Methuen, in an attempt to relieve Kimberley and Mafeking, again attacked a prepared Boer position at Magersfontein, where the enemy sheltered in cleverly sited trenches, from which they inflicted heavy casualties with accurate fire from their smokeless Mauser rifles.

However, the nadir of this terrible week for the British was the defeat of Buller at the battle of Colenso, as he and his 21,000 men tried to relieve Ladysmith. In this battle Buller was badly let down by two of his subordinates. Firstly, the initial British advance was led by Major-General Hart in double rank, close formation, into a salient of the River Tugela, and offered easy targets for the Boers' bullets and shells. Secondly, Colonel Long, of the Royal Artillery, showed no understanding of the importance and use of artillery on the battlefield and placed his guns within rifle range of the Boers. The volume of enemy fire soon picked off the artillerymen, and attempts to rescue the ten guns only resulted in more deaths, including that of Freddy Roberts, the son of Lord Roberts. Buller was forced to retire and accept a humiliating defeat. The only redeeming feature was the advance of the Queen's Regiment and the Devons on Colenso village. Led by Major-General Hildyard, a graduate of Evelyn's training at Aldershot, the men advanced in open order and suffered few casualties.[30]

Evelyn, like the rest of the world, was shocked by the ease of the Boer victories, although he had never accepted, like many commentators, that the war would be brief. This view had been confirmed in a letter Wood received from Churchill before 'Black Week'. Churchill stated, 'A long and bloody war is before us and the end is by no means as certain as most people imagine ... They [the Boers] firmly believe they will win and although I do not share their opinion, it must be admitted that it does not seem so unreasonable as it did only a month ago.'[31] In Britain the news of 'Black Week' did not immediately produce an outbreak of indignation and criticism – this would follow later – but rather a patriotic surge and a rush to the colours, which ensured that Evelyn would be kept very busy raising and training new contingents. He was also responsible for meeting Buller's plea for 8,000 mounted men to be sent to South Africa, by drawing up a proposal for an

Imperial Yeomanry, which were generally to serve on the lines of communication, thus freeing regular units to serve at the front.

On hearing news of Colenso, Wood wrote a series of letters and telegrams to Buller offering to serve under him. It was not until the end of the year that Buller found an opportunity to respond to Evelyn's offer: 'Your telegram offering to come and serve under me was a very great compliment, and also a temptation. I was twice on the point of telegraphing from Cape Town to ask that you might come out, and then I thought it was not fair to ask you to come and undertake a job that I in my heart thought only doubtfully possible.'[32] Evelyn had to resign himself to the fact that he was to be tied to his desk, and matters were further taken out of his hands when the Government, faced with the backlash from the disasters of 'Black Week', replaced Buller with Lord Roberts.

As the military situation worsened, pressure grew on the Government, Wolseley, and the other four members of the Senior Staff. Wood seems to have reacted to the criticism that the Army had been unprepared and ill-trained by throwing himself in his work, with his priority being the welfare of the troops in South Africa and ensuring that they were given the tools to do the job that was asked of them. He often worked more than twelve hours a day, and as this pressure on a man in his early sixties began to take its toll, his health and nerves suffered. Despite this, he remained constantly busy: from ensuring that new batteries of field-artillery were equipped and sent to the conflict to the apparently more trivial details of arranging for enough blacksmiths to be recruited and sent to the front so that sufficient horses remained shod and fit for use.

Whilst the Press was reviling the Government and the Army Command officers in South Africa, those who had benefited from Wood's training skills and foresight were quick to defend and to express their thanks to him. Major-General Sir George Marshall wrote to Wood to say: 'I thank you very sincerely for all the assistance you have given us in so promptly supplying all our heavy demands in the Artillery, in men and horses since we came out. I can assure you that the feeling of Gunners is one of amazement and admiration at such a large force of Field Artillery being sent out so efficiently and promptly. We owe you much for all you did to make us shoot, and improving our Tactical efficiency, and now when we succeed we give you the praise and gratitude.'[33] Evelyn was to later claim that he had been overwhelmed by masses of correspondence from officers in South Africa who had served under him at Aldershot, expressing their indignation at the criticisms the Press had levelled at Officers' training.[34]

In South Africa Lord Roberts achieved battlefield success at Paardeberg in February 1900, and he captured the capital of the Orange Free State, Bloemfontein, in March of that year. Buller finally managed to cross the Tugela River and the siege of Ladysmith was lifted at the end of February. In June, Roberts entered the capital of the Transvaal and it was hoped that this would bring an end to the war, but now the Boers avoided set piece battles and relied on guerilla warfare. In November 1900 Lord Wolseley retired as C-in-C and was replaced by Roberts. There seems to have been no thought that Evelyn as Adjutant-General, and thus officially the second most senior officer in the Army, should be considered for the top job. There was no doubt a feeling among members of the Government that Evelyn would be very much associated with an old guard which had apparently failed the test in South Africa. At least Roberts had the background of a successful commander in South Africa, and was not so tarred with the War Office brush, as he had served the majority of his career within the Indian Army.

As the war entered its guerrilla phase, the British, now commanded by Kitchener, responded to the Boer tactics by establishing lines of block houses and wire fences. British forces would then commence 'drives' towards these obstacles, in the hope of capturing the Boers. In reality this tactic did result in the capture of some combatants, but it was most effective in depriving the Boer commandos of the freedom to move and the supplies they needed to continue the fight. In early 1901 Roberts informally suggested that Wood should be sent to South Africa to serve under Kitchener. It was left to Sir Coleridge Grove, a military secretary, to write to Evelyn with the offer. Wood, still desperate for active service responded that, 'if I can serve our country by going out I will willingly go, and serve under Kitchener.'[35] However, Evelyn did stipulate that if Kitchener became a casualty he would not then serve under anyone junior to himself. In reality this meant that, unless Roberts was to return to South Africa, Wood would have become the commander of British Forces if Kitchener had been incapacitated in some way. It appears that it was Kitchener himself who rejected Evelyn's appointment, and perhaps with more diplomacy than actual truth, Kitchener responded to the War Office that, 'While he would be delighted to serve under Sir Evelyn Wood, if he were sent out, he felt he ought not to have him under his command.'[36]

It is debatable whether Evelyn and Kitchener could have worked effectively together, for Wood obviously viewed Kitchener's tactics with some disdain, and the different approaches to man-management adopted by the two men would surely have resulted in disagreement and discord. During a consultation with Dr Norman Moore, Evelyn candidly told his physician that he felt Kitchener treated his men as machines, not human beings, and consequently managed to get less out of his troops than if he treated them with some respect. Moore recorded that the disappointments Evelyn had experienced recently, such as not filling Wolseley's shoes and not serving in South Africa had made him look; 'anxious and worn'.[37]

Just before the possibility of Wood going to South Africa was raised for the last time, Evelyn's friend and patron, Queen Victoria, passed away on 22 January 1901. As Adjutant-General, Wood worked alongside the Lord Chamberlain and Viscount Esher to ensure that the funeral of 2 February went smoothly. There was a long military procession and huge numbers of visiting Royalty, including the Kaiser, and dignitaries who needed to be accommodated. Any sorrow Evelyn felt at the death of the Queen must have been overwhelmed by his own nerves on the day. Not only had the coffin to be transported from the Isle of Wight, via Portsmouth, but many of the mourners had to be taken from Buckingham Palace to Victoria Station, and then all had to be conveyed to St George's Chapel in Windsor. Evelyn, employing the same level of military precision he had displayed in army manoeuvres, came away from the day with credit for all his hard work.

Naturally events in South Africa lay heavily upon Wood. Not only did his three sons fight in the conflict, but many friends and comrades from his years in the Army were engaged. Evelyn was forced to make his contribution from behind his desk, but even from here his ability to think more laterally than some of the officers on the ground made his work of importance. For example, when Kitchener requested more Mounted Infantry, Evelyn responded by suggesting that, as the pattern of war had shifted away from set-piece battles, it would be simpler, and quicker, to train artillerymen in South Africa to shoot with a rifle, and add them to the ranks of the Mounted Infantry. This measure was adopted with satisfactory results. Wood was also aware of the need to maintain the support of the British public and he was one of the first Army officers to recognise the propaganda importance of the new moving pictures. He commissioned such early film pioneers as R.W. Paul to produce a series of twenty patriotic films on army life, which were shown to packed audiences in music halls throughout Britain.[38]

As the conflict drew to a close, the Government conceded to the clamours from the Opposition, the Press, and the public alike for a Royal Commission, chaired by Lord Elgin, to examine the military preparations for the war and the lessons to be learnt about training, tactics and equipment. It seems clear that Evelyn, still smarting from the criticisms which had been directed towards the Senior Army Staff, was determined to use his appearance in front on the Royal Commission to fight his own corner. He wanted to illustrate that he had been advocating better preparations before the war and he was even more desperate to show the Commission that, with the structure in place at the War Office, he had had no input on operational military decisions.

Evelyn, from the very start of his evidence, tried to impress on the members of the Commission that the structure of the War Office, created in 1895 and still operational in 1899, meant that power could not be exercised by the Adjutant-General himself, unless he was so instructed by the Secretary of State or the C-in-C. He went on to claim that, 'I had no responsibility on any one point ... I affirm that as Adjutant-General I never knew of any one plan as to military operations.'[39] Wood refused to discuss any matter of military preparation and he repudiated all responsibility for this area. He was asked to comment on such matters as the training of officers before the war, as well as rifle and artillery training. Although refraining from confrontation, Wood, in answer to all questions, refused to accept that he was personally to blame for any of the Army's failings in the Boer War.

Evelyn's performance on the day was described in a letter by one of the Commissioners, Viscount Esher, to the King. Esher wrote:

Your Majesty knows well the very superior intellectual equipment of this officer, and the singular precision of his ideas on all military subjects. Also, how elusive he can be, when face to face with a dilemma. Sir Evelyn's evidence was of importance, inasmuch as he travelled over most of the whole region of Army organisation, criticising most freely, and stating his own views upon all subjects, and the efforts he has made for 30 years to get them carried into effect. Of course Sir Evelyn found it a matter of some difficulty to explain how it was that having been Q.M.G. and A.G. for a period extending over nearly ten years, he had been unable to give effect to his ideas. His explanation generally was the helplessness of the military branch when brought into conflict with the civilian element, i.e. Sec. of State, the Permanent Under Sec., and the Financial Sec. Sometimes when reforms entailed large expenditure this excuse was valid; but there were many questions affecting the comfort of the soldier, recruiting, training of the officers, military organisation, methods of promotion and appointments to commands, upon which the military side of the W.O. could have carried their point, had the distinguished officers been agreed, or had they been firm enough to take the necessary initiative. He repudiated all responsibility for the preparations for war in

S. Africa. He contended that as Adj. Gen. he was never consulted either to the numbers required, nor the officers appointed to command. He told us privately that he was the 'whipping boy' between Lord Lansdowne and Lord Wolseley. The gist of his evidence, like that of every other officer hitherto examined, was that for all shortcomings at the W.O. it is Your Majesty's Civil Servants, and not the military Officers who are to blame.[40]

Although there is no doubt that Evelyn's evidence to the Commission was elusive and that he was quick to deny that he had responsibility for military operational matters in the run-up to the war, was Esher's judgement perhaps too critical? Wood had, more than any other senior officer, ever since his appointment to the Eastern District in 1885, worked at the joint issues of army reform and training. He had introduced the concept of night marches, as well as effective manoeuvres, to the Army. He constantly battled for improvements to the welfare of the men. With regard to training, Wood pointed out during his evidence that, 'the Army has only been trained in the last few years ... and the only people who can do field firing practically are those quartered at Aldershot, and that is only 20 battalions, you see, out of 110.'[41] Was it too much to expect that Evelyn's approach to training and reform could be extended across all 110 battalions in the space of a few years, especially, as he claimed, since he had little personal influence with the Secretary of State and the C-in-C. Evelyn repeatedly claimed to the Commission that his suggestions for improvements in training were blocked by the Financial Secretary or the Accountant-General, on the basis of cost, and he was to give the impression to the Commission that to a large extent his hands had been tied by the structure in place at the War Office before the outbreak of war.

It was left to Lord Elgin to get to, perhaps, the crux of Evelyn's position at the War Office, and thus the responsibility Wood had for some of the failings of the Boer war. In response to a question concerning the ability of the Financial Secretary to block expenditure on all matters, including training, Wood answered by saying, 'I have no further voice if my demand is rejected.' Elgin responded, 'Except, I suppose, that you can protest?' To this Evelyn said, 'One does that very often; but I think most soldiers, especially during war time, would think it very wrong, because they could not carry their views to resign, which is the only resource left to them.'[42]

While Wood's position during war time can be understood, for he clearly felt that the honourable course was to continue in his role as Adjutant-General, it can be less easily supported in peace time. It seems clear that during his time at the War Office Evelyn was blessed with more foresight than many of his contemporaries as to the impending dangers of conflict with the Boers, as well as the crucial requirements for the training of both officers and men. That he had succeeded, better than most, in awakening the desire among part of the Army to improve their tactics and skills, would seem to damn his lack of success across the Army as a whole. That he knew, more than anyone else, what needed to be done to produce an Army ready to face the threat from the Boers, and that he was not successful, leaves him open to criticism. In his defence, Wood was able to highlight the financial constraints imposed upon his attempts, as well as the structures in place in the War Office, yet it does seem clear that at no time did he consider resigning to highlight the problems he and the country faced.

It can well be imagined what an impact his resignation would have had on military thinking. For a holder of the Victoria Cross, a hero of the Zulu War, a friend of the monarch and the man who had clearly been very successful at Aldershot, to have acted in this way, would most certainly have brought the need for army reform to the forefront of political debate at a most crucial moment. That he did not resign can be viewed critically and as an opportunity lost. Evelyn had demonstrated in 1881 that he was not the kind of man to run away from a difficult situation by resigning. Furthermore, money still remained a pressing requirement, for he had a daughter and an expensive lifestyle to support, and it seems he preferred to slowly chip away at reform in a piecemeal fashion. Unfortunately, the events of the Boer war were to demonstrate that he should have acted more decisively in his role as Adjutant-General and should, perhaps, have considered his own resignation. The report of the Royal Commission was generally considered to be too timid, and the *Illustrated London News* stated that it was, 'the mildest mannered document that ever rebuked incapacity.'[43] Although the War Office may have lost public confidence, the individuals involved were to evade personal criticism. Evelyn was able to avoid any censure and he was to continue serving the new C-in-C, Lord Roberts.

Chapter Twelve

Service to the End

In March 1901 Evelyn was informed by the Secretary of State, Broderick, that he had decided to reduce the status of the Adjutant-General, and he asked Wood's views on the proposal. Wood reacted by overreacting and immediately offered his resignation. This was refused and, once Broderick had convinced Evelyn that his decision was not a personal slight directed towards him, Wood worked alongside the Secretary of State in his reforms aimed at introducing an Army Corps system. Broderick recommended that six districts be created in the United Kingdom, in each of which 'an army could muster, train, and manoeuvre in its entirety.'[1] The aim was to centralise responsibility in the districts and allow the Corp Commanders total authority for training, as well as to decentralise administration. Evelyn was given command of the Southern District, based at Salisbury, which he was to assume in October 1901.

During Evelyn's last few months in the position of Adjutant-General, he worked closely with the new Commander-in-Chief, Lord Roberts, and it appears the two men liked and respected each other. Roberts engaged Evelyn in decisions more than Wolseley had ever done, and Wood responded by offering support and advice. They accompanied each other on tours, in both May and July 1901, of Essex and of the Aldershot command, and both were able to relax and exchange ideas during these weeks. Indeed, correspondence between the two men seems to suggest an informal and friendly relationship, in which Roberts had already come to depend on Evelyn for advice. In July, Roberts wrote to Wood to say: 'I hope you will come with me to Shoeburyness [Artillery range] on the 18th, as previously arranged, unless you think you cannot spare the time. I should like to have the benefit of your experience on my first visit to places.'[2] The friendship the two men enjoyed was to serve both well when Wood assumed command of the Southern District.

Evelyn was able to impress upon Roberts his views on a number of training matters. These included Wood's belief that the physical training of recruits needed to be enhanced by placing in every Infantry depot a Sergeant Instructor, with full powers to improve the physique of the recruits by rendering the instruction more interesting. Wood was able to experiment with the new methods at Aldershot in 1900, and when he and Roberts saw a gymnastic demonstration there, Roberts was so impressed that he ordered its adoption across the Army.[3] Wood was also able to convince Roberts to consider a reduction in the number of companies in a battalion, from eight to four, on the basis that such a structure would allow closer working between officers and men.[4]

Although Evelyn had won over Roberts, he was unable to secure the respect of the new King. Just before Wood was to leave his position as Adjutant-General, Roberts went on leave for a month and Evelyn was thus nominally C-in-C. This situation obviously made the King apprehensive and an unsigned letter was sent from the Palace to Broderick which expressed the King's concerns: 'The K. understands that while Lord R. is on leave Sir E. Wood is to undertake the duties of C in C. He cannot help feeling that it is a pity Sir E.W. should be allowed practically a free hand when he is so soon to give up his appt. as A.G. The King is afraid Sir E.W. may try and introduce changes which he has been unable to carry out while Lord R. was present. He feels sure, however, you will be able to exercise some supervision over Sir E.W. (or as in the King's own words keep your eye on him).'[5] Clearly, Evelyn's reforming zeal was not appreciated by everyone!

Wood took up his new position as commander of the 2nd Army Corps, later known as the Southern Command, on 1 October 1901. Based at Salisbury, with easy access to Salisbury Plain for army manoeuvres, this new role provided Evelyn with the opportunity to continue his reformist approach, as well as indulge his passion for fox-hunting. However, there were some murmurings of disquiet over his appointment, which appeared in the columns of *The Times*. Having declared in March 1901 that the commanders of the new Army Corps would be the officers to lead the Corps in any future conflict, Broderick then appointed Wood, Buller and the Duke of Connaught to the first three Corps. An anonymous contributor to *The Times* letters page pointed out that it was highly unlikely that a Royal Prince or a failed commander in South Africa would lead troops into battle, nor did the writer feel that a man of Evelyn's age and deafness could be expected to take to a foreign field again.[6] Similarly, a month later, *The Times* reported that the feeling in the Indian Press was that Wood was, 'so deaf as to be incapacitated from active service.'[7] It is doubtful that there was an orchestrated campaign against Evelyn's appointment; more likely the criticism was of a political nature, directed at Broderick, but, whatever the motive, Wood weathered the slight storm and settled into his new command.

It appears that Wood's first few months in his new command were something of a revelation, as he discovered that many reforms which he had initiated at Aldershot more than ten years before, had not permeated into the Southern Command. For example, Evelyn discovered that soldiers were still being used for manual duties, such as postal collection and delivery, weeding, cleaning of barrack windows and superfluous sentry duty. Of course, when engaged in such tasks, the troops were not available to learn the art of soldiering. Although Wood took some joy in ending these practices across the Command, by using civilian contractors or retired soldiers, he must have been slightly depressed to discover how little reform had reached many parts of the Army.

Evelyn was able to assist Broderick in his attempts at the decentralisation of administration by highlighting to the Secretary of State some of the more ludicrous ways in which the War Office impinged on his command. Wood was able to show that he had to refer the simplest of building or camp improvements, such as the cementing over of a gravel path or the type of screen to be used in a wash area, to the Inspector-General of Royal Engineers. Together, Wood and Broderick were able to introduce delegation of authority to local Engineers. In terms of the men's welfare, Evelyn was able to persuade the principal Medical Officer at the War Office, Surgeon-General Evatt, that the regulation issue of two shirts for each man was simply insufficient to promote general cleanliness, and a third shirt was authorised. Again, working with Evatt, Wood was able to improve the overall hygiene of kitchens and canteens across the Southern Command.[8]

Evelyn was also encouraged to demonstrate his love of economy and detail by showing cost savings. Writing to Broderick in September 1902, he indicated that the Navy, based at both Plymouth and Portsmouth, was paying eleven per cent more for its bread than the Army in the same geographical area. He suggested to the Secretary that combined purchasing would result in considerable savings and he also pointed out that the same could be said for meat purchases, and indeed such savings were initiated.[9] In June 1902 Broderick appointed a committee to inquire into the education and training of officers, an area in which the Elgin Commission had highlighted significant problems. The Secretary asked Evelyn to be a member of the committee and Wood was not slow in coming forward with his own suggestions. Lord Roberts for one saw that the improved professional training of officers, as well as men, had to be the primary focus of army reform, and he was delighted that Evelyn was in a position to make a positive contribution to the debate. However, not all were so pleased with Wood's membership of the committee. *The Times*'s military correspondent enquired why Evelyn, who now expressed such forceful views on officers' training, had not put them in force, 'before the war discovered its necessity'. The article went even further in damming Wood, by stating that he had been, 'long enough at the War Office to have introduced changes which they [Wood and Coleridge Grove, Military Secretary] considered vital for the effective training of British officers'; at the very least, the paper concluded that Evelyn should have, 'insisted on the Secretary of State taking the onus of responsibility for refusing to accept their proposals.'[10] Wood remained silent and decided not to respond to these critical observations. He weathered this attack and made a positive contribution to the committee.

The main issue raised by the committee centred on the two opposing views held by Evelyn and Sir Coleridge Grove. Grove believed that subalterns should receive their training at the hands of their regimental commanders, after they had joined their first unit. This would leave Sandhurst, 'as a military university with the task of opening the cadets' minds to the higher aspects of their profession.' Wood felt that the lessons of South Africa suggested that Grove's views were incorrect. Evelyn argued that subalterns needed to know about the practical aspects of war before joining their regiment, for, once there, few regiments had the facilities to train them. Wood stated, 'If then it comes to a choice between the two systems, the theoretical and the practical, I should unhesitatingly decide in favour of the latter.' Partly as a result of Evelyn's protestations, after 1903, the courses at Sandhurst and at Woolwich, 'became more practical, with greater emphasis on outdoor work, tactics, engineering and topography.'[11] Such training was to allow the young officers to arrive at their regiments better prepared for regimental life, as well as encouraging them to consider all aspects of their profession.

However, once again, it was in the field of training and manoeuvres that Evelyn was able to best use his energies and talents. He made the most of the new resource of Salisbury Plain, particularly in the field of artillery training. Indeed, Broderick had tasked Wood with the development of Salisbury Plain into the greatest military facility in the country.[12] Whilst giving evidence to Lord Elgin's Commission on South Africa, Evelyn was able to report proudly on the improvements in artillery training that the acquisition of Salisbury Plain had permitted. He stated that, just two days before giving his evidence, he had supervised an artillery training course with firing over 5,000 yards, in which 476 shells out of 480 had penetrated the target. Wood also confirmed the fact that, in utilizing Salisbury Plain, he had been able to begin artillery training on moving targets and thus simulate the attack of an advancing enemy.

In April 1903, Evelyn, now the most senior General on the active list, received the news that he had been promoted to the pinnacle of his profession, when the King announced he had been appointed to the rank of Field-Marshal. He wrote to the King to thank him for the highest honour a soldier could receive and the monarch responded by stating: 'It has given me the greatest pleasure and satisfaction to promote you to the rank of Field Marshal, after the long and distinguished service you have rendered for the Crown and your country.'[13] It is clear that Evelyn owed his promotion to the patronage of Lord Roberts. Wood wrote to Roberts to thank him: 'I am most grateful to you for recommending me for the highest Army Rank ... It is very pleasant to me to feel I have satisfied you in my efforts.'[14] Even *The Times*, whose military correspondent had been somewhat critical of Evelyn's performance at the War Office, was able to write that Wood's, 'preferment will be welcomed everywhere with the greatest satisfaction, and all will rejoice that such a brave, tactful, and distinguished soldier should have been so worthily honoured by his Sovereign.'[15]

With his new honour, Evelyn continued his attempts at reform and improvement with renewed vigour. To encourage horsemanship amongst the cavalry, Wood introduced two separate prizes at Salisbury in the summer of 1903. The first was for compass-bearing rides across country and the second was for the best ride over a distance of twenty-five miles, without causing distress to the horse. In September he reported to Roberts that the trials of the new wireless sets by the Army had, 'succeeded up to about fifteen miles, and after that failed.'[16] The next month, again in a report to Roberts, Wood was able to state that trials of two horse blankets had reduced the incidence of sore backs considerably.[17] In the same month, Evelyn asked permission from Roberts to try a concentrated attack of cyclists during the manoeuvres on Salisbury Plain![18] Clearly, Wood's love of innovation did not diminish as he got older. Indeed, the amount of energy Evelyn exhibited in both fox-hunting and in the Southern Command appears to have been remarkable for a man of his advancing years. Wood's old comrade from Ashanti, Egypt and South Africa, Henry Brackenbury, was able to write that among their contemporaries, Evelyn alone 'seem to be evergreen.'[19]

Wood was to demonstrate the appetite that he still had for work during his last large-scale manoeuvres, held in the summer of 1903. He played a starring role as commander of an invasion force, the Blue team, which comprised two infantry divisions and a cavalry brigade, approximately 20,000 men in all. The defending force, or Red team, was led by Sir John French and was composed of a body similar in size to the Blue team, but with the addition of a detached force, under Bruce Hamilton, of one brigade and some mounted infantry. Evelyn's task was to draw the defending force away from their protection of the south coast ports and then try to destroy both French's and Hamilton's forces individually before they could combine to overwhelm his forces. Edward May again joined Wood's staff during the manoeuvres, and was able to observe at first hand Evelyn's continued energy and enthusiasm, despite his nearly sixty-seven years. May reported that Wood was, 'still able to ride as long and as far as any officer in the field.'[20]

In terms of public relations the four days of manoeuvres were a huge success, and the extensive daily Press reports were read with much interest. However, there was some criticism, once again, of Evelyn's appointment, with some papers commenting that it was a shame that the command of one of the forces was in the hands of a Field-Marshal who was so close to retirement, whereas a younger man might have benefited more from the experience.[21] Indeed, the rising star, General Archibald Hunter, who had been suggested as a commander of the Blue team, had to content himself with being the senior umpire on French's side, and Hunter's biographer certainly considers that Wood's appointment was an opportunity lost.[22] Over the four days, French's force moved up from the Petersfield area, whilst Wood led his command from Bristol, to capture the town of Swindon, before both armies clashed on the Marlborough and Wantage Downs. French's force received praise from the Press for its use of night-marching and its, 'admirable use of the ground.'[23] By the final day, Wood's force had been enveloped and had been forced back to entrenched positions. The dramatic conclusion was a surprise attack by Evelyn's full force into French's thin line of advancing infantry, which continued on to attack the Red team's artillery positions. With this final rush the manoeuvres concluded, although the correspondent of The Times could not resist commenting that, although Wood's attack had looked impressive, 'At what precise point will this principle of attack become applicable under modern conditions?'[24] Lord Roberts as senior umpire declared the manoeuvres a great success, and indeed the rapid movement of troops across such a wide area had been handled effectively. Evelyn's last demonstration of large-scale manoeuvres had been a personal triumph.

The scepticism that had met Broderick's initial plan for a six army corps scheme became more pronounced as it became clear that his estimates of post-war recruiting had proved to be incorrect. Broderick was forced to concede that, with the current level of recruitment, only the first three corps could be sufficiently resourced, and his murmurings of national conscription to meet the demands of a large six corps system were condemned by the Opposition, although both Roberts and Wood privately supported it. All this meant that the reforms that were initiated by Roberts and Evelyn, during the period 1901–4 were somewhat overshadowed by the political controversy surrounding Broderick.

Ignoring such political considerations, Roberts and Wood focused on officer training and the need to develop men who could act on their own initiative. The requirement for rapid-fire artillery pieces was impressed upon the Government, and Roberts was able to purchase over 100 pieces from Germany. Cavalry tactics were modified, with much more emphasis on the need to be able to use the rifle effectively in and out of the saddle. Both arms of the service were to receive new Drill Books, which reflected particular interpretations of the lessons from the Boer war. In a period when the politicians were still very much debating the larger picture of army reform and structure, Roberts and Wood saw the requirements and acted upon them. Both should be given credit for their much overlooked dedication to their profession.

With the departure of Broderick, in September 1903, and his replacement by Arnold-Forster, Lord Esher (an original member of the Elgin Commission) was tasked with proposing a new structure at the War Office. Esher's recommendations, which were to see the development of an Army Council and the Committee of Imperial Defence, were accepted by the Prime Minister, Balfour, and the position of C-in-C was abolished. At the same time as Roberts's departure, Evelyn's tenure at the Southern Command was reaching an end as he approached retirement. The news was received by Wood's old comrades with real regret. Lord Methuen was to write to Evelyn: 'You must let me write to you one line of real sorrow at your leaving us. You have always been so good a friend, and so valued a tutor to me that I shall miss you more than I can say, and the whole army ditto.'[25] At the end of December 1904 Wood retired from the Army, which had been his life and home for more than fifty years.

Naturally, a man of Evelyn's energy and character was not going to disappear from the public scene if he saw an opportunity to further the cause of the Army. However, in his first years of retirement Wood concentrated on writing his two-volume autobiography, *From Midshipman to Field-Marshal*, which was published in 1906. The popularity and renown of Evelyn amongst the British public meant that within its first month of publication it had reached a fourth edition. A fifth edition appeared in 1907 and, in 1912, an abridged pocket edition was produced. Other works were to follow, such as *The Revolt in Hindustan 1857–59*, in 1907, which included mention of his own exploits in India.[26]

Even though Evelyn was now on the 'Retired Army List', this did not stop him being showered with further honours. On the recommendation of the retiring Viscount Wolseley, he received the Colonelcy of the Blues. This honour was reserved for only the most eminent, and previous holders had included the Duke of Wellington. However, once again, monetary considerations made Evelyn somewhat reluctant to accept the honour, for as he was to explain to his friend, and editor of the *Daily Express*, Lord Blumenfeld: 'I hesitated for some little time as there are no earnings attached to the office, and the acceptance of the honour, which is great, involved the purchase of a new uniform, including those tin plates which on fine young men excite so much admiration in the minds of nursemaids.'[27] Despite this reluctance, the 'tin plate' must have appealed to Wood's vanity.

The Liberal victory in the 1906 General Election resulted in the appointment of a new Secretary of State, Richard Haldane, who entered office with a brief of not only reducing expenditure, but also revitalising the Army. Although opposed to universal conscription, Haldane saw the need for a larger, more flexible force, and decided upon a two-tier system. He intended to create an Expeditionary Force of regular troops and a Territorial Army, operated by local associations, in effect, a Reserve Army of part-time soldiers. This second force would be given intensive training and it was assumed that it would meet the obligation for home defence, whilst the regulars in an Expeditionary Force could be rapidly dispatched to conflict areas, wherever they might be.

Both Roberts and Wood, convinced that national conscription was the only solution for the Army's manpower problems, opposed Haldane's proposals. However, the two men had radically different approaches. Whilst Roberts became President of the National Service League, a pressure group dedicated to promoting national conscription, and actively campaigned against the Government, Evelyn felt he could not oppose the attempts to create a Territorial Force and he decided that it was his duty to offer his support to Haldane.

Haldane called upon Edward VII to add his support to the plans, and in turn the monarch requested that the Lord Lieutenants support the Territorial Force movement. As a Deputy-Lieutenant in Essex, Wood felt obliged to serve on the Essex County Association of the new force, which he did for three years. Haldane also asked Wood to take the additional responsibility of the Chair of the London City Territorial Force.[28] In both positions, Evelyn actively campaigned for new recruits and he frequently toured the two areas, giving lectures and presentations. Wood did not hesitate to use old friends and contacts to advance his attempts to enlarge the Territorial Force, or simply to keep up to date with the latest military thinking. Throughout 1908–11 Evelyn was a frequent visitor to Aldershot, where Smith-Dorrien was now in command. Here Wood could learn about new tactical thinking, as well as enjoy the company of former comrades. At one dinner party, Smith-Dorrien described how Evelyn had held court throughout the evening and later wrote in his diary that it had been, 'a most cheery evening, Sir E. Wood a marvel for his age.'[29]

Wood even used a friendly contact at the War Office, General Ewart, to obtain confidential papers relating to the new force structure. He wrote to Ewart: 'Can you produce me a copy of the Confidential Paper "Territorial Force, Draft Scheme". If too confidential for a copy to be sent me, perhaps I could be provided with page 113, which deals directly with the Essex Force, in which I am particularly interested.'[30] Apparently, Ewart did send Evelyn the page referring to Essex, for the following year Wood again wrote to ask, 'you kindly got me the "Essex" section Terr. Asso. – can you let me have the "City" one?'[31] By using his contacts to keep abreast of current War Office thinking, Wood ensured that he could still make a contribution to the larger public debate on army reform.

As the years passed, Evelyn was to suffer the loneliness of those who outlive their contemporaries and he frequently had to attend the funerals of old comrades. In June 1908, Wood, representing the King, said his goodbyes to his old friend Redvers Buller, in a funeral in Buller's home town of Crediton. Five years later, Evelyn paid the following tribute at the funeral of his old commander, Garnet Wolseley: 'Indomitable in action, undeterred by terrible wounds received fifty-eight years ago, with a most brilliant soldier's brain, he did more to improve the fighting efficiency of the Army than any soldier I have met.'[32] As one of the most senior surviving members of the army establishment, it also fell to Wood to attend services of remembrance for a number of figures associated with the reporting of Britain's colonial campaigns, many of which Evelyn had taken part in. In February 1909 he unveiled a memorial bust in St Paul's Cathedral to the reporter William Howard Russell, whose writings had done so much to inform the public about the logistical failings of the Crimean campaign. Three years later Wood was again in the Cathedral crypt to unveil a plaque to the memory of his old friend, the war artist Melton Prior. Evelyn's longevity also ensured that further honours were bestowed upon him. In 1911 he received the Court position of Gold Stick in Waiting on the King and, in the same year, the King approved his appointment as Constable of the Tower of London.

Evelyn maintained his desire to improve the standard of rifle shooting, both in the Army and in various associated bodies, such as the public school shooting competitions. Whilst still serving, he had established the annual 'Evelyn Wood marching and shooting' competition at Bisley, for sharpshooters serving in the Army. This event was reported each year in such papers as *The Times*, and for many years after his retirement Wood returned to Bisley to present the prize. He was also associated with the *Daily Mail*-sponsored 'Empire Day Rifle Contest,' in which teams from Britain and such far-flung colonies as Canada and Fiji would compete in England on Empire Day. Again, his involvement in this contest would be well reported in other newspapers.[33] Wood was also happy to attend speech days at a number of public schools, ranging from Marlborough to Beaumont, at which he advocated his own ideas of integrity and service to the Empire. On one particular occasion, he even impressed upon his schoolboy audience that if they were to fall whilst serving their country, their bodies would, 'make the foundation of one more pillar of Empire.'[34] When addressing the London Diocesan Church Lads' Brigade, Evelyn adopted a different approach, when he stated: 'In whatever position in life they might be knowledge was power, and if they wanted to be leaders instead of followers they must work harder than all their companions.'[35] It appears that Evelyn was speaking from his own experience of life.

Wood continued to work hard to increase recruitment into the London City Territorial Force and he was always keen to raise the profile of his district. With this in mind, he set about organising a 'march-past' of the Association in front of his Majesty, King George V. Despite a bad fall in March 1912 whilst out fox-hunting, which had followed a severe bout of flu in February, he had recovered sufficiently by the end of March to begin the planning of the ceremony. Evelyn first wrote to Lord Stamfordham to try to use his influence on the King to persuade him to attend a march past in Hyde Park. The date of Saturday 8 June was agreed upon and Wood set about planning and organising the day. First, he approached the twenty-eight London boroughs who had formed companies for the Territorial Force and asked them to encourage their men to register that they would attend the event. By April Wood was able to announce that he estimated that 25,000 men would attend and he, 'anticipated that there will be a considerable increase of strength in consequence of the parade.'[36] By May the expected figure had risen to 30,000 men. As the day approached, Evelyn realised that, because the review was timed for 6.00 pm, some men would not be able to leave work early enough to attend. In a last minute plea to employers, Wood wrote to *The Times*, asking that they allow those who had pledged to attend to leave work early so as to reach the parade on time.[37]

The papers, in reviewing the event, were full of praise for Evelyn, who had the honour of leading the men past the King and Queen. *The Times*'s military correspondent stated that, 'the gallant old Field Marshal, Sir Evelyn Wood, whose seat is as firm and eye as quick as in days of old, can never have lived through a happier moment than when he presented this noble array for the King's inspection.'[38] The paper also described the review as the, 'most remarkable and suggestive military gathering that has ever responded to the disciplined word of command.'[39] Although Wood had received much praise for organising the evening, he must have been disappointed that thousands of those who pledged their attendance did not materialise on the day. Whether this was because of work commitments or lack of interest cannot be known, but he must have been saddened that only 17,000 men were present at the review.

This event may have marked the realisation for Evelyn that, despite all his efforts, the recruitment figures for the Territorial Force were never going to reach Haldane's expectations. Although the initial up-take in 1908/9 was very encouraging, numbers began to dwindle and, at the time of the 1912 parade, the London Associations were a third under strength. In January 1914, at the annual meeting of the London City Territorial Force Association, Evelyn stated that the parade had not seen the anticipated rise in recruitment, that his Association was still 2,700 men short of its 11,000 quota and that, moreover, the numbers were actually falling. Wood was forced to admit that, despite his best efforts, he had failed to attract enough recruits.[40] He thus decided to tender his resignation and he used his final speech as Chairman of the London City Association not only to express his disappointment at the situation, but also to state his belief that the only solution to the manpower requirements for the Army was universal compulsory military service.

His resignation provoked near panic in the pages of *The Times*, which stated that the Territorial Force's failure to attract sufficient recruits, highlighted by Wood, left the country vulnerable and too dependent on the Navy for its defence. The paper hoped that Evelyn's action would further the public debate and illustrate the failure of the Government, 'to give us the garrison which we need.'[41] The Chairman of the National Service League, Evelyn's old friend and comrade Lord Roberts, was delighted by Wood's resignation and wrote to him: 'I cannot tell you the pleasure your resigning your position on the Territorial Forces has given me. It will do more to help than any number of meetings. I am most grateful to you. So long as men like you hold on to the force I felt I could do nothing, now I hope that other supports will follow your example.'[42] Wood, now released from his loyalty to the Territorial Forces, enthusiastically joined Roberts in campaigning for the National Service League, and in February he joined his old comrade in handing a petition to the Prime Minister which summarised the position of the League.[43] The outbreak of the First World War, just months later, would end the argument over the Territorial Forces. Haldane's reforms of the Regular Battalions would prove justified by the action of British Expeditionary Force in the first weeks of the war. Kitchener's disdain for the abilities of the Territorial Force would see him create his own 'Kitchener's Army' from the rush of volunteers, and the debate over compulsory military service was to be nullified by these events.

The outbreak of the war was to present Evelyn with yet another disappointment, for although he was nearly seventy-seven years of age and had been on the retired list for ten years, it seems he was still hopeful of a command. It appears that his optimistic approach to the War Office, seeking active service, was rather cruelly rejected. A letter to Wood, on which the sender's signature cannot be deciphered, stated: 'My heart bleeds for you and no language of mine could give expression to my feelings over the foul black ingratitude with which you have been treated ... What pains me is the manner in which the representations of a man who has done more for the British Empire up to today than any man living – who had he been given the chance would have added still more to his already unequalled record – has been treated.'[44] After being rejected for active service, Evelyn was forced to consider other means by which he could contribute to the war effort.

Despite this rejection, the outbreak of war aroused in Wood, as in most of the nation, a willingness to serve in whatever way he could. This seems to have taken the form of appearing at numerous army functions, where a speech or inspection by a senior figure was required. Thus, for example, in December, Wood was reviewing the march past of the North Midland Territorial Division in a 'certain provincial town'[45] as described by the military correspondent of *The Times*. Earlier, Evelyn had lectured to a meeting of Nonconformists at the Hackney Empire on their duty to join the ranks of those willing to serve in France. He declared: 'I ask every unmarried male adult who fulfils the physical conditions to enlist in the New Army for the war. I ask all qualified married men to enlist in the Territorial battalion for

Home Service for the war ... May God save the King, and enable him to defend the Right!'[46] Such duties and events were to keep Evelyn active throughout the war. In 1917 he visited the Down Hall Convalescent Home[47] to present a medal for bravery to a Corporal Carstairs, and he was to repeat such duties throughout the conflict. He was also kept busy receiving and responding to letters from bereaved parents and wives of fallen old comrades, as well as offering condolences to such friends as Dr Norman Moore, who lost his son in the conflict.

The war also allowed Evelyn to maintain contact with a number of his old colleagues. He regularly exchanged letters with the likes of French, Haig and Smith-Dorrien, and to all he offered advice and encouragement. He also received letters of thanks, one from an unnamed former Staff Officer, which must have greatly pleased Wood, for it stated: 'I think you can be proud of the Army that you have done so much to render efficient in war, and I should love to have you with me for an hour or two in a hot corner to see how splendidly the men behave.'[48]

Wood also continued to write throughout the war. His output varied from the production of a further volume of memoirs, to articles for periodicals, to the occasional letter to *The Times*. In 1916 he was engaged in an explosive debate, when he argued that Britain should not respond to the German Zeppelin raids on England by bombing German cities, but that British retaliation would be best served by the Army, on the battlefield, and that reprisals against German civilians would be useless. *The Times* was showered with letters which were critical of Evelyn's stance; many were not able to accept his argument and one writer stated: 'When the Germans shot at our men and our men shoot back, is it "reprisals"? I thought it was war.'[49] Even Arthur Conon Doyle joined the discussion and argued against Wood's view, but the debate soon disappeared from the paper, although Wood must have been upset by the tone of some of the correspondence directed against him. Wood also found the time to edit a two-volume work entitled, *British Battles on Land and Sea*, and a patriotic work with the title of *Our Fighting Services*. Evelyn's final memoir, *Winnowed Memories*, was published in 1917. This book was a collection of anecdotes, in which his wit or wisdom featured; some were poignant and others had rather dubious claims to hilarity. The book certainly did not do as well commercially as his earlier autobiography, although a cheaper edition did appear in 1918.

Evelyn spent the war years living in a large country property named Millhurst, near Harlow in Essex. From his study he would answer his daily correspondence and research and write his various books and articles. He still maintained his passion for fox-hunting and was a regular member of the local Hunt. Although he undoubtedly kept busy, the dwindling of his band of friends must have made him somewhat melancholy and, like all, he surely became war weary. As the war approached its final crucial stages, Evelyn, who was one of the few senior army officers to have served under three monarchs, wrote a perceptive letter to someone whom he only addressed as 'My dear friend', although it was probably addressed to Lord Stamfordham. The letter stated; 'I have thought often in my incurable optimism that it was well for our country that the Kaiser boiled over in this Monarch's reign, for granting all the merits of HM The Queen and King Edward I do not think that either would have got so much out of our people as King George has done, and that is the all important matter.'[50]

In February 1918, Evelyn received at letter from his friend, and former Secretary of State, Broderick, now Viscount Middleton. Although Middleton used the letter primarily to wish Wood a belated happy 80th birthday, he also reminisced about the time when the two men had worked together. Middleton hoped that when Wood looked back over his long period of public service, 'you realise how much the country owes to you. When history is written I feel that the Army of Mons [the British Expeditionary Force in 1914 which stalled the German advance on Paris] will be ascribed to Lord Wolseley, yourself and his other comrades who first broke down the old gang [the Duke of Cambridge] – and to you at Aldershot we owe the first real training of troops. People forget, and this war seemed to shatter every reputation after it is made, but the work which made our expansion possible will remain for ever on record.' Evelyn must have taken great satisfaction in these comments from his old friend.[51]

Ill health and the effects of injuries which his many accidents had inflicted upon his body began to take their toll on Evelyn. Even so, he remained remarkably active and the final end of the war meant that he had more time available for his passion of fox-hunting. In December 1918, during a routine medical check-up, Wood informed Norman Moore that he had managed nineteen days out with the Essex and Puckeridge Hounds, but admitted that anything over thirty days tired him too much.[52] However, from the spring of 1919, his health problems, which seem to have centred on a weakening heart, gradually worsened. In April, in a series of letters to his youngest daughter's former Governess, Miss Telford, he complained of bad nights, with little sleep, and said that he spent many days resting in bed.[53] Later in the year, Evelyn finally realised that his riding days were over and he announced that he was to give up altogether and sell his stud. Wood

237

and his family must have known that this act signalled that the end could not be far away.

Evelyn lived on through the summer and regained some of his strength. On many days he was able to rise from his bed and again enjoy writing and receiving correspondence. However, in his weakened condition he was susceptible to the influenza pandemic which was circling the globe in 1919, and he was struck down in November and forced to return to bed. It seems that the combination of the flu and Evelyn's weak heart meant that his condition deteriorated quickly. The Sunday before he died, he summoned his old valet, Walkinshaw, to Millhurst for one last meeting. Wood and Walkinshaw had shared many an adventure in South Africa in 1878–79 and again in 1881. It was Walkinshaw who had retrieved Evelyn's prayer book from his saddlebag during the battle of Hlobane, who had stood beside him as Wood fired at the Zulu chiefs during the crucial moments at Kambula, who had got drunk with Evelyn in Pietermaritzburg after the war, who was present at the signing of peace terms with Kruger in 1881, who had received a present of Gordon's evening coat when he had left for Khartoum and who had joined Evelyn in the army's attempts to rescue Gordon. Indeed, Walkinshaw had served Wood for over thirty years. During their last meeting, Evelyn said to Walkinshaw, 'I expect to die this afternoon and I wish to thank you for having risked your life to save mine not once or twice but many times and I thank you with all my heart.'[54] The meeting must have been both poignant and tearful.

Evelyn was to survive the afternoon and live on for two more days before passing away peacefully on 2 December 1919, three months from his eighty-second birthday. The *Daily Mail* was to report, perhaps with some licence, that Wood's last words were, 'My God, My King, My country.'[55] Grenfell, his old comrade from their days in the Egyptian Army, was told by one of Wood's daughters that, 'her father was quite worn out at last and that it was a happy release.'[56] Similarly, writing in response to a letter of condolence from Lord Blumenfeld, Evelyn's son Charles wrote: 'Your letter helps; you knew what he was to the country, and what he meant to all his kith and kind. I would not have kept him to live any life less active in mind and body than had been his wont, yet to me personally the loss is, as you know, beyond all imagination.'[57]

On hearing of Wood's death, George V sent a telegram to Evelyn's eldest son, Colonel Evelyn Wood, which read: 'The King is grieved to hear of the death of your father. His Majesty will join with the whole Army in mourning the loss of the gallant and distinguished Field-Marshal, who gave his services to the country during three successive reigns.'[58] Evelyn's death was reported extensively in all the national

238

newspapers and many, including the *Daily Mail*, devoted a whole page to his obituary. The *Pall Mall Gazette* of 2 December placed a photograph of Wood on its front page, whilst the obituary in the *Daily Telegraph*, written by its war correspondent, Bennett Burleigh, included a tribute from General Sir Ian Hamilton who stated: 'Sir Evelyn's vitality was so intense, his spirit so dauntless and so bright, that it seems strange, as well as sad, he should have become a memory within the lifetime of any of us ... I have never known Evelyn give expression to a selfish, vindictive, or jealous thought. His heart was young, and it was his constant endeavour to give youth a chance.'[59]

The Army authorities quickly decided that Evelyn was due full military honours in a funeral at Aldershot. It was clearly Wood's decision to be buried in the Military Cemetery at Aldershot, in a grave which adjoined that of his wife Paulina, and where he had spent many happy and successful years. The *Daily Telegraph* claimed that ten days before he died, whilst lying ill in bed, Wood, 'personally wrote to the firm at Aldershot who had conducted his wife's funeral giving minute instructions regarding his own interment.'[60] He was clearly organizing to the last. Evelyn's body was brought to Aldershot on the Friday before the funeral, to be held on Saturday 6 December. It lay in state in All Saints Garrison Church, guarded by Hussars and Lancers. A special train was laid on from Waterloo station to Aldershot on the Saturday morning, to convey the large number of military personnel who wished to attend the funeral, including many who had served under Wood, such as Wingate, Grenfell, Hamilton, Methuen and Haig, the latter representing the King. The funeral procession was confirmed by special orders from General Lord Rawlinson, commander at Aldershot, and comprised a number of regiments in which Evelyn had served, including the 17th Lancers.[61] After the funeral service, the coffin, draped in the Union Jack and surmounted by Wood's Field-Marshal's hat and sword, was borne on a gun-carriage in a mile-long procession to the military cemetery. Despite heavy rain, the route was lined by thousands of people, and all businesses in Aldershot were shut for the duration of the funeral. Flags were flown at half-mast and blinds were drawn. The church was filled with literally hundreds of wreaths and, following Evelyn's instructions, the flowers remained in the church for some days. Among the many wreaths was one from the Army Council which read, 'In affectionate admiration of a great soldier.'[62]

Evelyn's last journey was over, and within a few years one of the most famous soldiers of the Victorian age was all but forgotten. During his career, he had been mentioned in dispatches on twenty-five occasions. He was the holder of medals from the Crimea, India,

Ashanti, South Africa and Egypt, as well as the Victoria Cross, the Legion of Honour, the Medjidieh and the Khedive's Star. He was a Knight of the Grand Cross of the Bath and a Knight of the Grand Cross of the Order of St Michael and St George. *The Times* editorial of 3 December 1919 described him as the personification of the ideal of duty, which was performed with constant zeal, and recorded that he had an unusual gift for organization.

However, Evelyn's legacy was more than his evident bravery and an ability to inspire and organize. He had a foresight that many in the upper echelons of the Army of the late nineteenth century did not possess, and with this he recognised the flaws in the service, which could well have proved fatal. That he was an innovator and did much for the training of troops is evident, but it must not be forgotten that Wood was attempting to reform a system which was highly suspicious of change and was starting from a very low base of knowledge and experience within the Army. In his work of reform and training, Wood was undoubtedly brave and forceful, even if he can perhaps be criticised for not acting more decisively in the years preceding the Boer war. Viscount Middleton clearly felt that Evelyn's contribution was vital in preparing the British Army so that it was able to match and throw back a rampaging German Army in 1914. That the British battalions at Mons in 1914 were able to pour fifteen aimed rounds a minute into the advancing Germans, fire that was so intense that the German troops thought they were facing machine guns, can be considered a testament to the foresight of both Wood and Hamilton, who worked so hard together to improve the facilities available for musketry training. Yet, perhaps his greatest legacy was that he introduced a way of thinking, among all the officers who served under him, that encouraged a respect for the abilities of the rank and file, as well as promoting initiative from officers, and allowing men the opportunity really to think about and consider their profession and thereby gain an understanding of what was required to improve the Army.

That Evelyn's personality and character were somewhat flawed is without doubt. His vanity was well known, as was his love for money and advancement. Yet all who served under him thought him kind and considerate, with an ability to smile and make a joke even in the most trying of circumstances. *The Times* concluded its obituary by stating that Evelyn was a 'magnificent if not very great man, who lived a magnificent life and did his country service such as it has been given to few to do.'[63] A plaque was erected to him in the crypt of St Paul's Cathedral with the words: 'INTREPID IN ACTION, UNTIRING IN DUTY FOR QUEEN AND COUNTRY.' Evelyn would have certainly been very proud and happy to read such sentiments.

Notes

Prologue

1. Commander C.N. Robinson, RN (ed.), *Celebrities of the Army* (London, George Newnes, 1902), p. 12.

Chapter 1

1. K. O'Shea, *Charles Stewart Parnell*, Vol. 1 (Cassell, London, 1914), p. 6.
2. E. Wood, *From Midshipman to Field Marshal*, Vol. 1 (Methuen, London, 1906), p. 1.
3. C. Hibbert, *George IV* (Longman, London, 1973), p. 150.
4. Ibid, p. 152.
5. S. David, *Prince of Pleasure* (Simon & Schuster, London, 1998), p. 400.
6. E. Bradhurst, *A Century of Letters 1820–1920: Letters from Literary Friends to Lady Wood and Mrs A.C. Steele* (Thomas & Newman, London, 1929), p. 17.
7. C. Hibbert, p. 206.
8. C. Woodham-Smith, *Queen Victoria*. Vol. 1 1819–1861 (Hamish-Hamilton, London, 1972), p. 24.
9. E.A. Smith, *George IV* (Yale University Press, 1999), p. 131.
10. C. Woodham-Smith, p. 24.
11. Ibid, p. 29.
12. E. Wood, p. 5.
13. K. O'Shea, p. 11.
14. Ibid, p. 47.
15. Ibid, p. 43.
16. Ibid.
17. E. Wood, p. 11.
18. E. Bradhurst, p. 86.
19. Ibid, p. 87.
20. E. Wood, p. 5.
21. C. Williams, *The Life of Lieut-General Sir Henry Evelyn Wood* (Sampson Low Marston & Company, London, 1892), p. 3.
22. E. Wood, p. 5.
23. C. Williams, p. 5.
24. Ibid, p. 6.
25. E. Wood, p. 9.
26. B. Best, 'Evelyn Wood,' *Journal of the Anglo-Zulu War Historical Society*, IX June 2001, pp. 23–30.

241

27. E. Wood, p. 7.
28. Ibid, p. 10.
29. Ibid, p. 12.
30. Ibid.
31. E. Bradhurst, p. 7.
32. E. Wood, p. 19.
33. Ibid, p. 20.

Chapter 2

1. E. Wood, *From Midshipman to Field-Marshal* (Methuen, London, 1906), p. 21.
2. KCM 89/9/16/1.
3. KCM 89/9/16/2.
4. E. Wood, Vol. 1, p. 21.
5. E. Wood, *The Crimea in 1854 and 1894* (London, Chapman and Hall, 1895), p. 8.
6. E. Wood, Vol. 1, p. 27.
7. Ibid, p. 29.
8. Sir Norman Moore Case Box 18, 17 February 1895 (Private Collection), p. 159.
9. E. Wood, Vol. 1, p. 32.
10. Ibid, p. 33.
11. E. Wood, *The Crimea*, p. 87.
12. E. Wood, Vol. 1, p. 37.
13. E. Wood, *The Crimea*, p. 94.
14. E. Wood, Vol. 1, p. 40.
15. Ibid, p. 44.
16. Ibid, p. 45.
17. Ibid, p. 47.
18. C. Williams, *Life of Lieut-General Sir Evelyn Wood* (Sampson Low, Marston, London, 1892), p. 10.
19. Ibid, p. 51.
20. E. Wood *The Crimea*, p. 168.
21. E. Wood, Vol. 1, p. 55.
22. E. Wood, *The Crimea*, p. 168.
23. E. Wood, Vol. 1, p. 55.
24. Ibid, p. 57.
25. E. Wood, *The Crimea*, p. 202.
26. E. Wood, Vol. 1, p. 61.
27. Ibid.
28. Ibid, p. 62.
29. Ibid, p. 65.
30. E. Wood, *The Crimea*, p. 240.
31. E. Wood, Vol. 1, p. 67.
32. Ibid, p. 71.
33. E. Wood, *The Crimea*, p. 292.
34. E. Wood, Vol. 1, p. 83.
35. E. Wood, *The Crimea*, p. 293.
36. E. Wood, Vol. 1, p. 85.
37. Ibid, p. 88.
38. E. Wood, *The Crimea*, pp. 316–17.
39. For a detailed description of the failed assault see E. Wood, Vol. 1, pp. 82–93, and E.Wood, *The Crimea*, pp. 315–27.

40. Lushington to Michell, 19 June 1855, REF: KCM 89/9/16/4.
41. Michell to Raglan, 20 June 1855, and Raglan to Michell, 21 June 1855, REF: KCM 89/9/16/8 (a) and (b).
42. Michell to Burnett, 4 July 1855, REF: KCM 89/9/16/11.
43. C. Williams, p. 16.
44. Lushington to Wood, 28 February 1857, REF KCM 89/9/16/25.
45. Supplement to the *London Gazetter*, 4 August 1856, REF: KCM 89/9/55/1, and E. Wood, Vol. 1, p. XIII.
46. E. Wood, *The Crimea*, p. 27, and Supplement to the *London Gazetter*, 2 April 1858, REF: KCM 89/9/55/2.
47. E. Wood, Vol. 1, p. 101.
48. E. Wood, Vol. 1, p. 108.
49. Letter from Lady Wood to Sir William Page Wood, The Chancellor, 20 March 1856, REF: KCM 89/9/16/17.
50. E. Bradhurst, *A Century of Letters 1820–1920: Letters from Literary Friends to Lady Wood and Mrs A.C.Steele* (Thomas & Newman, London, 1929), p. 77.
51. Ibid.
52. E. Wood, Vol. 1, p. 109.
53. Ibid.
54. Letter Captain Peel to Evelyn Wood, 11 May 1856, REF: KCM 89/9/16/18 and Captain Peel to Evelyn Wood, 18 June 1856, REF: KCM 89/9/16/19.
55. B. Farwell, *Eminent Victorian Soldiers* (London, Viking, 1986), p. 243.
56. E. Wood, Vol. 1, p. 113.
57. For a thorough, and well-researched, approach to the reasons behind the Mutiny, and its consequences, see S. David, *The Indian Mutiny* (London, Viking, 2002).
58. E. Bradhurst, p. 78.

Chapter 3

1. E. Wood, *From Midshipman to Field-Marshal* Vol. 1 (Methuen, London, 1906), p. 119.
2. Ibid, p. 120.
3. Letter Capt. Sir William Peel to Evelyn Wood, 9 April 1850, KCM 89/9/17/1
4. E. Wood, *The Revolt in Hindustan 1857–59* (Metheun, London, 1908), p. 331.
5. E. Wood, Vol. 1, p. 133.
6. Ibid, pp. 139–41.
7. Ibid, p. 147.
8. B. Farwell, *Eminent Victorian Soldiers* (Viking, London, 1986), p. 245.
9. E. Wood, Vol. 1, p. 157.
10. Ibid, pp. 159–61.
11. S. David, *The Indian Mutiny 1857* (Viking, London, 2002), p. 369.
12. Letter Major-General Sir John Michel to Chief of Staff, India, 14 April 1859, REF: KCM 89/9/17/3 (a).
13. Letter Brigade-General Somerset to Asst. Adjt General, 14 April 1859, REF: KCM KCM 89/9/17/4.
14. Letter Colonel Hurling, Military Secretary, to Major-General Sir John Michel, 17 May 1859, REF: KCM 89/9/17/3(b).
15. Letter Major-General Sir John Michel to Lady Wood, 15 June 1859, REF: KCM 89/9/17/6.
16. Ibid.
17. C. Rathbone Low, *Soldiers of the Victorian Age*, Vol. 1 (Chapman & Hall, London, 1880), p. 266.

18. E. Wood, Vol. 1, pp. 171–2.
19. Ibid, p. 168.
20. Letter Lieutenant Wood to Adjutant-General, 26 March 1860, REF: KCM 89/9/17/15.
21. E. Wood, Vol. 1, p. 184.
22. Letter Lieutenant Wood to Adjutant-General, 26 March 1860, REF: KCM 89/9/17/15.
23. Ibid.
24. E. Wood, Vol. 1, p. 173.
25. Ibid, p. 178.
26. Ibid, pp. 179–80.
27. Letter Captain Hutchinson to Lieutenant Wood, 2 January 1860, REF: KCM 89/9/17/9.
28. Letter Colonel Shakespear to Cecil Beadon, 9 January 1860, REF: KCM 89/9/17/10.
29. Letter Colonel Shakespear to Lieutenant Evelyn Wood, 9 February 1860, REF: KCM 89/9/17/13.
30. C. Williams, *The Life of Lieut-General Sir Henry Evelyn Wood* (Sampson Low, Marston, London, 1892), p. 28.
31. E. Wood, Vol. 1, p. 181.
32. E. Bradhurst, *A Century of Letters 1820–1920: Letters from Literary Friends to Lady Wood and Mrs A.C. Steele* (Thomas & Newman, London, 1929), p. 78.
33. C. Williams, p. 29.
34. Letter Lieutenant Wood to the Adjutant General, Indian Army, 26 March 1860, REF: KCM 89/9/17/15.
35. E. Wood, Vol. 1, pp. 186–7.
36. Ibid, p. 194.
37. Letter Lieutenant Mayne to Lieutenant Wood, 15 July 1860, REF: KCM 89/9/18/3.
38. E. Wood, *The Revolt*, p. 336.
39. Letter Lieutenant Wood to Lieutenant Mayne, 17 July 1860, REF: KCM 89/9/18/3.
40. Letter Colonel Shakespear to Lieutenant Mayne, 2 August 1860, REF: KCM 89/9/18/8.
41. Letter Lieutenant Wood to Lieutenant Mayne, 6 August 1860, REF: KCM 89/9/18/9.
42. Letter from Brigade Major Mayne to Colonel Sir R. Shakespear, 7 August 1860, REF: KCM 89/9/18/5.
43. Letter from Colonel James Travers to Lieutenant Evelyn Wood, 4 October 1860, REF: KCM 89/9/18/13.
44. C. Williams, p. 36.
45. Ibid, p. 37.

Chapter 4

1. E. Wood, *From Midshipman to Field-Marshal*, Vol. 1 (Methuen, London, 1906), p. 202.
2. B. Best, 'Evelyn Wood', *The Journal of the Anglo Zulu War Historical Society*, Vol. IX, June 2001, p. 23.
3. E. Wood, *From Midshipman to Field-Marshal*, p. 204.
4. War Office to Captain Evelyn Wood, 17 July 1862, REF: KCM 89/9/19/3.
5. E. Wood, Vol. 1, p. 206.
6. Ibid, p. 209.
7. Ibid, p. 211.
8. Ibid.
9. Ibid, pp. 221–2.
10. Ibid, p. 223.
11. Mitchell to Wood, 28 March 1867, REF: DUK XVIII-H.

12. E. Wood, Vol. 1, p. 227.
13. Lady Emma Wood to the Hon. Paulina Southwell, 23 August 1867, REF: KCM 89/9/3/2.
14. Hon. Paulina Southwell to Wood, 25 August 1867, REF: KCM 89/9/3/3.
15. Lady Emma Wood to the Hon. Paulina Southwell, 28 August 1867, REF: KCM 89/9/3/4.
16. Evelyn Wood to the Hon. Paulina Southwell, 28 August 1867, REF: KCM 89/9/3/6(a).
17. E. Bradhurst, *A Century of Letters 1820–1920* (Thomas & Newman, London, 1929), p. 29.
18. Ibid, p. 28.
19. M.R. Callaghan, *Kitty O'Shea: The story of Katharine Parnell* (Pandora, London, 1989), p. 38.
20. Wood to the Hon. Paulina Southwell, 4 September 1867, REF: KCM 89/9/3/8.
21. E. Wood, Vol. 1, p. 228.
22. Lady Emma Wood to Evelyn Wood, 6 September 1867, REF: KCM 89/9/3/10.
23. C. Williams, *The Life of Lieut-General Sir Henry Evelyn Wood* (Sampson Low, Marston & Co., London, 1892), p. 46.
24. Ibid.
25. I. Beckett, *The Victorians at War* (Hambledon, London, 2003), p. 28.
26. Ibid.
27. Wolseley to his wife, 11 October 1887, REF: HOV W/P 16/85.
28. I. Beckett, p. 28.
29. J. Marlow, *The Uncrowned Queen of Ireland – the Life of Kitty O'Shea* (Weidenfeld & Nicolson, London, 1975), p. 11.
30. E. Wood, Vol. 1, p. 232.
31. Ibid.
32. C. Williams, p. 49.
33. E. Wood, Vol. 1, p. 239.
34. Ibid, p. 246.
35. Ibid.
36. Ibid, p. 249.
37. Field Marshal Sir Henry Evelyn Wood 1872–1881, WO 27/489.
38. B. Farwell, *Eminent Victorian Soldiers* (Viking, London, 1986), p. 248.
39. E. Wood, Vol. 1, p. 254.
40. All the surviving responses Wood received can be viewed at REF: KCM 89/9/21/5-26.
41. Viscount Southwell to Paulina Wood, March 1873, REF: KCM 89/9/1/10.
42. Report on the introduction of Pioneers in the British Cavalry, 1876, REF: KCM 89/9/54/5.
43. A. Clayton, *The British Officer* (Longman, London, 2006), p. 100.
44. B. Farwell, *Queen Victoria's Little Wars* (Allan Lane, London, 1973), p. 182.
45. G. Powell, *Buller: A Scape Goat?* (Leo Cooper, London, 1994), p. 23.

Chapter 5

1. C. Williams, *The Life of Lieut-General Sir Henry Evelyn Wood* (Sampson Low & Marston, London, 1892) pp. 52–3.
2. B. Farwell, *Queen Victoria's Little Wars* (Allan Lane, London, 1973), pp. 190–1.
3. E. Wood, *From Midshipman to Field-Marshal*, Vol. 1 (Methuen, London, 1906), pp. 254–5.

4. H. Kochanski, *Sir Garnet Wolseley – Victorian Hero* (Hambledon, London, 1999), p. 62.
5. E. Bradhurst, *A Century of Letters 1820–1920* (Thomas & Newman, London, 1929), p. 80.
6. E. Wood, Vol. 1, p. 255.
7. B. Farwell, p. 191.
8. E. Wood, Vol. 1, p. 257.
9. H. Brackenbury, *The Ashanti War of 1873–4*, Vol. 1 (Frank Cass, New Impression, London, 1968), p. 144.
10. W. Walton Claridge, *A History of the Gold Coast and Ashanti*, Vol. 2 (Cassell, London, 1964), p. 50.
11. C. Williams, p. 55.
12. E. Wood, Vol. 1, p. 258.
13. H. Brackenbury, p. 176.
14. J. Lehmann, *Sir Garnet: A Life of Field-Marshal Lord Wolseley* (Jonathan Cape, London, 1964), p. 174.
15. L. Maxwell, *The Ashanti Ring – Sir Garnet Wolseley's Campaigns 1870–1882* (Leo Cooper, London, 1985), p. 27.
16. J. Lehmann, p. 175.
17. H. Brackenbury, pp. 177–81.
18. L. Maxwell, p. 29.
19. C. Williams, p. 55.
20. Letter from Secretary of State, Edward Cardwell, War Office, to Major-General Sir Garnet Wolseley, 18 November 1873, REF: KCM 89/9/22/3.
21. Letter Col. Evelyn Wood to Major-General Sir Garnet Wolseley, 15 December 1873, REF: HOV. Wood Letter No. 5.
22. E. Wood, Vol. 1, p. 263.
23. Ibid, p. 261.
24. L. Maxwell, p. 32.
25. E. Wood, 'The Ashanti Expedition of 1873–74', *Journal of the United Services Institution*, Vol. XVIII (1875), pp. 331–57.
26. E. Wood, Vol. 1, p. 267.
27. E. Wood, The Ashanti Expedition, pp. 331–57.
28. J. Lehmann, p. 180.
29. E. Wood, Vol. 1, p. 267.
30. L. Maxwell, p. 38.
31. E. Wood, Vol. 1, p. 265.
32. W. Ward, *A History of Ghana*, 4th Edition (George Allen & Unwin, London, 1969), pp. 274–5.
33. W. Walton Claridge, p. 77.
34. E. Wood, Vol. 1, p. 271.
35. F. Boyle, *Fanteland to Coomassie* (Chapman & Hall, London, 1874), p. 212.
36. Ibid, p. 269.
37. E. Wood, Vol. 1, p. 273.
38. E. Wood, The Ashanti Expedition, pp. 331–57.
39. E. Wood, Vol. 1, p. 275.
40. H. Brackenbury, p. 181.
41. E. Wood, Vol. 1, p. 276.
42. Ibid, p. 277.
43. L. Maxwell, p. 70.
44. H. Brackenbury, Vol. 2, p. 183.
45. Letter Lt. Eyre to Col. Wood, 2 February 1874, REF: KCM 89/9/22/10.

46. C. Williams, p. 61.
47. E. Wood, Vol. 1, p. 279.
48. Ibid.
49. H. Stanley, *Coomassie and Magdala* (Sampson Low, Marston & Co., London, 1874), p. 176.
50. Letter Col. Wood to Lady Eyre, 14 March 1874, REF: PIET I/2/1.
51. H. Brackenbury, Vol. 2, p. 225.
52. Letter Lady Eyre to Col. Wood, 22 March 1874, REF: KCM 89/9/22/14.
53. I. Beckett, *The Victorians at War* (Hambledon, London, 2003), p. 75.
54. H. Brackenbury, Vol. 2, p. 212.
55. Ibid, p. 217.
56. E. Wood, Vol. 1, p. 283.
57. L. Maxwell, p. 86.
58. E. Wood, Vol. 1, p. 284.
59. L. Maxwell, p. 88.
60. H. Brackenbury, Vol. 2, p. 359.
61. C. Williams, pp. 63–4.
62. Letter Capt. R. Buller to Col. E. Wood, 26 June 1874, REF: DRO 2065M/SS4/9.
63. E. Wood, Vol. 1, p. 288.
64. Ibid, p. 291.
65. Ibid, p. 295.

Chapter 6

1. L. Maxwell, *The Ashanti Ring, Sir Garnet Wolseley's Campaigns 1870–1882* (Leo Cooper, London, 1985), pp. 94–5.
2. P. Gon, 'The Last Frontier War', *The South Africa Military History Journal*, Vol. 5, No. 6.
3. For a more detailed examination of the Ninth Frontier War see P. Gon, *The Road to Isandlwana* (A.D. Donker, Johnannesburg, 1979).
4. Ibid, p. 154.
5. E. Wood, *From Midshipman to Field Marshal*, Vol. 1 (Methue, London, 1906), p. 309.
6. P. Gon, p. 155.
7. A. Greaves and B. Best (eds), *The Curling Letters of the Zulu War* (Pen & Sword, Barnsley, 2001), p. 43.
8. C. Williams, *The Life of Lieut.-General Sir Henry Evelyn Wood* (Sampson Low, Marston & Co., London, 1892), p. 70.
9. E. Wood, Vol. 1, p. 322.
10. A. Greaves and B. Best (eds), p. 59.
11. Letter Capt. Haynes to Col. Wood, 6 June 1878, REF: KCM 89/9/25/4(a).
12. Letter to District Adjutant General [DAG] Col. Bellairs from Col. Wood, 6 June 1878, REF KCM: 89/9/25/4(b).
13. E. Wood, *From Midshipman to Field-Marshal*, Vol. 2 (Methuen, London, 1906), p. 2.
14. Ibid, p. 3.
15. Ibid, p. 6.
16. Ibid, p. 9.
17. F. Emery, *The Red Soldier – The Zulu War of 1879* (Hodder & Stoughton, London, 1977), p. 43.
18. E. Wood, Vol. 2, p. 11.
19. Letter Col. Wood to Lord Chelmsford, 22 October 1878, REF: KCM 89/9/26/5.
20. Letter Lord Chelmsford to Col. Wood, 26 October 1878, REF: KCM 89/9/26/6.
21. Letter Major Crealock to Col. Wood, 31 October 1878, REF: KCM 89/9/26/7.

22. Letter Col. Wood to Major Crealock, 11 October 1878, REF: NAM 6807-386-18-7.
23. E. Wood, Vol. 2, p. 16.
24. Ibid.
25. Letter Col. Wood to Gen. Lord Chelmsford, 10 November 1878, REF: NAM 6807-86-9-75.
26. E. Wood, Vol. 2, p. 22.
27. S. David, *Zulu* (Viking, London, 2004), p. 192.
28. Letter Col. Wood to Major Crealock, 15 December 1878, REF: NAM 6807-386-6-16.
29. For more detailed explanations as to the motives behind the outbreak of war see S. David, *Zulu*, and A. Greaves, *Crossing the Buffalo: The Zulu War of 1879* (Weidenfeld & Nicolson, London, 2005).
30. I. Knight and I. Castle, *Zulu War 1879* (Osprey, Oxford, 2004), p. 146.
32. S. David, p. 192.
32. E. Wood, Vol. 2, p. 29.
33. A. Greaves, *Crossing the Buffalo*, p. 107.
34. E. Wood, Vol. 2, p. 31.
35. Ibid, p. 32.
36. Ibid, p. 33.
37. F. Emery, p. 155.
38. S. David, p. 198.
39. E. Wood, Vol. 2, p. 34.
40. Ibid, p. 56.
41. L. Maxwell, p. 101.
42. J. Sydney, 'Field Marshal Sir Henry Evelyn Wood – A Distinguished Soldier and his Medals', *Coins and Medals*, Vol. XVIII, 2, February 1998, p. 28.
43. L. Maxwell, p. 101.
44. F. Emery, p. 155.
45. B. Best, 'Evelyn Wood', *Journal of the Anglo Zulu War Historical Society*, IX (June 2001), p. 25.
46. Letter Col. Wood to Sir Theophilius Shepstone, 7 February 1879, REF: NAM 6807-386-9-15.
47. Letter Col. Wood to Sir Theophilius Shepstone, 8 February 1879, REF: NAM 6807-386-9-17.
48. Letter Col. Wood to Lord Chelmsford, 11 February 1879, REF: NAM 6807-386-9-101.
49. Letter Col. Wood to Lord Chelmsford, 11 February 1879, REF: NAM 6807-386-9-102.
50. J. Paine, 'From Midshipman to Field-Marshal – The Centenary of Sir Evelyn Wood, V.C., *The Cavalry Journal*, Vol. XXVIII, 1938, p. 232.
51. R. Edgerton, *Like Lions They Fought* (Macmillan, London, 1988), p. 117.
52. E. Wood, Vol. 2, p. 41.
53. L. Maxwell, p. 103.
54. C. Williams, p. 85.

Chapter 7

1. R. Lock, *Blood on the Painted Mountain* (Greenhill, London, 1995), p. 97.
2. S. David, *Zulu* (Viking, London, 2004), p. 250.
3. For a full description of the British defeat at Ntombi Drift see D. Morris, *The Washing of the Spears* (Simon & Schuster, New York, 1965), pp. 471–5.
4. S. David, p. 251.
5. Ibid.

6. A. Greaves, *Crossing the Buffalo – The Zulu War of 1879* (Weidenfeld & Nicolson, London, 2005), p. 267.
7. R. Lock, p. 134.
8. A. Greaves, p. 271.
9. R. Lock, 'The Battle of Hlobane – New Evidence & Difficult Conclusions', *Journal of the Anglo-Zulu War Historical Society*, Vol. VI, December 1999.
10. E. Wood, *Winnowed Memories* (Cassell & Company, London, 1917), p. 290.
11. S. David, p. 258.
12. Campbell's father, the Earl of Cawdor, was to write to Wood to thank him for burying his son and stated, 'I am told the universal feeling that your burying my son and Lloyd under the circumstances was one of the bravest acts ever done. These are the acts that make a man in command beloved and admired.' Letter Earl of Cawdor to Col. Wood, 6 May 1879, REF: DUK.XVIII-H.
13. E. Wood, *From Midshipman to Field Marshal*, Vol. 2 (Methuen, London, 1906), p. 51.
14. S. David, p. 261.
15. R. Lock, *Blood on Painted Mountain*, p. 178.
16. E. Wood, Vol. 2, p. 53.
17. R. Lock, *Blood on Painted Mountain*, p. 179.
18. E. Wood, Vol. 2, p. 54.
19. S. David, p. 267.
20. For a fuller description of the battle of Kambula see A. Greaves, pp. 279–87 and S. David, pp. 268–77.
21. F. Emery, p. 179.
22. E. Wood, Vol. 2, p. 64.
23. L. Maxwell, *The Ashanti Ring* (Leo Cooper, London, 1985), p. 118.
24. E. Wood, Vol. 2, p. 62.
25. R. Lock, *Blood on Painted Mountain*, p. 197.
26. Ibid, p. 200.
27. Lord Chelmsford's Letters & Correspondence REF: NAM 6807-386-14-18.
28. C. Norris-Newman, *In Zululand* (W.H. Allen, London, 1880), p. 155.
29. Lord Chelmsford's Letters & Correspondence REF: NAM 6807-386-14-19.
30. Marquis of Zetland (ed.), *The Letters of Disraeli to Lady Bradford and Lady Chesterfield 1876–1881*, Vol. 2 (Ernest Benn, London, 1929), p. 215.
31. C. Rathbone Low, *Soldiers of the Victorian Age*, Vol. 1 (Chapman & Hall, London, 1880), p. 276.
32. R. Lock, *Blood on Painted Mountain*, p. 180.
33. Letter from Col. Wood to Lord Chelmsford, 10 April 1879, REF: NAM 6807-386-23-28.
34. S. David, p. 267.
35. Letter Brigadier-General Wood to Lord Chelmsford, 18 April 1879, REF: NAM 6807-386-9-116.
36. A. Greaves and B. Best (eds), *The Curling Letters of the Zulu War* (Pen & Sword, Barnsley, 2001), p. 121.
37. A. Greaves, p. 290.
38. E. Wood, Vol. 2, pp. 77–8.
39. Ibid, p. 72.
40. F. Emery, p. 195.
41. L. Maxwell, p. 120.
42. Ibid, p. 123.
43. Norman Bagalgette to Major Blake, 24 October 1879, REF: KCM 89/9/31/17.
44. C. Williams, p. 107.
45. For a full description of the battle of Ulundi see D. Morris, pp. 545–75.

46. Lord Chelmsford's Letters & Correspondence REF: NAM 6807-386-16-60.
47. S. David, p. 347.
48. Ibid, p. 349.
49. F. Emery, p. 22.
50. S. Manning, 'Private Snook and Total War', *Journal of the Anglo-Zulu War Historical Society*, XIII, June 2003, pp. 22–6.
51. S. David, p. 356.
52. Ibid, p. 380.
53. J. Lehmann, *Sir Garnet A Life of Field-Marshal Lord Wolseley* (Jonathan Cape, London, 1964), p. 255.
54. C. Williams, p. 105.
55. E. Wood, Vol. 2, p. 82.
56. Sir Garnet Wolseley to the Duke of Cambridge, 18 July 1879, REF: HOV SA/2/52.
57. Sir Michael Hicks Beach to Sir Bartle Frere, 8 July 1879, REF: KCM 89/9/28/2.
58. E. Wood, Vol. 2, p. 82.
59. Letter Sir Garnet Wolseley to the Duke of Cambridge, 18 July 1879, REF: HOV SA/2/52.
60. E. Wood, Vol. 2, p. 84.
61. Letter Captain Woodgate to Col. E. Wood, 19 July 1879, REF: KCM 89/9/28/11.
62. Letter from Sir Garnet Wolseley to Col. E. Wood, 28 July 1879, REF: DUK XVIII-H.
63. E. Wood, Vol. 2, p. 85.

Chapter 8

1. E. Wood, *From Midshipman to Field-Marshal*, Vol. 2 (Methuen, London, 1906), p. 86.
2. C. Williams, *The Life of Lieut-General Sir Henry Evelyn Wood* (Sampson Low, Marston, London, 1892), p. 109.
3. F. Greenwood to Lady Wood, 9 September 1879, REF: KCM 89/9/2/5.
4. General Sir Evelyn Wood to Rear Admiral J.W. Whyte, 10 November 1879, REF: NAM 5501-8.
5. RA/VIC/QVJ/1879: 9 September.
6. E. Wood, Vol. 2, p. 89.
7. B. Farwell, *Eminent Victorian Soldiers* (Viking, London, 1986), p. 257.
8. Ibid, p. 92.
9. S. David, *Zulu* (Viking, London, 2004), p. 382.
10. E. Wood, Vol. 2, p. 86.
11. John Murray to Lord Hatherley, 3 November 1879, REF: KCM 89/9/32/4.
12. Sir Bartle Frere to Sir Evelyn Wood, 2 November 1879, REF: KCM 89/9/32/3(a).
13. Francis Power Cobble to Sir Evelyn Wood, 18 October 1879, REF: KCM 89/9/31/13.
14. W. Saunders to Sir Evelyn Wood, 28 July 1880, REF: KCM 89/9/34/2, and F. Greenwood to Sir Evelyn Wood 6 January 1881, REF: KCM 89/9/35/3.
15. J. Lehmann, *Sir Garnet – A Life of Field-Marshal Lord Wolseley* (Jonathan Cape, London,1964), p. 255.
16. Ponsonby to Sir Evelyn Wood, 16 December 1879, REF: DUK II/2/7.
17. A. Preston (ed.) *The South African Journal of Sir Garnet Wolseley 1879–1880* (A.A. Balkema, Cape Town, 1973), p. 278.
18. T. May, *Military Barracks* (Shire Publications, Princes Risborough, 2002).
19. E. Wood, Vol. 2, p. 95.
20. A. Preston (ed.), p. 277.
21. Wood's Proposed Route 1880, RA/VIC/R9/148.
22. RA/VIC/R10/21 and RA/VIC/R10/21a.

23. J. Laband, *The Transvaal Rebellion – The First Boer War 1880–81* (Longman, London, 2005), p. 177.
24. Ibid.
25. W.F. Butler, *The Life of Sir George Pomeroy-Colley* (John Murray, London, 1899), p. 294.
26. *The Graphic*, 26 February 1881.
27. J. Lee, *A Soldier's Life – General Sir Ian Hamilton 1853–1947* (Macmillan, London, 2000), p. 13.
28. Wood to Dr Norman Moore, 18 January1881, Private Collection.
29. J. Laband, p. 156.
30. Ibid, p. 172.
31. W.F. Butler, p. 314.
32. J. Lehmann, *The First Boer War* (Jonathan Cape, London, 1972), p. 226.
33. A. Forbes, *Souvenirs of Some Continents* (Macmillian, London, 1885), p. 358.
34. M. Prior, *Campaigns of War Correspondents* (Edward Arnold, London, 1912), p. 128.
35. Ibid.
36. J. Lehmann, *The First Boer War*, p. 231.
37. For a detailed explanation of the reason for the assault annd the defeat at Majuba see J. Laband, pp. 198–212.
38. E. Wood, Vol. 2, p. 112.
39. Major-General Sir Evelyn Wood to the Duke of Cambridge, 2 July 1881, REF: RA/VIC/Add E1/9672.
40. Major-General Sir Evelyn Wood to Lt. General William Napier, 25 April 1881, REF: PRO 30/86.
41. Major-General Wood to Queen Victoria, 13 April 1881, REF: RA/VIC/040/27.
42. Acting Governor Sir Evelyn Wood to Lady Wood, 5 March 1881, REF: RA/VIC/039/51.
43. J. Lehmann, *First Boer War*, p. 268.
44. Ibid.
45. Major-General Wood to Lord Kimberley, 5 March 1881, REF: DUK III/6/3.
46. RA VIC/QVJ/1881: 3 May 1881.
47. J. Laband, p. 215.
48. J. Lehmann, *The First Boer War*, p. 274.
49. Lord Kimberley to Major-General Wood, 22 March 1881, REF: BNL MS.Eng.c4126, fols. 89–90.
50. *Pall Mall Gazette*, 28 March 1881.
51. *Daily News*, 23 March 1881.
52. *Illustrated London News*, 26 March 1881.
53. J. Lehmann, *The First Boer War*, p. 270.
54. Letter Queen Victoria to Sir E. Wood, 31 March 1881, REF: RA VIC/039.207.
55. Letter Sir Evelyn Wood to Queen Victoria, 13 April 1881, REF: RA VIC/040/27.
56. Letter Sir Evelyn Wood to Queen Victoria, 4 May 1881, REF: RA VIC/040/144.
57. Letter Queen Victoria to Sir Evelyn Wood, 14 June 1881, REF: RA VIC/040/225.
58. H. Kochanski, *Sir Garnet Wolseley – Victorian Hero* (Hambledon Press, London, 1999), p. 111.
59. J. Lehmann, *The First Boer War*, p. 291.
60. Ibid, p. 292.
61. E. Wood, Vol. 2, p. 122.
62. J. Laband, p. 221.
63. Lord Grenfell, *Memoirs* (Hodder & Stoughton, London, 1925), p. 64.
64. J. Lehmann, *The First Boer War*, p. 297.
65. Letter Sir Evelyn Wood to Queen Victoria, 22 July 1881, REF: RA VIC/041/11.

66. Sir Evelyn Wood to Lord Kimberley, 6 June 1881, REF: RA VIC/040/209-11.
67. E. Wood, Vol. 2, p. 129.
68. Letter Sir Garnet Wolseley to Sir Evelyn Wood, 3 July 1881, REF: DUK IV/2/4.
69. E. Bradhurst, *A Century of Letters 1820–1920: Letters from Literary Friends to Lady Wood and Mrs A.C. Steele* (Thomas & Newman, London, 1929), p. 205.
70. C. Williams, p. 156.
71. J. Laband, p. 222.
72. Sir Evelyn Wood to Godfrey Lagden, 31 August 1881, REF: RH MSS Afr.s 211 Box 3 ff. 1.
73. Childers to Sir Evelyn Wood, 3 October 1881, REF: DUK III/5/2.
74. Lord Kimberley to Sir Evelyn Wood, 11 October 1881, REF: DUK III/5/3.
75. Lady Florence Dixie to Sir Evelyn Wood, 12 September 1881, REF: DUK VII/1/6.

Chapter 9

1. C. Woodham Smith, *Florence Nightingale* (Constable, London, 1950), p. 556.
2. E. Wood, *From Midshipman to Field-Marshal*, Vol. 2 (Methuen, London, 1906), p. 146.
3. C. Williams, *The Life of Lieut-General Sir Henry Evelyn Wood* (Sampson Low, Marston, London,1892), p. 158.
4. RA VIC/QVJ/1882: 20 February.
5. E. Wood, Vol. 2, p. 148.
6. Wood to Harcourt, 24 March 1882, REF: BNL MSS.Harcourt dep.fols.53–9.
7. RA VIC/QVJ/1882: 4 July.
8. C. Williams, p. 159.
9. *The Times*, 4 August 1882.
10. J. Lehmann, *The First Boer War* (Jonathan Cape, London, 1972), p. 226.
11. J. Paine, 'From Midshipman to Field-Marshal – The Centenary of Sir Evelyn Wood, V.C.', *The Cavalry Journal*, Vol. XXVIII, 1938, p. 231.
12. Bigge to Victoria, 6 November 1882, REF: RA VIC/0 18/24.
13. *The Times*, 15 September 1882.
14. *The Times*, 28 September 1882.
15. C. Williams, p. 166 and Colonel J.F. Maurice, *The Campaign of 1882 in Egypt* (Naval & Military Press, London, reissue 2001), p. 39.
16. E. Wood, Vol. 2, p. 150.
17. Wood to Victoria, 27 August 1882, REF: RA VIC/015/76.
18. C. Williams, p. 167.
19. Wood to Ponsonby, 5 September 1882, REF: RA VIC/015/153.
20. J. Lehmann, *All Sir Garnet: A Life of Field-Marshal Lord Wolseley* (Jonathan Cape, London, 1964), p. 319.
21. E. Wood, Vol. 2, p. 151.
22. C. Williams, p. 169.
23. Ibid, p. 170.
24. E. Bradhurst, *A Century of Letters 1820–1920: Letters from Literary Friends to Lady Wood and Mrs A.C. Steele* (Thomas & Newman, London, 1929), p. 207.
25. *The Times*, 18 September 1882.
26. J. Paine, p. 232.
27. *The Times*, 2 October 1882.
28. Wolseley to Wood, 14 November 1882, REF: KCM 89/9/38/8.
29. Ponsonby to Childers, 13 November 1882, REF: RA VIC/0 18/51.
30. Colonel J.F. Maurice, p. 148.
31. Grosvenor to Wood, 13 November 1882, REF: KCM 89/9/38/6.

32. Grosvenor to Wood, 13 November 1882, REF: KCM 89/9/38/7.
33. M. Asher, *Khartoum the Ultimate Imperial Adventure* (Viking, London, 2005), p. 76.
34. Granville to Wood, 28 November 1882, REF: KCM 89/9/38/9.
35. Lord Grenfell, *Memoirs* (Hodder & Stoughton, London, 1925), p. 75.
36. Ibid.
37. P. Johnson, *Gordon of Khartoum* (Wellingborough, Patrick Stephens, 1985), p. 95.
38. C. Williams, p. 177.
39. Wood to the Duke of Cambridge, 23 January 1883, REF: RA VIC/Add E1/10313.
40. Wood to Queen Victoria, 19 February 1883, REF: RA/VIC/019/26.
41. Wood to the Duke of Cambridge, 25 February 1883, REF: RA VIC/Add E1/10340.
42. Wood to the Duke of Cambridge, 20 May 1883, REF: RA VIC/Add E1/10417.
43. Wood to the Duke of Cambridge, 18 December 1883, REF: RA VIC/Add E1/10573.
44. A. Hunter, *Kitchener's Sword-Arm* (Spellmount, Staplehurst, 1996), p. 12.
45. E. Wood, Vol. 2, p. 157.
46. Wood to Victoria, 1 April 1883, REF: RA VIC/Z209/3.
47. Dufferin to Wood, 1 May 1883, REF: KCM 89/9/39/4.
48. Wood to the Duke of Cambridge, 25 February 1883, REF: RA VIC/Add E1/10340.
49. Wood to His Highness The Khedive, 13 July 1883, REF: RA VIC/Add E1/10457.
50. C. Williams, p. 182.
51. Wood to Victoria, 10 December 1883, REF: RA/VIC/019/105.
52. Wood to Baring, 6 January 1884, REF: RA VIC/Add E1/10585.
53. Wood to the Duke of Cambridge, 18 December 1883, REF: RA VIC/Add E1/10573.
54. J. Marlowe, *Mission to Khartoum – The Apotheosis of General Gordon* (Gollancz, London, 1969), p. 123.
55. Wood to the Duke of Cambridge, 21 January 1884, REF: RA VIC/Add E1/10606.
56. Wood to Victoria, 21 January 1884, REF: RA VIC/020/30.
57. R. Wingate, *The Life and Times of General Sir Reginald Wingate* (Greenwood Press, Westport, reprint 1975), p. 50.
58. E. Wood, Vol. 2, p. 164.
59. General Sir Horace Smith Dorrein, *Memories of 48 Years Service* (John Murray, London, 1925), p. 47.
60. Wood to the Duke of Cambridge, 31 January 1884, REF: VIC/Add E1/10617.
61. Wood to Moore, 20 April 1884, Private Collection.
62. J. Marlowe, p. 52.
63. Wood to the Duke of Cambridge, 31 January 1884, REF: VIC/Add E1/10617.
64. Wolseley to Wood, 4 June 1884, REF: DUK XVIII-H.
65. A. Preston (ed.), *In Relief of Gordon – Lord Wolseley's Campaign Journal of the Khartoum Relief Expedition 1884–1885* (Hutchinson, London, 1967), p. 4.
66. Ibid, pp. 31–2.
67. Ibid, p. 126.
68. Ibid, p. 179.
69. C. Williams, p. 193.
70. J. Symonds, *England's Pride: The Story of the Gordon Relief Expedition* (London, 1965), pp. 98–9.
71. B. Farwell, *Eminent Victorian Soldiers* (Viking, London, 1986), p. 256.
72. Wood to Victoria, 2 December 1884, REF: RA VIC/023/71.
73. Wood to Victoria, 26 December 1884, REF: RA VIC/023/77.
74. C. Melville, *The Life of General Sir Redvers Buller*, Vol. 1 (Edward Arnold, London, 1923), p. 203.
75. A. Preston (ed.), p. 49.
76. P. Johnson, p. 95.

77. Wood to Victoria, 23 January 1885, REF: RA VIC/023/115.
78. Wood to Victoria, 29 October 1884, REF: RA VIC/023/61.
79. E. Wood, Vol. 2, p. 177.

Chapter 10

1. C. Williams, *The Life of Lieut-General Sir Henry Evelyn Wood* (Sampson Low, Marston, London, 1892), p. 205.
2. A. Preston (ed.), *In Relief of Gordon – Lord Wolseley's Campaign Journal of the Khartoum Relief Expedition 1884–1885* (Hutchinson, London, 1967), p. 85.
3. J. Lehmann, *The First Boer War* (Jonathan Cape, London, 1972), p. 224.
4. Wood to Wolseley, 15 October 1885, REF: HOV, Wolseley Papers, Wood Letter No. 7.
5. Ibid.
6. B. Farwell, *Eminent Victorian Soldiers* (Viking, London, 1985), p. 258.
7. E. Wood, *From Midshipman to Field-Marshal*, Vol. 2 (Methuen, London, 1906), pp. 184–6.
8. Ibid, p. 186.
9. C. Williams, pp. 224–5.
10. E. Wood, Vol. 2, p. 187.
11. C. Williams, p. 223.
12. Wolseley to Lady Wood, 16 August 1888, REF: DUK XVIII-H.
13. Wood to Moore, 2 November 1888, Private Collection.
14. Wolseley to Ponsonby, 12 November 1888, REF: RA VIC/Add A15/5199.
15. Queen Victoria to Stanhope, 27 November 1888, REF: RA VIC/Add E63/33.
16. Bigge to Ponsonby, 27 November 1888, REF: RA VIC/Add A34/40.
17. I. Beckett, *The Victorians at War* (Hambledon, London, 2003), p. 28.
18. Bigge to Ponsonby, 30 November 1888, REF: RA VIC/Add A34/41.
19. Letter WO to Wood, 6 December 1888, REF: KCM 89/9/43/8.
20. Ibid, pp. 114–15.
21. J. Marlow, *The Uncrowned Queen of Ireland – The Life of Kitty O'Shea* (Weidenfeld & Nicolson, London, 1975), p. 191.
22. E. Bradhurst, *A Century of Letters* (Thomas & Newman, London, 1929), p. 38.
23. Dr Norman Moore Papers. Private Collection.
24. Wood to Broderick, 1 September 1902, REF: PRO 30/67/10.
25. J. Marlow, pp. 194–5.
26. Ibid, p. 18.
27. F. Lyons, *The Fall of Parnell* (Routledge, London, 1960), p. 56.
28. M. Brady, *The Love Story of Parnell and Katharine O'Shea* (The Mercer Press, Dublin, 1991), pp. 55–7.
29. M. Callaghan, *Kitty O'Shea – The Story of Katharine Parnell* (Pandora, London, 1989), p. 124.
30. F. Lyons, p. 68.
31. J. Marlow, p. 196.
32. *Pall Mall Gazette*, 15 November 1890.
33. *Reynolds Newspaper*, 23 November 1890.
34. Ibid.
35. M. Brady, p. 132.
36. B. Farwell, p. 261.
37. Wood to Harman, 17 October 1890, REF: PRO WO 27/489.
38. Wood to Moore, 2 August 1890, Private Collection.
39. E. Wood, Vol. 2, pp. 206–7.

40. M. Ramsey, *The Citizen Soldier & Minor Tactics in the British Army 1870–1918* (Westport CT, Praeger, 2002), p. 62.
41. E. May, *Changes and Chances of a Soldier's Life* (Philip Allan, London, 1925), p. 162.
42. E. Wood, Vol. 2, p. 217.
43. Wood to Moore, 23 May 1891, Private Collection.
44. RA QVJ 11 May 1891.
45. PRO WO 279/1 Autumn manoeuvres in Hampshire, in September 1891, 20 November 1891.
46. E. Wood, Vol. 2, p. 221.
47. F. Maurice and G. Arthur, *The Life of Lord Wolseley* (William Heinemann, London, 1924), p. 259.
48. Wolseley to Wood, 6 February 1892, REF: KCM 89/9/49/6.
49. Methuen to Wood, 21 August 1892, REF: DUK XVIII-H.
50. Bigge to Wood, 26 August 1892, REF: DUK XVIII-H.
51. E. Wood, Vol. 2, pp. 222–3.
52. Wood to Roberts, 30 November 1892, REF: NAM 7101-23-91-5.
53. Report of 1892 Manoeuvres. Wood to Roberts, REF: NAM 7101-23-91-4.
54. E. May, p. 169.
55. Ibid, p. 172.
56. E. Wood, Vol. 2, p. 226.
57. *The Times*, 7 October 1893.

Chapter 11

1. E. Wood, *From Midshipman to Field-Marshal*, Vol. 2 (Methuen, London, 1906), p. 230.
2. Wood to Wolseley, 31 July 1895, REF: HOV WP24/77/4.
3. H. Gordon, *The War Office* (Putnam, London, 1935), p. 70.
4. Royal Commission on the War in South Africa (HMSO, London, 1903), p. 171.
5. E. Wood, Vol. 2, p. 235.
6. E. May, *Changes and Chances of a Soldier's Life* (Philip Allan, London, 1925), p. 187.
7. M. Ramsey, *The Citizen Soldier & Minor Tactics in the British Army 1870–1918* (Westport CT, Praegar, 2002), p. 93.
8. Arthur Davidson to Queen Victoria, 7 April 1897, REF: RA VIC/E64/54.
9. Wolseley to Bigge, 27 July 1897, REF: RA VIC/W73/179.
10. Wood to Napier, 2 September 1897, REF: PRO 30/86/9.
11. E. Wood, Vol. 2, p. 239.
12. War Office Misc 1900–01, REF: DRO 2065M/SS4/32-34.
13. WO Memorandum, Evelyn Wood, 1 December 1898, REF: RA/VIC/W 14/89.
14. J. Lee, *A Soldier's Life – General Sir Ian Hamilton 1853–1947* (Macmillan, London, 2000), p. 44.
15. Kitchener to Wood, 10 February 1898, REF: NAM 6807/234.
16. E. Spiers (ed.), *Sudan the Reconquest Reappraised* (Frank Cass, London, 1998), p. 41.
17. G. DeGroot, *Douglas Haig 1861–1928* (Unwin Hyman London, 1998), p. 55.
18. Ibid, p. 54
19. Papers of General Sir Horace Smith-Dorrien, IWM REF: 87/47/6.
20. J. Pollock, *Kitchener the Road to Omdurman* (Constable, London, 1998), p. 126
21. P. Magnus, *Kitchener Portrait of an Imperialist* (John Murray, London, 1958), p. 118.
22. For a detailed background of the Boer War see T. Pakenham, *The Boer War* (Weidenfeld & Nicolson, London, 1979).
23. Royal Commission, p. 37.
24. Ibid, p. 125.

25. H.O. Arnold-Forster, *The War Office, The Army and The Empire* (London, 1900), p. 40.
26. E. Wood, *Winnowed Memories* (Cassell, London, 1917), p. 292.
27. Ibid, p. 293.
28. G. Powell, *Buller: A Scapegoat?* (Leo Cooper, London, 1994), p. 119.
29. H.O. Arnold-Forster, p. 72.
30. T. Pakenham, pp. 224–38.
31. Churchill to Wood, 10 November 1899, REF: DUK V/1/3.
32. Buller to Wood, 27 December 1899, REF: KCM 89/9/50/18.
33. Marshall to Wood, 24 January 1900, REF: KCM 89/9/51/2.
34. E. Wood, Vol. 2, p. 250.
35. Wood to Grove, 1 February 1901, REF: NAM R91/11.
36. E. Wood, Vol. 2, p. 256.
37. Moore Case Book No. 29, pp. 13–14 (Private Collection).
38. A. Rankin, *The History of Cinema Exhibition in Exeter 1895–1918*, Ch. 2, The Boer War, Synchronised Sound and Pantomime (1900–1902), Unpublished Thesis University of Exeter, Bill Douglas Film Centre, 2002.
39. Royal Commission, pp. 171–2.
40. Esher to HM King, 29 October 1902, REF: RA VIC/W38/48.
41. Royal Commission, p. 176.
42. Ibid, p. 174.
43. *Illustrated London News*, 8 September 1903.

Chapter 12

1. E. Spiers, *The Army & Society 1815–1914* (Longman, London, 1980), p. 243.
2. Roberts to Wood, 12 July 1901, REF: DUK XVIII-H.
3. Wood to Roberts, 18 July 1901, REF: NAM 7101-23-91/14.
4. E. Wood, *From Midshipman to Field-Marshal*, Vol. 2 (Methuen, London, 1906) p. 260.
5. Letter to Broderick, unsigned and undated. REF: RA VIC/W22/36.
6. *The Times*, 28 September 1901.
7. *The Times*, 26 October 1901.
8. E. Wood, Vol. 2, pp. 274–5.
9. Wood to Broderick, 1 September1902, REF: PRO 30/67/10.
10. *The Times*, 9 June, 1902.
11. D. French, *Military Identities: The Regimental System, the British Army, & the British People, c.1870–2000* (OUP, 2005), p. 70.
12. *The Times*, 5 September 1901.
13. E. Wood, Vol. 2, p. 278.
14. Wood to Roberts, 9 April 1903, REF: NAM 7101-23-91-44.
15. *The Times*, 10 April 1903.
16. Wood to Roberts, 28 September 1903, REF: NAM 7101-23-91-72.
17. Wood to Roberts, 1 October 1903, REF: NAM 7101-23-91-75.
18. Wood to Roberts, 13 October 1903, REF: NAM 7101-23-91-76.
19. Brackenbury to Wood, 9 February 1904, REF: DUK XVIII-H.
20. E. May, *Changes and Chances of a Soldiers Life* (Philip Allan, London, 1925), p. 276.
21. *Daily Telegraph*, 9 September 1903.
22. A. Hunter, *Kitchener's Sword-Arm – The Life & Campaigns of General Sir Archibald Hunter* (Staplehurst, Spellmount, 1996), p. 188.
23. *The Times*, 18 September 1903
24. *The Times*, 21 September 1903.
25. Methuen to Wood, 29 November 1904, REF: DUK XVIII-H.

26. J. Paine, 'From Midshipman to Field-Marshal – The Centenary of Sir Evelyn Wood, V.C., *The Cavalry Journal*, Vol. XXVIII, 1938, p. 233.
27. Wood to Blumenfeld, 17 November1907, REF: H/L BLU/1/2/WOO.14.
28. E. Wood, *Winnowed Memories* (Cassell, London, 1917), p. 382.
29. Sir Horace Smith Dorrien Diaries 1905–1914, 9 May 1908, REF: IWM 87/47/2.
30. Wood to Ewart, 25 November 1907, REF: H/L TD74/11.
31. Wood to Ewart, 2 December1908, REF: H/L TD74/11.
32. *The Times*, 26 March 1913.
33. *The Times*, 5 May, 1909.
34. Speech Made by Sir Evelyn Wood at Beaumont, 2 July 1904, REF: KCM 89/9/53/15.
35. *The Times*, 28 March 1911.
36. *The Times*, 22 April 1912.
37. *The Times*, 7 June 1912.
38. *The Times*, 10 June 1912.
39. Ibid.
40. E. Wood, *Winnowed Memories*, p. 382.
41. *The Times*, 28 January 1914.
42. Roberts to Wood, 28 January 1914, REF: DUK XVIII-H.
43. *The Times*, 28 February 1914.
44. Letter from undeciphered signature to Wood, 29 September 1914, REF: DUK XVIII-H.
45. *The Times*, 5 December 1914.
46. E.Wood, *Winnowed Memories*, pp. 334–5.
47. *The Times*, 6 November 1917.
48. E. Wood, *Winnowed Memories*, p. 385.
49. *The Times*, 7 February 1916.
50. Wood to 'My dear friend', 6 April 1918, REF: RA PS/GV/O 1320A.
51. Middleton to Wood, 16 February 1918, REF: DUK XVIII-H.
52. Dr Norman Moore, Case Book No. 59, 10 December 1918, Private Collection.
53. Wood to Miss Telford, April 1919, REF: KCM 89/9/9/18-23.
54. Dr Norman Moore, Case Book No. 58, 8 April 1920, Private Collection.
55. *Daily Mail*, 3 December 1919.
56. Lord Grenfell, *Memoirs* (Hodder & Stoughton, London, 1925), p. 231.
57. Charles Wood to Blumenfeld, 17 December 1919, REF: H/L BLU/1/22/WO.1.
58. *The Times* 3 December 1919.
59. *The Daily Telegraph*, 3 December 1919.
60. *The Daily Telegraph*, 8 December 1919.
61. Special Order for the Funeral Procession of Field Marshal Sir Evelyn Wood, 4 December 1919, REF: KCM 89/9/54/10.
62. *Daily Telegraph*, 8 December 1919.
63. *The Times*, 3 December 1919.

Bibliography

(Note: Place of publication London, unless specified)

Arnold-Forster, H., *The War Office, The Army and The Empire*, (1900).

Asher, M., *Khartoum: the Ultimate Imperial Adventure* (Viking, 2005).

Beckett, I., *The Victorians at War* (Hambledon, 2003).

Boyle, F., *Fanteland to Coomassie* (Chapman & Hall, 1874).

Brackenbury, H., *The Ashanti War of 1873–4*, Vol. 1 (Frank Cass, New Impression, 1968).

Bradhurst, E., *A Century of Letters 1820–1920: Letters from Literary Friends to Lady Wood and Mrs A.C. Steele* (Thomas & Newman, 1929).

Butler, W., *The Life of Sir George Pomeroy-Colley* (John Murray, 1899).

Brady, M., *The Love Story of Parnell and Katharine O'Shea* (The Mercer Press, Dublin, 1991).

Callaghan, M., *Kitty O'Shea: the story of Katharine Parnell* (Pandora, 1989).

Clayton, A., *The British Officer* (Longman, 2006).

Walton Claridge, W., *A History of the Gold Coast and Ashanti*, Vol. 2 (Cassell, 1964).

David, S., *Prince of Pleasure* (Simon & Schuster, 1998).

David, S., *The Indian Mutiny* (Viking, 2002).

David, S., *Zulu*, (Viking, 2004).

DeGroot, G., *Douglas Haig 1861–1928* (Unwin Hyman, 1998).

Edgerton, R., *Like Lions They Fought* (Macmillan, 1988).

Emery, F., *The Red Soldier – The Zulu War of 1879* (Hodder & Stoughton, 1977).

Farwell, B., *Eminent Victorian Soldiers* (Viking, 1986).

Forbes, A., *Souvenirs of Some Continents* (Macmillan,1885).

French, D., *Military Identities: the Regimental System, the British Army & the British People, c.1870–2000* (OUP, Oxford, 2005).

Gon, P., *The Road to Isandlwana*, (A.D. Donker Ltd, Johannesburg, 1979).

Gordon, H., *The War Office* (Putnam, 1935).

Greaves, A. and Best, B. (eds), *The Curling Letters of the Zulu War* (Pen & Sword, Barnsley, 2001).

Greaves, A., *Crossing the Buffalo: the Zulu War of 1879* (Weidenfeld & Nicolson, 2005).

Grenfell, Lord, *Memoirs* (Hodder & Stoughton, 1925).

Hibbert, C., *George IV* (Longman, 1973).

Hunter, A., *Kitchener's Sword-Arm* (Spellmount, Staplehurst, 1996).

Johnson, P., *Gordon of Khartoum* (Patrick Stephens, Wellingborough, 1985).

Knight, I. and Castle, I., *Zulu War 1879* (Osprey, Oxford, 2004).

Kochanski, H., *Sir Garnet Wolseley – Victorian Hero* (Hambledon, 1999).

Laband, J., *The Transvaal Rebellion – the First Boer War 1880–81* (Longman, 2005).

Lee, J., *A Soldier's Life – General Sir Ian Hamilton 1853–1947* (Macmillan, 2000).

Lehmann, J., *Sir Garnet: a Life of Field-Marshal Lord Wolseley* (Jonathan Cape, 1964).

Lehmann, J., *The First Boer War* (Jonathan Cape, 1972).

Lock, R., *Blood on the Painted Mountain* (Greenhill, 1995).

Rathbone Low, C., *Soldiers of the Victorian Age*, Vol. 1 (Chapman & Hall, 1880).

Lyons, F., *The Fall of Parnell* (Routledge, 1960).

McClelland, V., *Cardinal Manning – His Public Life and Influence 1865–1892* (OUP, Oxford, 1962).

Magnus, P., *Kitchener Portrait of an Imperialist* (John Murray, 1958).

Marlow, J., *The Uncrowned Queen of Ireland – the Life of Kitty O'Shea* (Weidenfeld & Nicolson,1975).

Marlowe, J., *Mission to Khartoum – the Apotheosis of General Gordon* (Gollancz, 1969).

Maurice, Colonel J., *The Campaign of 1882 in Egypt* (Naval & Military Press, reissue 2001).

Maxwell, L., *The Ashanti Ring – Sir Garnet Wolseley's Campaigns 1870–1882* (Leo Cooper, 1985).

May, E., *Changes and Chances of a Soldier's Life* (Philip Allan, 1925).

May, T., *Military Barracks* (Shire Publications, Princes Risborough, 2002).

Melville, J., *The Life of General Sir Redvers Buller*, Vol. 1 (Edward Arnold, 1923).

Morris, D., *The Washing of the Spears* (Simon & Schuster, New York, 1965).

Norris-Newman, C., *In Zululand*, (W.H. Allen, 1880).

O'Shea, K., *Charles Stewart Parnell*, Vol. 1 (Cassell, 1914).

Pakenham, T., *The Boer War* (Weidenfeld & Nicolson, 1979).

Pollock, J., *Kitchener the Road to Omdurman* (Constable, 1998).

Powell, G., *Buller: a Scapegoat?* (Leo Cooper, 1994).

Preston, A. (ed.), *In Relief of Gordon – Lord Wolseley's Campaign Journal of the Khartoum Relief Expedition 1884–1885* (Hutchinson, 1967).

Preston, A. (ed.), *The South African Journal of Sir Garnet Wolseley 1879–1880* (A.A. Balkema, Cape Town, 1973).

Prior, M., *Campaigns of War Correspondents* (Edward Arnold, 1912).

Ramsey, M., *The Citizen Soldier & Minor Tactics in the British Army 1870–1918* (Praegar, Westport CT, 2002).

Robinson, Commander C.N., R.N. (ed), *Celebrities of the Army* (George Newnes, 1902).

Smith-Dorrien, General Sir Horace, *Memories of 48 Years Service* (John Murray, 1925).

Spiers, E., *The Army & Society 1815–1914* (Longman, 1980).

Spiers, E. (ed.), *Sudan the Reconquest Reappraised* (Frank Cass, 1998).

Spiers, E., *The Victorian Soldier in Africa* (MUP, Manchester, 2004).

Stanley, H., *Coomassie and Magdala* (Sampson Low, Marston & Co., 1874).

Symonds, J., *England's Pride: the Story of the Gordon Relief Expedition* (1965).

Ward, W., *A History of Ghana*, 4th edition (George Allen & Unwin, 1969).

Williams, C., *The Life of Lieut.-General Sir Henry Evelyn Wood* (Sampson Low Marston & Company, 1892).

Wingate, R., *The Life and Times of General Sir Reginald Wingate* (Greenwood Press, Westport, reprint 1975).

Wood, E., *The Crimea in 1854 and 1894* (Chapman and Hall, 1895).

Wood, E., *From Midshipman to Field-Marshal*, Vols I and II (Methuen, 1906).

Wood, E., *The Revolt in Hindustan 1857–59* (Metheun, 1908).

Wood, E., *Winnowed Memories* (Cassell & Company, 1917).

Woodham Smith, C., *Florence Nightingale* (Constable, 1950).

Woodham-Smith, C., *Queen Victoria, Vol. 1, 1819–1861* (Hamish Hamilton, 1972).

Zetland, Marquis of (ed.), *The Letters of Disraeli to Lady Bradford and Lady Chesterfield 1876–1881*, Vol. 2 (Ernest Benn, 1929).

Journal Articles and Theses

Best, B., 'Evelyn Wood', *Journal of the Anglo-Zulu War Historical Society*, IX June 2001, pp. 23–30.

Gon, P., 'The Last Frontier War', *The South Africa Military History Journal*, Vol. 5, No. 6.

Lock, R., 'The Battle of Hlobane – New Evidence & Difficult Conclusions', *Journal of the Anglo-Zulu War Historical Society*, Vol. VI, December 1999.

Manning, S., 'Private Snook and Total War', *Journal of the Anglo-Zulu War Historical Society*, Vol. XIII, June 2003.

Paine, J., 'From Midshipman to Field-Marshal – The Centenary of Sir Evelyn Wood, V.C.', *The Cavalry Journal*, Vol. XXVIII, 1938.

Rankin, A., *The History of Cinema Exhibition in Exeter 1895–1918*, Ch. 2, The Boer War, Synchronised Sound and Pantomime (1900-1902), Unpublished Thesis University of Exeter, Bill Douglas Film Centre, 2002.

Sydney, J., 'Field Marshal Sir Henry Evelyn Wood – A Distinguished Soldier and his Medals', *Coins and Medals*, Vol. XVIII, 2, February 1998

Wood, E., 'The Ashanti Expedition of 1873–74', *Journal of the United Services Institution*, Vol. XVIII (1875).

Newspapers

Broad Arrow, The Daily Mail, The Daily News, The Daily Telegraph, The Devon Evening Express, The Graphic, The Illustrated London News, The Pall Mall Gazette, Reynolds, The South Molton Gazette, The Times.

Index